Business without Boundary

THE STORY OF GENERAL MILLS

T0338417

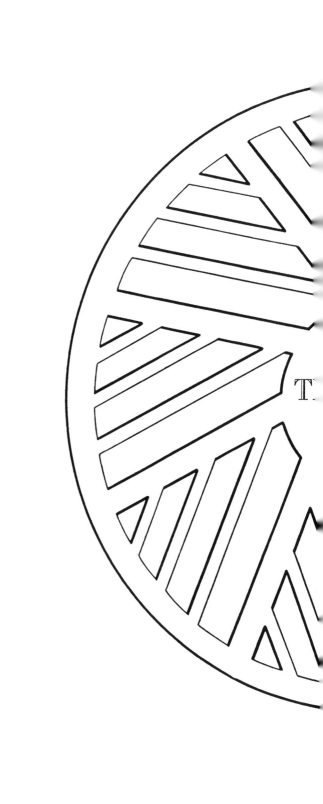

Business without Boundary

ORY OF GENERAL MILLS

James Gray

University of Minnesota Press, Minneapolis

PRINTED AT THE NORTH CENTRAL PUBLISHING CO., ST. PAUL

Library of Congress Catalog Card Number: 54-10286

PUBLISHED IN GREAT BRITAIN, INDIA, AND PAKISTAN BY
GEOFFREY CUMBERLEGE: OXFORD UNIVERSITY PRESS, LONDON, BOMBAY, AND KARACHI

Foreword

T H E date June 20, 1953, marked the twenty-fifth anniversary of the incorporation of General Mills. To a vigorous enterprise, just as to an ambitious young man, such an occasion seems to call for a summing up of progress, for an appraisal of past performance and a steady scrutiny of prospects for the future. This book undertakes to tell the story of General Mills in terms of its historic growth from small beginnings on scattered frontiers into a closely integrated organization devoted to a wide variety of interests. It undertakes to tell the story also in terms of the contribution made to the problem of feeding America well and appetizingly. It undertakes finally to tell the story in terms of industry's growing sense of responsibility toward its significant task so that, as one of General Mills' own men has expressed the point of view, the object of the twentieth century must be "the welfare of the common man as citizen of the world."

It is an obvious fact that the food industry serves an essential function. Nature is its silent partner and, to quote a sharp observer, "as long as a growing population gets hungry three times a day, each year will bring bigger markets." This outlook is something over which an enterprise may legitimately rejoice. But even in the most benign of realms, success is never the free gift of nature. This account of the growth of General Mills will examine the steps by which an enterprise may advance securely in the midst of the hazards of circumstance and the threats of change.

One enormous advantage has been the leadership of General Mills and of the earlier companies that went into its formation. Men of sober insight have seemed, again and again, to anticipate change and to make it their ally. Both in the development of practices and in the formulation of principles they have seen the light of the future before them and been in the vanguard now of a technological revolution, now of a managerial reform.

Another advance has been made possible by falling into step with science. The men responsible for the progress of General Mills have not been content merely to be the passive ally of nature. Rather, they have assumed the initiative in exploring nature. They have sought out her hidden values and her secret strengths and have presented these nourishing attributes to the public in attractive form. Specifically this has meant making an intimate study of the inexhaustible wealth of cereals. Milling has been described as the simple conversion of a primary product — grain — into flour. The conviction that has animated the minds of the men of General Mills is that infinitely more could be done to recover from wheat and corn and oats the good that is in them and so to enrich both the nourishment and the pleasure of the daily diet.

Research has led General Mills not only into the exhaustive examination of its own field but into the exploration of many that lie near by. The result is that the corporation has developed a diversified program of activities that has quite literally made it a business without a boundary in either geography or type of product.

It is under the stimulation of the twentieth-century doctrine of service that General Mills has made its steady and unwavering day-by-day progress. In the view of its leaders, it has been far from enough to develop old products to the limit of their resources and to create new products from the discoveries of science. Equally necessary to success is the full use of the merchandiser's skill. And that skill must be wholly honest, drawing effectiveness and persuasiveness from ability to serve. General Mills has concentrated, throughout its history and throughout the several histories of the companies that went into its making, on teaching men and, more particularly, women how to eat well. Through its cooking schools it has educated the public in matters of diet and stirred desire for what serves human needs best. Its advertising programs have further emphasized the contribution that its own products could make to the art of eating. Through its vigorous merchandising campaigns it has carried these products along the "avenue to the home" and straight into the housewife's kitchen.

The leadership of General Mills in all these particulars has been preeminent. Its adaptability and readiness to change before change itself could corrupt its usefulness has made industrial history. Its preoccupation with research has helped to find out much hidden wealth in the materials with which it has dealt. Its Home Service Department has achieved prominence not merely as practitioner of the art of cooking but as trusted teacher in the fundamentals of the balanced diet. Its pioneering adventure in radio advertising has made history not in one industry but in two. Its skills as merchandiser have enabled the company to multiply its interests until it now handles a vast complexity of goods as adeptly as it once handled one.

Twenty-five years is not long for the life of a corporation. But General Mills had forebears whose history carries the record back for more than a hundred years into the clamorous days of the mid-nineteenth century. Four major groups of interests came together starting with the formation of General Mills in 1928: the Washburn Crosby Company with headquarters in Minneapolis and its associate companies; the Sperry Company whose mills in California, the Pacific Northwest, and Utah were presided over from San Francisco; the Kell group of mills in Oklahoma and Texas; and the Larrowe Milling Company, specialists in animal feeds with Detroit as its base. The largest of these was Washburn Crosby which had come into being at the Falls of St. Anthony during the period of expansion that immediately followed the Civil War. The oldest was the Sperry Company which sprang out of the needs of the forty-niners, who as they devoted themselves feverishly to the search for gold had to be fed by someone.

This report on the progress of General Mills deals with both the period before and the period after consolidation of the several companies, but the greater amount of attention is devoted to General Mills itself. As the largest of the companies to be associated in the corporation and the one from which sprang the initiative for consolidation, the Washburn Crosby Company is required to sit longest for its portrait. Accounts of the development of the other companies have been concentrated in one chapter, which sketches the events of the Sperry Company from the days of the Gold Rush on to the turn of the century, traces the development of the Kell group from the time when Oklahoma lands were opened to settlement, and outlines the enterprises of James Larrowe in the feed business. From the 1928–29 period the four move forward, of course, as a team.

Through the conscientious effort of a hundred years and the highly disciplined effort of the last twenty-five years in particular has run the sustaining and unifying belief that prosperity is closely related to service. Worth is established for an enterprise only by making an economic contribution and the successful company is the one that deserves well by serving well.

This is the central theme of the story of General Mills.

J. G.

Minneapolis, Minnesota
June 1954

Contents

Business without Boundary

List of Illustrations

xi

Business without Boundary

A recurring symbol in Gold Medal Flour advertising from 1900 to 1920 was a "cleanly maid"

"How a well bred maid makes well made bread," a recipe in verse

Streetcar placards brought news of the Gold Medal Cooking School to Atlanta housewives

Billboards across the country echoed Benjamin Bull's crisp slogan

In 1852 the Sperry mill of Stockton, California, took gold dust in trade for flour

"Drifted Snow" was the Sperry equivalent of "Gold Medal" in flour

A Sperry company outing in the days of the flivver

Charles Staff and the research farm that was based on the principle of "asking the animals" what was good for them

Leaders of four milling dynasties that came together in 1928 to form General Mills — Austin Sperry, Frank J. Kell, James Larrowe, and James Ford Bell

The feminine touch in company advertising through the years — from a sprightly young housewife to Betty Crocker

BETWEEN PAGES 210 AND 211

Harry A. Bullis took over a "third shift" when he became president of General Mills in 1942

Charles H. Bell brought a familiar name to the presidency in 1952

J. F. Bell and Donald D. Davis were colleagues in the Food Administration of World War I and at General Mills

John Crosby II and Charles C. Bovey, lifetime associates in both Washburn Crosby and General Mills

Leslie N. Perrin, J. F. Bell, and Harry A. Bullis help T. A. Erickson celebrate his eightieth birthday

Harry A. Bullis, Leslie N. Perrin, Walter H. Barry, and Samuel C. Gale bake a cake in the Home Service kitchen

Business without Boundary

THE STORY OF GENERAL MILLS

1

Wheat and Men

THE MIGRATION TO MINNESOTA

MA N Y minds have studied the impulse that drove the American pioneer west, out of the comparative comfort of settled communities into the hazards of the wilderness. He was taking the highway to the future, says the champion of the gospel of progress. He was looking for escape from a desiccated civilization, says the romantic interpreter of the gospel of individualism. He was following his "manifest destiny," says the patriot, by taking effective possession for democracy of the vast expanse of land that lay beyond the Mississippi.

The pioneer himself might well have said, more simply, that he was determined to lay his hands on better rewards than he could ever have had at home where his elders already owned the earth. But this hard-headed fortitude did not transform him automatically into a superman, able to meet the enormous challenges of a new, untried world. The pioneer grew a formidable beard to hide the fact that he was not much more than a boy and also, perhaps, to mask the insecurity that might otherwise have shown in his face when ruin threatened his audacity. Having precipitated himself into a realm that was furnished chiefly with promises, he rattled about in it, sometimes lacking a place to lay his head, often without bread to put in his mouth. The chances must often have seemed to be heavily against his ever being able to lay firm hold on the natural wealth he had traveled so far to find.

Yet within three decades of his arrival on the soil of an unfamiliar, even hostile, world, he had transformed it into an ordered, if not always orderly, society. By act of will he had created a vivid new version of the civilization that he had left behind.

Wheat and Men

The rise of Minneapolis to a dominating position among the milling interests of the country offers an eventful dramatization of that story. By the year 1880 its leadership in the market for breadstuffs had become secure. Yet it was not until 1849 that Minnesota had been formally organized as a territory and several more years were to pass before lands could be opened for settlement. Through years that were shaken by panic, war, and social upheaval of many kinds, men of energy and imagination worked indefatigably at bringing about an achievement that would have been striking in any circumstances and at any time. It was accomplished, in large part, by the fact that pioneer millers' gifts of organization were supported by a determination to offer the best product that milling method could bring to market.

In the early days of the westward migration visitors supposed that the continental climate and soil of Minnesota did not promise well for the production of the major raw material of milling. But in 1853 a writer observed, "No one competent to judge doubts the efficacy of Minnesota as a wheat-growing region, although the crop has not been thoroughly tested yet." This was just a decade and a half before Minnesota farmers harvested a wheat crop of 15,380,000 bushels.

It was the hard red wheat that proved to be the answer to the physical conditions of the North Central states. Planted in the spring and harvested in the summer, it escapes the blight of the severe weather that would kill the winter variety. The texture of its kernel is relatively hard, a characteristic that baffled American millers and bakers before the year 1860 when they began to learn its virtues. Much preferred were the white, soft winter wheats which processors regarded as more manageable. But the higher degree of hardness in spring wheat usually results from a higher proportion of gluten to starch and this, as the processors came presently to know, gives it special value as bread flour. A technological revolution that was soon to come made spring wheat flour the most desired of all such products, putting Minnesota and its millers in a fortunate position to serve the industry and giving Minnesota a name as "the great spring wheat state."

At the moment of Minnesota's beginnings as a state these values were not even suspected and the milling industry was still a modest affair. It came, first, with the movement of population, setting up in business to feed the lumbermen who arrived on the first wave of migration in the 1840s; it grew as wheat production spread westward and the

4

immigrants turned to agriculture as a way of life in the 1850s. As the population increased from 2500 in 1849 to 20,000 in 1853, 30,000 in 1855, and 150,000 in 1858, mills were established to grind the local product. The market, too, was exclusively local. Indeed, before 1859 there was not enough wheat grown in Minnesota to satisfy immediate needs, and additional supplies had to be shipped in by steamboat. Widely scattered mills at Hastings, Northfield, and Dundas served their immediate neighborhoods. They could attempt to reach no broader market for lack of transportation facilities to the east and even of adequate facilities within the borders of the state.

Presently the figure of a man was cast large across these interests. Cadwallader Washburn in the course of his comparatively short association with the milling industry established one of its important companies; helped significantly to cure its transportation difficulties by encouraging the creation of railroad links to the great highways of trade; revolutionized the industry's technical processes; became author of the prestige of his own patent flour; and found a wide market for its distribution.

He was, indeed, a kind of universal genius of business enterprise, the archetype of American entrepreneur who laid his hands on any project that could return him a profit but who touched all his interests with a fastidiousness that allowed the dictates of idealist and patriot to dominate those of the man of affairs.

Washburn had a high brow and a fine shapely promontory of a nose both of which features lent themselves fortunately to the image of the statesman, classic style. Though he was of less than average height, his broad shoulders and erect carriage suited his natural affinity with stateliness and a deep chest lent resonance to the word of authority which he was later to speak in the Congress of the United States and in the governor's office at Madison, Wisconsin.

But in 1839, at the age of twenty-one, this young adventurer was on the threshold of his career in Livermore, Maine. From his eighteenth birthday he had been on his own, working hard on the family farm to hold together the family unit. This consisted of a father who did not enjoy good fortune, a mother who had an intense passion for all things of the mind, and an astonishing assortment of brothers all of whom became distinguished.

The Washburns were men for whom the native mythology must

5

be deeply grateful. "All the brothers were valiant." Israel became governor of Maine. Elihu, long a public servant in Washington, served as Grant's secretary of state and went in 1869 as minister plenipotentiary to France. When all the other diplomats of the world left precipitately for home at the outbreak of the Franco-Prussian War, Elihu stayed at his job and played foster father, during the siege of Paris, to the frightened and bewildered victims of the crisis from whatever country they came. Algernon Sidney served as banker extraordinary to all his enterprising brothers. Charles Ames penetrated to the Pacific Coast where he edited the *San Francisco Daily*, went as Lincoln's minister to Paraguay and wrote a history of that county. Samuel became a seaman and rose to the rank of captain before an injury to his hip incapacitated him for life. William Drew followed Cadwallader to the West where he made and lost fortunes with the zest of one determined to earn the nickname "young Rapid." He represented Minnesota first in the state legislature and later in the United States Senate, erupted with a new enterprise each year, juggling mills, lumber companies, railroads with great energy if not always with great virtuosity.

Mutual admiration and its corollary, mutual dependence, are striking features of the lively family correspondence. The Washburns educated each other, borrowed money from each other, supported each other's enterprises. Each wrote a fine hand and their letters constitute a set of documents out of which flows steadily the tireless enthusiasm of the creative man.

The Washburns offer a composite portrait of the pioneer that is in many ways unlike the hackneyed image of the ruthless builder of empires. They dressed well; they lived well; their very silhouettes were stately and their manners tended to be elaborate. Yet they never lost the rugged integrity of their origins or the simple directness of their basic intentions. In Washington Elihu served so vigilantly on the "committee of commerce" that he earned the nickname "watchdog of the treasury." On one occasion Cadwallader as a member of Congress had succeeded in engineering an appropriation for his state and the question was raised by a jealous rival as to where Elihu, as guardian of public funds, had been when this coup was accomplished. A Washington wit responded: "Don't you know that a watchdog never barks when a member of the family approaches?"

Though oratory was their second language, the vernacular came easily to their tongues. Elihu answered a question about the desirability of leaving Livermore by saying spiritedly, "The West is the place for this child." He anticipated by many years the use of a cherished American-ism when he wrote to one of the brothers that as a means of earning a living the legal profession was "O.K." In the course of the Washburns' endless conversation (by mail) as to who should run for what political office, Cadwallader once described Webster as an "old envious jealous 'cuss'." When Algernon Sidney ("Dear Sid") pressed William Drew for payment on a note, the senator-to-be answered briskly admonishing his brother to "keep cool and let your hair grow." As members of a family they wrangled with hearty impudence but helped each other make permanent contributions to community welfare. As members of a democracy they showed almost exactly the same pattern in relation-ship to their country.

Back in Livermore, Maine, "Cad," as he came inevitably to be called in the loose family slang, had taught school as a side line to farming and read law with an uncle for his own improvement. Then, having dis-charged what he considered to be his apprenticeship duties, he set out to see what his mature talents might earn in the world. He had his eyes on the Mississippi River and there on its banks he eventually established the mill from which a great flour empire grew. It is no mere lip service to tradition that makes General Mills claim Cadwallader Washburn as one of its most illustrious forebears.

But between 1839 and 1842 he wandered widely in the Mississippi Valley seeming to try various communities for size. From one he turned away in disgust when he found business to be "most horrid dull." He read law in another town and clerked in its local store. In a third place he served as surveyor. At Mineral Point in "Wiskonsan" Territory he finally found a home. He was now twenty-four and eager to settle down to the practice of law. All his neighbors seemed to be gratifyingly em-broiled in suits and the community, he reported, was "not so much thronged with lawyers as most places." Within two years he had estab-lished himself as a leader in his profession.

Washburn's partner was Cyrus Woodman, local agent of the Boston and Western Land Company. Among its clients were veterans of the Mexican War who were entitled to grants of land in Wisconsin Territory in payment for their service. Many of them wished to exchange for cash their share in the dubious bounty of a wild new world. Washburn and Woodman, knowing where the mineral riches lay and where the best timber stood, bought up the best of these lands and took their treasure.

Thus Washburn acquired the foundation of his fortune. But it gave him no pleasure to be merely a rich man. The tragedy of his personal experience (his wife had lost her mind early in their marriage) left his private life meager and he turned to new enterprises as an outlet for his imaginative powers as well as for his capital. Presently his eyes turned toward the Mississippi, where at the Falls of St. Anthony an impressive drop of water offered power.

It was the priest-explorer Father Louis Hennepin who had given the Falls their name. As the first representative of European civilization to see them, he claimed the right as discoverer to dedicate them to his patron, St. Anthony of Padua, "in gratitude for favors God did me through the intervention of this great saint."

For nearly a century and a half the Falls continued to serve chiefly the uses of beauty and of grace. The Sioux Indians also considered them to be the shrine of a great spirit. Then in 1823 the United States government built a small gristmill for grinding corn to feed the soldiers at Fort Snelling. The officers in charge tried also to grow wheat and to make flour. But the men did not like the product and rejected it bitterly. They "cursed the bread" in the traditional manner of soldiers who were also sovereign citizens without, however, discouraging the efforts of their superiors. For twenty-six years the government mill at the Falls of St. Anthony continued to be the scene of a monotonous comedy of errors, with officers and men locked in stubborn struggle over the production of bread that no one wanted to eat.

In 1849 when Minnesota began to look like a promising place in which to have interests, a congressman from Alton, Illinois, Robert Smith, developed a long-distance love of the Falls of St. Anthony. On the representation that he wanted a farm on which to establish his family, he was able to persuade the secretary of war to lease him the government mill and a large tract of land on the west wing. It was necessary to pass a special act to permit settlement on a government reservation but this, too, Smith managed. Actually he never occupied the land or operated the mill. In 1851, having bought outright title to the best water power sites for a modest $750, he leased them to Calvin Tuttle, who announced in the *St. Anthony Express* on May 31 that he was "now in readiness for the grinding of Corn, Rye, Oats, Peas, Buckwheat and whatever requires grinding, including salt."

The properties which Smith had spent so much ingenuity in acquiring seem to have served him not at all except as items to be juggled nervously in endless dealings with creditors. In 1855 he became eager to sell eighty-nine acres of his land and, with them, the water power privileges. Washburn paid well and promptly, not realizing how long it would be before their active utilization could begin. For the purpose of leasing his power rights to mill operators he formed the Minneapolis Mill Company and a year later his cousin, Dorilus Morrison, also out of Maine, entered into partnership with him. The corporation, chartered on February 27, 1856, had Smith as president though, except for his low-pitched and wearisome complaints, he remained the most silent of partners. At the same moment "young Rapid" rushed out of Bowdoin College to become his brother's agent at the Falls. (Cadwallader maintained his residence all his life in Wisconsin and he required a local representative for each of his distant enterprises. Tours of his widely scattered properties became magnificent operations rather like royal progresses. Minneapolis and the Nicollet House awaited his arrival with the respect owed to creative man on the march.)

Young Rapid reached the West in an evil hour. The panic of 1857 was about to cast its shadow and its all but deadly chill over the region. The nationwide depression was particularly acute in the Midwest, where the distresses were no mere matters of paper losses and of hopes deferred. The people were bankrupt; they went hungry. One prominent citizen who wore out his shoes in the service of his community had no money with which to buy new ones. Frugally he cut an old leather valise in half, tied the two parts to his large feet with rags and went about his business leaving a strange trail through the Minnesota snowdrifts.

One of the charter obligations of the Minneapolis Mill Company was to carry out an agreement with its neighbor on the east bank of the Mississippi River, the St. Anthony Water Power Company, for the construction of a modern dam to control and share water power. The handsome, audacious pioneer Franklin Steele, who had been on the east bank since 1838 always deep in enterprise and often equally deep in debt, had managed to satisfy his obligation as head of the St. Anthony company. Now in an atmosphere of crisis and threat of disaster young Rapid had to find $60,000 to build his share of the dam and a year later to find

9

$20,000 more for a power canal. He saw the difficult project completed in 1858.

This sea of troubles and expenses, however, engulfed some of the owners, Smith among them, threatening to sweep away the very existence of the Minneapolis Mill Company. Young Rapid improvised strenuously in an effort to make some use of the power rights but the company itself was forced to mark time. It was almost a decade before Cadwallader Washburn's organizing genius could put the Falls effectively to work once more. Meanwhile the major crisis of the Civil War had intervened. To Washburn it seemed clear that the place of a man of spirit was in the army. He refused to consider that his job in Congress made him indispensable. Instead of another term in office, he accepted a commission as colonel and began recruiting the second regiment of Wisconsin cavalry.

Three Washburns had been in Congress simultaneously during the period when the Civil War was still a war of words. Israel, representing Maine, Elihu, representing Illinois, and Cadwallader, representing Wisconsin, all had had their share of eloquence and even of action. (On one occasion when a southern member had made a physical attack on an opponent Cadwallader intervened and, catching the instigator of the trouble by the hair, found that he had all too easily scalped him; the gentleman wore a wig.) As patriots they were opposed to secession and, as humanitarians, to the expansion of slavery as "a great moral, social, and political evil."

Cadwallader was the only one of the brothers actually to serve as a soldier. He fought through three and one-half years, first in the Arkansas campaign and later at Vicksburg and in Texas. His letters to his brothers flowed on, offering accounts of his experiences with the Army of the Tennessee and with the Army of the Potomac that were often luminous with insight, still more often electric with disgust at incompetence or cynicism. (Washburn once rejected with appropriate scorn the offer of a $40,000 bribe to spare certain citizens of a New England town the inconvenience of army service.)

In 1865 as the Civil War moved toward its close, Washburn began to think eagerly of his own affairs. Wishing to clear up the complications of the Minneapolis Mill Company, he wrote from Vicksburg to Robert Smith. The mercurial opportunist had continued to be president because he still controlled land that was important to the operation; but the fluctuations of fortune had made his own temperature seem to shudder between that of fever and that of torpor. Washburn reminded Smith with asperity of these waverings. When the company had seemed likely to be "swept away by the mortgage" Smith had declared that he "could never pay a cent," but "a change of times" had made him eager to share in possible profits. From his army headquarters Washburn negotiated briskly, determined to be free at last of what had been "an unpleasant business." In the end he bought out his partner and Smith retired to the corner of limbo that is reserved for indecisive manipulators.

The company was firmly under Washburn's control when, after the close of the war, he resigned with the rank of major general and returned to his own world of affairs — a much more orderly and progressive world than the one he had left. The Homestead Law of 1862 and the ceding of the Red River Valley by the Chippewa a year later had opened up much land for permanent, inexpensive settlement. The population had increased to 172,000 in 1860 and to 250,000 in 1865. Half of the newcomers were native-born Americans who had taken a zigzag course out of New England. The rest were made up of industrious Germans, politically alert Irishmen, Canadians who were well acquainted with conditions of life in the region, and easily assimilated Scandinavians who found the new country comfortably like the old.

Wheat had established itself securely as a major crop. Enthusiasts began to talk of Minnesota as "the banner wheat state." Production had risen, between 1850 and 1865, from less than 2000 bushels to 2,500,000. Flour milling prospered correspondingly under the stimulus of a price rise from fifty cents in 1860 to $1.50 at the end of the war. Measured even by the standards of pioneer growth the development was fabulous. In 1860 four mills at Minneapolis produced 30,000 barrels of flour; in 1865 seven mills filled 98,000; in 1869, the year after wheat production had reached 15,000,000 bushels, thirteen mills turned out more than 250,000 barrels. These thirteen mills represented an investment of almost half a million dollars and the value of the product had averaged over $1,500,000. It was, in fact, worth more than all the lumber produced in the state.

In 1865 when he returned to the Midwest, Washburn had put behind him an assortment of careers as teacher, farmer, lawyer, real estate dealer, legislator, and soldier. Several more lay ahead as chief executive

11

of his state, as financier, as miller. But it was as a miller that he liked to identify himself.

Actually he never became in any sense a practical worker. He was always the organizer, the director, the instigator of plans which others carried out. But the fact that his approach was theoretical proved in the end to be an enormous advantage. His mind was bound by no commitment to tradition and he used his capital freely to develop a better product than any that had existed before.

So in his late forties, this vigorous, imaginative, imperious, and lonely man began a new career, one into which circumstances had edged him but which was destined to make Minneapolis the center of leadership in the making of flour.

2

Trade into Science

THE MILLING REVOLUTION

T H E Y called it "Washburn's Folly." For, as everyone in the frontier village of Minneapolis knew, a substantial stone mill of six stories, costing a fabulous $100,000 (for structure and brand-new equipment, transported all the way from Buffalo) could not possibly prosper. Twelve "run of stone" (that is, twelve pairs of millstones in working order) would produce more flour than existing markets would be able to absorb.

But Cadwallader Washburn was not in the habit of listening to old wives' gossip or to old husbands' gossip, either. He completed his mill, later called the "B mill," in 1866, knowing that in this summertime of enterprise broader markets could be discovered by men of energy. The rapidly growing midwestern world, full of Civil War veterans with bonus money in their pockets, offered more opportunity than the unimaginative supposed. And beyond this realm there was the eastern market to be invaded and across the Atlantic the not unattainable market of England and the Continent.

Before the limitations arising out of the transportation problem could be overcome, however, two other major difficulties had to be resolved. There was, first, the matter of management since Washburn himself had no intention of attempting to become a mill operator. The second was a matter of method of studying the raw material, hard spring wheat, and of discovering how to utilize fully its fine qualities.

In choosing men to act for him, Washburn had sometimes been more loyal than fortunate. His brother William Drew had served him well in certain instances. While Cadwallader was absent at the Civil

13

Trade into Science

War, the Senator (as he later came to be called) had made what he could of the assets of the Minneapolis Mill Company, leasing parts of its power rights for $100 a year to a buyer here and there (shaving that figure to accommodate friends).

But W. D. Washburn was too mercurial, too opinionated, and too easily distracted to be the best of delegates. He seems to stamp in and out of the story of Minnesota, of its politics, its milling, lumbering, railroad building, always imperiously demanding attention and even more imperiously rejecting any judgment made against him. An eyewitness of the days of the Senator's grandeur recalls a characteristic scene that places this dramatic man in his relation to the world he ruled with autocratic authority. The episode was typical and frequently reenacted in his family circle.

Surrounded by his four sons and two daughters, all as opinionated as himself, Washburn would dominate their discussion even as its crescendo of challenge and defiance grew higher and higher. One of the sons was deaf and dumb, a handicap which with characteristic Washburn determination he refused to acknowledge. At the peak of a family wrangle he would demand, by sign language, to be told what the argument was about. It would then begin all over again at the tips of flying fingers. To conclude the matter, the Senator would refer the point at issue to the encyclopedia and if this authority failed to sustain his own opinion he disdainfully hurled the corpulent volume across the room.

Just so, he hurled away any criticism of his conduct as lawmaker, railroad executive, or businessman.

Full-time work as manager of a big mill would have been too humdrum for a man with many interests of his own in Minneapolis. Though the brothers were still close allies, Cadwallader turned outside the family circle to find experienced men. But there his first choice proved disappointing. The firm of Judd and Brackett had made a success in operating the Cataract Mill, built in 1859. To these men Washburn leased his property at an annual rental of $12,000 a year. Within two years Judd and Brackett had to admit failure. They returned the property to Washburn, and the search was begun all over again for manager or lessee.

Meanwhile another disaster threatened the mill. On a day in October 1869 it was thought that the Falls were "going out" and Minneapolis faced the grim possibility of seeing its livelihood swept away.

The millers of the early days were dramatic men. Their gift of ceremoniousness invites treatment in the traditional style of the pageant. They wore profuse beards and high silk hats and spoke to one another in the grand manner. But they were also men in a great hurry to make their fortunes. They were particularly jealous of the water rights on which their activities depended, and it was a dull day on the river front that did not see stately gentlemen losing their poise and their high hats in a grimly enthusiastic exchange of blows in a water power dispute

Such an impatient man, determined to get more power, decided to dig a tunnel under the Falls and divert to his use a swift flow of water directly from the river.

The result was disastrous. For several years the Falls had been receding as the limestone wore away. The tunnel caused a collapse of the rock formation and water gushed through threatening everything in its way. For days desperate citizens devoted themselves to the task of trying to fill the gap, flinging logs, underbrush, loads of hay into the whirlpool. Still the water rushed on and for a time it looked as though only rapids would be left. In a grand climax of destructiveness three mills were carried away. Finally, a group of cofferdams stopped the flow through the many breaks long enough for government engineers to take over. A wooden apron was thrown over the exposed limestone ledge to prevent further damage. This thick protection stretching across the river and deep into each bank added nothing to the beauty of the Falls. The chronic rhapsodist Father Hennepin might have grieved over this dese-cration to his discovery. But the usefulness of the Falls had been pre-served for generations of grateful citizens.

With the saving of the Falls the milling industry seemed to take an-other spurt forward. At this moment Charles A. Pillsbury arrived in Minneapolis and purchased an interest in a mill. Later he drew his uncle, John Sargent Pillsbury, and others of the family group into a major enter-prise with which Washburn was presently involved in a stimulating rivalry that lasted down the years. In the same period (1869–76), the number of mills increased at the rate of two a year and the annual output of flour multiplied many times over. It rose from 585,000 barrels in 1873 to 727,000 in 1874, to 843,000 in 1875, and reached 1,000,000 barrels in 1876.

If he were to play an effective role in this development, Cadwallader Washburn had to have an active ally in management. On June 3, 1869, W. D. Washburn told his brother that the search was over.

Trade into Science

"I believe I have found the man who will fill the bill in the mill question," he wrote. (Graceful rhetoric was never one of W. D.'s assets even when he occupied a desk in the United States Senate.) "It is George H. Christian, who has been operating in flour here [Minneapolis] for the past three years and who is undoubtedly the best operator in the state, honest, economical and cautious."

Christian was a great deal better than this ungrudging, yet guarded, estimate managed to suggest. Qualities of insight, industry, and imagination enabled him to serve not merely himself but the wheat and flour workers of the entire country.

Born to be an original investigator, George Christian made his debut in a most improbable place. His boyhood home in rural Alabama offered little in the way of formal education. But an enthusiasm for the occupations of the mind had been communicated to him as a boy by a frail eccentric known to his neighbors only as "the ghost." This strange figure haunted Christian all his life, prompting him to teach himself French, German, Italian, and even a little Greek. He taught himself also to play the organ, and it was characteristic of his particular kind of self-discipline that he once set himself the task of mastering the scores in a book of compositions. Having played them through, seriatim, without error, he never played again.

Like many another miller and lumberman of the region, the seasonal aspect of whose work allowed them, now and again, a little leisure, Christian was a mighty traveler. In the course of his journeys back and forth across the world he became a sensitive appreciator of the fine arts and a collector in many fields.

Henry James would have understood such an American pilgrim but even the novelist's intuition would not have enabled him to encompass this man's variety of interests. Christian lived richly and exultantly in the realm of business, an atmosphere which James did not understand at all so that his rich Americans seem always to float poetically, but unbelievably, on a vague tide of dollars. The first million made by this miller came so easily that he was able to retire (though only temporarily) while still a very young man. Once when he sold one of his enterprises he complained quizzically that he had not received enough for it. Why, then, had he not held out for more from his buyer? "Because," said Christian gleefully, "I had already got all he had."

This able man of affairs drove a succession of shrewd bargains with

16

Washburn. Their final contract called for the contribution by Washburn of the mills and the water power to match Christian's contribution of management. In addition, each man was to invest $12,000, and net profits were to be distributed on the basis of five eighths for Washburn, three eighths for Christian. Washburn was to be so silent a partner that the company was to bear only Christian's name.

At last a fruitful agreement had been made for the operation of Washburn's Folly. Christian had an unappeasable appetite for knowledge in and out of his own field and to him must go much credit for solving the milling problems involved in the use of hard spring wheat.

This variety of grain had come to the Northwest out of Canada. Earlier it had migrated from Russia to Germany, then from Germany to Scotland, prospering in all these places because, though their severe climates would have killed fall-sown wheats, their spring and early summer weather favored the perfect maturing of the berry with its gluten-rich endosperm.

Before 1870, however, millers did not know how to make the most of this asset, and spring wheat was quoted in Chicago at ten cents a bushel less than winter wheat, while flour made from it sold for a dollar a barrel less than flour made from its much preferred rival.

A series of improvements in milling method, all developed in Minnesota properties, exactly reversed this situation and made spring wheat the aristocrat among grains, able to command a high premium on the Chicago Exchange. The "milling revolution," as this event of technological history came to be called, wrote finis to the primitive practices that had endured for centuries and opened the modern chapter.

The gristmill of the pioneer world to which farmers took their wheat used a method similar in essential respects to the process that man had employed for hundreds of years. The many successive grinding and sifting operations by which the kernel is gradually reduced to flour in the modern mill had as their wasteful substitute only a few rigorous steps. Millstones were in universal use and millers tried to pulverize as fine as possible and to make as much flour as they were able at one grinding. The products of this initial attack on the wheat berry were three: flour consisting of pure endosperm, the starchy interior of the kernel; bran, the fibrous outer covering; and middlings, a term used in the milling language of the day to describe the less fine particles of floury matter to which bits of bran might still adhere.

17

Milling method required, in these mid years of the nineteenth century, that millstones be set close together and run at a high rate of speed. The "fast reduction" method "bolted" out a reasonably satisfactory amount of flour but the by-products were of no great value. Middlings though they contained valuable endosperm could not, because of their inadequately refined state, be sold as flour of first quality. In the early days they were offered only to the Indians under the disparagingly impolite name "red dog."

With the debut of the spring wheat in Minnesota it became evident to leaders that something must be done to improve milling methods. The fast reduction process presented here particularly exacting problems. It tended to shatter the hard, friable grain, mixing the bran through the flour. Sifting operations recovered far too little of first-rate flour, far too much of the by-product middlings. Furthermore, even the flour was discolored by pulverized bran.

The economic problem was serious. A method must be found to treat the middlings in a second process to purify them of contamination from bran and so to recover larger quantities of flour.

It was the country miller who took the first step. At his fine mill in Hastings it was the practice of Stephen Gardner to reduce the pressure of the millstones and to increase the number of grindings. By doing so he produced a flour which sold in the East at one to two dollars higher a barrel. And under its own name, too, instead of masquerading mendaciously, as did some Minnesota flour, under the label "Made in St. Louis."

Before he joined Washburn, George Christian had been trained as buyer for a flour commission house. Now that he had exchanged his role for that of seller he devoted the best of his professional knowledge to improvement of his product. He knew of the work of Gardner, whose mill he had visited often in making his rounds. He knew also of the accomplishments of the Archibald brothers at Dundas. The Archibalds milled a flour which bakers called "the doctor," because, when blended with other flours, it seemed to cure any ill. Christian, who liked nothing better than experimentation, set out to develop such a doctor of his own.

His efforts had not gone far when by happy accident there appeared in Minneapolis a wandering engineer, Edmond La Croix, who had come with his brother Nicolas out of Montreal looking for a place to employ the family talents. The La Croixs had been educated in France at the

Ecole des Arts et Metiers. As professional engineers they had built mills in Minnesota and experimented with a mechanism that came to be known as the "middlings purifier." This device cannot be called the invention of any one experimenter. Edmond La Croix had become familiar in France with the theory of the purifier and with one machine — that of Perrigault — designed to make it function practically. But the intensive work that he did for George Christian in the remodeled Washburn B mill proved to be decisive in finding a solution for the ancient problem.

His model, produced in great secrecy behind locked doors, was, as Christian reported later, "a small crudely built arrangement of moving sieves." These received the middlings for the second treatment required to reduce a large part to first-rate flour. It exposed them to a rising current of air which held in suspension the lighter particles of bran and allowed the pure middlings to pass through the sieves without the branny contamination.

The new machine did not work perfectly. Many years later Christian still remembered its "good and evil moods" with a certain bitterness. One of its evils was the fact that the belting (or sifting) cloth became clogged so badly that it was necessary to have a workman stand over it to brush the lower surface by hand. This stutter in technique was presently corrected by a head miller, George T. Smith, who devised an automatic traveling brush to keep the cloth clean. Smith improved upon La Croix's machine in other ways, by putting air currents under more complete control and by devising a method which partially graded the middlings.

In the end, the combined brains of many men, working on the practical application of an already established principle, produced a machine which revolutionized milling, transformed spring wheat from a kind of Cinderella of the trade to heiress of its best tradition, and profoundly affected the economy of the Midwest.

In accordance with the respectable tradition of the time, which advised a sensible man to keep a good thing to himself, Christian tried to keep the development of the purifier a secret. But ideas have a way of eluding locked doors and armed guards. Smith went to work for Charles Pillsbury, taking his knowledge with him. La Croix left Christian's employ to install a purifier in the Cataract Mill. And at last the principle of middlings purification passed, as was proper, into the keeping of the entire trade.

Trade into Science

The product of the "new process" was called "patent flour" and all millers who used the purifier were entitled also to the prestige that attached to this identification of their high-grade flours. Buyers paid well for the new commodity. In 1871, just before the development of the "new process," profits per barrel had averaged fifty cents. In 1872 they rose to $1, in 1873 to $2, and finally in 1874, before competition began to check the upward tendency, to between $4 and $4.50. It was sound practice to pay such prices, for, as the bakers themselves said, a barrel of Minneapolis flour made 12½ per cent more bread than did the best winter wheat flour. The supremacy of spring wheat was established.

For his willingness to support Christian in theoretical experimentation Cadwallader Washburn had been abundantly rewarded. In an issue of 1877 the *Northwestern Miller* estimated that his B mill had made profits in a three-year period of $650,000. In addition, he was delighted with the realization that "my mills," as he called them proudly, had become recognized as a kind of laboratory for the entire industry. Further experiments which served to complete the "milling revolution" were generously encouraged and supported by his financial aid. He was a close follower of Christian's innovations and on each of his trips abroad had made extensive studies of European methods.

Then circumstances took a clumsy hand in these matters and tragedy revealed the necessity of making further fundamental changes.

At 6:30 on the evening of May 2, 1878, as Minneapolis had just finished its work for the day and was on its way home to dinner, the pleasant hum of daily routine on river and highway was suddenly interrupted by a loud, inexplicable sound. One observer reported seeing "a bunch of heavy dark smoke" rising above the Falls. On the surface of the water "a red glare" shone for a moment and then "fell back and was dissipated." Down in the mill district "a sheet of flame" seemed to flutter along the street while burning timbers were hurtled in the air.

There had been an explosion. The Washburn A mill (built in 1873, seven years after the B mill but larger in size) lay in ruins with eighteen men buried under its collapsed walls. Three neighboring mills had been wrecked in a chain of secondary explosions; three more caught fire; a cooper shop and lumber yard went next; in what seemed like the repetitive frenzy of insanity, the whole river front shouted disaster.

The cause of the explosion was, of course, a question of terrifying interest both to the community and to the industry. Nearly half the city's milling capacity had been destroyed at a stroke and such a risk could not be run again. The answer found eventually was that the milling process tended to fill the air with fine flour dust which was likely to explode if ignited by a stray spark. To eliminate this hazard there must be more efficient equipment to collect dust, and during the next few years adequate machines for that purpose were evolved. But Cadwallader Washburn needed a new mill as well as better dust collectors. He wanted — and he wanted quickly — the best mill that could be designed.

On his first visit to the ruins he paced out the exact space that the new plant was to occupy. The next step, taken at the same brisk rate, was to select for the planning and equipment of the structure the best engineer he could find. George Christian had left him in 1875 for other interests — cultural and managerial — but even without his aid, Washburn was determined to proceed steadily toward the future under the guidance of science.

William de la Barre was the man he chose, a man admirably trained to help in the work of completing the revolution in technique. His formal instruction in mechanical engineering had been received at the Polytechnic Academy in Vienna; for a short time, before emigrating to America, he had served in the engineering corps of the Austrian navy; and in his new American home he had held important posts, like that of engineer for the Centennial Exposition at Philadelphia in 1876.

An important figure in the history of milling at Minneapolis, de la Barre seemed to dramatize in his own person the story of the immigrant's transformation into an American. He was a composite of all the cultures his life had touched, as genial and courteous as a Viennese headwaiter, as direct and forthright as a midwestern merchant. His memoirs, written when he was eighty-six years old and blind, reflect a touching enthusiasm for the pioneer work of the past and an unbaffled patience under the hardship of the moment. He made the best of his two worlds.

At the Centennial Exposition de la Barre became acquainted with all the new technological devices of the time including the Hungarian roller mill for the gradual reduction of flour and Gustav Behrn's machine for the ventilation of millstones, the great asset of which was an exhaust preventing the diffusion of flour dust through the mill. As the representative of Behrn's American agent, de la Barre visited Minneapolis on appointment with Washburn to show him the value of the new machines.

When he arrived the ruins of the mill were still smoldering, but he had not come fast enough to suit Washburn who received him briskly, saying: "You were slow in getting here. Sit down and tell me all that you know and make it short and to the point."

What de la Barre knew was that the Behrn exhaust was a good safety device and of this he was able to convince Washburn (after a free demonstration for which Washburn later paid voluntarily both in money and in gratitude). When discussion of equipment for a new mill proceeded to Hungarian rollers and gradual reduction, de la Barre could tell Washburn something of the process, but he was not familiar with all the technological details. Since 1873 there had been great curiosity in America about the new European method of passing grain through a series of rollers instead of feeding it between millstones. Experiments with this technique had been made at Winona and also by Christian at Minneapolis. But cast-iron rollers wore down too quickly, porcelain ones tended to chip.

Now Washburn was determined to overcome the difficulties and he engaged de la Barre to help solve them. For the practical work of adapting European method to American conditions a Bavarian engineer, Oscar Oexle, was imported and Oexle, in his turn, imported a professional millwright as assistant. Neither of these accomplished workers spoke English and the difficulty of communication was increased further by the fact that Oexle was blind. Whenever a drama of international conflict threatened to explode, de la Barre served as interpreter, liaison officer, and diplomatist extraordinary; but even his tact could not prevent occasional breakdowns in the course of which differences of language, of scientific faith, and of technological practice seemed to rage hopelessly together. Washburn, in the role of "grand old leader," kept everyone encouraged and ego-fed while the work approached completion. In the end, de la Barre made a significant contribution by suggesting the substitution of steel for porcelain rolls. Eliminated all at once by this stroke of inspiration were the intolerable noise of the porcelain rolls, their tendency to become heated and to crack, the likelihood of their falling out of balance, and their limited capacity for work. The very description of the porcelain sounds like a diagnosis of hysteria; by comparison the steel rolls were sane, stable, enormously productive workers.

Yet even after the whims of the new process had been disciplined theoretically, a practical daily routine had to be established. Washburn interrupted de la Barre in the work of rebuilding the A mill and sent him again to Hungary to study roller-mill methods. Though many changes had been made in the process of adapting European ways to American needs, still it was hoped that short cuts to competence might be discovered by watching the operation actually at work. The conscientious de la Barre hesitated. After all, he said, he knew little about the new process. "In that," Washburn answered "you are like the rest of us here. You have everything to learn and nothing to forget. Go ahead and learn all you can in the shortest possible time and then we will proceed."

In Europe an atmosphere of international intrigue enveloped de la Barre. As he traveled to Switzerland, to Germany, to Austria, to Hungary, his reputation preceded him and, one after another, the mills were closed at his approach. Jealous of their prestige and their markets, the Hungarian millers guarded their secrets. In the end a grand conspiratorial crisis was reached, appropriately enough in Budapest where conspiracy always has flourished. After a furtive meeting and a whispered conversation with a millwright who proved to be amenable to reason, de la Barre went into the plant heavily disguised as a workman. He learned what he needed to know and made a hasty departure to the comparative security of easygoing Vienna. There he drew his plans for the installation of machinery in the new Washburn A mill.

And now the milling revolution was complete. The development of the middlings purifier and of the roller-mill process had established the technique of gradual reduction whereby a better flour, a more reliable flour, a cleaner flour, and much more of it could be produced more safely and more economically. Traditionalists complained bitterly for a time that milling had lost all its picturesqueness. The steel rolls and their patent flour must, these people thought, be somehow less desirable than the product of the picture-postcard mill and of its sentimental-ballad operator. But the realistic learned very soon to appreciate and to want the advantages of the new processes.

Washburn was not possessive of them. Once de la Barre was called upon at his home by rival millers and questioned about the "new process." He told Washburn of the episode. "You were right to give full information and advice," his employer told him. "My mills are only a small part of the whole. I can't make all the flour people want, even if I wished to. I have no liking for any dog-in-the-manger business."

He meant it. All his life had been lived in the atmosphere of experimentation. He had begun to study the techniques of milling because his spontaneous impulse was to find the best way of accomplishing a purpose. The explosion had proved to be an experiment by ordeal, completing his own education. He was glad to pass on the fruits of that education to others.

But he was, to be sure, no quixotic philanthropist. After the explosion the insurance companies fought his claims, protesting ingeniously that his policies had protected him against fire but that it was an explosion that had destroyed his property. With the intimidating austerity of an uncompromising moralist, Washburn stood on his rights. Finally every cent was paid, for Washburn would accept no compromise with truth and justice. It was, as the insurance companies learned, quite impossible to make a deal with this solid, granitic, out-of-Maine embodiment of moral principle.

Fortunately for his associates, Washburn's awareness of what he owed was as sensitive as his awareness of what was owed to him. After the explosion he planned generously to provide relief for the families of the men who had lost their lives and found work for the men made idle by the shutdown of the old mill in the building of the new.

A benevolent autocrat, Washburn often demonstrated his desire to serve the whole milling district. On one of his royal progresses through Minneapolis he noticed with distaste how deep in mud lay the only path by which the men and their employers made their way to work. A sidewalk must be built at once, he ordered.

On his next visit he inspected the result and was still dissatisfied. The carpenter was summoned. Why had his instructions been disregarded, Washburn asked. He had ordered a walk two planks wide.

"But, Governor," the carpenter protested, thinking perhaps of the fist fights on the water front, "you never saw two millers walking side by side on the street."

"Nevertheless," Washburn repeated gravely, "the sidewalk must be two planks wide."

He did as much as any man of his time to persuade millers to walk side by side. As a eulogist once said, by championing the development of new techniques, he had transformed "a trade into a science." By virtue of that leadership he had taught himself and his neighbors as well to make a superior product; and by virtue of having a product of quality to sell he and his rivals together had come into acknowledged command of the milling industry in America.

3

Minneapolis in Command

THE MILLING CENTER OF THE WORLD

CADWALLADER WASHBURN, having made his distinguished contribution to quality in his product, began in the 1870s to address himself vigorously to the new problem of quantity. As a large-scale producer he had to face two challenges: first, that of finding markets for his rapidly growing output of flour; second, that of attracting a sufficient flow of wheat to his mills to maintain their great capacity.

Minneapolis, thriving and growing as it was, had long since outgrown the local market for the disposal of its flour. The glittering reputation of the product of the "new process" made eastern millers anxious to have large supplies of it for blending purposes. The great question of the moment for Minneapolis was how to get its flour from the Falls to the distant customers.

Up to 1867 traffic had been chiefly by water. But the troubles of winter weather created all kinds of harassing difficulties that hampered industrial development. During the late 1860s W. D. Washburn was forever writing to his brother, then representing Wisconsin in Congress, about these trials:

"The Northern line of steamboats has been running their boats quite regularly for the past few weeks. While the water remains at the present stage there will be no difficulty in their coming. But after a while they will commence hitting boulders, a few of which remain in the channel. The two government steamboats are lying idle in St. Paul and could as well as not be employed in taking out these boulders. Can you not write to the War Department on the subject?"

Minneapolis in Command

What was needed for all the trade was a system of railroads that would link the lumber operations, the wheat fields, and the mills with the East. There had been frustrating delays due to the failure of over-ambitious efforts in the 1850s when, despite munificent land grants, companies crippled by hard times had not produced much in the way of track. The state had been left holding the worthless bonds issued to advance these operations and it was a miller, John Sargent Pillsbury, who, as governor of Minnesota, insisted that his administration would not countenance defalcation on the bonds but that Minnesota's public honor must be kept immaculate.

A second spurt of energy in the late 1860s and early 1870s brought the outline of the state's railroad system into existence all within a period of ten years. By 1871 direct service to the East was complete and a network of rails tied in such major interests as those of the Red River Valley, where the "bonanza" operations in wheat farming were already established. These roads into the wheat fields had their natural meeting place in Minneapolis and, as early as 1868, the *Minneapolis Tribune* was able to boast that the community had become "the acknowledged railroad center of the upper Mississippi." This development was largely spontaneous and the millers did little to stimulate it. Their business represented an important factor in the success of the railroads and, in the end, the mills profited also by this success.

But relations between mills and railroads did not resemble an uninterrupted love affair. There were many quarrels to be worked through before a lasting amity could be achieved. In two major crises the railroads failed or refused to satisfy the millers' needs. Each time the milling fraternity joined hands to supply lines of their own; each time, the Washburns — Cadwallader and William Drew — were in the center of the enterprise.

The first new railroad line came about as a result of the effort of the city of Milwaukee, supported of course by the railroads, to keep its position as a grain center. Before the time of Minneapolis' ascendency that of Milwaukee had been unchallenged.

A letter from W. D. Washburn stated the problem succinctly:

"Dear Cad: The autocrat of the Milwaukee [the Chicago, Milwaukee and St. Paul Railway] has been here and overawed the whole crowd. His treatment of the millers has been infamous. He has put in buyers, thereby putting up the price of wheat ten cents a bushel. He regulates freight on his road to suit himself. 'Tis said that the scoundrel has made for himself in the last three years half a million dollars. We have got to have other railroad connections or we are gone up."

It was not in the nature of the Washburns to "go up" without a struggle. Like the other millers of Minneapolis they had looked toward Lake Superior to provide them with an alternate route to the East by way of the Great Lakes. Such a comparatively cheap means of transportation would provide them with an effective argument in future discussion of freight rates with the railroads themselves. When in 1870 the Lake Superior and Mississippi Railroad opened a branch line from St. Paul to Duluth, the millers had only to supply the last link of the chain. This the Minneapolis and St. Louis provided, adding the second advantage of spanning the distance between the mills and the fertile wheat fields of southern Minnesota and northern Iowa.

The older railroads were not, of course, immediately chastened in spirit. They continued to produce extraordinary conundrums of finance by dreaming up freight rates that made it as expensive to ship goods from one Minnesota community to another as to send them halfway across the continent. The newly organized Patrons of Husbandry were outraged and in the grange meetings passed eloquent resolutions against discriminatory rates. Politicians were not eager in that moment to talk very severely to the railroads and it was only in periods of comparative quiet between elections that the cautious governors of Minnesota cared to make fine rumblings of protest. In such an interval one chief executive did growl that the time had come "to take these robber corporations by the scruff of the neck and shake them over hell."

The Grangers managed at last to get a law passed by the state legislature calling for the creation of a commission of three men to establish rates and, if necessary, to bring suits against violators. But by 1874 an end had come to the spurt of railroad-building energy. The panic of the preceding year had thrown them on evil days and it seemed unsporting to nag at the fallen. A milder law of 1875 reduced the commission to a single member and this man had power, as the historian Folwell has said, only "to hold down a swivel chair" and to transmit without comment the required reports of railroad presidents. Finally, in the year 1876, the United States Supreme Court, in a decision reached in the case of Munn vs. Illinois, established firmly the right of state legislatures to regulate rates and fares. This precedent, together with the competition offered by the water route, prevented railroads from absorbing all the profits of Minnesota's farming and milling enterprises.

The Washburns were leaders also in the revolt that led to the creation of another passageway to the East. In 1873 W. D. Washburn as president of the Board of Trade in Minneapolis invited his brother Israel, then governor of Maine, to address a meeting of his associates. Israel spent the evening urging that because the lake route was open only part of the year, millers must provide themselves with a direct escape to the Atlantic seaboard by rail. A meeting at Sault Sainte Marie with lines which Canada was building would bring about a union of East and West. The idea was more than a generation in germinating but out of it there developed an important project, the building of the Soo Line with W. D. Washburn as its president. Construction was begun in 1885 and in 1888 the Canadian Pacific Railroad linked the Soo with its own main line. In that year through train service was established between Minneapolis and Boston, providing effective competition to the services through Chicago.

The development of the Soo Line coincided with the second spurt of energy in building Minnesota's railroads. By 1890 six thousand miles of track existed to satisfy almost any need that agriculture or industry might feel.

Cadwallader Washburn's second challenge, that of maintaining a sufficient flow of raw material to his mills, required equally vigorous handling.

In the days before Minneapolis established its dominating position in the milling world, the city was not the natural outlet into which the streams of grain flowed. Wheat went by steamer to St. Louis and later by rail to Milwaukee and Chicago. Under the stimulus of the "new process" and the roller-grinding method, the mills at the Falls grew prodigiously and were constantly wheat hungry. Their output rose from 850,000 barrels in 1875 to 2,000,000 in 1880, to more than 5,000,000 in 1885 and to nearly 7,000,000 in 1889.

To get supplies for this great industrial animal required something of the ingenuity of the hunter. The millers went hunting — and not singly. Though rivalries in production and in selling were intense, alliances entered into to gain particular common ends were frequent and reasonably harmonious. The prominent members of the two great firms — the one dominated by Charles A. Pillsbury, then the larger company, and that dominated by Cadwallader Washburn — served together on the boards of the millers' railroads. Again in 1869 they joined hands to form the Minneapolis Millers' Association.

At first this was an informal coming together (the association was not incorporated until 1876). However, its purpose was final. It was to serve as a buying pool for millers and eighteen out of the twenty firms then active in milling were members. It maintained an office in Minneapolis from which agents went out into the country to buy supplies. The grain purchased by these agents was distributed to the mills according to their capacity. The advantages of the system from the miller's point of view were, first, that it deflected streams of wheat from other milling or market centers; second, that it eliminated competition in a period when many other American businesses were taking similar steps to avoid having their throats cut; and third, that it reduced buying expenses.

For their part the farmers did not like the association at all. They considered that this union of buyers fixed prices arbitrarily and that the close cooperation between millers and the managers of elevators owned or controlled by railroads worked to the wheat growers' disadvantage in the matter of grading. The issue came to a head in 1878 during the "brass kettle" election campaign, so called in derisive salute to the brass tester which the farmer so distrusted in the hands of the grain inspector. Two of the region's most striking personalities were pitted against each other for one of Minnesota's seats in the federal House of Representatives, and they chose to fight as champions of miller and farmer in a battle over the issue of monopoly. W. D. Washburn flung his aristocratic person and his weight of authority at Ignatius Donnelly and Donnelly, not in the least reluctant, flung back the humorous rotundity of his figure and the noble petulance of his oratory.

Washburn won, for though the millers could not deny that they took all the wheat they could get, they were able to show that they paid higher prices, generally, than grain growers received at Chicago and Milwaukee. A point was made, however, in the farmer's favor by the campaign. The millers no longer were willing to be blamed for the sins of the elevator men and they began to construct their own chain of elevators for the storage of grain. The area of wheat growing and of wheat supplies became too large for anyone to wish (or hope) to control it. Further, in 1881 the Minneapolis Chamber of Commerce — later known as the Grain Exchange — was created by a group of businessmen, some representing commission houses, to serve as an organized grain market. Though the millers fought it for a time they chose at last to dissolve their own organization and henceforth did their buying on its floor. In 1885 the legislature established a state system of grading intended to eliminate the evils of which the farmers had complained so long. All things conspired to make the millers wish to woo and to win the good will of the farmers.

Glimpses of this midwestern world in the decades of the 1870s and 1880s show it effectively exploiting its resources. Capital and men had been pouring in from the eastern states and from Europe for more than a quarter of a century and were still coming. The prairie had been opened for settlement as free homesteads or as farm units bought from the railroads. A new kind of steel plough had broken the fertile but heavy soil. The harvester, the binder, and the threshing machine had enabled a small labor force to evolve what was virtually mass production. The railroads that crisscrossed the land, the elevators, the box cars, the practice of grading grain, and the competition between the railroads and lake carriers had given the farmer cheap mass transportation. The "new process" had converted a previously intractable grain into superior flour. A midwesterner might well feel that here was "a tide in the affairs of men which taken at the flood leads on to fortune."

The fortune would have to be found in the great expansion of markets, in discovering new demand to absorb the mounting supply. The home market was growing as the population increased (30 per cent during the 1870s) and as eastern farmers turned their attention more and more to corn, hogs, or dairy produce, leaving to the midwesterner the task of filling the nation's breadbasket. But beyond the 50,000,000 American customers of 1880, tens of millions across the Atlantic were coming within reach of the midwestern farmer. The populations of Scandinavia, Germany, and still more the United Kingdom were multiplying rapidly. By 1880 the British Isles housed almost 35,000,000 people, despite the exodus of the Irish. Britain's inability to produce all her own breadstuffs had been officially recognized in the repeal of the protective corn laws in 1846, thereby throwing her ports open duty-free to grain from all over the world.

For a time the supplementing imports came from European farms — those of Russia, those of rural Germany, sometimes those of France. Only when Europe's crop was short and America's abundant did the British price rise high enough to make American exports profitable after the heavy freight rates to the eastern seaboard and across the ocean had been paid. The Anglo-American grain trade, therefore, had grown slowly with violent oscillations between deep troughs and high peaks. By 1870, however, the upward trend had become more rapid.

The laying of the transatlantic cable in 1866 helped grain merchants to operate in a world market, for they could know at any moment the price in Chicago or New York as well as in Danzig, Hamburg, or Odessa. Competition between the old sailing vessel and the new cargo steamship was paring ocean rates. It was the moment for the American producer to get one foot firmly planted in the transatlantic trade.

Nature helped him almost overnight to get in on two feet by deluging the European grain fields with an almost unbroken series of cold wet seasons between 1874 and 1882. Bleak springs, sunless summers, icy rains, flooded fields, scanty crops, mildewed wheat, potato blight, mold in hops — these were the advance guard that ushered in twenty years of agricultural depression.

The Old World's tragedy was the New World's opportunity. British imports of wheat jumped from less than 30,000,000 bushels in the early 1870s to more than 80,000,000 bushels in 1879. In smaller measure, only because the countries themselves were smaller, Belgium, Holland, and Scandinavia became dependent on America, and their farmers, like the British farmers, had to turn painfully in search of other ways of scratching sustenance from their land.

As Cadwallader Washburn watched this development during the 1870s, he reasoned, if Europe must have American wheat why should it not be persuaded to accept American flour? He urged his associates at the Falls to join him in an attempted invasion of the British market. But the others did not immediately perceive the opportunity and Washburn decided to make the attempt alone. He chose a good time, for in 1877 the British had a particularly bleak season and he had a good salesman to send.

Even within the limits of the domestic market Washburn's affairs had been prospering. His mills had expanded their operations steadily under the stimulus of new capital, largely the reinvested profits of the boom years when the "new process" had sent the price of patent flour high. But problems of management still plagued him. George Christian's retirement in 1875 had been prompted by competition and the general depression of 1873, which sent the price level down. Christian said bluntly that if "a man could no longer make more than a dollar's profit on a barrel of flour, it was time to quit." His retirement caused Washburn to split his interests. Under the name John A. Christian and Company the A mill was managed by George H. Christian's brothers, John and Llewellyn. By a partnership arrangement with Christopher G. Hazard the B mill became the owner's acknowledged responsibility under the firm name of Washburn, Hazard.

This adjustment was not to last long either. Then, at last, in 1877 there came to Washburn's assistance two men who were to give permanent form and special character to his milling enterprises. John Crosby and William Hood Dunwoody fulfilled Washburn's purposes and they survived him — one by five, the other by thirty years — as the perfect disciples for whom he had long been looking.

John Crosby, first of his name to be associated with the flour-milling firm, came into the milling community through family and geographical association. In Bangor, Maine, he had married a sister of Mrs. W. D. Washburn. When the Minneapolis mill needed new management in 1877, his brother-in-law recommended him as a potentially congenial and thoroughly competent partner. It helped to catch Cadwallader's favorable attention that Crosby, like all the Washburns, was Maine born and bred. Tragic circumstances made him ready to move. His wife had just died of tuberculosis and he was looking for a new home in which to rear his children. Part of the contemporary folklore was that the "bracing" climate of the Midwest, while it challenged endurance, ensured survival. In that belief he accepted the invitation to Minnesota.

At 47 he was a stocky, well-made man with a fine ruddy beard, a great booming voice, a spontaneous capacity for making friends, and a gift for keeping them thanks to a broad humanitarianism that made everyone call him "Honest John." He demonstrated this trait well on one occasion when the millers of Minneapolis urged him to join in a plan for wage cutting. "Gentlemen," said Crosby, who never wasted a word even in his affectionate letters to his children, "I shall pay my men what they are worth to me." He did so all his life and had, in return, the intense loyalty of his employees.

In Maine he had done well, working first for his father in a paper mill, later for his father-in-law in an iron foundry. His father before him had been good at many things — banking, loading his own lumber onto his own ships, making rum — any task that served the spirit of man.

The same strenuous impulse took John Crosby at nineteen around Cape Horn during the rush to the gold fields. But he found them lonely fields and he returned to Maine to get on with more familiar tasks. It was a quarter of a century later that he moved to Minnesota.

The second recruit to Washburn's team, Dunwoody, had had a busy career in flour milling before he reached Minneapolis at the age of thirty-six. In his native Philadelphia he had served an apprenticeship among Quaker friends and relatives who taught him to be patient, silent, and thorough, and to keep a close eye on the books.

A curious figure in the business world, he looked like an exquisite, limited edition of a diplomatist, with the face of an aristocrat, a delicately nurtured Van Dyke beard, and a gentle, reassuring manner. A man of frail health in his middle years, dedicated to intellectual interests and stubbornly sedentary ways, he later submitted to a complete revision of his personal life, becoming an out-of-doors man, a mighty fisherman, and a tireless pursuer of game.

There was about Dunwoody a kind of soft persistence that gave him a triumphant career in business. It made him precisely the person to send to England in 1877 when it was his task to force open the door for Minneapolis flour. Washburn, aware of his long experience as flour merchant, appointed him to the newly created post of foreign representative. Without his polite and patient refusal to accept rebuff a start could not have been made toward the establishment of the huge export trade that did so much to give Minneapolis its prestige in the milling world.

In the course of his mission Dunwoody visited all the flour houses and large bakeries in Liverpool, London, and Glasgow. He was not made welcome. Their tempers sharpened by problems that seemed great enough without any aggravation from upstart foreigners, the heads of these organizations often met his request for an interview with the hint that his visit was mere "meddlesome interference." The English did not like the whiteness of American flour. Knowing nothing of the middlings purifier, they assumed — and sometimes said so bluntly — that the product Dunwoody had to offer must be mixed with alum, marble, or dust to be so pale. They were used to working with flour that contained more moisture. They complained of a lack of uniformity. In short they wanted none of it.

Through many tense months (1877–78), before he wrote a single order, Dunwoody went on saying with Quaker firmness that his flour was of a uniformly high quality and uniquely pure consistency. The only dealers who would listen to him, at first, advised cynically that he yield to the very practices against which the *London Miller* often protested, that he put his flour into the hands of wheat receivers and allow them to mix it with their own. He must not attempt to establish his own brand but wink at the practice of putting on any flour any name that happened to be in demand.

Through clouds of insults, uncertainties, and rumors of a Russo-Turkish war which might cut off supplies of Russian grain through the Dardanelles, Dunwoody made his quiet way. First in Scotland where his family name recommended him to men of his own background he was able, as he reported modestly, to "gain a foothold." By going directly to bakers and giving them samples of his flour with which to make independent tests he was able to crack the solid barrier of prejudice. When English bakers found that American flour was stronger and made more loaves per barrel than their own native product, they were able to force British middlemen to buy. Later, English housewives, too, learned the value of the American product and the family "patent" flours were also made welcome.

It was useless to have resisted Dunwoody, for he represented the new age when the goods of the New World must flow back to the Old. Again the tragedy of Europe's agricultural depression served the American merchant miller. He could outsell his English counterpart because he had the best and cheapest of wheat supplies to draw upon and also he had far better methods of manufacture. As the export trade developed, the railroads, rivaling one another for this new business, lowered their rates, made convenient arrangements for handling, and secured direct connections with steamships so that there should be no delay in shipment.

The new business boomed. Direct exports of flour from Minneapolis rose from the few hundred barrels for which Dunwoody had worked so hard in 1877 to one hundred thousand the next year and after that from two million in 1885 to four million barrels in 1895.

Dunwoody's trip, which seemed so bleak in its first months, must be set down as the salesman's dream of glory. It changed the outlook for an entire industry, placed Minneapolis incontestably at its head, and set patterns of operation for many years to follow.

The expanding market had a marked effect on the structure and personnel of Caldwallader Washburn's enterprises. John Crosby's administration at home while Dunwoody sold flour abroad had been very successful and put him in a position to demand a greater share in prestige and in rewards. The contract by which he had entered into partnership with Cadwallader Washburn in 1877 called for investments by him and by W. D. Washburn of $25,000 each. These two active partners were to "give all necessary attention to the prosecution of the said business in all its branches." The original agreement referred only to the B mill; the A mill continued to be under the management of the Christian brothers. Within a year it had become abundantly clear that another adjustment of managerial responsibility must be made. W. D. Washburn had not given time to prosecuting the business in any of its essential branches. Instead he had become deeply involved in politics once more with his election to Congress in 1878.

Whenever he happened to enter the office, he and Crosby disagreed on everything having to do with the company's affairs. Crosby was betrayed by his irrepressible gift of humor into many an admission of incompatibility. Once when tension was high between the partners a stencil cutter put before Crosby a new design for a barrel head. The firm name was crowded into a crescent shape which left room at the tip for only a small letter to begin Washburn's name. Crosby, remembering his associate's habitual arrogance, eyed the design with rueful delight and then made the great renunciation. "It will never do," he said, " you might as well try to spell God with a small g as Washburn with a small w."

W. D. Washburn's return to politics offered a good moment for Crosby to ask Cadwallader to make a final choice between himself and the busy brother. From the new partnership formed in 1879, W. D. was dropped. Now for the first time the firm name Washburn Crosby appeared. The original document, written in long hand, included the name of Dunwoody too. But in the end Quaker temperament prevailed and Dunwoody decided to be the silent member, sharing equally with Crosby in investment and in reward but keeping to the economic strategist's shelter of anonymity.

The value of each man's investment had grown impressively during this period of large-scale success. John Crosby's $25,000 of the first contract (1877) was worth $66,666 under the terms of the 1879 agreement. Later when the activities of Washburn Crosby were broadened to include the A mill, from the management of which the Christian brothers had retired, his total share became $166,666. For a man who had had to borrow to make up the $25,000 of his original investment, John Crosby had done well.

The year 1880 brought a fine and significant moment for the new firm. At the Millers' International Exhibition in Cincinnati, Washburn Crosby's three brands took the gold, the silver, and the bronze medals. It is from the day when these awards were made that the use of the name Gold Medal Flour dates.

As the importance of Minneapolis grew, it became evident to Washburn that he must have men who could go out and carry the news of Gold Medal Flour into new domestic as well as foreign markets. The first of these salesmen actually engaged himself by walking into the mill, pointing out where there were new worlds to conquer, and coming out with the assignment to go and conquer them.

George Barnum was very close to being the perfect pioneer of heroic tradition, vital, violent, and gentle. Many times in the course of his adventures as an officer in the Civil War and as the head of railroad surveying crews, he had to deal with stubborn, ruthless, undisciplined men and always his extremely heavy fist could be counted upon to meet the emergency. Once a group of men in his charge attempted to follow the nightmare whim of using a group of Indian women and children, at work gathering wild rice in a Minnesota lake, as objects for their marksmanship with revolvers. Barnum promptly "put the fear of God" into the "irresponsible bums." He had his own kind of chivalry and his response to its commands was spontaneous, thunderous, and thorough.

Barnum sold flour by methods that were equally direct and forceful. On his first trip he disposed of a carload of flour to the manager of the Palmer House in Chicago, invaded the strongholds of many rival brands in towns all across the Midwest, doing very well by his employer in each, and finally covered the Atlantic Coast from Portland, Maine, to Washington, D.C. The legend is that while he was on one such journey, John Crosby, looking desperately through a great pile of new orders, called to his clerk to "wire Barnum to come home. He's selling more flour than I can make."

In his latter days Barnum headed a grain firm of which the chief stockholders were Washburn Crosby men. He once twitted these associates as slack businessmen because they never had his books audited. Merely as a courtesy to him, they presently sent two young experts tc do so. Happening to catch Barnum in a busy season, the auditors found him also uncooperative. If they did not get out, they were told, Barnum would pitch them out the window. In the estimation of young idealists there was only one reason why a man would refuse to open his books. Their nostrils quivering with the scent of guilt, the auditors wired Minneapolis for instructions. Back from the head of the company came the formal order: "If Uncle George told you to get out, get out." (The anecdote has the authentic ring of the paternal voice of James Stroud Bell, then the company's president.)

Another pioneer of salesmanship, quite different but no less picturesque, was Colonel Charles C. G. Thornton. He was a tall, stately man with an affinity for Boston and bankers which proved to be useful to the company on many occasions.

The military title to which Thornton clung all his life was the souvenir of a distinguished career in the Civil War. (Like Washburn in many respects, Thornton resembled him also in the high sense of responsibility that he brought to his interlude of soldiering. But it is perhaps fortunate that he did not press comparison and competition too far by being a general.)

After being mustered out of the army, Thornton settled in Wisconsin where he operated a flour mill at Madison until he lost it by fire. Presently he joined the Washburn Crosby Company as chief salesman at Minneapolis. But he had always longed to return to his native Boston and after two years at the Falls he was happy to go back as manager of Washburn's first branch office for sales and distribution.

He might, had he wished, have been Washburn's partner. Even lacking that distinction he made his Boston responsibilities much broader than those of salesman. His intimacy with the Massachusetts Medici made it possible for him to get unusual support for his developing enterprise and, as the market for Washburn Crosby flour spread out over New England, he built up an effective administrative unit.

During the 1880s the pattern of milling in Minneapolis began to be clearly established. The tendency was toward concentration in a few large mills. In the last quarter of the nineteenth century the number of mills increased by very few — from twenty to twenty-four — but the aggregate capacity of these well-organized plants increased between seven and eight times over. In 1876 the twenty mills belonged to seventeen different firms. In 1889, 87 per cent of the capacity at the Falls was in the hands of the four great corporations. These were Pillsbury, Washburn Crosby, the Northwestern Consolidated, and the Minneapolis Flour Manufacturing Company. The first two were in 1889 close rivals, each with a daily capacity of 10,000 barrels.

After 1880 every advantage lay with the large mill: economy of operation; ability to buy wheat at the best price and in the best area; the means to experiment with new machinery; the authority to command special freight rates; an organization that justified sending out salesmen instead of depending, as the small mill must, on the commission house; the experience to find and hold new markets in the East and across the Atlantic.

Already established also were the conservative practices of the midwestern millers. In a letter of advice to a young businessman, Dunwoody presented himself as the prophet of caution. He urged against carrying a larger stock of wheat than "would seem [to be] absolutely necessary." Even when conditions were favorable, he pointed out, there was risk. "I have never tried to make money by forecasting the market. I have noticed that competitors who have done this continuously have, as a rule, failed in business."

Out of this conservative impulse to be, as millers said, "never long or short at the end of the day" there arose the practice called "hedging" which is still a vital feature of daily practice. It was already in extensive use in the 1880s. Hedging is a device to protect the mill against loss caused by a price decline or rise in the wheat market. It has been called "the price insurance feature of trades in the futures market."

Consumption of wheat products is relatively uniform year after year but the marketing of wheat is seasonal. The inevitable result is that flour buying is periodic because buyers — bakers, in particular — wish to avail themselves of any advantage in the price of flour that may result from fluctuations in the price of wheat. The miller, therefore, cannot hope to be perfectly "in balance." His flour commitments are almost certain either to exceed or to be under his stock of physical wheat.

In the after-season flow of wheat the miller may not have an immediate need of grain but he knows that he will need it presently and he must buy it when the opportunity is offered him to get grain of the best quality. He cannot wait.

Nor is he willing to assume the risk involved in the possibility of a drop in price between the time when he buys his grain and when he sells his flour. Therefore, with the spot-cash purchase of wheat at, perhaps, $2.65 per bushel, he simultaneously sells what he calls "futures contracts" for a like amount of wheat.

The term "futures contract" refers to trading not in specific parcels of actual wheat but in contracts calling for the delivery of a certain grade of wheat at a time in the future named in the contract. These legal agreements are written under rules controlled today by the Federal Commodity Exchange Authority. There is a practical reason why millers feel that they must trade in futures and it is related to the conditions under which the raw material is produced. Wheat is produced in temperate zones all over the earth. In every month of the year a wheat crop is coming to maturity somewhere. The futures markets provide a free and open record of the day-by-day price of wheat and of its fluctuations. Traders with large investments in milling plants or grain elevators are unable to assume the risk involved in dealing with a commodity that fluctuates widely in price. This risk has been assumed by a trading group whose job it has become to assume this risk and to deal in contracts for future delivery. Imperfect as the system may be (and it has been widely criticized) it has the advantages of ensuring the processor of wheat against adverse price fluctuations, of providing public knowledge of price, and of providing, also, a continuous market.

To return to the illustration, the average price at which futures have to be sold may be $2.60 a bushel. In such a circumstance if, when the wheat is sold in the form of flour, the market has declined ten cents, the miller will have lost ten cents a bushel on the grain he has used. But since the value of cash wheat usually parallels the value of futures contracts, rising or falling at approximately the same rate, the loss of ten cents a bushel on the actual wheat is offset by the opportunity to repurchase the futures at a profit of ten cents a bushel.

This, then, would be the pattern of a "perfect hedge": actual wheat bought at $2.65 is sold at $2.55; but futures sold at $2.60 can be repurchased at $2.50. The balance redressed. The ill effects of price fluctuation offset and the milling program steadied.

It is significant to notice that this practice came so early into the miller's program as to fix in him the habit of conservative operation.

The year 1882 usually is named as the one in which the prestige of the Minneapolis mills achieved world-wide recognition and their dominating position was acknowledged. It is also, by dramatic coincidence, the year in which Cadwallader Washburn died. He had suffered a stroke of paralysis more than a year before but continued to conduct his affairs from his bed, faltering occasionally but going on under the stern discipline to which he had so long inured himself. He had always spoken a little grandly of "my mills," calling them "the largest, the cleanest, the most perfect in the world." Whatever may have seemed vainglorious in such utterances took on at the end the touching tone of devotion to duty. His mills came to be the most important interest of his life. Into the responsibilities of the entrepreneur he had canalized all of the abundant energies that an empty personal life left to him. He deserved to know — and did know — that he had used his talents well.

After Washburn's death John Crosby continued to profit enormously by the foresight with which he and his partner had captured for their company a comfortably large part of the export trade. What had started, with Dunwoody's visit, as an audacious adventure had become less than a decade later a steady, reliable business. In August 1884 the *Northwestern Miller* reported that "The great export trade which has had a mushroom-like growth in the past five years is getting down to a sound basis."

For their part English commentators had begun to regard the situation with philosophic calm. In January 1887 the editor of the *London Millers' Gazette* reported "more in sorrow than in anger" that "There does not seem to be much falling off in the American flour shipments or in the output of American mills." London and Glasgow were the chief customers, he added, seeming to mean that they were the chief culprits.

On December 29, 1887, John Crosby fell ill of pneumonia and died. He had had fifty-eight years of usefulness all supported by good will and colored by lively humor. Once more circumstance seemed to dramatize in a man's death the end of an era. For the year 1887 did, in fact, bring down the curtain on one of the glittering phases in the development of the milling industry. One of quite different character was to follow.

4

Competition and Crisis

DEBUT OF A MODERN MERCHANDISER

On THE masthead of the *Northwestern Miller*, oracle of the trade, a symbolic figure appeared for the first time in the issue of June 1, 1888. This plump little winged god stood beside a sack of flour seeming to measure its stocky rotundity against his own.

The editorial paragraph just below explained the significance of this creation, taking a rueful tone. The reader was invited to notice that the figure was "unclothed — which will probably be the case with the millers unless the disparity in flour and wheat values is shortly removed."

This was a journalist's lively exaggeration of the millers' plight. The boom in the export business was by no means over. Indeed it had still to reach its peak in 1900, when approximately one third of the output of the Minneapolis mills — an average of 2,700,000 barrels — was shipped abroad, chiefly still to England.

But difficulties had begun to show themselves. Stiff competition had sent flour prices down. Shippers much preferred to handle wheat and made special rates to encourage exports in that form. The milling industry in England began to adopt rollers and the "new process," to build modern plants, and to make a patriotic issue of patronizing home brands. After 1890 the export market had become relatively less important than it had been in the day of John Crosby's comfortable success.

In the course of these adjustments many millers at the Falls had moments of blank misgiving. Years later one of them recalled that as he stood facing his children's Christmas tree in one such season of doubt, he fingered in his pocket his total resources — a few very small coins.

Competition and Crisis

Some of the small mills went under and some of the larger were obliged to undergo drastic reorganization. Others, including Washburn Crosby, began to be aware that heavy dependence on a single market was dangerous because local conditions of depression might wipe out profits. There were many indications that foresighted leadership must develop new policies and new programs.

The reaction against America's trade invasion was evident – and politically more militant – in other parts of Europe besides free-trade England. When wheat supplies from across the Atlantic began pouring into the industrial area of western Germany, the result was a general decline in prices. German landlords of the grain-growing group presently joined with industrialists in a movement for protection. Pressure from these elements combined to produce Bismarck's tariff of 1879. In France also the protectionist movement was successful in obtaining a tariff on grain imports. In both countries the rates were raised step by step to nearly prohibitive figures and in both of them the milling interests cast aspersions on the purity of American flour.

In the awkward period of transition the *Northwestern Miller* undertook to preach the gospel of "forbearance." The decline in prices must be accepted since it was world wide and affected industrial as well as farm products. It did no good to say to foreign buyers, as the editor suggested millers had lately been inclined to say : "You fellows have been getting our stuff altogether too cheap. You will either pay our prices or go hungry." People in England would "eat mud" before they would "pay fancy prices for the product of American mills."

The solution? Call a conference of millers, suggested the editor. Arbitrarily limit output. When the industry failed to respond to this suggestion, the *Northwestern Miller* showed its little cupid in a still more deplorable state. Now wilted over the barrel, he seemed fatalistically to await further punishment. "We tried to stand him up," the editor explained, "but he was too sick and shaky on his legs to bear it."

For the large miller there was, however, an alternative to that of curtailing output. This was, of course, a thorough and consistent exploration of the domestic market such as had not been attempted before.

It was in this atmosphere of uncertainty that James Stroud Bell made his debut in milling with Washburn Crosby at Minneapolis. Throughout the first two years of his midwestern career he endured nearly every trial that a man of affairs must face. He had to cope with the exacting demands of absentee owners. He had to match the arrogance of one close associate in the task of reorganizing the company with a graciousness that was strong enough and effective enough to offset the destructive influence. He even had to accept responsibility for the mistakes of others and so preserve the morale of his whole staff. That he managed to do all these things with cool serenity is perhaps all the proof that is needed of the deep sincerity of his Quaker philosophy.

Indeed, the joint career of Dunwoody and Bell — Quakers, both — suggests that theirs is the kind of self-discipline that is needed for the conduct of business. When the signs and portent of disaster hurtled through their skies, they seemed deftly to catch them and toss them back

The Bell family had long been dealing with flour. Two early nine teenth-century representatives, James and Isaiah, had owned and op erated a gristmill for twenty years on the Wissahickon Creek near Philadelphia. The sons of Isaiah, William and Samuel, became flour merchants in Philadelphia, and later Samuel organized a new firm in which he and his sons were partners.

James Stroud Bell, one of those sons, entered the business while still in his teens. At forty-one, when Minneapolis wanted him, he was already a veteran, well acquainted as a professional buyer of flour with the Washburn Crosby product, and well acquainted also through his Quaker associations with William Hood Dunwoody.

In many editorials concerned with the changing times, the *North western Miller* undertook to suggest what kind of new leader the industry needed. He must be "no longer simply a miller, but a manufacturer, a merchant, a man of affairs." He must know more than the mechanics of his trade; he must "know what the people who buy his flour are doing and thinking and hoping to do." The shrewd Dunwoody, at the moment a vice president of the company, realized how true this analysis was. He knew, also, that for the past twenty years Bell had been training himself to be just such a man. In the spring of 1888 he went to Philadelphia to get Bell.

It was not easy to lure a Quaker out of his natural habitat. Despite all the reassuring, persuasive sounds that Dunwoody made, Bell hesitated. Two opposing impulses in him kept the question in delicate balance. (It would be incorrect to say of so essentially pacific a man that they were at war within him.) He was modest, even shy; he was unwilling to go anywhere unless he was sure that he was wanted. Yet he

43

was a natural campaigner. Long before the word "aggressive" had come into general use as the epithet of highest praise for effective salesmanship, it was a favorite in Bell's vocabulary. But his aggressions were of the rare sort that are designed to convey benefits; in these he believed with all the quiet ardor of his Quaker temperament.

A glowing center of faith warmed and informed this temperament. Bell could speak or write only to encourage. When his business associates faced threats to their very existence, his letters written in answer to complaints seem to have been whisked through a bath of confidence, so that even when they say little they give off a scent of hope. When his son faced the routine crises of growing up the letters from his father that reached him at school were not merely dipped in confidence but immersed in it. To the most difficult of human relationships he lent an art that achieved daily masterpieces of tact and affirmation.

Even his rebukes were administered with grace supported by generosity. The most fastidious of men, Bell himself looked always as though a smooth shave, fresh linen, and a good suit of clothes were gifts of the gods to their chosen ones having nothing to do with the labors of barbers, laundresses, and tailors. He liked to have well-groomed men about him and insisted, in a characteristic way, on the preservation of reasonable standards of smartness. When he went into the plants and found, here and there, a man in need of a haircut or a shave, he would surreptitiously leave a coin on the offender's desk, enough to finance a trip to the barber for emergency treatment.

The firm to which he came as managing partner was a reorganized company known as Washburn Martin. Bell had wished to retain Crosby's name but at the moment this had not seemed to be feasible. The officers included Bell; W. D. Washburn, who had slipped in once more as executor of his brother's will and as representative of the other heirs all of whom lived in Philadelphia; John Washburn, a nephew of Cadwallader and the latest recruit from Maine; Charles J. Martin who had been Cadwallader's companion and aid in the Civil War, in public office, and at the Falls and who was now the perfect secretary-treasurer of the company; and A. V. Martin.

By July 1889 it had become evident that another reorganization of the company was essential before Bell's policies could be put into effect. First of all, W. D. Washburn must go out again and go he did, trailing clouds of malediction. ("There you are," he had said to the most modest of Quakers, J. S. Bell, "all swollen up like a great bullfrog.") Second, Dunwoody must be brought back into the firm. He had refused to join the partnership of 1888, even after drawing Bell into it, because of the serious division of authority. Now he returned. Third, the Crosby name must be restored, so that old customers would realize this was the old company doing business at the old stand. To accomplish this purpose, John Crosby's son, John II, then a law student at Harvard, was made a member of the board of directors.

W. D. Washburn whenever he retired from anything left trouble, as well as maledictions, behind. He still had Cadwallader Washburn's surname and he had mills of his own. These he combined with the Pillsbury interests to form the Pillsbury Washburn Flour Mills Company, bringing the daily capacity of the new organization to 14,500 barrels. That there should be at the Falls a Pillsbury Washburn Company and a Washburn Crosby Company, the two not associated in any way but rather the most intense of rivals, for a time puzzled the trade. But the circumstance was so dramatic that it arrested attention and in the end brought new prestige to the Washburn name.

Another acute problem for Bell was that of water power. Stock in the old Minneapolis Mill Company, leasers of power, had been from the beginning in the hands of the Washburns (including W. D.) and their cousin, Dorilus Morrison. Cadwallader Washburn had had the foresight throughout his lifetime to assign to his own plant certain mill rights "in perpetuity." But with rivals in control of the water power, Bell was by no means sure of receiving his share. Often he was obliged to run the B mill with steam power while, as it appeared to him, another plant was "making two thousand barrels daily" though its steam power was "sufficient to make only eight or ten hundred." The classic struggle for water power was on once more and though fist fights between silk-hatted gentlemen had now gone out of fashion, a new element had been added — one that was peculiarly unsympathetic to a Quaker — intrigue.

Yet another danger cast its shadow over the Falls in the late 1880s — a threat to the independence of the milling industry. American flour had invaded England and now there was a counter invasion from England. The quality of Minneapolis flour had inevitably attracted the eyes of capitalists looking for outlets in a period when British investments were yielding only meager rewards. Such capital had been flowing into America for a long time but it had not interested itself previously in the milling industry. Enterprises at the Falls had grown through investment by new partners and through reinvested profits.

First to attract the interest of foreign buyers were the mills of Cadwallader Washburn, whose heirs were known to be restless under the burdens of absentee landlords. Once a year these men and women assembled in Minneapolis to dine on bear steak (for were they not making a pilgrimage into the wilderness and must they not make appropriately rugged gestures?), to tell one another the same stories and to complain of declining profits. They were in a mood to sell.

While Bell managed to hold off this threat, an English syndicate acquired the Pillsbury Washburn properties. Charles A. Pillsbury became the managing director of a new company, organized in England, at a salary that was said to be the highest ever paid up to that time in the history of American business. Other members of the original Pillsbury family group also purchased considerable stock in the Pillsbury Washburn Flour Mills Company Ltd.

This dramatic event left everyone at the Falls with the fatalistic feeling that all the other mills were bound to go the same way. Indeed in September 1889, when Bell had been in Minneapolis just a year, he learned that an option to buy the mills from under him had been acquired by the English syndicate. Not in the least nonplussed by the fear of losing his foothold at the Falls, Bell began to look about for a new base. He knew that though the center of flour production may move, flour itself never moves completely out of the economy. He was prepared, if necessary, to move with flour anywhere. On October 30 he wrote to George Barnum in Duluth to say that he and Dunwoody would presently arrive there "to look over the ground." By November he was certain that he would be forced to leave Minneapolis and he had considered invitations from as far away as Canada and Indian territory. He himself favored either Duluth or Buffalo.

In a kind of last-ditch effort to beat off the British, Dunwoody went to Philadelphia to see the Washburn heirs. It was his task to assure them that, despite the declining market, the present management had done well by them and could be relied upon to do so in the future. Unfortunately, at this crucial moment, secretary-treasurer Charles Martin made the one mistake of an otherwise blameless life. In his estimate for October of the previous year he recorded a purchase of Red River grain at the local elevator price, forgetting to add the freight cost of getting it to Minneapolis. When the error was detected and clarified the company found itself poorer than it had thought itself to be by $16,000 — a substantial slice out of an annual profit of approximately $75,000.

It is characteristic of Bell that in all his letters to Dunwoody this serious mistake is never referred to as Martin's fault but as "our error." Dunwoody accepted the polite fiction of shared responsibility, offering no reproach. Quaker forbearance could hardly go farther.

The tempo of the drama quickened as economic conditions themselves approached a crisis. Overexpansion during the boom period of the early and mid 1880s needed to be redressed. The *Northwestern Miller* began to preach that "combinations of forces" were inevitable. But the editor did not wish to see "combination" translated into "expatriation."

Meanwhile Bell fought a war of nerves with the forces that wished to take his mills from him. The plants returned an honorable profit annually. He was reluctant to mention the figure ($75,000) for fear that it might be regarded as a bid which would send that of the English company higher. Instead he urged his brother-in-law, R. O. N. Ford, the company's New York representative, to maintain the good sales record in that area; he wrote regularly to Thornton, his sales executive in Boston, reporting each development that might interest the banking fraternity there; he negotiated with Wall Street for large-scale backing with which, if the chance came, to buy out the Washburn heirs. His mind had achieved its own kind of fluid drive so that he could move quickly in any direction that might prove to be desirable and to do with the least amount of mechanical adjustment.

In May 1890 the fight to keep the mills seemed to have been finally lost. John Gest, the Philadelphia banker who represented the heirs, wrote to Bell saying prematurely that the offer of the Pillsbury Washburn Flour Mills Company of London had been accepted. The proposal called for a "rental of $75,000 per annum for five years clear of all expenses and charges of any kind with the option of purchasing the stock held by the Company within the five years at $125 per share." Mr. Gest regretted that an old association must end but, he said, "acting entirely in a fiduciary capacity" he could not do otherwise.

But he had spoken without full authority. The stockholders of the C. C. Washburn Flouring Mills Company (it was under this name that the heirs conducted business) had to act officially on the offer. At their June meeting this was considered with favor. Though it was still not voted upon formally, the curtain seemed to be about to fall on the episode. It remained only, so it seemed, for the newly elected directors to sign the necessary documents.

This was a bad moment for the *Northwestern Miller*. Once more its little symbolic figure, whose attitudes — bellicose, frustrated, desperate — dramatized the state of the industry, collapsed over the barrel.

Bell still refused to admit defeat. In his unobtrusive way he enjoyed a sense of drama and now, like an improvising actor, he seemed to have caught the stage manager's eye and to be urging him not to ring the curtain down. "We have only one chance in a hundred of obtaining the mills," he wrote to Thornton, "but until the question is finally decided we will hope for the best. I wish you would say to our friends and customers that there is some doubt about the lease being ratified. We will ask them to remain loyal to us and to our flour."

The difficulty was that the Washburn heirs wished to keep owner- ship of the brand names and were determined that these should continue to be used in honor of their originator, not lost to distinction in a great family of flours such as the English syndicate would have. The integrity of the Washburn name must be preserved.

It is possible, as Bell in his private correspondence surmised, that the Washburn heirs had become difficult deliberately. It seemed to him likely that they wanted to toss monkey wrenches about because the legal status of a Minnesota company, chartered in New Jersey, carrying a London address as headquarters, began to seem a little too complex to further their own interests well. For its part, the London company be- came reluctant to be committed to so many promises. Everyone suddenly became rigid and noncooperative. Everyone, that is, except Bell, who stood smiling on the side lines with a contract in his hands.

The rest of the story reads as though its details had been contrived by a writer of romantic fiction with a taste for feverish climax. It is a matter of intrigue within intrigue, of last-minute reversal of situation, of victory snatched from defeat. There is even a neat little race against time, lost by those who, in the eyes of the community, deserved to lose.

A revolt against the idea of leasing to the English syndicate had de- veloped within the group of those most intimately concerned. It was led by John Washburn, who, though he was an heir of Cadwallader Wash- burn, was also a Washburn Crosby partner in whose interest it was to see the company remained intact.

Most of the Washburn relatives had returned to Philadelphia after the indecisive stockholders' meeting without having signed the proffered lease. But Cadwallader Washburn's son-in-law, Charles Payson, remained behind to look after other interests. It was to Payson that John Washburn turned with the suggestion that a special meeting be called to reconsider the matter.

By this time all but two of the directors had been brought around to the attitude that it was best for their interests to renew the agreement with Washburn Crosby. With full legal formality a lease was executed, signed, countersigned, and delivered and the meeting promptly adjourned. The dissenting directors had not been present at this session though they had been properly informed that it was to take place.

A scene that might have been designed by and for Hollywood followed. No sooner had Bell and his associates closed the meeting and left the building in which it took place than a carriage drove up before the door. Out of it there rolled a heavy, breathless sheriff (the time was mid July) ready to serve an injunction, also piping hot. It had been issued at the request of one of the dissenting directors and was intended to keep Payson from executing a lease. But the document had been delivered. The law could do nothing.

At the moment of great relief Bell managed to remain calm. He wrote a full account of the episode of the sheriff and the injunction for the benefit of Thornton, concluding with a masterpiece of understatement. "Fortunately," he commented mildly, "we had all left the office so there can be no doubt about the lease being completed."

Still the curtain was not quite down. There was an epilogue of judicial fireworks in the course of which everyone threatened to sue everyone else. The *Northwestern Miller* had never witnessed, so the editor said, such a spontaneous outburst of "injunctions, mandamuses, posse comitatuses, habeas corpuses and riot acts." Everyday life, it declared with the jocularity of relief from strain, had become so exciting that "millers generally are afraid to look out of their office doors lest they be struck by some Latin term let loose by one or another" of the embattled litigants.

But when the last pinwheel had sizzled out and the eyes of the community were turned toward center stage, J. S. Bell was seen to be occupying it solidly with a lease clutched in his hand.

The contract demanded much of him. He was to risk all the capital, do all the work, bear all the expense in return for half the profits. He had to be content not to own but merely to lease use of the brand name, Gold Medal. Bell believed in his ability to meet all difficulties and to justify the investment. So, too, did Dunwoody.

The victory was more than a purely personal one. Bell and Dunwoody had set their quiet resolution against a force in international finance which they considered to be dangerous. Circumstances were later to justify their judgment when the mills acquired by the London company were surrendered and repurchased by the original owners. If the Washburn Crosby mills also had been involved the round trip home might have been even more complicated.

Bell had had an exhausting initiation in Minneapolis. But it ended in triumph and he was not displeased. He revealed his satisfaction in a small dramatic gesture which even a modest Quaker might permit himself. Existing volumes of his business correspondence, copied by the old letter-press method onto flimsy sheets of paper, seem to follow no formal pattern, beginning and ending with the dates of either the calendar or fiscal year. He closed each when it seemed to be full enough. The one concerned with the battle for the mills ends dramatically with a letter dated July 29, 1890. Its last paragraph reads: "The English syndicate is after us and injunctions are flying around in all directions, but as we have possession of the Mills and with a lease to operate them we hope to hold the *Fort* against all intruders."

Now he had an opportunity to cope with the problems of competition. To that task he brought a brilliant understanding of the domestic market that won him admiration among his fellow millers as "the greatest merchandiser" of his time.

On the banks of St. Anthony Falls a great flour
empire was to grow

The first mill at the Falls was built by the government in 1821–22

Early builders of Washburn Crosby's prestige in the milling world

"Washburn's Folly," the B mill built by Cadwallader
Washburn in 1866

The Washburn Crosby mills — A, B, and C — in the 1890s

The *Northwestern Miller*'s symbol of the American miller in 1888 appeared vigorous, if unclothed, in his first appearance on the journal's masthead

But a few weeks later, in sympathy with the millers' plight, he had wilted over the barrel, "to sick and shaky on his legs" to stand up

The interior of an early Minneapolis mill sketched for the *Northwestern Miller*

The explosion of 1878 as seen by a photographer-artist, who added his impression of the blast to a photograph of the Minneapolis milling district taken a few days before the disaster

In the nineties the barrel was the symbol of flour, as shown (above) in a parade and (below) in a delivery wagon, called a "barrel rack"

Left, James Stroud Bell, "the greatest merchandiser" of his time. Right, James Ford Bell, "statesman of business" during World War I, pictured here with a visiting Belgian general

J. S. Bell and his team, about 1905

JOHN GERARD   FRANK W. LUND   JAMES F. BELL   H. O'B. HARDING   W. A. JONES   H. R. McLAUGHLIN

T. C. ESTEE   WILLIAM H. BOVEY   BENJAMIN S. BULL   WILLIAM G. CROCKER   G. A. THOMAS   JOHN H. MULLIKEN   WILLIAM SHERMAN

F. F. HENRY   FREDERICK G. ATKINSON-WILLIAM H. DUNWOODY   JAMES S. BELL   CHARLES C. BOVEY   SAMUEL BELL, JR.   P. B. SMITH

In 1893 Washburn Crosby displayed its wares at the World's
Columbian Exposition in Chicago

An advertisement of the following year stressed the Gold Medal trademark,
adopted after the company received an award at an earlier exhibition

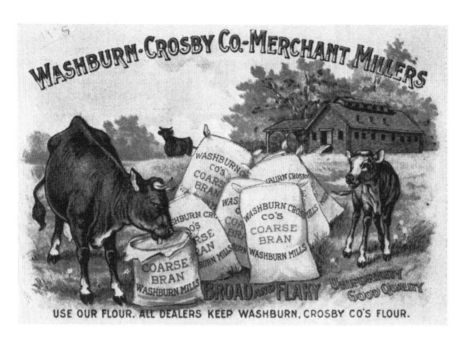

Advertising cards like these were popular with
merchants in the nineties

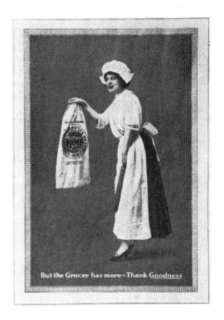

A recurring symbol in Gold Medal Flour advertising from
1900 (left) to 1920 (right) was a "cleanly maid"

"How a well bred maid makes well made bread,"
a recipe in verse

NEXT stir the flour into the
mixture that's stood
Waiting to play its part, to
make the bread good.
Mix it up thoroughly, but not
too thick;
Some flours make bread that's
more like a brick.

NOW grease well a bowl and
put the dough in,
Don't fill the bowl full, that
would be a sin;
For the dough is all right and
it's going to rise,
'Till you will declare that it's
twice the old size.

BRUSH the dough with melted
butter, as the recipes say;
Cover with a bread towel, set
in a warm place to stay
Two hours or more, to rise
until light,
When you see it grow, you'll
know it's all right.

AS soon as it's light, place
again on the board;
Knead it well this time. Here
is knowledge to hoard.
Now back in the bowl once
more it must go.
And set again to rise for an hour
or so.

FORM the dough gently into
loaves when light,
And place it in bread pans,
greased just right.
Shape each loaf you make to
half fill the pan,
This bread will be good enough
for any young man.

NEXT let it rise to the level
of pans—no more,
Have the temperature right—
don't set near a door.
We must be careful about draughts;
it isn't made to freeze,
Keep the room good and warm
—say seventy-two degrees.

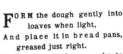

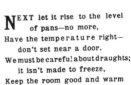

Streetcar placards brought news of the Gold Medal Cooking
School to housewives of Atlanta

Billboards across the country echoed Benjamin Bull's crisp slogan

In 1852 the Sperry mill of Stockton, California, took gold
dust in trade for flour

"Drifted Snow" was the Sperry equivalent of "Gold Medal" in flour

A Sperry company outing in the days of the flivver

The original research idea of Charles Staff (above) to "ask the animals" what was good for them prompted the Larrowe Milling Company to establish a farm for research on feeds (below)

Austin Sperry, founder of the
Sperry mills of the Pacific Coast

Frank J. Kell, "the man who
made milling in Texas"

Four milling dynasties came together in 1928 to form General Mills

James Larrowe, who built an
animal feed industry from a
waste product

James Ford Bell, president of
Washburn Crosby, founder of
General Mills

Before the advent of Betty Crocker, a sprightly young housewife was pictured in advertisements for Gold Medal Flour

In the 1920s Betty Crocker had not yet sat for her portrait to Neysa McMein, but she was fast becoming "the first lady of food"

By the mid-thirties Betty Crocker "belonged to the great tradition of symbolic figures"

The feminine touch in company advertising through the years

5

Nationwide Marketing

J. S. BELL AND HIS TEAM

T H E place of the Washburn Crosby Company within the millers' world during the period just before and just after the turn of the century was well "up front." This was due in part to the fact that it was one of the largest of American mills. Further, the organization was still traveling under the impetus given it by Cadwallader Washburn's three acts of initiative in sponsoring major technical improvements, making a tremendous asset of spring wheat, and opening up the export market.

Now, in the 1890s and 1900s, fresh impetus was supplied by the intense, ideally controlled purposefulness of J. S. Bell. Better than any man of his time he understood what the future pattern in milling affairs must be. He recognized that the purveyor of food must have an unwavering sense of responsibility toward standards of craftsmanship. There must be no room for manipulation or exploitation in the task of helping to feed a growing nation.

His strong sense of obligation suggested that an intimate relationship must be preserved between manufacturer and customer. It was not enough to put one's flour in the hands of jobbers and let these powerful middlemen dictate policy. The miller must preserve and promote his own brands, communicating directly to the user his confidence in their special merit.

Another implication of such a program was that many well-trained men must be available to carry it out. If a manufacturer were to take full advantage of the size of his organization, if by improved method he were to produce quality goods at reasonable price, he must have a team of

51

experts about him. He must choose assistants and associates who could develop with — or a little ahead of — developing opportunity.

In all these respects the insights of J. S. Bell were distinguished. His success as a man of affairs was the direct result of his ability to extend his energies through those of the young men who came to him as millers, salesmen, executives.

What Bell realized as soon as he had taken firm possession of his mills was that their output must inevitably decline, along with the falling off in the export trade, unless a new formula of distribution could be discovered. He found it in the intensive development of domestic markets.

To direct this big campaign he brought together a group of young men who regarded themselves almost as his foster sons. These men — the Atkinsons, the Boveys, the Crosbys, Frank Henry, B. S. Bull, William Crocker, and the rest — had a wide variety of backgrounds. Some had had considerable formal education, others almost none. The talents of several were highly specialized, those of others had to be shaped shrewdly to make them useful to the milling business. There were among them boisterous young men, timid young men, men who went to bed at nine o'clock and others who rioted away their private resources long before pay day. Bell drew them all together into a unit as close as a congenial family, but much less contentious than even congenial families are likely to be. A gift to which every major executive must aspire was so effortlessly at the disposal of J. S. Bell that the whole milling fraternity recognized him as a "builder of men."

The first demand for teamwork came with the building of a new mill at Great Falls, Montana. It began, not as a Washburn Crosby project, but as an independent venture of the chief men of the company. The Royal Milling Company was incorporated in 1892 and later became an associate company.

It was J. J. Hill who prodded Dunwoody, as an officer of Washburn Crosby, into making this experiment. Believing that the hard spring wheat area would spread through all the region, Hill had pushed the Great Northern Railway westward even before there were settlers for it to serve. Montana, described by a later admirer as "high, wide and handsome," was indeed spacious but it was also nearly empty with only a few grain farmers. Hill was sure that there would soon be more of them if mills became available and Dunwoody dutifully went to test his foresight.

Bell, whose interest was in selling, opposed this production job. His judgment was sustained when it was discovered in the first season of operation that there was not enough Montana wheat in existence to keep the mill going for ninety days. Additional raw material was shipped in from Dakota. The flimsy little plant, perched high on the bank of the Missouri River and driven by rope belt from a powerhouse below, struggled on losing money every year for a decade before the corner was turned and the minute book was able to report a modest profit.

Long before this pleasant climax, Dunwoody had grown weary of the undertaking and complained bitterly of its load. With characteristic charity of spirit Bell offered to buy him out and with a sudden access of shrewdness — also characteristic — Dunwoody declined. The Royal Milling Company survived to become, at last, one of the original units to be absorbed into General Mills.

The significance of the episode lies in its dramatization of Bell's patience in bringing to final success, as market conditions improved, a project that he had resisted. Great Falls also served as a dress rehearsal for a movement of expansion which proved to have far greater significance. This was the move to Buffalo, first impulse of an eastward migration in the course of which other Minneapolis millers were to follow the Washburn Crosby Company.

A first step was taken in this direction in 1893 when Bell, seizing a new advantage in lake transportation, established warehouse facilities at Buffalo. The New York Central and the Erie railroads offered space for blending and for repacking flour intended for eastern and for overseas markets. Bell found exactly the right man to direct this project. Frank Henry brought to the team the sturdy usefulness of an all-American tackle. For half a century his rugged resourcefulness served successive presidents, their boards of directors, and their operating boards, first in the Washburn Crosby Company and later in General Mills. An indefatigable lover of theoretical analysis, he filled the files of the home office with long, but readable, dissertations on every kind of problem — tariff, freight rates, and what to do with the politicians for whom he had no love.

The high color of Henry's individuality tended to emphasize any pallid inadequacy in an associate. As a result many men who worked for him were challenged by his vividness into the early discovery of strength in themselves. In his own didactic way Frank Henry became a builder of

53

men. At least, the men about him had to build themselves briskly in order to stand up to him.

Henry was born on the Indian Ocean to a mother who liked traveling with her shipmaster husband. The boy's first six years were spent aboard the various barques sailed by his father. The strong beat of the sea was in his pulse all his life. He liked to boom sea chanteys out of his deep chest and there was an echo of the romantic tradition of the sailor in his lifelong devotion to the art of invective. Never ribald, his language was thorough in its exploration of the power of destruction.

No narrow specialist, Henry had turned from ships to railroads and had worked as a young man for the Lehigh Valley Transportation Company. His usefulness to Bell was great because he had acquired during his first career a full knowledge of transportation problems.

Bell's next step was in energetic pursuit of new domestic markets. He and his team committed themselves to a strenuous seven day a week campaign to capture new customers. As one of his men, Fred Atkinson, once wrote of the period and of its temper:

"The United States was our field and it had hardly been touched on a national basis by a mill of consequence. All auspices were favorable. Every crossroad town in the country had flour buyers who purchased in car loads or mixed car lot loads. Bakeries of large size had not yet come into existence. Ninety per cent of the flour consumed in the country found its distribution through the retail grocer. Home-baking prevailed everywhere."

With the zeal of an evangelist and the indefatigability of a very young man, Atkinson, as head of sales, set out to attract these home bakers.

Envious rivals sometimes spoke of J. S. Bell's collection of young assistants not as his team but as his "kindergarten." But this effort at disparagement could hardly have been more transparent. For there was nothing in the least infantile about the energy with which each went at his assignment. Atkinson, for example, was a quiet, meticulous man with an endless interest in observing details and a passion for organizing them into patterns. It was his particular gift to put ideas under a regimentation at once precise and imaginative. It was said of him that when he went on a tour of inspection he would enter a branch office saying, with the mild almost deprecatory air of being an innocent bystander, that he was going to look about for a day or two. At the end of that time he left, as he once wrote, "with a notebook full of ideas" and a head full of encyclopedic information about management, method, character of employees, and prospects for the trade.

Timed even better than Dunwoody's European invasion was Atkinson's invasion of St. Louis. For many years this had been closed territory to any but purveyors of flour made from soft red winter wheat. Habit, dating back to the time of the Revolution, had fixed this preference. Many northern firms had tried to break through the barrier; always they had been driven off like latter-day carpetbaggers.

In 1895 and 1896, however, a severe crop failure in the southern states accomplished what years of battering at the gates had failed to do.

Atkinson was first in the field. "We let no grass grow under our feet," he once commented gleefully. To large buyers he brought the welcome news that spring wheat flour could be had for less than their own inadequate supply of winter wheat flour. As zealot he proclaimed the faith that spring wheat flour was as good as it was plentiful. Through successive levels of resistance the Atkinson team penetrated: first, the wholesale grocer; second, the retail grocer; and finally, the housewife and her cook. In this last stronghold of prejudice, the task was most difficult of all. The Negro expert (knowing very tenaciously what she knew) refused to believe that any biscuit could be made properly from that Yankee stuff. Canvassers went from door to door explaining how to bake with the new flour. The campaign was supported by advertisements in St. Louis newspapers and by widely distributed pamphlets. The result was a really spectacular triumph. To a region that had previously used no spring wheat flour at all the product was sent in by the trainload.

In "building men" Bell knew how to fit a job to a man as well as a man to a job. Henry and Atkinson knew what they wanted and their mentor gratefully made way for them. Other members of his team came simply looking for work and Bell had to help them to discover their talents. Such an enrollee was Charles Cranston Bovey, who came to the company in 1891. With Bell's help he created two important jobs, one technical, one commercial; to them he gave fifty years of conspicuous service.

There was nothing about milling in which Bovey was not interested, from tests for new-made flour to its sale in the domestic or foreign market. As a beginner he made some crude experiments in washing wheat (simply sloshing it about in a lard pail) but the importance of this concern prompted Bell to send him abroad for serious study. There he set out to become familiar with the serviceable wheat-washing machines of England and the even more adaptable ones to be found on the Continent. Hungary still offered the best postgraduate training school for millers but continued to be hard to enter. The Haggermackers of Budapest were courteous, ceremonious, and strictly noncooperative. They whisked Bovey through the mills, letting him see as little as possible. Nonetheless he managed to learn much in spite of his instructors and came home well acquainted with the latest techniques for washing wheat and for testing the color of flour. A year later, Dunwoody brought back the best of German equipment. The immediate result was an impressive increase in production. High-grade wheat which previously had been unusable because of the presence of smut could now be milled successfully, thanks to the new washing process.

Bovey's trip had the welcome effect also of refreshing the personal character of relations with European importers. Even more than Dunwoody before him Bovey had the ambassadorial touch and as he greeted buyers in Dublin, Belfast, Bristol, London, Glasgow, and Aberdeen, he was able to hold their loyalty firm. Year after year the sales to Bruce and Wilson of Glasgow, to Byrne and Mahoney of Dublin, to Grippeling and Verkley of Amsterdam went on until the submarines of World War I cut off all communication. They were picturesque — these European customers — adding drama to the routine of the trade. No firm was more so than that of A. I. With, who carried Gold Medal Flour into the farthest reaches of Scandinavia traveling sometimes behind reindeer teams.

There were other problems of the export trade which Bovey made his special province. One concerned the exportation of wheat. In the free-trade countries, British, Dutch, and Scandinavian millers liked to attract American grain and grind it themselves, selling the product at a price with which American makers could not compete. Meanwhile, American railroads played favorites against their own countrymen. They set up discriminatory rates to the advantage of wheat over flour insisting that the difference in charge for handling corresponded with the difficulty of handling.

But neither railroad nor steamship handler actually took much trouble on this account. The steamship companies, in particular, seemed to the Millers' League, organized to try to get relief, to be particularly cavalier. Sacks of flour were the orphans of the transport business. They were dumped into dirty holds in all kinds of weather, unprotected against contamination by water. Flour was classified scornfully as "ballast freight" subject to "optional delivery." This translated out of the jargon of the trade meant that it would be delivered whenever the steamship companies found it convenient and not before.

Bills of lading on which flour was transported were masterpieces of literary and legalistic ingenuity designed to drug the shipper into surrender of his rights. In the 1890 struggle of flour against the sea, millers bitterly nicknamed the shipping document the "Captain Kidd Bill of Lading." It permitted stevedores to handle sacks with tools like lumberjacks' canthooks — "murderous looking instruments," the *Northwestern Miller* called them, ending in "sinister curves" of sharpened iron. Not many jute bags survived, quite whole, the shock of its attentions.

The millers made brisk frontal attacks against these enemies. One of their own number, M. D. Harter of Ohio, was persuaded to run for Congress with the express intention of getting protection for the industry. The Harter Bill became law in 1893 despite the vigorous opposition of the steamship lines. It worked well enough (though not perfectly), and the inclination to slither past its regulations finally died. A major victory had been won for the flour interests.

Bovey continued to be the millers' eloquent defender against the shortsighted policies of the railroads. "The fallacy of exporting wheat" became his theme in many solid arguments offered in print and on the platform. The Midwest, he pointed out, would have continued to be a howling wilderness had it been the policy of leaders to remove its resources of lumber and grain and to ship all these assets elsewhere for processing. Instead, civilization had followed the manufacturers. By cutting logs into lumber and grinding wheat into flour, wealth had been put to work in its own place. The advantages of a secure society had been extended to many men. In the future, as farmers broadened their interests with diversification and branched out more and more into stock raising, their cattle would require the large supply of feed that the milling process made available. These feeds consisted of bran itself and "shorts," a low-grade flour containing germ and dine bran. Even the railroads themselves, Bovey insisted, would profit in the end by having a continuous traffic in flour supported by traffic in the by-products of flour manufacture and the by-products of diversified farming.

Nationwide Marketing

This kind of foresight about economic trends showed itself frequently among Bell's young men and helped him to form the policy of expansion which gave his organization its success.

A curious figure of "Bell's kindergarten" was the rugged Tully Estee who first opened the South American market to Washburn Crosby flour. This changeling child of a Latin professor, who had christened his son Tullius Cicero, began his career as a manual laborer in the Minneapolis mill and ended it as head of the New York branch office.

Given to pugnacity, practical jokes, and vehement laughter, Estee brushed away all the froth of his temperament when his gift for selling became active. He discarded the old formula of disposing of flour to an exporter who was then at liberty to sell it under his own brand name, and entered Brazil with his own salesmen. These men spoke Portuguese and under their chief's inspiration made it their job to create a demand for Gold Medal Flour. This new type of emissary had little difficulty in taking customers away from competitors who had long followed a sterile routine of salesmanship. Estee was credited with putting together a new trade almost literally "sack by sack."

The tendency toward consolidation in the milling industry so that in each center a few large corporations controlled activity was evident again in the 1890s when Washburn Crosby acquired two more mills at the Falls. The Minneapolis Mill was leased in 1893, bought outright in 1898; the Humboldt was bought in 1896.

Prosperity by production was the unwritten motto of the Bell administration. Since the margin of profit on a barrel of flour was small, it was necessary to add many small profits together, in many barrels of flour, in order to achieve a satisfactory total. With these acquisitions Bell expanded modestly and securely, bringing the total of his output at the turn of the century to 15,000 barrels a day.

With the new mills he acquired also two additions to his team — William Crocker and Benjamin Seth Bull — long emotion-stirring names in the company. Crocker joined the firm in 1894 shortly after the absorption of his father's Minneapolis Mill; Bull in 1895, just before the acquisition of the Humboldt.

Crocker — round, ruddy, and jovial — took as his function that of transforming a by-product of milling from a liability into an asset. In the early days it had been the habit of millers to pile what they called screenings outside the plant and invite farmers to take the stuff away at a dollar a load. By 1893, however, the value of bran as animal feed had begun to be appreciated and Crocker assumed the responsibility for development of the new department.

The emotions stirred by the name of Bull were strong and mixed. To his office he brought each day the temperament of an inquisitor and the grave, pervasive doubts of a man who had seen his father ruined in an early panic. The pessimism of the pioneer character dominated Bull's mood as clearly as the optimism of the pioneer character dominated Bell's.

A wit once said of Bull that he was creator of the atmosphere of "addition, division, and silence" in which the affairs of the company were conducted. Yet this taciturn man was an early advocate of advertising. He knew that personal appeals must be made to the buying public over and over again if they were to be persuaded to accept the manufacturer's claims for his product. Out of his tormented silence Bull spoke the first widely used phrasing of Washburn Crosby's appeal on behalf of Gold Medal Flour.

To Bell, the tirelessly explorative expansionist, belongs credit for the discovery as far as his product was concerned that advertising offered a new dimension in which to operate. Penetration into the consciousness of the woman buyer seemed to him, even in 1893, a project worth $10,000 a year. To pay money for space in a magazine seemed to his more conservative partners like wanton extravagance. It was proper to notify the trade about new plans in the advertising columns of the *Northwestern Miller* but to attempt to speak to customers far away through the pages of the *Ladies' Home Journal*, that was another matter. Bell insisted that it was a vitally important matter, the confident word spoken between friends in the interest of good living. So his campaign began. A year later the daring $10,000 appropriation had been increased to $220,000. This sum would be the small change of an advertising budget today but, in 1894, it seemed fabulous.

Bull added a slogan. There are many legends about how his words were introduced into the folklore of American wit. The most probable is this.

A long and highly argumentative text had been prepared for Bull's approval as advertising manager in which the writer set forth the superior quality of Gold Medal Flour. Each of his sentential paragraphs began with the word "Eventually." Bull's taste for silence was revolted by all this chatter and one after another he struck out the loquacious sentiments. In the end only the word "Eventually" remained. Then with characteristic imperiousness he was prompted to add: "Why not now?"

It is also part of the legend that having had this bright idea Bull was struck with self-doubt. He tossed the bit of paper with the slogan written on it into the wastebasket, from which it was retrieved by a young member of the firm (James Ford Bell).

Thereafter for many years the words "Eventually — Why Not Now?" lettered out in a copy of Bull's own hand appeared on billboards across the land. The omniscient Bull checked on them constantly. On one occasion he assigned a young assistant, Chester Lang, the task of counting display billboards that could be seen from the window of a train traveling between Minneapolis and Lang's home in Erie, Pennsylvania. The assignment was carried out with dogged conscientiousness until night fell eclipsing the observer's efficiency. The incident still troubles the memory of Lang, now vice president of General Electric in New York.

Few slogans have taken so firm a hold on public fancy. Thousands of variants on the formula were contrived by bright young people to serve every kind of social emergency. Eventually — the slogan itself had to be discarded, but not before a rival had put it to ingenious misuse. Next to a Washburn Crosby signboard bearing the familiar message, one was acquired by Pillsbury and on it appeared what purported to be an answer to the question: "Because Pillsbury's Best."

The closing years of the century were crowded for millers with the kind of drama that makes for headlines and headaches, the Leiter corner, for example, and the McIntyre experiment. Each started a landslide of incident that carried many firms to ruin, but not Washburn Crosby.

In June 1897 the activities of Joseph Leiter, a young Chicago financier, began to interest the trade and by the year's end to alarm it. He had secured title to a large proportion of the outstanding wheat contracts in the Chicago market. He had also acquired a substantial part of the small stocks of the cash wheat of contract grade and a significant share of the cash wheat of all the surrounding country. He seemed to be in a position from which he could dictate terms to all dealers. The price of wheat rose in Chicago, crazily out of balance with the price structure in the country as a whole. When grain receipts proved to be heavy,

Leiter found himself obliged to accept delivery of 9,000,000 bushels and those who had suffered as a result of his maneuvers hoped for a collapse. In February the *Northwestern Miller* began to predict cheerfully that this "Most Puissant King" would presently find himself dethroned. But Leiter, quite as cheerfully, clung to his crown. He surprised friends and enemies alike by providing himself with great strings of freight cars to receive his wealth in wheat.

In April 1898 world affairs fell tragically into step with Leiter's line of march. The United States declared war on Spain, and Europe, alarmed by the cold wet weather that threatened its crops, began buying American wheat more heavily than ever before. Again Leiter profited. But, in the end, circumstance turned upon him. The 1898 harvest was uncommonly abundant. Leiter was unable to buy enough of it to prevent a price decline. Literally engulfed in wheat, he drowned and his holdings were transferred to others for liquidation. The *Northwestern Miller* saluted his downfall as the release of the industry from "thralldom to speculation."

These congratulations proved to be premature. In the same year, 1898, a much more threatening episode, also engineered outside the industry, was written into milling history at the Falls. But the crisis conferred indirect benefits. Millers clinging stubbornly to their view of themselves as craftsmen, rather than promoters, held tight also the control of their enterprise and kept adventurers out.

In the mind of a New York promoter, Thomas A. McIntyre, there evolved during the time of grandiose trust schemes, the idea of uniting the country's flour interests in a great combine. Backed by eastern bankers he embarked upon a grand tour of the country picking up such properties as fell easily into his hands — mills in New York, Syracuse, Milwaukee, Duluth, and Superior. Essential to his success was possession of one of the large, well-established firms in Minneapolis. The three to which he presently laid siege were the Pillsbury group, then run by C. A. Pillsbury for the British operating company; the Northwestern Consolidated Milling Company of which A. C. Loring was president, representing a partnership of tired pioneers; and the Washburn Crosby mills still merely leased by the managing partners from the absentee heirs.

Any one of these might have been expected to pass quietly into the keeping of McIntyre's United States Milling Company. The foreign owners of the Pillsbury mills were interested chiefly in making money on their investment. The owners of the Consolidated mills were concerned with escaping from their burdens. The Washburn Crosby mills always had been for sale to the highest bidder.

But McIntyre loved his plan unwisely. He made extravagant claims; he betrayed a lack of knowledge of the industry and a far greater interest in selling stock than in selling good flour; he seemed to prefer his champagne parties to any meal based on bread. The millers regarded him uneasily. Schemes of his kind were more likely, they thought, to undermine what they had built up than to extend their usefulness.

In the end only the Consolidated group capitulated to his overtures. The Pillsburys quietly sent to London and bought up enough stock to prevent a sale. Dunwoody, quite as unobtrusively, went to Philadelphia to deal once more — and this time finally — with the Washburn heirs. His large private resources and his access, as banker, to more had enabled the Washburn Crosby group to maintain its steady course of expansion. At a moment when he might have been expected, as a man approaching his sixtieth year, to consult his comfort rather than his ambitions, he made a new commitment to industry by buying 75 per cent of the stock of the C. C. Washburn Flouring Mills Company. Now for the first time in a history of several decades the operators of the plant became its owners.

It was fortunate not only for themselves but for the industry that they managed to do so. Within a year of McIntyre's capture of Consolidated mills, the whole combine was in the hands of receivers. The *Northwestern Miller* followed the corpse of the United States Milling Company to its grave without regret. The men involved had been mere "Waldorf-Astoria millers," the editor wrote tartly, and "the defects of the organization were inseparable from those of Wall Street." As money men, the whole McIntyre group had failed to show anything of the professional *savoir-faire* that millers exacted of themselves. By their rejection of the whole effort millers had served notice that they expected to retain control of their industry, basing their hope of usefulness and of prosperity on their sense of personal responsibility to the job.

By the turn of the century Bell was in secure possession of his mills and of his program for them. The team was working well and the representatives of the older generation continued to be stanch allies. To be sure, C. J. Martin had taken, as he grew older, to giving audible expression to the thoughts he had for so long kept sternly to himself. In bad moments Bell would sometimes comment dryly: "What can you expect when your silent partner starts talking to himself?" But this pleasantry merely emphasized the truth that there were no really bad moments in this time of broad expansion.

Restating his formula for achieving prosperity by increased production, Bell told the board in his annual report of 1901–2 that, with the facilities that existed already for "obtaining and storing wheat" nothing was needed "to complete our organization and keep pace with its rapid growth" but "additional mills favorably located."

A chief necessity, the team in consultation decided, was a mill at Buffalo, New York.

There were two reasons for this. The first had to do with the fact that it had become cheaper to ship wheat than to ship flour, via the Great Lakes, from the Midwest to eastern markets. In 1901, the railroads, under orders from the Interstate Commerce Commission, readjusted their freight rate structure to the disadvantage of Minneapolis. Struggling with this new problem, Charles Bovey sat up night after night with a scratch pad before him trying to arrive at a mathematical formula that would make the cost of handling the finished product able to compete with the cost of handling grain. But, as Bell told him with his usual tolerant finality, he was looking for a magical device that did not exist.

Frank Henry agreed. For several years, as manager of the Buffalo warehouse, he had been urging that instead of maintaining transit facilities at this strategic point of navigation, the company should build a real mill. There it could receive an abundant supply of wheat, process it as reasonably as at Minneapolis, and have the flour ready for eastern and overseas markets without heavy transportation cost. In short, Mohammed must move sensibly and without protest to the mountain.

Another argument in support of the proposal to mill heavily at Buffalo was the size and excellence of the Canadian wheat crop. Since 1896 the Canadian prairies had been swept by a wave of immigration comparable to that which had inundated the American wheat land three or four decades earlier. Canada's "growing time" had come, at last, and much of the effort of the new agricultural community was devoted to high-grade, high-protein wheat for export, chiefly to Europe.

Though the Canadian Pacific Railroad (opened in 1885), together with the St. Lawrence Waterway to Montreal, offered an outlet to the sea, the route across American soil, through Buffalo to New York, was still attractive to shippers because a great deal of shipping was available all year round, while the St. Lawrence–Montreal route was closed part of the year by weather conditions. As Bell was the first to see, by moving into Buffalo a miller could recapture some of the export trade that was being lost to Canada. Its wheat could be bought and milled in the United States, preserving for the manufacturer a fine source of raw material and, to the trader, a European outlet for his product. Once more the members of the team agreed that a mill at Buffalo, directly in the line of march of Canadian wheat, was a necessity.

The formula for this operation was provided by the tariff regulations put into effect by the McKinley administration. In 1897, the President, determined to overcome the effects of the depression that followed the panic of 1893, called a special session of Congress, the purpose of which was to revise the tariff law in the interest of industry. The Dingley Act, as the measure was popularly called, pushed the principle of protection farther than it had ever gone before.

Its provisions, as they applied to milling, were flexible and, in consequence, susceptible to misinterpretation even within the inner circle of the industry. The law stated that "no articles or materials [like wheat] received into a bonded manufacturing warehouse shall be withdrawn or removed therefrom excepting for dock shipment and exportation under bond." This practice came to be known, in its application to the flour industry, as "milling in bond." Its importance to the miller was that it permitted him to purchase Canadian wheat duty-free if the flour made from it were exported.

But the law provided also that "where imported materials on which duties have been paid are used in the manufacture of articles manufactured or produced in the United States there shall be allowed on the exportation of such article a drawback equal in amount to the duties paid on materials used, less 1 per cent of such duties." This modification of the system was described in the trade as "grinding duty paid wheat with privilege of drawback." Its advantage to the miller was that it permitted him to retain the by-product of flour manufacture, mill-feed, the supply of which in the United States was inadequate to domestic needs.

The principle of the drawback (its very name melancholy-sounding and prejudicial) was so imperfectly understood that even trade editors assured readers that the Minneapolis fraternity was "getting weary of the endless talk about the importation of Canadian wheat." What "with the many trying and annoying features," said the *Northwestern Miller*, "the game is not worth the candle."

Much later "the privilege of drawback" was subjected to quite another interpretation which conceived of it as tending to encourage devious, unfair practice. The Minneapolis miller, said the miller of the Southwest, imported high-protein wheat from Canada, pretended to comply with the regulations by exporting an equivalent amount of flour, but actually exported flour made from inferior wheat. Envy so tormented the minds of certain groups of millers that they came to believe this libel unshakably.

In 1902, however, the features of wheat importation which so annoyed the *Northwestern Miller* did not trouble Bell. He bonded his Humboldt Mill and ground a million bushels of Canadian wheat there, adding greatly to the success of his operation for the season. Once more he had taken the initiative in starting a new practice and broadening his field of opportunity.

Having disposed of other immediate problems of operation, Bell's team turned in January 1903, after many months of study, to the task of making the mill at Buffalo a reality. The whole group was involved in this major project: Bell as over-all planner; Dunwoody, who liked to think that he was "always in advance even of Bell in plans for spending money," as provider of funds; Frank Henry, as chief instigator of the idea; Charles Bovey and Fred Atkinson, as adaptable lieutenants; Will Bovey and John Gerard, as engineers of the plant itself. Henry, who knew the lake front as he knew the inside of his pocket, suggested the spectacularly handsome site. By May ground had been broken.

The debut of Washburn Crosby at Buffalo caused a local sensation. Before this turn of circumstance the community had not been important as a milling center. Its chief claim to distinction was that in 1842 one of its citizens, Joseph Dart, had devised the world's first system of handling grain by machinery for commercial purposes. (Before this achievement "Irishmen's backs had been considered the cheapest elevators.") Only a few mills of small capacity survived the combinations and closings that marked the economic hazards of the 1890s. At the time of Bell's arrival there was nothing to suggest that Buffalo would become one of the world's great milling centers.

The team made the prospects brighten year by year and almost day by day. In September 1903 the mill was completed; in January 1904 it was in full operation, producing as much flour as did all other local mills combined; by 1906 it had reached the most active kind of maturity, receiving huge cargoes at its elevator directly from shipboard and delivering these to its mill by conveyor belt. This spectacular innovation enabled the Buffalo plant to handle the largest shipment ever consigned up to that time to one mill — 351,000 bushels. The original capacity of the mill — 3500 barrels daily — proved very soon to be quite inadequate and was presently doubled. Elevator capacity was similarly increased and the whole plant became a model of teeming energy and resourcefulness, a glittering and enviable attraction that drew other Minneapolis millers to Buffalo.

In 1904 Bell assumed a leading role in a drama of great importance to the trade. This had to do with the question to bleach or not to bleach. Millers long had known that by aging flour for six or eight weeks they were able to achieve the pure white effect and, more important, its baking properties were superior to those of new flour. It was also common knowledge in the trade that customers preferred flour of light color to the creamy product of the original grinding process.

But storage itself presented a problem. Small mills could not afford the space required. In Great Britain the first experiments were made in search of a way to accelerate the process by artificial means. Chlorine gas, sulphur, pure ozone — all were tried without producing a feasible method.

James N. Alsop, a St. Louis miller, took out patents for a new process in 1904. This involved exposing flour to air containing traces of nitrogen peroxide produced by a flaming discharge of electricity. Professor Harry Snyder of the University of Minnesota, reporting on independent studies made at the time when to bleach or not to bleach was the question of the hour, described this phenomenon as being like a "miniature flash of lightning." In the confines of the bleaching chamber this chemically controlled stroke of lightning united the nitrogen and the oxygen of the air. The nitrogen, as Professor Snyder's experiments indicated, served merely as an efficient carrier of oxygen enabling it to act quickly on the unstable yellow coloring matter of freshly milled flour and to bring about a change by oxidation exactly as does air in the natural aging process.

Bleaching by electrical method, Snyder concluded, was a natural process involving no chemical change, leaving the physical properties of fat and gluten exactly what they were in unbleached flour.

The milling fraternity rejoiced over this discovery. All the leaders in the industry came together in an organization called the American Milling and Purifying Company, with headquarters in St. Louis, to share the benefits of a process which they regarded as the greatest advance since "the milling revolution." There was no commercial advantage to a privileged group. Under the leadership of Bell everyone was invited to join the controlling unit and buy rights to the Alsop process in the modest confidence that a general improvement of the product would inevitably result.

But this was not the opinion of certain zealots who believed that any tampering with nature was mischievous. Dr. Harvey Wiley, author of the Pure Food and Drugs Law, passed in 1906, launched a crusade against mischief, directing his stinging verbal fire particularly at bleachers of flour. To be accused of criminal intent was startling to an industry that had always been jealous of its reputation. Millers had fought the battle against adulteration with success from within.

Prominent scientists, and much later the Supreme Court itself, exonerated the bleaching process of any tendency to injure flour. But at the moment when James Wilson, secretary of the United States Department of Agriculture, joined with chief chemist Dr. Wiley in the campaign against bleaching, and had its practice forbidden under the Food and Drugs Law, millers behaved with nearly unanimous docility. They would not fight their government, even in a cause where they believed the government to be wrong, because of a conviction that the Department of Agriculture and the milling industry shared a responsibility to the public which could only be injured by a struggle between them.

Bell had led the movement to make bleaching a general practice because he was convinced of its merit. Now he led the retreat, unwilling after his long career of building confidence in his product to play the role of dissenter. In his diary for December 1908 he wrote: "The decision of Mr. Wilson is the law of the land. There will be no bleached Gold Medal Flour after June 9, 1909."

In March 1908 Bell on one of his many journeys wrote a long letter in meditative mood to an associate at home. The Roman background evidently reminded him that monuments to human effort sometimes endure gratifyingly and he thought of his own organization as such a monument. It made him feel proud, he wrote, to see how the company grew and to know that when its elder members were gone the younger generation would go on to "build a still greater organization."

The old members began now to disappear one after another. In June 1910 Charles Martin talked to himself for the last time, murmuring half-incredulous, wholly outraged cries against that radical fellow recently in the White House, Teddy Roosevelt. He died with no other unforgiveness in his mind and the city of Minneapolis became by the terms of his will a chief heir.

Bell himself fell seriously ill in 1913 and the period of his lingering invalidism was shadowed by new anxieties. An unwritten rule of the company was that its stock must be closely held. Dunwoody required Bell and the younger men each to take up his share of the Martin stock that it might not be thrown on the market. This crisis had barely been passed when, in February 1914, Dunwoody died. He, like Martin, left large benefactions to the city of Minneapolis. But again, for the younger partners, there was an obverse side to this generosity. It was necessary this time to sign joint notes for two and a half millions from Philadelphia bankers to "buy in" the Dunwoody stock. Once more a time of crucial anxiety had just been passed when Bell himself died on April 5, 1915.

For several days thereafter the Minnesota press was full of his praise. He had been, the obituaries agreed, the best of his kind, the "greatest merchant miller," the most understanding "builder of men."

If Bell's last months were shadowed by private problems he escaped, by his death, public problems of much greater complexity. In the spring of 1915 it became clear that the war in Europe was to be a prolonged and agonizing struggle; shrewd observers had begun to say that America could not expect to avoid participation in it. A period of man's experience was over, one that had been dedicated to large creative effort and cheered by prosperity no matter how often high expectation had been punctuated by panic.

To many members of the inner circle of one American industry it seemed clear that J. S. Bell had managed to be the embodiment of the temper of that time — of its energy, its imagination, and its confidence. He and his team had conquered a nationwide market. The team, with Bell's own son now a prominent member, remained to deal with the exacting complexities that were to follow.

68

6

Statesman of Business

JAMES FORD BELL

J OHN WASHBURN, who occupied the president's chair in the Washburn Crosby Company from the time of Bell's death in 1915 until May 1919, when he became chairman of the board, was a displaced Yankee all his days, complete with drawl and solemn, dry comic style. He had a habit of teasing rejection which amused, but baffled, his associates as he allowed it, quite uncritically, to invade all his relations, social and professional. Fortunately, he did not reject factual knowledge of grain and he became a recognized authority on wheat prices, wheat quality, and wheat markets. Nor did he reject Bell's program, and his own relaxed method of taking command of the momentum for which his predecessor was responsible enabled the Bell team to make the most of their opportunities.

The two leading members of that team now were John Crosby, son of the first Crosby to reach Minnesota out of Maine, and James Ford Bell, son of the late president.

Crosby, made a director in 1889 while still a student in college because of the company's desire to preserve the prestige of its name, had been first a legal adviser to Washburn Crosby and, after the death of Martin, its secretary-treasurer.

Tall, slender, wearing his immaculate and always formal dress as though it were a natural covering, Crosby managed to look a little like a Maine pine tree; Maine clung to his crisp, tart speech. To his associates he wrote laconic letters, signed with a spidery hand, and through these there ran strains of civilized irony and the subtle charm of reticence. His enormous value to a business enterprise lay in his ability to use intelligence as a precise instrument for measuring opportunity and risk. "Acumen" was the word used most often of this asset. But Crosby's mind was not merely quick; it penetrated deep into the realms of finance and the law, touching the rock bottom of wisdom that should support both. Intimates felt that a temperament the core of which was caution seldom had shown so fine a fruit of charm, and that a fixed habit of re-serve had seldom made room for so much of lively humor.

The younger man who became Washburn's chief ally had begun in his early youth a lifelong love affair with experimentation. From boy-hood young Bell had been an inventor of gadgets. In 1900 while he was still a student of cereal chemistry under Professor Harry Snyder at the University of Minnesota he had created the first laboratory for testing flour. In this enormous room, up an alley and over a saloon, the young members of the team studied wheat and flour chemistry assiduously. In later years, his capacity for action erupted in a pyrotechnical display of enthusiasms and he became known as a collector of rare books on American history; creator of a natural history museum; founder of a station for the preservation of wild life; authority on a wide variety of arts, with a particular interest in American silver; author of many essays on finance and economics; regent of a university. These activities rode on the tide of his major preoccupation with milling and its development as a feature, basic and permanent, of world economy. Rising above all this was a spray of interest in hobbies: music (he once composed a song sung by Galli-Curci), fishing, hunting, cooking. Inexhaustible and in-destructible, he has vibrated between the world of ideas and the world of action, letting the discoveries of the first serve the campaigns of the second and the excitement of the second suggest new adventures for the first.

In 1901, after Bell's graduation from college, his father flung him headlong into the business saying: "I'm going to turn you loose against a bunch of fellows who'll steal your shirt if you let them. I can't help you." And for all the high intensity of his paternal feeling, he never did. The apprentice worked as millwright, carpenter, electrician, clerk, bill collector. He stamped the company's name and brand identification on its first cookbook. He was "Jim" to the men in the mill and "Tinker" to some who had watched with amusement his wide variety of experiments.

Eventually he became a salesman with Michigan as his territory.

Very promptly the hereditary silver spoon was dislodged from the none-theless resolute Bell mouth. Travel conditions were primitive and so were the towns. Food in the hotels merely sustained life and did nothing for the spirit. The salesman went from town to town by train and from customer to customer often making his way in winter through unploughed drifts. His schedule called for visits each day to a new community. As his trip progressed, hardships mounted because, since travel time had to come out of the workday, he began his round of calls later and later at each successive stop.

Little initiative rested with the salesmen. Atkinson did much of the major campaigning by letter from Minneapolis. He himself handled all orders, telling salesmen merely what firms needed flour and whether the territory was gaining or losing volume.

But Bell learned much. As a salesman in his twenties he began to evolve the philosophy of merchandising that led at last to the formation of General Mills. His letters and reports from Michigan indicate clearly that already he had accepted the principle, formulated in later writing, that "the miller's job isn't finished when flour is sold but only when it is consumed." He felt even then that the objective was to "maintain a continuous drive to get the flour out of the grocer's stock and baker's bins and off the kitchen shelves to the table in forms appealing to the appetite." He saw that the larger the organization devoted to that work, the lower the cost could be made and "the greater the satisfaction to the consuming public." Anticipations of what he was later to accomplish occupied his mind as he wrote his long reports from lonely Michigan hotels.

With the experience of salesman to fill out his background as practical man of affairs, Bell accepted executive assignment. In 1909 he was made a director of the company and in 1915, after his father's death, a vice president.

It was a time of opportunity and of risk when an administrator could not operate by a book of established rules but must improvise decisions to match each day's crisis. Europe, at war, was cut off from its normal sources of flour for bread, an item always basic to its diet. Its own farming districts were devastated; belligerent Germany lay between Russia and the Allied countries; difficulties of transportation made India and Austria as remote as though they belonged to another planet. North America had to make up the difference.

71

Statesman of Business

The Washburn Crosby Company, long important in the export trade, was in the drama from the start. Even before the outbreak of actual hostilities, the directors had felt an anticipatory shock of war when the German government announced firmly that it had seized $140,000 worth of flour en route through Hamburg to buyers in the Scandinavian countries. This was only part of the resources, some $400,000 worth in all, committed to the sea in German ships. In the end these problems were adjusted through international agreement and not a cent was lost.

In 1915 war conditions had begun to seem normal. The Buffalo mill tapped the flow of Canadian wheat and sent it on in the form of flour to satisfy the vastly increased demands of Great Britain. Belgium and Switzerland were also heavy buyers and even France and Italy, normally self-sufficient, were enrolled as customers. Bell's diary for June recorded the fact that "We have secured a large amount of this desirable new business." To a special meeting of the directors called in October he reported that "bookings now amount to 3,122,963 barrels, one million greater than our best previous year [1912] and twice as much as our average at this time of year." In December he made a grand tour of the mills and came home "thrilled with the spirit of accomplishment."

The year 1916 presented a more confused picture. To seize opportunity it began to be necessary to dodge with a certain agility through the missiles of circumstance. By April it was clear that the crop would be disappointing. Overwork of equipment in many plants caused mechanical difficulties. There were threats of labor trouble. To Bell's tasks were added those of placating prima donnas among his engineers and patching up equipment. All this he managed in addition to his major jobs which were to outline policies, to keep the practice of hedging sound even in the midst of the wild fantasy of war, and to anticipate movements in the wheat market so that the company might always have enough raw material without ever being, as a company grain expert put it, "long, short, or sleepless."

The crop year ended well, after all. A fine harvest in Montana's Flathead Valley made up for failures elsewhere and the company's output was 2,000,000 barrels ahead of any previous year.

Each day, however, brought a new crisis. In October all prospects for the immediate future were "knocked in the head" by the cynical success of Germany's unrestricted submarine warfare. Nine vessels were destroyed off the American coast. The stock market was shaken, looked "nasty," and a tremor of uncertainty ran through the wheat world. The market was "nervous"; quality in grain itself seemed no longer to be reliable; there were threats that Canadian wheat might pass out of American reach. As Bell wrote: "It is evident that the English government would gladly commandeer the crop and embargo shipments except for the bullish effect on American markets in which they are making heavy purchases."

Yet through these harassing difficulties, he managed to keep all his mills running to full capacity. Balancing opportunity against risk in each new circumstance, he kept output and sales ever on the increase.

A resilient temper helped him through these crises. A secretary remembers a shock that he once administered to her inadvertently at a moment when problems were many and pressing. The time was the Christmas season in the year before America's entry into World War I. Bell was wanted urgently on the telephone, but the secretary could not find him in his office. She visited the office of each executive and found them all empty. The question of what had become of the whole administrative force was resolved when the young woman saw a light shining under the door of the directors' room. There was no answer when she knocked, so, greatly daring, she walked in.

A strange, even frightening, kind of ritual appeared to be in progress. The directors' table had been pushed into a corner and, in the center of the room, all the officers of the Washburn Crosby Company were grouped in a circle on their knees. The idea suggested itself disturbingly that this might be a session of prayer for guidance in a time of disaster. But presently the secretary saw that this was not so. In the center of the group was James Ford Bell. Even on his knees he towered above the others. He was demonstrating the operation of an electric train bought as a Christmas present for his young son.

On April 2, 1917, President Wilson asked Congress to declare that a state of war existed between the United States and Germany and a new phase opened for the milling industry.

The situation recently had been precarious. The poor harvest of 1916 together with unrestricted buying by foreign governments had, as Bell feared, sent the price of wheat high and drained away American reserves. Many millers hesitated to buy the grain that was available

73

because they feared that a break might come just in time to crush them in bankruptcy. Before the declaration of war, mills all over the country were preparing either to curtail their activities to a minimum or to retire from business altogether.

Once war had been declared, millers felt required by duty to themselves as well as to their country to do an abrupt about-face. That they were able to execute this maneuver with smart military precision, in the very midst of crisis, testifies to the strength of their habits of self-discipline.

But the new situation which changed the millers' minds did not change the market. Indeed, the weather in the milling world grew worse rather than better. Now it was clear that there must be government control of food; but until it became equally clear by what means the public interest was to be protected, the miller still could not afford to buy. Speculation continued to call the wild tune. During May and June 1917 the price of wheat leaped to $3.40 a bushel and flour to $18 a barrel. The probability that the administration would ask that the price of wheat be pegged together with the certainty that Congress would not do so quickly trapped the miller in a blind alley of uncertainty.

Exactly a month after the declaration of war Herbert Hoover returned to America from Belgium where during 1914 and 1915 he had been in charge of providing food for noncombatants threatened by starvation. On the same day President Wilson asked him to take over the new and vastly greater problem faced by the United States at war. This was to provide sufficient food not only for the American people and their men in the armed services, but also for a large number of the civilians and soldiers of the Allies and of neutral countries. Within four days the first steps were taken toward the creation of a war agency that came to be known as the Food Administration.

The scope of its responsibility was enormous. As Hoover himself has said, the authority of the chief "must cover every phase of food administration from soil to stomach. That included direct or indirect control over production, farm policies, conservation, exports, imports, buying for our military forces and those of the Allies, prices, rationing, processing, distribution and consumers."

For this purpose Congress gave Hoover's organization a capital of $150,000,000 with which to buy and sell food. The Food Administration Grain Corporation became, for example, the only agency with a right to buy wheat. This tremendous project was intended, as Wilson explained to the American people, not to interfere arbitrarily in a time of crisis with the normal processes of production, but rather "to benefit and assist the farmer and all those who play a legitimate part in the preparation, distribution and marketing of foodstuffs."

Wilson and Hoover had managed to cut briskly and effectively through the clutter of routine considerations in their effort to set this vital plan in motion. No such direct action followed in Congress. The announcement of Hoover's appointment as "food czar" (the picturesquely inept phrase adopted by the headline writers in search of nice short words) brought from chronic viewers-with-alarm the traditional attack on his personal character. Because of his long residence abroad in the service of British mining interests he was greeted as a designing foreigner. Startled by this reception, Hoover thought of withdrawing to his home in California to await the result of congressional dispute. But there was no time for morbid delicacy of feeling. Within the barricade of his formidably high collar (which seemed in those days to be the symbol of his rectitude), his neck stiffened and he stayed on to fight the battle of the food bill. Through May, June, and July the struggle continued without decision from Congress.

Meanwhile the milling industry was virtually paralyzed. Hoping to stimulate action, William G. Edgar, editor of the *Northwestern Miller*, went to Washington to interview Hoover with whom he and J. S. Bell had worked intimately on the task of feeding the Belgians. Hoover had spoken of wishing to turn over responsibility for details of food administration to the various trades and of eliciting their voluntary cooperation. Edgar presently volunteered to call to his side the young executive James Ford Bell. Straight from a sickbed, Bell joined Edgar in Washington.

The first meetings of this informal and unofficial committee were not always placid. Hoover was positive, emphatic, impatient of criticism, ready to receive only such ideas as seemed to implement his own. To the others he seemed sometimes to be "lost in the force of his own logic." Edgar, irascible, sharp-tongued, had a kind of punctilious obstinacy that made him dash off notes to Hoover in which he threatened "to return home and advise millers to liquidate as speedily as possible." It was Bell's task, as young conciliator, to intercept such threats and keep the discussion going until agreement could be reached.

75

Statesman of Business

At a first session with Edgar and Bell, Hoover dashed off in long-hand on a piece of hotel stationery a list of problems faced by the Food Administration in the miller's realm. Then, under the heading "Hypothesis," he proposed a design for control. This hastily improvised scheme conjured up before Edgar's frightened eyes the image of a huge government monopoly in charge of nonexperts who would dictate what kind of flour was to be manufactured, to what means of transportation it would be committed, and to whom it would be sold. In short, Edgar saw his friend the miller reduced to the status of a clerk, with his initiative destroyed and his all-important relationship to his customer damaged perhaps past repair.

Fortunately, Hoover had meant it when he said that he wished to give responsibility to the trades themselves. The solution to all problems was the same: to find a professional miller who would recognize the necessity of concerted action and who would be capable of securing the voluntary cooperation of fellow millers.

During a season of record heat in Washington when the asphalt seemed about to melt in the streets, Bell commuted between Minneapolis and Washington. Edgar was usually at his side, but, more and more, the younger man was pushed forward by the milling fraternity as its spokesman. That he might not seem to speak alone, he had drawn about him a group of men who represented the liveliest intelligence of the industry: A. C. Loring of Minneapolis; Fred Lingham of Lockport, New York; Mark Mennel of Toledo; Andrew Hunt of Arkansas City; and A. P. Husband of Chicago. At this moment in June, Congress had not acted to give Hoover and the Food Administration authority. The volunteer committee, surrendering all old habits of competition, met together to pool their knowledge and to work out patterns for cooperative effort. Delighted with this generous sacrifice of personal advantage, Hoover met frequently with the millers' committee and accepted in principle its proposal for a program of control.

The agreements reached in these discussions included several that were broad and basic. The miller was to conform to a price for wheat stipulated by the government. He was to sell his flour at cost plus a fixed margin of profit. He was to accept as his share of available supplies a fair percentage of the amount he had used, on an average, over the past three years. In return, the government was to guarantee him against loss on wheat bought at the pegged price.

On June 29, Hoover wrote to Bell as chairman of the millers' committee: "I wish to express deep appreciation for the patriotic manner in which the millers have come forward. You have been of the greatest assistance in setting advance standards for the whole administration."

It was no surprise when, four days later, he named Bell as supervisor of the milling operations under the Food Administration. The chief, just turned 38, asked only that his appointment be endorsed by the milling fraternity. His old committee offered him an immediate vote of confidence. By August 10, when the Lever Bill creating the Food Administration finally was passed by Congress and signed by the President, the Milling Division was already organized and poised at the starting line. Within ten days of the first official action by the Milling Division, 90 per cent of the entire industry was committed to its discipline. Bell had resigned from the Washburn Crosby Company and turned all his energies to the task of justifying the slogan "Food Will Win the War."

The exigencies of the program required him to be two places at once: New York where, each month, 2,000,000 barrels of flour had to be brought together for shipment to the Allies, and Washington where high policies were constantly being made or revised. Bell managed this neatly by spending virtually every night of his mission on trains plying between the two cities. Importunate millers, looking for favors, learned of his habit and pursued him down the labyrinthine ways of the Pennsylvania line. Once, realizing that he had been trapped, Bell hid in a coach car and feigned sleep for hours while the hunter, having found him, stubbornly and steadily kept the bead of his attention on him from the next seat until Bell could endure it no longer and opened his eyes.

Members of his own firm were scrupulous in asking no favors. Indeed, he was so determined to be immaculate in his role as government servant that he refused to know anything about an individual mill that might be to his advantage later when competition was restored. All accounts of the Milling Division were known to him only by number. He himself never saw the key to this record, leaving it in charge of his first assistant.

Having created on paper a unique design for an untried form of cooperation on a very large scale, Bell had to implement it with an organization. In New York he drafted Richard Fenby Bausman, who had been representing Washburn Crosby's export interests in New York since 1914, and set about looking for a business home. The suite selected at 76

Broadway looked down into the tight, tense pattern of the financial district and out across the splendid sweep of the harbor. This office must have pleased the eye of a man whose temper understood both the powerful drive of human effort and the impulse after freedom which the scene dramatized.

Bausman, long a member of Bell's team, assumed the responsibility of export manager for the Milling Division. He purchased all flour needed by the Allies.

The choice of an executive manager led Bell to a man who was to have an important place in the subsequent history of his private affairs. Donald D. Davis, recommended by a banker of the J. P. Morgan organization, had been a "trouble shooter" for ailing companies and he had learned to detect waste, inefficiency, looseness of organization as accurately as a master mechanic identifies a faulty part. He was, much later, to inherit various kinds of executive responsibility from Bell. In the first association of the two men, both had the satisfaction of hearing their division called the model of efficiency among units of the Food Administration.

It was Dr. Raymond Pearl who offered this judgment. The Johns Hopkins biologist and research expert in many fields of agricultural experimentation had been borrowed by Hoover as special adviser. Wearing his thick-lensed glasses and trailing a cloud of academic abstraction, Pearl put the Milling Division under his own kind of microscope and ended his investigation by pronouncing it a perfect specimen. This was the beginning of a long friendship between Bell and Pearl, one that lasted through many years of mutual preoccupation with problems of improving nutrition.

Another academic whom Hoover added to his collection of brains and whose genius passed later into Bell's keeping was the physiological chemist Dr. Alonzo E. Taylor. In the hastily run-up offices of the Food Administration Building in Washington where Bell lodged momentarily on his flights to the capital, a thin partition separated him from a neighbor whom he called The Voice. The power of this organ would roar toward the partition, recede in volume, fall into silence, and then roar out full again. It was a fascinating but distracting performance, obviously that of a pacer who prowled constantly as he dictated. The Voice, Bell discovered, belonged to Dr. Taylor, later to become director of the Food Research Institute at Stanford University and author of the most important studies of wheat movements in all the literature of science and business. Dr. Taylor, after his retirement from the academic world, became director of research for General Mills.

A commission appointed by the President and headed by Harry A. Garfield, president of Williams College, assumed the responsibility of estimating what would be a fair price for wheat of the 1917 crop. A chief member of the group was Professor Frank Taussig, whose exhaustive knowledge of the tariff problem and of tariff legislation seemed to impart to his person, when he was only fifty-eight, the bulk and grandeur of the patriarch. By a simple and sensible formula of consultation with the industry, the commission arrived at the conclusion that the price for the basic commodity, number one northern spring wheat, at the central distributing point, Chicago, should be $2.20 a bushel. The Grain Corporation adopted this figure and the millers respected it scrupulously.

The formula chosen for arriving at a price for the individual miller's flour was that of adding a twenty-five cent profit to the cost of manufacturing each barrelful. Bell was convinced from the first that this short cut to decision was economically unsound. To put a premium on extravagance was certainly no part of the intention of an executive like Bell, who had spent a busy youth fighting extravagance in his own organization. Yet as head of the Milling Division he was in the position of seeming to countenance it, for slack and heedless habits of manufacture were bound to be the result of allowing millers to tabulate their own expenses and base the price of their flour on these costs. But time was of the essence of the voluntary agreement and a reconsideration of this problem had to wait for a more favorable moment.

Bell did not, however, side-step the basic problem. In January 1918 he created the Mechanical Department of the Milling Division, the purpose of which was to supply manufacturers with free advice — plans, drawings, specifications, and the like — by which they might improve their techniques, lower their costs, and save wheat. Under the direction of a brilliant engineer, James H. Hammill, this exercise of the principle of cooperation had a permanent, beneficial effect, bringing the outposts of the industry into the enlightened sphere of modern technology.

Another lasting effect of the Milling Division's service had to do with business method. Many of the small organizations had been operated by individualists whose ruggedness tended to defeat its own high, exhilarating purpose. Lack of discipline and training made it impossible for them to keep orderly books. To this Donald Davis and his corps of accountants addressed their attention, instructing all units under the Milling Division in modern method. Even the most stanchly independent of operators learned that statistical records have a blessing to offer. The establishment of a uniform system of accounting was perhaps the largest incidental benefit derived by the industry from an experience that imposed significant sacrifices.

Chief of these sacrifices was loss of the privilege of making their flour to suit themselves. In order to stretch scanty supplies and make them feed all the Allies and the neutrals, as well as American civilians and soldiers, Hoover offered his own variation on the parable of the loaves. In his "hypothesis" set down for Edgar and Bell, he proposed that millers should make "war flour," stressing the "psychological advantage" of doing so since it would indicate that the United States was ready to share all burdens of war with England and France. By grinding 80 to 90 per cent of the wheat berry into human food those countries had produced the dark flour of which "war bread" was made.

American millers were reluctant to follow their example. There were many objections to this high-extraction grinding. First, it produced a flour that spoiled quickly. Only the fact that shortage tended toward quick consumption kept the loss in Europe from being serious. Second, it eliminated the by-product of the milling process, feed for cattle. Third, as a result of the loss of feedstuffs, herds of cattle tended to decrease in size and in number. Fourth, as a result of the scarcity of milk and dairy products, prices of these goods soared.

A counter suggestion was presented by the millers through their representatives in the Milling Division, and the American government, anxious to dislocate industry as little as possible, listened to it sympathetically. This called for a program of increasing supplies by mixing wheat flour with flour made from barley, rye, oats, and corn. All these grains had lately produced plentiful crops. Samples of bread made from such mixtures were presented for Hoover's inspection and in January 1918 he consented to adoption of the substitution program. Again the Mechanical Department was called upon to help millers the country over adapt equipment and techniques to the new demands. Bell had once suggested that a mill in full operation had the significance, from the standpoint of over-all strategy, of a regiment of soldiers. The readiness of his fellow millers to follow him in any campaign indicated that they had begun to think of themselves as having immediate military importance, indeed as soldiers in dusters.

During the spring of 1918 it became evident that the wheat crop would be much larger than that of the year before. The strict regulation necessary in a time of shortage was not necessary in the new circumstances. Hoover began to seek a new formula for carrying on and so did Bell.

The two men met in Washington for a discussion of possible changes. Hoover, surcharged with enthusiasm, offered an account of his proposal. "What do you think?" he asked at last. "It has merit," Bell answered, "but I have been thinking of something a little different." In his turn he outlined a plan. As Bell concluded, Hoover made a gesture of self-abnegation that was rare with him. He reached for the notes of his own plan, tore them into shreds, and dropped them into the wastebasket.

The new plan, while it took account of the need to conserve wheat supplies, made possible an immediate return to the normal conditions of competition within the industry. Each mill was given a "fair price schedule" for its flour and millfeed, but the formula that determined price was changed. Instead of allowing the miller his "manufacturing price plus a 25 cent profit on each barrel," he was permitted to charge $1.10 a barrel to cover cost of manufacture and profit.

Again the manufacturers agreed. In 1918 as soon as the program could be put into effect the Milling Division went out of existence and the United States Grain Corporation assumed such supervision of the plants as was still necessary.

Relieved of the daily routine of administration, Bell under the compulsions of social conscience and a love of busyness accepted the next chore assigned him. This was to travel abroad with Hoover to study conditions among the harassed Allies. To an ambassador without portfolio the perils of life with royalty seemed to be the most exacting feature of the tour. King Victor Emmanuel III of Italy once questioned him rigorously through a five-hour dinner and then continued the interview for three hours more while both men stood. As Bell later commented: "At 11 P.M. the rate of shifting body weight from one foot to the other was approaching the frequency of radio transmission" and he had, finally, to risk international relations by excusing himself from a king who happened also to be the world's most ruthless conversationalist.

The war was still in progress when Bell returned to the United States

81

in the fall of 1918 and Hoover had still another assignment for him, this time as treasurer and general manager of the Sugar Equalization Board. Not until March 1919 was he able to resign and return to his own affairs.

The contribution made by millers to the tremendous, unfamiliar effort of World War I was definite and distinguished; it could be measured in dollars and cents. By their voluntary submission to government regulation they reversed the upward trend of prices in their field. Without such control wheat might have gone to $5 a bushel and flour to $25 a barrel. Actually the price of the latter was stabilized at approximately $10 a barrel. It has been estimated that the saving to the public was half a billion dollars.

They made many sacrifices, too. The individual brand of flour, which is all that the miller has to offer in competition, tended to lose its distinctive character in conformity to government rules in the stretching program. Mills that were close to the best available grain were able to maintain their standards while others that were required to take what wheat they could get suffered serious losses. Also, the war emergency encouraged an increase in capacity in an industry already overexpanded. The war left a heritage of problems to be faced during the critical adjustments of the 1920s.

To Bell, who had had to deal with all these difficulties in their most aggravated form and who had learned to cope with men and crises patiently and philosophically, the war bequeathed also a special gift, matured by emergency. He emerged from the experience a statesman of business with a speculative interest in the largest aspects of affairs, a widened acquaintance with men who were to make valuable contributions to the nation's economy in the years ahead, an insight into the character of his craft and its problems, and a generous view of his duty toward it.

Bell's first communication to his partners, upon his return to Minneapolis, indicated clearly that it was with the attitude of a statesman of business that he approached his own professional challenges. These, as he saw them, were serious. The consumption of flour was falling off. During the war the conservation program had undertaken to teach people to save wheat and to develop tastes for other foods. Dutifully they had done so with a result that now shocked the millers: the per capita consumption of flour had declined markedly.

The mores were changing, too. Housewives who had once expected, when the morning chores were done, to spend long hours baking bread, pies, cakes, did so no longer. They went, Bell suspected, to the movies, letting bakers supply their needs. He quoted Jim Hill's witticism (but without echoing its censorious tone) that the trouble with America was not so much the high cost of living as "the cost of high living." What was of interest to the miller was that he must look for buyers in new places.

Of interest to the Minneapolis miller in particular was the further evidence that he must look for wheat in new places. Minnesota had begun to turn to diversified farming. Wheat lands were moving south and west. The ultimate development of the immediate region as producer of grain had been reached.

It followed inevitably that competition would be more keen than in the "good old days" of the company's early growth. During the war all millers had learned to operate more efficiently and there were more of them — too many.

If the Washburn Crosby Company were to maintain its high level of production, it must begin to look for new opportunities. In a bold plan of reorganization, presented to his partners in 1919, Bell urged the invasion of the Southwest; the establishment of still more plants close to the new centers of wheat production; a close collaboration with bakers, one that would enable millers to become "participants in their growth"; and a similar closeness to the new "chain stores." Bell wanted to create new food commodities bearing the Washburn Crosby trademark. These were needed not merely to add new margins of profit but actually to preserve the identity of Gold Medal Flour itself. Without such bolstering, its name might be lost in the great, teeming impersonality of many chain stores.

The passing of the old order was marked for the Washburn Crosby Company in a particular way by the death of John Washburn. He had served as chairman of the board for six months, exercising now a little languidly his drawling talent for the rejection of the ideas of the younger men. The reorganization put John Crosby II into the president's chair in acknowledgment of his fine business judgment. Bell assumed, still as vice president, the responsibility of running the mills.

Before his program of industrial expansion could be put in motion it was necessary to do some tidying up after the unexpectedly early conclusion of World War I. Millers dreaded the period of transition, the withdrawal of government control, and the return to the competitive system. They foresaw chaotic markets, cutthroat price wars, collapse of the export market, and confusion of authority. None of these disasters occurred immediately. Though the first crop harvested after the war in 1919 was a good one, the export trade continued to be lively. Distant wheat-growing countries like Australia were still cut off from the European market by the scarcity of ships (these were wanted in great number to bring American soldiers home) and nearby countries profited accordingly. The American grain surplus was readily absorbed.

Nor did the government hastily withdraw its hand. Wilson, thinking the war likely to drag on in France, had pledged further support to farmers early in 1918. To make good his promise of stable prices, the Wheat Guarantee Act of 1919 was passed. Through the Grain Corporation and its wheat director, the government stood ready to buy any grain that the producer found himself unable to sell. In its turn the Grain Corporation disposed of these holdings in the export market. Despite the fact that it played an anomalous role, that of buyer who did not want to buy and was quite willing to sell at a loss, the United States Grain Corporation managed, through certain "unavoidable profits" of its operation, not merely to remain solvent but to end its career with money in the bank.

Throughout this period of transition, Bell was called upon by the exigencies of circumstance to serve in peculiarly difficult circumstances. Having accepted an assignment as chairman of an advisory committee appointed by the Millers' National Federation, he had to renegotiate the closeout of the Milling Division, or, in his own phrase "to unscramble the eggs" he had beaten so thoroughly during the war period. The millers, feeling insecure about their future and now once more intensely jealous of their constitutional rights, were an edgy group of men, given to outbursts of irrelevant eloquence at almost every session. Even while they still clung doggedly to the protective hand of the government they distrusted its intentions, suspecting it unjustly of entering into direct competition with them by throwing on the domestic market at a low price the flour left over from the war stores intended for the Allies.

Bell checked the flow of charges and countercharges, representing simultaneously the government he had served during the war and the industry of which he was once more an important member. It required both diplomacy and a gift for paternal discipline to keep the committees at their job of unscrambling. Once at a great session in New York a majority of the members showed an inclination to play hookey and go off to see the sights of the town.

"Gentlemen," said Bell firmly, "I intend to sit exactly where I am all night if necessary to get this work done and I expect every one of you to sit with me." The recalcitrants from Kansas City and St. Louis sat.

No sooner had the affairs of the Milling Division been finally resolved than the menacing aspects of change in the economic outlook for millers showed themselves in earnest. In 1920 Dr. Alonzo Taylor pointed out with characteristic acumen that transition from old to new, from war economy to peace economy, from control to full competition, threatened to bring about "one of the worst known periods in the history of the modern world." The situation, he said, was "pregnant with difficulties for agriculture."

The chief problem was that war conditions had encouraged an over-expansion of wheat production. A surplus existed which European countries, now on their own once more but seriously handicapped by postwar deflation, could no longer absorb. In the general downward trend of spring 1920, wheat prices plummeted abruptly. At first farmers refused to believe that they were living in a stern time once more. They had seen the value of wheat go up spectacularly and were understandably reluctant to surrender their peak. When the reverse process began they tried defiantly to hold themselves in mid-air. Shortly before World War I when wheat went to $1 a bushel grain men paraded the streets of Minneapolis headed by a brass band. The phrase "good as dollar wheat" had come into the language. During the war the government had pegged wheat at $2.20 a bushel. Just after the close of the war the price of the grain reached $3.20. Here, the agricultural community decided cheerfully, was the level on which its life must be lived forever.

Then the collapse came. In huge mass meetings the newly created American Farm Bureau Federation, which enrolled whole families as members and encouraged in all its sessions the temper of impassioned solidarity, called a "wheat strike." The huge crop was withheld from the market. But the crops of subsequent years also were large. The surplus grew and prices went lower and lower. In the face of slowly declining agricultural costs and rapidly declining prices, farms were abandoned, workers drifted into the cities to aggravate the crisis and a sharp depression was on.

The second half of the year 1920 was, in the words of a writer for the

Northwestern Miller, "the most trying and disastrous in the history of American milling." The price of flour fell along with that of wheat; buyers canceled orders in panic and seized upon excuses to repudiate contracts. What spared the Washburn Crosby Company acute discomfiture was that its method of operation had always been conservative, untouched by speculation on the price of wheat. The miller's margin of profit, the company's leaders knew, lay in the efficiency of manufacturing techniques. The price of flour simply reflected the price paid for wheat. If both were low, the margin of profit, always narrow, need be squeezed no narrower in the worst of seasons. A prompt adjustment made within this pattern kept the company secure.

Despite the fact that an island of security had been achieved for his own organization within the wide range of the storm, Bell did not fail to interest himself in all the theoretical discussions of justice for agriculture that rose out of the whirlwind. The years 1921, 1922, and 1923 covered a period when he commuted between Minneapolis and Washington, or Minneapolis and Chicago, with a strenuous regularity that recalled the days of his career-on-wheels during World War I.

The activities of the American Farm Bureau Federation held his fascinated and far from unsympathetic eye during a period of its most vigorous activity. On February 16, 1921, its Committee of Seventeen came briskly forward with a proposal to grain growers that they establish a cooperative National Sales Agency for the disposal of their crops through farmers' elevators or local associations. This great combine was to put the farmer in direct and powerfully eloquent communication with buyers of his product. As one of these Bell listened attentively and undertook to woo leaders into agreement with his views on tariff matters.

The Committee of Seventeen numbered several members with picturesque habits of speech, one of whom assured his followers that the purpose of the plan was to sell grain actively, not to sit on the heap armed with a shotgun and an order pad. But when Bernard Baruch suggested that a contribution of one third of his crop should be *compulsory* for every farmer-member, enthusiasm for the idea cooled and the discussion dwindled off into idle dissension.

In January 1922 President Harding called a great Agricultural Conference at Washington, and he addressed the opening session with the encouraging word that "an industry more vital than any other, in which half the nation's wealth is invested," must be supplied with working capital. The wonder was, he said, that agriculture "deprived of easy access to both investment and accommodation capital" had prospered as well as it had.

On hand, bringing the first outline of a plan for solution of the surplus problem which later took shape in the several versions of the Mc-Nary Haugen Bill, were Bernard Baruch, George Peek, and Hugh Johnson, "the youngest general" the United States army had ever created. Johnson, who was to be strenuously active in the early years of the New Deal, had just begun to find his voice as an advocate of causes. His difficulty then, as later, was that he could not learn to keep from that voice the formidable tone of the professional soldier, "full of strange oaths."

On hand also was Bell who, as he once observed, remembered that Minnesota had "been good to him" and realized that he must make a return, during a time of trouble, for its many benefits. But no amount of impersonal idealism could persuade that the right formula for relief of the farmer's distress had been found. As he and Congressman Sydney Anderson (later to be a vice president of General Mills) studied the proposal, they reached the conclusion that such legislation as Peek and Johnson offered would have more ill effects than good.

What the plan proposed, in essence, was to raise agricultural prices by isolating the surplus and dumping it unceremoniously on other countries. This was certain to bring retaliatory action from importing countries. The theory, they believed, was unrealistic because it took no account of interests other than those of the United States. The machinery for its operation would be costly and would constantly become greater. Benefits would be impermanent and the final effects would be to narrow the farmer's market rather than to broaden it and to raise his costs higher than it raised his rewards. It was, as they saw it, a desperate remedy recklessly offered as stimulant to a patient quite likely to be killed by such kindness.

Bell had his own cure for the surplus problem. It was to reverse the orders of World War I to conserve wheat and, in a great nationwide educational campaign, to teach people once more that bread was their best quick energy food.

The Eat More Wheat campaign which Bell launched with the verve of a showman in March 1923, and carried on for a year with the indefatigable energy of a man in love with an idea, attempted to turn back

87

a tendency on the part of the American people to change dietary habits. Since the turn of the century it had been evident that the native table offered more milk, more vegetables, more sugar, and less bread than it had done before. The reasons were many: decrease in the need for energy because machines had begun to perform much of man's heavy labor; new ideas of beauty in the human figure (the wheat line, a wit said, had shrunk along with the dimensions of woman's waist line); new habits associated with the increased use of the automobile. This decline in the per capita consumption of flour took a dizzy plunge during the conservation period of World War I. It continued to go down until 1935 when once more it leveled off. This decline has, of course, been more than offset by the increase in the population so that flour, which as Bell has observed never leaves the economy, has been present in it ever more significantly.

But if Bell did not manage the impossible in reversing a trend in human habit, he did give it a highly dramatic pause. In the middle years of the 1920s the downward trend in per capita consumption of flour seemed to hesitate and then for a time it rose perceptibly. This was exactly the moment of the Eat More Wheat campaign when Bell launched a great advertising program in newspapers and on billboards. He escorted wheat ceremoniously into the center of the consciousness of the American people by arranging for various experts to go on the air to explain the physical virtues and the economic importance of wheat. He persuaded governors of five states to issue formal proclamations endorsing the effort. He engineered the calling of a great Wheat Conference in Chicago to which representatives were sent by railroads, banks, manufacturers of farm implements, universities, the great foundations, and the labor movement, as well as representatives of farmers' organizations, mills, and bakers. The final result was the creation, with Sydney Anderson as its head, of a Wheat Council, with headquarters in Chicago, the purpose of which was to survey agricultural conditions in all regions of the country. The Eat More Wheat campaign did not accomplish a miracle but it demonstrated the power of an idea in action and produced many important indirect results of benefit to the industry.

In March 1924 the Wheat Council ended its task and closed its offices. Circumstances had begun to bring about an improvement in the wheat situation. The crop of that year had been excellent in America while crops in Europe, Canada, and Australia were poor. The deficits elsewhere were made up out of the American surplus. At the same moment the report of Charles G. Dawes and his committee on the hopeful outlook for European recovery revived world confidence. Big private loans went to Europe making its countries buyers once more. Business was good.

Out of this period of trial James Ford Bell emerged a recognized leader, dedicated to the service of common sense and man's innate good will. He had demonstrated that he was capable not merely of successful administration, but also of taking the broad view of general problems of economic welfare. Idea, he saw, was more important than immediate profit because only by satisfying the basic needs of agriculture could a permanent prosperity be assured.

At home, in his own world, he had earned once more the name statesman of business.

7

The Wide Open Door

NEW MEN, NEW METHODS

T HE period of six or seven years just before the formation of General Mills in 1928 was a time of industrial expansion for America. To claim a legitimate share in that development Bell saw, at the very beginning of the period in 1921, that what he called "the ancient and honorable profession" of milling must be brought down to date. Clearly out of date was the idea that a miller could sit in his plant and wait dutifully for the wheat crop "naturally tributary to his mill" to flow to him. That way led to all the hazards of uncertainty — frequent reductions of output, shutdowns, invasion by competitors of one's trade. The alternative was to move into the areas now favored by circumstance and to establish mills of one's own at the best strategic points.

To Bell it seemed equally clear that new appeals on behalf of his product must be made to the human appetite. As he once expressed the idea, it was unreasonable to demand of the palate that it "send in favorable reports for us on samples of the same food three times a day, three hundred sixty-five days in the year. No food ever devised by nature, or by nature and man together, could stand such a test." In short, he realized that, to share in the growth of industry, he must have new products.

To develop new plants, new fields, new projects, new products, and new responsibilities required new men. Crosby and Bell, with the perfect combination between them of insight and initiative, caution and drive, devoted themselves to the work of expanding in all these directions. As Bell observed hopefully at the start of the journey: "There is no limit to the possibilities before us. The door is wide open."

90

Among men, the first important acquisition was Harry A. Bullis. This tall, thin young man had come out of Nebraska and Iowa and in his teens made his way to the University of Wisconsin where Richard T. Ely and John R. Commons offered exactly the kind of instruction in economics that he wanted. Schools of business administration were young and most of them moved on a comparatively elementary level, but Wisconsin was a leader in the advanced level. Its engineering faculty was also strong. Out of these interests — economics, commerce, and engineering — Bullis charted a course of study all his own. He earned his way through college as a salesman of sewing machines, emerged with a Phi Beta Kappa key in his hand, and headed for a job at the Chase National Bank in New York. There he put his brand-new theoretical education to work, making his way through most of the departments, identifying and analyzing any slackness of procedure that came under his eye. The crisp impersonality of his confidential reports so delighted his superiors that they felt deeply wronged for a moment when he announced that he had joined the army. But in 1917 the uniform seemed to be the only proper wear for a conscientious and highly responsible young man. Bullis enlisted as a private and later as a member of the A.E.F. rose to the rank of captain. After the Armistice he was chosen among promising students in the American army to go to Oxford during the interval before transportation home could be provided. He chose to go instead to the famous London School of Economics.

Back in America at last and out of uniform, he decided that his next job should be in the Midwest. The next job proved to be the last. He heard that Bell was making a collection of promising young men and he went to Minneapolis for an interview with Bell and his associates.

He got the job, but during his first days it seemed to him sometimes that the war had started all over again on an intensified scale. Bell, as a young executive with original ideas, had his own old guard to combat. Rooted firmly in the midst of this bloc stood Benjamin S. Bull almost without a hair to his head and quite without a concession to tact in his nature. A man whose name not merely invited but virtually compelled punning never resented the inevitable so bitterly. Much more than any tampering with his name, he resented any tampering with his system of business administration, a strangely inspired weaving together of obscurities and complexities which he alone understood. It was in his realm that a man with Bullis' background belonged. He wanted nothing of

91

Bullis and his college-bred theories. Whereas Bell was convinced that both were necessary.

Bell and Bull bit their mustaches in a crisis of intramural warfare while Bullis went on with his plan of starting in the mill. There, too, he encountered an old guard and a tradition of seniority. Old-fashioned millers believed that the only proper way to advance was step by step through the levels of a firmly established hierarchy. A man spent two years as a sweeper before he could reasonably expect to become an oiler; he must learn to oil with distinction and authority before he could pass on to the next assignment. Head operators had all their calculations "on the cuff" and did not like to be challenged or even questioned by a young theorist.

Bullis was more than ever a young man in a hurry and he was determined to cut through the red tape of tradition to improve operations in the mill. From boyhood he had had the habit of doing his day's work on the first shift and then of lingering about to see what the second shift was up to. He did so at the mill despite suspicious opposition and managed to learn everyone's task. This made him invaluable to superintendent Will Bovey who was coping with the 1919 upsurge in export business and running his mill at top capacity. Bullis streamlined trucking operations, introduced a new accounting method, and devised an inventory system that promptly put an end to petty larceny. He exercised his talent for morale-building by introducing a cafeteria for workers into the mill and organizing basketball teams, baseball teams, and Christmas parties.

Presently Ben Bull died. He had made his department so inviolably his own that no one wished to enter it for fear of encountering his stern shade. Only Bell had the hardihood to do so. He would take over, he announced with the zest of a protean artist who, having played seven or eight roles, saw no valid reason why he should not play nine or ten. Bullis changed from his overalls to the good blue suit of a young executive and came up from the mill to join the accounting committee. He was put in charge of two departments, the statistical and the misnamed profit and loss, and he had under him a score of people all paralyzed by the frightful silence left by the cessation of the voice of Bull. Bullis promptly snuffed out and buried the profit-and-loss department, which had actually to do not with the casting up of accounts of the whole company but only with those of the scattered branch offices. Its functions were merged with those of the statistical department to which Bullis gave the full treatment of modern science. From his own and other universities he brought in a group of young assistants — Gordon Ballhorn, later to become vice president and comptroller, Ralph Stiles, Harold Frohbach, and Charles E. Olson. Thorough surveys of all departments were conducted by these statisticians and accountants. Ancient and decrepit practices were thrown out. Mill procedures were accelerated dazzlingly. Even Bullis' passive backers who had gone along with him dubiously, just for the ride, began to find it exhilarating. A new accounting system and a new classification of accounts wrote finis to the old days of improvisation.

While he lived, the solitary, unapproachable figure of Bull had delayed the debut in the milling industry of another young man who was to make an important contribution to the development of the Washburn Crosby Company and of General Mills. Bell had wanted, after the close of World War I, to gather in Donald Davis, the man who had been his chief assistant in the Milling Division. Davis had left in the midst of that operation to put on the uniform of a major of the air service and to help produce planes at Dayton, Ohio. When he returned to civilian life Bell wanted him again as executive associate. But the prevailing ubiquity of Bull seemed to block advancement and Davis went back instead to New York, first in the service of the Liberty National Bank, later of the New York Trust Company.

Davis liked to think of himself as an engineer of business. As a boy he had made a blueprint for personal progress which called for experience in many fields before settling to one. He had, in fact, traveled a long, picaresque journey before he reached Minneapolis. While he studied engineering, accounting, and business law at Ann Arbor, he had operated the projector in a nickelodeon to earn his way through school. Later at the Hayes Wheel Company at Jackson, Michigan, his assignment was to help in switching from the manufacture of wheels for wagons to wheels for automobiles, thereby enabling him to claim a small but significant share in the pioneer work of mechanizing the American economy. After leaving college he served at various times as head of the staff of certified public accountants for the Detroit Trust Company, manager of a Philadelphia tractor factory remodeled to make brass shell cases for the British army, and trouble shooter for indigent business organizations. After the death of Ben Bull in 1922, he was at last persuaded to become secretary of the Washburn Crosby Company.

The Wide Open Door

At thirty-four, when he entered the milling industry as its youngest top executive, he was a tall, powerfully built man, who rode horseback, played a fast game of tennis, an able one of golf, and made something resembling a second career of fly fishing. He was regarded as austere but the mask of resolution that he wore at his desk was intended, in part, to conceal his youth. Intimates knew that his austerity was well ventilated by high spirit and gaiety.

Davis knew how, first, to choose a policy and, second, to reduce that policy to a plan. His preoccupying concern was with the world of objective reality. "Facts, not opinions," he would say briskly, even dismissively to anyone suspected of having indulged in a flight of speculative fancy. His love of factual data was supported by a gift for analysis which tended to reduce reality to something that could be weighed, measured, and evaluated in concrete terms. He was a good man to have about in a time when new programs were being developed daily.

Bell had not waited, however, for these men to come to his side before he had begun to deal with the company's other needs, notably with the need for new facilities. In his statement to the board, made in 1919 just after his return from government service, Bell had urged the necessity of following the march of wheat wherever it should go. He had experience to support his judgment that now was the moment to move into new fields.

The success of the Buffalo mill had established beyond doubt the anticipatory wisdom of Bell's father in scattering the hazard of the operation. Canadian wheat had flowed through this natural gateway en route to the export trade. Throughout the many changes of international policy, through the American wheat farmers' demands for tariff protection, the younger Bell, with the highly articulate support of Frank Henry, fought to keep the advantage gained by the existence of a mill that utilized the facilities of the Great Lakes system.

Woodrow Wilson's tariff law, the Underwood Act of 1913, had been based on the principle of free trade; both wheat and flour were on the list of goods to be admitted duty-free. But this was theory only. Because Canada continued to impose a duty of 10 cents a bushel on imported wheat, the United States did the same. In 1917, however, when the war gave the two countries shared responsibility as the granary of the Allies, all restrictions were removed. Wheat and flour flowed freely back and forth across the border.

This arrangement continued for four years until worried farmers in the United States appealed to the new Republican administration for protection and the Emergency Tariff Act put a duty of 30 cents a bushel on wheat. A 20 per cent ad valorem duty on flour was later added. The Fordney-McCumber Act of 1922 confirmed the protectionist policy and the duty on wheat went to 42 cents a bushel.

But under agreements which, with every shift in the balance of power, the Washburn Crosby men used their powers of persuasion to keep, Canadian wheat continued to reach the Buffalo mill without payment of duty. The milling-in-bond principle still permitted the miller to bring in wheat and ship abroad the flour made from it, paying duty only on the feed that was kept in this country for sale. The mill became a manufacturing way station of the export trade. The alternative principle of the "drawback" also continued to be at the miller's disposal if he chose to use it. The beneficent working of these regulations had kept the Buffalo mill busy and made it an enormous asset to the company.

But possession of the Buffalo mill was, as Bell had seen, not enough to ensure prosperity. King of kings in the wheat realm, the hard variety which had made Minnesota's reputation at the time of the "milling revolution" was beginning to be grown in other regions. Strong grain of this kind is produced, not in areas of heavy rainfall, but rather in places where the rainfall is just plentiful enough to sustain plant life. The rule of survival of the fittest, as applied here, means that wheat which survives under rigorous conditions has the richest and most rewarding life.

During the war when there was a premium on the production of wheat, high prices encouraged the development of a vast new field in the semi-arid country west of the 100th meridian. This land had been considered to be fit only for grazing. To the delight of some and the consternation of others, it was discovered that hard wheat grown in this country of meager precipitation was of fine quality. It produced flour of the kind the baker wanted. The Midwest's hard wheat now had serious competition from the hard wheats of other regions.

This change was occurring at exactly the moment when dairying and diversified farming had begun to push wheat out of Minnesota. Here, then, were Kansas, Nebraska, Colorado, Oklahoma, and the Panhandle of Texas offering competition that the Midwest had not known before. Within another quarter of a century the wheat acreage of this

95

new region was to be almost twice that of the older wheat-growing states, Minnesota, the Dakotas, and Montana.

As Minnesota produced less wheat herself, she adopted during the war the practice of bringing in grain from other areas. The demand for flour was great and, at one moment, wheat from fifteen states was being ground at Minneapolis. The fact that this was an economically unsound procedure bothered no one, for the monstrous recklessness of war itself threw into obliterating shadow any such minor recklessness of business operation. But with the return to sharp competition this situation could be endured no longer.

Shipping rates which govern the flow of grain always have sent it from west to east, never from south to north. Following the cheap water routes and later the railroad routes, streams of grain converged at certain strategic points. The Minneapolis-Duluth region constituted such a point; Buffalo another. But the flow of the hard winter wheat of the Southwest could not be diverted to Minneapolis except at exorbitant cost. It was far more expensive to ship Kansas wheat to Minneapolis than to ship it to Chicago. The problem of the "out-of-line" haul was creating new centers of milling.

A further damming up of the flow of wheat to Minneapolis occurred when the railroads withdrew the privilege of milling in transit, an agreement by which a through shipment of wheat could be detained at Minneapolis for processing without any increase in freight charges. Later most of these privileges were restored in the form of proportional rates; but, meanwhile, the strategy of milling had shifted its drive toward Buffalo and the adjustments were not of sufficient significance to prompt a shift back to Minneapolis.

Because Chicago was the gateway for wheat from the Southwest, it seemed inevitable to Bell that the Washburn Crosby Company must go there. The idea was not new. Since 1914 several members of the firm had been urging an invasion of this territory. P. D. McMillan of the grain department had written a report, as precise and as neat in its succession of climaxes as an outline for a well-played chess game, in which he had pointed out the importance of Chicago. In 1917, H. R. McLaughlin, sales manager for the Chicago area, took up the theme that it would be "a wonderful place for our company." With a kind of meditative reticence he expressed the belief that the "variety and volume of wheat at all times available" would "insure interesting profits."

The Star and Crescent Mill of Chicago was purchased in 1922. It had been in existence only a little less long than Washburn's first mill at St. Anthony Falls. From 1868 on through the time of Chicago's bucolic innocency the Star and Crescent had done business on the Chicago River. Old-fashioned millstones had ground the grain and wagons had taken the flour away through winding lanes that did not anticipate the glaring splendor of "the Loop."

By 1903 the neighborhood had become too busy to accommodate an expanding mill. The Star and Crescent moved to South Chicago and there on the Calumet River it continued to grow to twenty times its original capacity. When Washburn Crosby bought it — literally lock, stock, and barrel — a complete rejuvenation treatment increased capacity by another 50 per cent bringing it to 4500 barrels a day.

In 1923 the Washburn Crosby Company built at Chicago on land adjacent to the Star and Crescent a new plant for the preparation of packaged foods that were to be sponsored by a new unit, the Gold Medal Food Products Company. Among the offerings were a pancake flour, a whole wheat flour, a buckwheat flour, a cake flour, and a wheat flake breakfast food. With this company of comestibles Washburn Crosby courageously undertook a lateral invasion of a market already pre-empted by firms of established reputation in the packaged foods business. Its own products were good, well designed to appeal to "those sensitive little nerves that fringe the tongue," as Bell once described the vital points of attack in a food merchant's campaign. The same little nerves, he went on to say, "carry messages from the human tongue to the human pocketbook."

But in this instance the message was not automatically conveyed. Indeed, it took years for the full force of its logic to be felt. For five years, between the establishment of the Gold Medal Food Products Company and the formation of General Mills, the fate of these offerings stood in doubt. The annual reports and minute books of the period reflect the conscientious care with which techniques of manufacture were developed, the earnest zest with which sales campaigns were conducted, and the misgiving with which officials looked into the unfamiliar face of loss. Year by year the red figure shrank but it was still disturbingly red. Indeed, the problem had yet to be solved at the time when General Mills was formed. But out of this first experiment in expansion by way of new markets for new products a triumph finally emerged. Though several of the products were dropped, two remained which were to add lively chapters to later history. These were the cake flour, rechristened Softasilk, and the wheat flakes, rechristened Wheaties.

Kansas City as gateway to the Southwest was another of Bell's objectives. Early in 1919 he had begun negotiating for a plant there. One potential seller who had enjoyed himself greatly at the conference table turned so suddenly and so skittishly away from the dotted line that for a time a lawsuit seemed to be indicated. But Bell had no taste for drastic operations and he preferred to continue his search in other quarters.

This ended in 1922 when the backers of a partially completed mill in Kansas City found themselves without money to continue. Purchase was made in the spring and so eager were the men from Minneapolis to get on with their belated pioneering in the Southwest that machinery had been installed and the elevator was ready to receive the wheat even before it was time for the crop to arrive in July.

"Bring your own desk," new recruits to the staff were soberly advised; the workday, they were told, would be just half over at 5 P.M. This schedule did not include Sunday. On that day everyone was piously urged to "knock off at six o'clock."

To Kansas City went one of Atkinson's young men. The career of William Morris offers an excellent example of the design for the American pioneer, revised model. He was born in 1880 in Mineral Point, Wisconsin, which by curious circumstance was the place from which Cadwallader Washburn had launched himself on a midwestern career. With the help of a small inheritance Morris put himself through the University of Iowa, where he was a high-grade student of mathematics and where he played a powerful game of football. It had been his plan to teach school while studying law at night, but he was persuaded by the "big money" ($7 a week in 1899) to go to work for Atkinson. He continued to work for Atkinson's successors throughout a career that covered nearly half a century.

There was one interruption. Atkinson set Morris up in business as a jobber to sell Gold Medal Flour to Chicago retailers. The arrangement proved to be unsatisfactory chiefly because of Ben Bull's famous profit-and-loss system. In sympathy with its creator's unhappy temperament, the system tended gloomily to ignore profits and highlight losses. Morris retreated for three years into the bakery business in St. Paul. There his patron, Atkinson, visited him once a month and finally led him home to Washburn Crosby, a much more useful man for knowing just how the mind of the professional baker works.

The adventure in the Southwest prospered almost immediately. The company grew so rapidly that within a decade it had become a close rival to the older units. This success at first gave other southwestern millers acute anxiety. So much strenuous effort on the part of a new recruit might, as they whispered to one another, "rock the boat." Old hostilities shook the conferences of the Southwestern Millers' League, and there was a moment, during Morris' first year in Kansas City, when the membership was ready to pass a resolution urging upon Congress legislation that would end milling-in-bond at Buffalo. As the representative of a company with important interests in Buffalo, Morris was regarded almost as an enemy within the gates, and he had to suffer the suspicion that attaches to a minority leader. But he argued with the skill of a statistician and the power of a football player that milling-in-bond should be encouraged rather than discouraged. As long as Canadian wheat went to Buffalo and immediately left the United States as flour bound for Europe, it offered no rivalry to the southwestern mills in the domestic market. If milling-in-bond were to end, Canadian wheat might well be thrown on the American market where it would dislocate business at home. His voice prevailed.

And fortune continued to be with the southwestern millers. Everyone prospered and the cooperative temper flourished accordingly.

Among the Minneapolis men who made up the group of latter-day pioneers at Kansas City was Walter Barry who was to have a dominating role in later developments of General Mills.

Once in a mildly riotous session that preceded a sales conference, Barry's confreres greeted him in song as "A hell of a hell of a hell of a hell of hell of good looking guy . . ." They referred to a self-evident fact which an admirer of the similarly fortunate Edward Stettinius, Jr., acknowleged when he said to a neighbor in a meeting at which Stettinius rose to speak, "There you see what God can do when he really tries."

From his Irish forebears to whom Barry owed his handsomely assembled collection of rugged features, he inherited also an imaginative vigor that served new projects well. Within ten minutes of his arrival in the uncompleted Kansas City plant, he had asked: "Where's the code book? Where's a stenographer? Where's the surplus department?

Where's the sales record department?" All of them had to be created on the spot to satisfy his impassioned need to sell.

The success of the Kansas City experiment offered a kind of final endorsement of Bell's policy. And now more urgently than ever young men were needed to help him carry his program to the full extent of its implications. The elder statesmen of the company — even ones as useful as Frank Henry always had been — tended to draw away from new commitments. Henry, though he had been the real instigator of the Buffalo project, had been dubious about the southwestern invasion. Bell, occupying high ground from which he could survey all operations impartially, continued to look for lieutenants who could share his broad view.

Such a young man was Gerald S. Kennedy, who was dispatched to Buffalo in 1920 to become Frank Henry's second in command. Except for the interruption of World War I, Kennedy lived his life with the Washburn Crosby Company and its successor, General Mills, from the age of nineteen. Several years before that he had spun up to his full height of six feet and shame for this adolescent impetuosity of growth had prodded him into a kind of academic sprint. He had completed three years at St. Thomas College — all he proposed to allow himself — when he started to look for a job in 1914.

The terrifyingly decisive Ben Bull engaged him saying that it was a great mistake to have stayed in school past the eighth grade but that, if he would promise to conceal his background, he might begin as an office boy. Kennedy and the century proceeded through their teens together placidly up to America's entry into the war. The great interruption took the young man from second or third rung of an upward climb and sent him as an enlisted man to France. (Surveying the biographies of his prominent contemporaries, Kennedy sometimes remarks that he appears to have had the distinction of being "the only private in the A.E.F.") For a time after his release from the army he returned to his old job as bookkeeper in the grain department. But the monastic seclusion of being "back of the books" bored him. He asked for an assignment in which he could renew his acquaintance with the human race and was sent to join Frank Henry.

The Buffalo plant long since had come to be regarded as the private property of "the boss" by that powerful, dominating man himself and by all his staff. Every decision must be Henry's and he could see no one to whom he thought it possible to delegate authority. Actually, he had divided himself up so fine that the need for technical assistance had become crucial. Kennedy set himself to learning every detail of the business of the mill. By a habit of unobtrusive friendliness he avoided involvement in old feuds. From men who regarded anonymity as their only protection in their jobs he mastered the mysteries of the cost card and became its chief interpreter. He accomplished improvements in technique, efficiency, and morale by dropping hints at the psychological moment and then remaining discreetly in the background while Henry went strenuously about the business of carrying them out. He entered sales "by the back door." In short, he had quietly, and at first unconsciously, created a new function, "operations control," which with the formation of General Mills was to have wide and significant applicability. It meant coordinating the work of various departments to the end that wheat might be put easily and efficiently into proper condition for milling.

One of the minor but amusing manifestations of Kennedy's success as Henry's second in command was the skill that he developed in forging the boss' name. Never again was Henry quite sure whether or not his signature was genuine. Only the humorous tone of a memorandum could supply the clue. Henry's humor was inclined to be stately; he wrote his jeremiads with the thunderous authority proper to a prophet. Kennedy's tone was sly, characterized by engaging modesty. Designed to elude the cluttery, roundabout clichés of business, his style cleared the way to a full view of fact.

During the 1920s the facilities at Buffalo grew impressively. Flour for export was loaded directly from its docks. As the practice of intercompany shipments developed, the activities of this strenuous center became more important still. And all the while production grew until Buffalo's name led all the rest.

The search for new products and, as Bell once wrote, "new services of worth to the American people," led also during this period to a program of milling durum wheat. This drought-resisting, rust-resisting variety, developed on the arid lands of eastern Europe, had been introduced into Minnesota during a moment of panic when its own spring wheat was seriously threatened by blight. The amount of land given in spring to its cultivation grew slowly but steadily especially in North Dakota. After 1919 the crop averaged 40,000,000 bushels the country over. Bell saw that the emergency which had made farmers grow durum might well be transformed into a blessing conferring on the miller and on his customers a permanent benefit in the form of a new product. In 1919 he began to mill durum wheat at the old D mill in Minneapolis, calling the product Bull Durum in sly salute to the famous Bull Durham tobacco.

By 1925 Washburn Crosby was active in the manufacture of Gold Medal Semolina made from durum wheat for use in macaroni products. A pamphlet on the subject, published in that year for the benefit of housewives to whom macaroni was new, pointed out the error of most contemporary dictionaries in their treatment of the subject. Definitions erred rather sweepingly in calling macaroni "an edible Italian paste of flour made into slender tubes." Macaroni is not necessarily Italian; it is not a paste; and it is not made of flour.

Semolina, the article continued, is like flour in that bran particles and impurities have been removed but essentially unlike it in that it is not a powder. Rather it is the wheat berry itself broken into granules. These have a texture like granulated sugar. The peculiar character of the gluten in durum wheat is that it binds these granules together, and the advantage of the granulated form is that it provides a porous substance which permits the instant permeation of water in cooking. Some macaronis (the pamphlet admitted more in sorrow than in anger) were made of flour or of flour blended with Semolina, but these tended to cook to pieces and become soggy. The clear amber kind manufactured by the Washburn Crosby Company constituted more than 90 per cent of the product in the United States. It did not need to be washed in cold water after boiling; it was a highly nutritious food, comparable to meat in food value but far more easily digested; a pound of it contained half again as many calories as a pound of medium fat beef. In short, this gastronomic immigrant from Italy should be made welcome at the American table.

So the manufacture of macaroni became a part of the Washburn Crosby design for feeding the nation. The new activity served simultaneously the company, the public, and the growers of grain. For as Bell wrote: "Such new products represent an increase in the consumption of grain as food; they actually compete less with other cereal products than with types of foodstuffs outside their own field."

A part of Bell's program for expansion during the prosperous 1920s called for the discovery of new resources in merchandising techniques.

He was quite out of sympathy with the impulse of the miller who under the pressure of competition flung himself headlong into a ruinous price war. Such two-fisted tactics were doomed in advance. For what did it profit a man to gain increased sales if he were left in the end with operating losses? There was a limit, Bell pointed out, beyond which low prices "ceased to be socially beneficial even to the consumer." Society was bound to suffer in a price war because such violence involved "a sharp deterioration in goods and services."

A "proper constructive competition" should lead to a "sharpening of brains" rather than "a sharpening of red pencils." For himself and his associates he decided on a policy of making his products, old and new, ever more appealing to the imagination of the housewife.

Gold Medal Flour, so long the aristocrat in its realm that little could be done to improve its prestige, nonetheless was reexamined critically by selling experts. In Bell's philosophy, a merchant did not merely sell a "thing" but also "the attributes of that thing." Therefore, the artful, though completely legitimate, approach to the problem of finding still more customers for Gold Medal Flour was to "sell the results" of using Gold Medal Flour. It was the sincere faith of the Washburn Crosby laboratories that in their studies all the housewife's problems had been anticipated and solved. The daily baking tests detected in advance any weakness in a batch of flour and no inferior product could reach the market. The buyer's good was doubly protected, in fact, for Gold Medal Flour was not merely laboratory-tested for ordinary baking quality but tested in the kitchen as well for performance under exactly the conditions that a woman faced in her own home. A way had been found to "sell results," to make a merchandisable commodity of faith in the outcome of a morning spent over the stove.

"Kitchen-Tested" became the title of nobility attached to Gold Medal Flour as a flour to be sold for family use. The letters GMKT — Gold Medal "Kitchen-Tested" — came to have as much authority as had once been possessed by the formula "Eventually — Why Not Now?" They had, however, much more actual value, for they represented, in the mind of the seller, a mixture of faith and reason. The salesman believed as intensely as before in what Bell once called "the enduring virtue of wheat" as transformed into flour. But now he undertook to communicate to the buyer the "reason why" he held his faith so securely and why he felt he could recommend his faith to the buyer. "Reason why" advertising had begun to take the place of the old style of advertising by incantation.

On July 22, 1925, John Crosby made public announcement of the fact that the Washburn Crosby Company intended "as soon as the legal technicalities can be complied with to make Mr. James F. Bell president and himself Chairman of the Board."

Bell's private diary made note of this event in a half-dozen words and went on briskly to other matters, the installation of a new milling unit at Kansas City, further extension of facilities at Buffalo, and search for other new men to assume chief executives' jobs. Though he loved to theorize, there was at the moment no time for such indulgence. He must get on with the next new project.

With the temper of the time, stirred by the liveliest kind of economic ferment, Bell at forty-five was in perfect sympathy. His official portrait of the period showed him as a dark and challenging man. The broad brow was being unveiled already by baldness; the characteristic expression, even in repose (or in Bell's nearest approach to repose), seemed to echo the sentiment often on his tongue: "We must have the courage to seize opportunity."

But the most revealing thing about this camera study is an item of dress: a bow tie quite unlike any other bow tie in the history of haberdashery. It did not lie close to the collar but had been jerked by the tier into blade-like shapes so that it looked like the propeller of an airplane. The sympathy between Bell and the idea of flying always had been great. As a young man he had gone to Dayton to order a biplane which was to be especially made for him by the Wright brothers. The idea of becoming the pilot of a private plane was dropped out of deference to his father's objection. Later Bell was to do most of his traveling in a company-owned plane. And at every period of his life he has looked, despite his bulk, as though he might suddenly take to the air under the powerful propulsion of his nervous drive.

During the first years of his presidency, Bell took off, with the same kind of spontaneity, into the atmosphere of change and progress. To seize new occasions, presented both by adversity and prosperity, and to make them all serve the purposes of growth, this was his formula for enterprise. By the exercise of a kind of practical prescience, by coordinated effort in disciplining opportunity, he was able to advance the consumption of wheat products within his own realm at the very moment when it was declining in the American home. In his often witty, always realistic way, he refused to have anything to do with the psychology that bemoans losses and longs for the "good old days." In moments of misgiving he had only to remember that the wheat berry was "rich in miracles." The "service to humanity stored up in its kernel" was limitless. To ensure success one had only to improve one's own product and then, through similarly improved advertising and merchandising methods, to recommend it sensibly to the public. The "enduring virtue of wheat" could be counted upon, if it had proper cooperation from a merchant.

The problems involved in bringing together a new staff, creating new products, building new facilities, Bell had faced with gusto. A greater challenge was immediately to follow, for the formation of General Mills meant putting a new idea into action.

8

Milling Empires

A PANORAMIC VIEW

T H E idea that has been developing in the background of Bell's speculative mind was the truly dramatic one of bringing together a combination of elements within the industry which would ensure the cooperative enterprise of mills in many parts of the country. In anticipation of his lively campaign to effect such a consolidation, it is time to take a sweeping panoramic view of those areas of the miller's world in which Bell was particularly interested.

The Washburn Crosby Company with its important properties at Buffalo, at Chicago, at Kansas City, and in Montana already had seized the initiative in establishing a unity of effort by linking the various wheat areas. The mills with which Bell was now prepared to invite affiliations were those of the Sperry Flour Company which had extended its sphere of influence all along the Pacific Coast into the Northwest and also inland as far as Utah; the "Kell group," scattered through Oklahoma and Texas; the Red Star Milling Company of Wichita, Kansas; and the Larrowe Milling Company with its base in Detroit.

Before Bell's plan could be perfected several stutters in negotiation had to take place. These will be discussed in subsequent chapters. But in the end his persuasions did prevail. So it is toward the Pacific Coast, the Southwest, and feed-milling interests centered in Detroit that this account must turn to fill in details of the early history of the companies which were shortly to come together as General Mills.

Flour milling in California has a long history. Indeed its records go back far into the time of Spanish control. Missions like San Gabriel

Arcángel and San Jose were centers of community life over which the priests presided with parental authority, teaching their Indian converts how to develop large crops of wheat.

By the mid years of the nineteenth century flour milling had become a profitable business and there were plants sprinkled about the bay at Yerba Buena (San Francisco). In 1848 a famous Swiss adventurer, John Augustus Sutter, the enormously wealthy proprietor of an estate in the Sacramento Valley, ordered construction of a gristmill on his land. But before it could be finished gold had been discovered nearby. The forty-niners quite literally rushed in carrying and destroying all before them. Among other things that they stole were all the parts of the mill equipment. As Sutter commented ruefully: "There is a saying that men will steal everything but a milestone and a millstone. But they stole my millstones."

It was in this hysterical drama of hope and hatred that Austin Sperry made his contrastingly quiet debut. A tall, thick, enormously sturdy, enormously friendly young man of thirty, he had come from a farm in Vermont to have a fling at prospecting. But he lacked the temperament for it. A man who had whiled away the long journey around Cape Horn by organizing a glee club among the passengers and accompanying their performance on the flute could not be expected to like the loneliness of placer diggings. After twenty-three days he had had enough of prospecting. But in that short time he had managed to put $500 of gold dust into his poke. With this small fortune he went back to Stockton to establish what he called "a proper business."

This was the beginning of the great Sperry flour empire of the Pacific Coast.

The first step was to cater modestly to the miners who obviously were in no mood to try to grow food for themselves. Sperry sold them groceries. Presently he saw a greater opportunity. The San Joaquin Valley grew fine wheat. Why not mill the product himself to feed the miners? He established his first plant at Stockton in 1852. Both wheat and Sperry flourished. The harvest multiplied seventeen times over in a few seasons. Flour made from it sold at forty dollars a sack. With brisk candor Sperry showed the price, as XXXX, just below the maker's name. His mills became a combination clubhouse for lonely miners, bank where they could exchange their gold dust for cash, and a forum for the discussion of politics. The Sperry enterprise grew and made a sizable fortune for the founder's descendants. At his death in 1881, its several properties passed into the keeping of widow, sons, and brother.

Other figures of early milling history in California combined, as Austin Sperry's career seemed to do, the glitter of success with the shining zeal of good will. Such a man was Horace Davis. This son of a governor of Massachusetts had left Harvard to join the forty-niners. But he, too, preferred a more orderly way of life and found it as owner and operator of the Golden Gate Flouring Mills at San Francisco. There he made flour so good that as a eulogist once reported it was "blessed [alike] by hardy yeomenry and the most fastidious."

The career of Horace Davis shows striking points of similarity to that of Cadwallader Washburn. He had an intense sense of public responsibility and an inexhaustible interest in things of the mind. In the midst of a vigorous career as a man of affairs, he found time to represent California in Congress, to serve as president of the University of California and during another period as trustee of Leland Stanford, to write a small book on the sonnets of Shakespeare and another on the ministry of Jesus.

But the making of flour was his "proper business" and he continued to work at it effectively for nearly seventy years.

By 1870 California had entered into its greatest period as wheat producer. The term "grain factory" had come into general use to describe the operations of these cheerful vandals of the soil who worked tracts of 50,000 to 100,000 acres and who worked them finally into exhaustion. These men owned fleets of ships to carry their surplus across the sea. It was the time, as Horace Davis wrote, when "the valleys were waving with grain" and San Francisco's Golden Gate was "white with the sails of ships bearing out the harvest of wheat" to Europe and the Orient.

The export business in flour was also enormously profitable, for many years, to both Sperry and Davis. Their products went chiefly to the Orient where there were then no mills to offer competition or to process American wheat. The East liked American flour and its reputation benefited by the fact that it was carried in iron ships and so protected against the effects of sea change.

But there is no finality in milling supremacy. The quality of California wheat began to deteriorate as the overworked soil rebelled. At the same time competition began to move in on all sides with the heavy tread of inevitability. Mills in Washington and Oregon, which had carried on inconspicuously from the time of the Hudson Bay Company's operations, were inspired suddenly to go in for large-scale production. Direct shipments from these northwestern plants to the Orient ended California's comfortable monopoly of the export market. Even the home market had been invaded. Flour was reaching California, Davis pointed out ruefully, from as far away as Minnesota.

It was time, as that shrewd analyst saw clearly, for a reconsideration of the basic program. As far as wheat was concerned *less* of it must be grown *more* scientifically. "I grieve," wrote Davis in an article called "American Breadstuffs," "to see the state wearing out its soil to give cheap bread to Europe." He preached the doctrine of smaller holdings and of diversified farming. To cure the ills of sharp competition in the flour market there must be fewer mills, better mills, more strategically situated mills, and ones that could be operated more economically.

To serve that end Davis suggested a major consolidation of California plants. On August 5, 1892, a new corporation was created made up of twelve mills, chief of which were the properties of the Sperry family at Stockton and of Davis at San Francisco. The new combine took the already famous Sperry name. Davis was chosen as president and until he died in 1916 a routine item of business at the annual meeting was to reelect him.

There was need of shrewd reorganization in the first crucial year of the corporation's history. The country was heading directly into one of the most severe panics of its history. Davis moved fast to close up plants that had survived their economic usefulness and his own Golden Gate mill at San Francisco was one of the first to be eliminated under his sternly realistic program. Then in May 1893 the bottom fell out of the financial world. Interest rates soared, banks failed, confusion was everywhere. With livelihoods at stake, men complained bitterly of the Sperry "trust" and newspaper editorials fumed sulfureously about "this writhing octopus." But Davis had long since foreseen this crisis and prepared for it. Universal adversity had been aggravated in California by local conditions — dwindling supplies of wheat, competition from beyond its borders — and it was undoubtedly the timely discovery of the formula survival by consolidation that saved the Sperry enterprise. Davis was the first leader of a large company to adopt this drastic but effective policy.

109

Milling Empires

One serious threat to Sperry's position had been fought off by consolidation of the California mills but another presently emerged. California found that it had a new rival in the export trade. The Pacific Northwest had waked to opportunity and begun to seize an important part of this business. A picturesque feature of the flour merchant's life in San Francisco had been the regular visit of the great Chinese man of affairs. This superb creature, mandarin-like in his dress, serenely aloof in manner, had sat many times at the conference table with Sperry or with Davis buying on a very large scale. His patronage was valued and he himself was deeply respected.

Now he showed an inclination to take his business to the ports of the Northwest. Steamship lines originating in the Orient made these places their objectives, and boats laden with flour began to make their way directly to Hong Kong. A tremendous impetus was given to the tendency when, in the season of 1897–98, the world wheat crop proved to be poor while that of the Northwest was magnificent.

In that moment of triumph, the Portland flour mills began to grow impressively. Local wheat was cheap, much cheaper than the raw material available to Sperry. Moreover this soft Sonora grain made ideal pastry flour, which in turn made exactly the kind of food that pleased the Oriental palate. The railroad lines of the region showed a tender solicitude toward the mills in their territory, and all things conspired benignly to give flour milling in the Northwest great success.

On the principle that it is good strategy to take over as one's own a stronghold that one has failed to defeat, Davis invaded the Northwest in 1903. At Tacoma he acquired an interest in a warehouse and elevator and provided most of the money for erecting a fine new mill nearby. With a daily capacity of 1500 barrels this unit proved to be an eminently satisfactory recruit to the job of recapturing the export trade. Three years later the Sperry Company bought the Tacoma plant outright and, in the course of the next decade, doubled the mill's capacity.

Always a shrewd analyst of markets, Davis knew how, when, and where to expand. In February 1903 he told his board that "in order to hold the southern California trade" it must have a mill at Los Angeles. The territory was broad and destined to grow. (That Davis should have known this clearly in 1903 is testimony to his foresight, for Los Angeles jumped from 100,000 in 1900 to 320,000 in 1910.) There was a demand for flour; raw materials were to be had nearby; investment capital was available; a good labor reservoir existed; transportation facilities were satisfactory. To maintain its prestige as the "oldest, largest, and most efficient milling concern in California" Sperry must serve this area. Within a year the company had begun that service with a mill that stood for twenty years.

In 1910 Sperry drew into its alliance another large unit, the Port Costa Milling Company, and acquired along with it a young executive, Seward McNear, who was to be a major figure in the subsequent history of the industry in California.

McNear's father, George Washington McNear, had been a distinguished pioneer on the Pacific Coast. Beginning simply as a shipper of grain out of Port Costa, the elder McNear had become involved, in spite of himself, in several related enterprises. First, he acquired a mountain of wheat when, during the panic of 1893, frenzied speculations failed in an attempt to corner the market. To protect his livelihood as shipper he was obliged to acquire these holdings. Then, with more grain than he could possibly send to sea, he was forced into becoming a miller as well. A bankrupt plant at Vallejo shortly fell into his hands and to his son, who had just graduated from Harvard, he turned over the active management.

Seward McNear continued through many years to be a business executive of foresight and an enormously useful citizen as well. In war, peace, fire, famine, panic, and prosperity he was never far from the center of the drama of public life.

He had been his father's chief ally only a few years when he made his first significant contribution to the technique of flour milling. It occurred to him one day that something must be done about the enormous nuisance of fumes from the mill's smokestack which daily let wealth escape as waste. If its exhaust could be controlled, some $100,000 worth of raw material might be saved each year. Harry East Miller, an American chemist who had been educated in Germany, found a solution for the problem.

But a more important by-product of the experiment was the establishment of a chemical laboratory. Discussions with Miller had broadened McNear's interest in the possibility of making chemistry an active business partner. At Miller's suggestion he engaged a young scientist, Bert Ingels, to become permanent head of a research staff. Soon after James Ford Bell had created at Minneapolis the first such research

111

laboratory in the industry, McNear, a man of similar outlook and background, had embarked on the same adventure.

The year 1906, through the agency of the San Francisco earthquake and fire, literally burned a curious little item into the history of the Sperry Company. Its minute book (still preserved) offers tacit testimony to having faced and survived ordeal. The heat of the vault in which it was filed became so intense that the cover melted quite away and the edge of each page was reduced to a form that crumbled to powder at a touch. During the moment of immediate disaster officials of the company with Seward McNear at their head were too busy directing problems of relief to be concerned about their books. McNear directed 180 food distribution stations and found time besides to deal tactfully with the chambers of commerce scattered about the country which tried to rush second- and third-grade flour into the San Francisco market although of this commodity there was no shortage.

When at last the effects of the tragedy had been brought under control the directors of the Sperry met to consider their own affairs. The first entry in the minute book for May 1906 suggests their rather astonishing *sang-froid*: "The regular monthly reports could not be made on account of the fire of April 18 having prevented access to the account books. Business generally as far as could be reported was unusually good."

Business continued to be not merely good but better and better during the years between the fire and the close of World War I. Even though conflict at sea forced radical changes in the basic program of the company, the adjustment was made easily in a time when it had become America's task to feed the world.

Before World War I a third of Sperry's flour was shipped to the Orient. It went chiefly into the magnificent harbor of Hong Kong where it was transferred to sampans, junks, and a great variety of picturesque Chinese vessels and carried up the rivers to the big, consuming centers of the interior. With the outbreak of fighting, this activity was gradually drained away until the spring of 1918 when it had virtually ceased to exist. The last of the ships that had carried flour to the East were commandeered by America at war for the transportation of military supplies and men. The Oriental trade dwindled and China got flour from Australia or went without.

Nonetheless the war years were a heyday for Sperry. Europe was the only market (except the west coasts of Central and South America) that the government permitted the company to supply and to it went flour by the shipload. Business was all that the most driving executive could wish. Stimulated by this prosperity, which continued on the West Coast as elsewhere even after the signing of the Armistice, facilities were greatly expanded. A new unit at Ogden, Utah, one of the largest of the Sperry system, was started in 1919.

Then suddenly came the shocking collapse of 1920. Fortunes and reputations were crushed under it. One Sperry executive who had held three important posts simultaneously and still found time for such elegant pastimes as breeding race horses lost everything in one moment as crowded with disaster as any ever imagined by a scenario writer. But "the oldest milling firm in the West" fought for its life. The Sperry Company had powerful banking friends and one of them, Roy Bishop, came up from the Crocker bank to put things right. He served first as director-extraordinary, working chiefly behind the scenes; later, openly, as president.

Bishop once said that he had learned self-discipline while shoeing mules as an enlisted man in the Spanish-American War. Trouble-shooting had been his profession ever since. Because the wife of his employer at the Crocker bank had been born Sperry (daughter of Austin), the matter of curing the flour company's ills was particularly urgent. Bishop devoted his striking talents to exploring and developing the domestic market lately opened up by the enormous new population of the Pacific slope. He set about the recovery of the export market. Like Davis before him, he dismantled mills that had outlived their usefulness and acquired new ones in fortunate locations. In the end he had created a tight and serviceable pattern for the organization.

Through his staff he did much more. Indeed one of the company's chief contributions to the wealth of the community was the development of a finer wheat than had been grown before on western soil.

Seward McNear had retired from the Sperry Company even before the appearance of Bishop but the emphasis that he had put upon research still prevailed. Every mill in the system had its own laboratory and its staff of chemists all looking for ways to improve the raw material with which they worked, the flour made from that raw material, and the bread made from that flour.

The effort really had begun in 1915 at the time of the Panama

Pacific International Exposition at San Francisco. Crocker had backed the undertaking enthusiastically. On the fair grounds the Sperry Company had set up a complete mill and, next to it, a no less complete modern bakery. Booths in which cooks of all nations displayed their special arts provided outlets for the bread and cakes produced hot from the oven. The venture had had great publicity value in establishing the name of Sperry even more firmly than ever before in the public mind.

At the same Exposition, G. R. McLeod, head of research in the Stockton mills, purchased samples of twenty-nine varieties of wheat developed by the experimental stations of New Zealand and Australia. He set out immediately to learn if among these imported varieties there was a grain that would grow well in California soil. Four of them did, indeed, reveal excellent possibilities in crop yield, and flour made from them had a gluten content some 10 per cent higher than that of any of the varieties then grown in California.

This important new variety was early Baart and its development proved to be a minor miracle. It grew well under local conditions, produced a flour of fine quality, one that proved to be precisely what the bakers wanted. The whole industry had undergone a fortunate revolution. Baart took over. A more compact example of how industry may make a free gift to the economy it serves could hardly be found.

To develop the potentialities of the new grain further the manager of the Stockton plant leased a 286-acre farm and established a staff of investigators on it. Varieties of Baart multiplied so rapidly that presently it became necessary to add a second and, at last, a third experimental farm.

This work with wheat led naturally to the study of new possibilities for cattle and poultry feeds. This was also a necessary development because it concerned the miller's ancient problem of what to do with his by-products. During the second decade of the century the supply of these materials exceeded demand on the West Coast and the feed plant remained the unloved child of the Sperry family.

Help came, finally, from the federal and state departments of agriculture, which began at this moment to advocate the practice of giving cattle and poultry a variety of nutrients. Seizing on this suggestion, the Stockton experimenters on the Sperry farm set out to develop a line of feeds. To these they gave names than sang with promise — Suregrow for chicks, Surelay for hens, Suremilk for cows. They briefed salesmen with detailed knowledge concerning the nutrients that each item contained and the benefits that might reasonably be expected from them. They helped poultrymen and dairy farmers to build up proper feeding programs. Such service was not regarded as altruism but as part of a sound business policy. For, as one of its interpreters observed dryly, "Dead cows and chickens don't eat."

The feed problems of the Sperry Company were not solved once for all by the creation of a Special Stock and Poultry Feed Department. There was still to be faced the difficulty of competition from the Pacific Coast region. The Olympic Cereal and Feed Mill at Portland had been offering strong rivalry. Borrowing from diplomacy the principle "If you can't fight them join them," Bishop offered to consolidate. The offer was accepted almost eagerly because the Portland mill like the Sperry units had fallen on evil times in the days of postwar deflation. In January 1923 the Olympic was absorbed into the Sperry system along with the Portland Flouring Mills Company.

Bishop's lively campaigning claimed a broad market for his products. The new population of the Pacific slope was wooed intensively in more than a score of cities where there were branch offices — seven in Washington, two in Oregon, and thirteen in California. Flour in large quantity was shipped by the Panama Canal route into the southeastern corner of the country and out of Ogden by rail into Florida for distribution through jobbers. A gift for showmanship kept Sperry products in the public eye. Salesmen drove cars enameled a gleaming white to suggest the purity of their flour product, Drifted Snow. Even the delivery trucks in which goods were delivered displayed the same immaculate face to the world. At one period salesmen carried as official assistants flocks of homing pigeons. These were released from their cages, one at a time, to carry orders from each town back to the home base. (Actually, the plan was more picturesque than practical. Sperry did not quite trust the birds and the orders sent by carrier pigeon were duplicated by ordinary post.)

By 1924 the Oriental trade had been brought under control once more after the disruptive influence of World War I. China was still the world's greatest consumer of pastry and Sperry provided the kind of flour needed for its favorite delicacies. During the latter half of the 1920s, the export business absorbed from two and a half to four million barrels of West Coast flour annually.

Milling Empires

By the late 1920s Bishop had put the Sperry Company on a solid foundation. It owned nine mills at Spokane, Tacoma, Portland, Ogden, Vallejo, Los Angeles, and Pasco (Washington). The total milling capacities of its various properties added up to 14,500 barrels of flour a day, compared with the 20,350-barrel capacity at Minneapolis and the 20,000 capacity at Buffalo.

The brand names of the Sperry Company were familiar throughout the region and buyers respected them almost as though they were part of the historical tradition of the country. (Incidental intelligence: Black Bart, the most famous of the early highwaymen, had worn a Sperry flour sack over his head when he held up stagecoaches.) For seventy-five years the name Sperry had never been missing from the roster of the coast's great industries. The leadership of the organization was respected, too, for its devotion to the service ideal. A touch of personal commitment bound merchant and customer together.

Bell was determined that into his proposed consolidation he would invite only companies that had represented their special fields with real business distinction. When he surveyed the animal feed realm his eyes inevitably fastened on the Larrowe Milling Company. Already its founder had made a tremendous reputation for his firm as leader in the great industrial adventure of transforming waste into wealth.

Larrowe had come by a long circuitous route into the feed business. In 1887 his father, Albertus Larrowe, had created a milling company at Cohocton, New York, for the purpose of manufacturing and selling buckwheat flour. His two young sons were his partners and, just a decade later, the company had extended its activities to include the brokerage of grain on the New York Produce Exchange. James Larrowe had gone to New York to represent his father. He had engaged on his own initiative in many side lines. One of these was the beet sugar industry, an infant enterprise just struggling into existence in that last decade of the nineteenth century.

The residue of sugar extraction, under conditions that prevailed at the time, was a pulp of peculiarly unpleasant character. Its odor when fermentation began was nauseating. Because it contained 95 per cent water it was prohibitively expensive to haul away for disposal. It could not be ploughed under the soil. Sportsmen raised lusty howls of protest when it was sluiced into rivers because, they said, it killed fish. A

116

nuisance to owners, it became a threat to their very existence in business when legal action began to be taken against them.

Yet it had long been known in Europe to have value as a substitute for other animal feeds. No effort was made in America to capitalize on this knowledge until in the nineties a German engineer set up a pulp-drying machine, at Alma, Michigan, in the strategic center of the sugar beet country. Believing that he would be able to sell his dried pulp easily he had taken the first year's output in payment for his work. But no one wanted his pulp; no one would accept it as a gift. Now nearly desperate he took samples of his product to New York, hoping to find among traders help in breaking through the massive barrier of indifference. There, after many trials and disappointments, he encountered Larrowe whose curiosity was immediately aroused. For ten dollars a ton — less than the cost of production — Larrowe bought a carload of what he called skeptically "the stuff." Charles Staff, Larrowe's "stenographer, bookkeeper, and general utility man," headed straight for the public library to learn all that could be learned about beet pulp.

Larrowe and Staff offered a humorous study in contrasts: the former tidy and austere; the other, windblown and approachable. But they shared a lifelong passion for research and each, in his way, served it scrupulously.

Staff looked always as though he had got into his clothes during a cyclone. At once untidy and meticulous, he kept mountains of statistical data on a desk so littered with unclassified material that it looked to everyone except Staff himself like the final ruin of the world of ideas. The owner of the desk made his way about in it with the majestic confidence of a seasoned explorer of jungles.

His eccentricities were so numerous that simply to catalogue them would require pages of case history. The most inconvenient of these was a chronic irascibility with those who failed to understand his completely unintelligible system. The most endearing was his habit of wearing carpet slippers in his office and of sitting with both feet squeezed into a wastebasket where with a kind of conscientious regularity he moved them up and down as though he were very busy working a treadle.

All the incidental wonders of his temperament were dwarfed by the genuinely impressive phenomenon of his genius. A man without formal education, Staff transformed himself, by the sheer force of his gift, into an able research scientist. Beginning as an undisciplined, even flighty amateur, he was able to make a notable contribution to the practice of animal husbandry.

In 1903 when Larrowe and Staff received their first carload of pulp, they had little money and their product had less than no prestige. To get impartial tests of its value they gave away free samples. About the results of these experiments one of the three dairies failed to report at all, one commented indifferently, and one answered with sufficient enthusiasm to order a carload of what was still called "the stuff."

A long, patient, frequently disheartening program of education began. Feed merchants ignored the company's mail campaign, shrugged their shoulders in the faces of salesmen. The next approach was to the farmers themselves. More shrugs, more condescending smiles. But by now the faith had become something almost mystical, and its devotees were so obsessed that they were willing to lose money on every ton of pulp that came to their hands, giving away more than they sold.

For three years the losses continued while agricultural experiment stations threw semiofficial doubt on the value of pulp. It was not economical, they said. It had less nutritive merit than wheat bran. Its protein and fat content were nearly negligible. Its only possible use was as a kind of appetizer.

Manufacturers of prepared feeds were of the same stern, unalterable opinion. Dried beet pulp, they insisted, contained little beside fiber and carbohydrates. It was good only as filler and filler could be had for much less than the cost of preparing beet pulp.

Inadvertently the doubters did Larrowe a service by leaving the field wide open to him. But in 1906 when a demand for beet pulp began to be evident Larrowe's position became exposed as well as commanding. If he were to proceed with his venture he had to do so entirely on his own initiative. One sugar manufacturer, even in the face of an injunction compelling him to dispose of waste in a sanitary way, refused to invest money in a drying plant. To protect his commitment to the pulp business and to provide himself with the product itself, Larrowe was forced to enter the engineering business. From a German firm, originator of the drier, he bought the American rights and prepared to build the plants he needed. As president of the Larrowe Construction Company he had to be his own financier as well and find the money to support his program.

At this critical moment the panic of 1907 loosed its storm of fear across the land. The collapse of the copper industry started a run on the

Trust Company of America. Banking everywhere was affected. The interest rate on call money rose to 125 per cent and there was none for Larrowe when he needed it badly to complete his plant. Only the indulgence of creditors helped him through his crisis.

The malevolence of circumstance continued to be heavily weighted against him. No sooner had he erected his plant than the machine itself went wrong, refusing capriciously to dry the pulp properly. Three weeks of uninterrupted effort were required to coax it back into working order. When this problem had been solved by a stubborn refusal to admit failure another suddenly shattered Larrowe's prospects. The walls of the five furnaces fell in and the plant was reduced to a state of hopeless collapse. With operations at a standstill, the decaying vegetable matter of the beet pulp seemed more offensive than ever. The complaints of neighbors deepened in bitterness; government officials appeared on the scene waving injunctions; everyone glowered threateningly at Larrowe.

Nothing had been omitted from the traditional moving picture pattern of disaster except the labor strike and this oversight the workers promptly corrected. Larrowe himself undertook to replace the whole company of them. He stayed in the plant day and night, repairing machinery, shoveling coal, performing all the tasks of the operation. Fastidiousness forgotten and aloofness sacrificed, he wore the same clothes for days at a time and slept at night on a pile of bags.

Contrary to probability the plant was completed. The machinery began to function. The venture prospered and by 1908 Larrowe was in a sound position. Both as constructor of driers and as salesman of pulp he had made himself indispensable to the industry. Indeed the whole fraternity of sugar beet refiners clung to him so closely that one of his chief clients insisted upon his moving into the center of operations at Detroit. During the next two years he equipped nearly all the well-situated sugar factories with driers and began to build sugar factories of his own the most important of which was at Toledo.

In 1910 the spur of competition prodded Larrowe and Staff into another imaginative leap forward. The American market for dried pulp, largely created by them, was now invaded by products from other countries. It became difficult once more to sell pulp at a profit.

At this moment when another sort of man might have faced the future with blank misgiving, Staff got a glimpse of his future lifework. It had always been necessary to mix other ingredients with beet pulp

119

in order to achieve a balanced ration for dairy cows. Part of the job for which Larrowe's salesmen were trained was to give advice about this blending. But why not, Staff now reasoned, do the blending for the farmer in one's own laboratory? Would it not be better to sell a finished product?

Larrowe was dubious. To solve the selling problem of one business by building an entirely new one sounded like the suggestion of a visionary. He was right, to be sure. Staff was a visionary but he seemed always to see his visions against a background of solid reality. With the demoniac persistence of a man possessed by an idea, Staff nagged at Larrowe for funds with which to make experimental tests. Eventually Larrowe yielded. Staff's estimate of his requirements had been modest. They must be, his partner insisted, or the whole idea would have to be shelved.

So into a coach house on his own property at Pleasant Ridge, a suburb of Detroit, Staff introduced a herd of eight cows. While he was quarantined at home with an outbreak in his family of a children's disease, he improved his enforced leisure and began to gather and analyze the data on cattle growth for which he has become famous.

It was Staff's policy, in effect, to "ask the animals" what was good for them. Though his first procedures were crude as compared with those of a modern experimental farm, he became by a kind of grim persistence in this cross-examination of cattle the discoverer of principles upon which the preparation of many formula feeds of today are based.

He was a stubbornly independent analyst of what the cows told him. Tradition held, in 1910, that a dairy feed must carry not less than 24 per cent protein. Staff reached the conclusion that 20 per cent was the proper level, basing his belief on the evidence, supplied by the animals themselves, that an excess even of an excellent nutrient cannot be absorbed but is merely eliminated as waste. Staff studied the habits of his cows daily, and hour by hour, until he was convinced that he understood their requirements and had provided for them in a feed that was "right."

Again, briskly defying the tradition that a feed manufacturer must supply a great variety of feeds for a great variety of purposes, Staff dared to suggest that he and Larrowe go before their public with a one-feed program. Larrowe agreed, accepted Staff's formula, and installed machinery for its preparation in a warehouse on his brother's property at Cohocton. "Vegeto" they thought of calling it at first but better judgment prevailed and Larrowe bobbed his own name to provide "Larro."

The success of the feed was immediate. Sales soon ran far beyond the production capacity at Cohocton. In 1913 Larrowe built a new plant at Rossford, Ohio. It prospered so greatly as to distract attention from all other enterprises. The Larrowe Construction Company, created to build and operate driers, went out of existence and the founder devoted his full time to the manufacture and sale of his unique feed.

But the alternation of good and bad fortune, which has kept American industry intensely alert throughout the present century, frequently shook the interests of James Larrowe out of any possible tendency toward complacency. In 1917, the sugar beet growers and processors were treated to a kind of preview of the depression. The crop of that season was a failure. A succession of freezes and thaws, each coming at precisely the wrong moment, thoroughly demoralized growth and left the prospective supply wretched. Since there was no new pulp available Larrowe could stay in business only as long as his holdover stock lasted, or perhaps a little longer if a new formula for feed could be found.

Inevitably, the voice of cynicism counseled compromise. Was it necessary to make his feeds of 20 per cent beet pulp? Could he not use 2 per cent and stretch the rest through a long season? But such advisers misunderstood completely Larrowe's philosophy as businessman. He looked his most austere as he refused, once for all, to consider such an idea.

However, there was something else that he could do. This would be to put out a new product, one that would be candidly a substitute but that would relieve the emergency both for himself and for the growers. He prodded Staff into removing his feet from the wastebasket and speeding up a new research project. The eventual result was a feed called Big Six, the chief substitute element of which was hominy. "This," Larrowe said in effect, "is the best that we can do for you in the circumstances. It is not a Larro feed but until we can make Larro as it is supposed to be made, it will not be on the market. We shall never temporize with quality."

Ironically, the substitute product, born of the emergency, developed its own devoted following. Three years later when Larro feed was back in the stores certain livestock growers continued to ask wistfully for Big Six.

This preoccupation with the ethics of workmanship came to be known within the company as "Larro religion." The conscientiousness

121

displayed by Larrowe and Staff in protecting their own standards of quality has proved to be a highly communicable attitude and each succeeding generation of workers has shared the faith. Neither Larrowe nor Staff fancied himself as an unselfish benefactor of humanity, but each, quite without display, felt himself to be dedicated to the idea that the quality of the product of which they were joint creators must be kept to the highest standard forever.

After the 1917 difficulties were over and while the war boom still was on, the Larrowe Milling Company built up its production phenomenally. Original facilities were outgrown and Larrowe, under the intoxication of success, began, like everyone else, to expand. He sold preferred stock and immediately ploughed his new funds into projects for further development.

One of these was the replacement of the original research farm (the backyard improvisation of which had become entirely inadequate to current needs) with a modern, fully equipped laboratory. Staff's undemanding temperament had made him willing to get on with modest arrangements. For years he had drawn on his genius to make up for the limitations of physical facilities. But now the Larro salesmen were clamoring for new products and a fresh start had to be made in fundamental investigation. Competitors had appeared offering a whole line of poultry feeds and to maintain its position the Larrowe Milling Company must branch out. So the exponents of Larro religion went to work again.

A 200-acre tract near Detroit was purchased in 1920. (Thirty-two years later even this proved to be inadequate to new responsibilities and plans were put in motion to replace it with a larger experimental farm to be situated in a strategic area somewhere in the Midwest.) The process of "asking the animals" what they wanted to eat continued on a much larger scale with chickens included along with cows and pigs among the experimental subjects. Long-range tests were devised to determine on what combination of nutrients each kind of livestock could be expected to thrive. Growth records covering representative periods of maturation were made available to experimenters. At the end of three years the greatly expanded staff offered their first poultry feed and by 1925 the company was ready to go before the agricultural world with a full line of feeds equal in quality to the first one.

The Larrowe Milling Company had made a conspicuous place for itself in American industry. Its Rossford plant was able to turn out dairy feeds at the rate of 140 tons an hour; its poultry mash units produced another 60 tons an hour. The Ohio factory was one of the most strenuously busy institutions of its kind in existence and often 200 cars stood on its tracts being loaded or unloaded. It was exactly the sort of disciplined and mature partner for the flour milling enterprise needed to fulfill J. F. Bell's design.

The story of the development of flour milling in the Southwest has, as its first significant event, the settlement of the Mennonites on Kansas land in 1872–73. These far-wanderers in search of freedom of religion and conscience brought with them from Russia a rare skill in growing wheat on lands of low rainfall. They brought also supplies of Turkey Red seed which they had used successfully in the Crimea.

Their labor quickly turned into a vast wheat field a tract of 200,000 acres bought from the Santa Fe Railroad. Turkey Red became popular with other settlers and was soon being produced in great abundance. At first local millers did not welcome it because it was hard. But the "new process" developed at Minneapolis, which had made such a docile ally of hard spring wheat, solved the problems of Turkey Red as well. By 1880, another great permanent wheatfield had come into existence and Kansas had many mills to match and to complete the effort of the farms.

An even more striking event marked the opening up of Oklahoma as agricultural country. On April 22, 1889, at the border of the state that was to become Oklahoma there assembled under the eyes and the guns of federal troops some 50,000 land-hungry homesteaders, ready at a signal to plunge over the line and start a free-for-all scramble to establish claims. To the swiftest went the best sites, or to the shrewdest, or to the luckiest.

Within eight months of this mingled race, gamble, pageant, and brawl, towns stood where there had been wilderness. The citizens lost no time in getting started.

Oklahoma began presently to produce its millions of bushels of fine winter wheat (18 million in 1906) and the outlook was bright indeed. The bulk of the flour produced by the region was freighted by wagon all the way to the West Coast where Horace Davis viewed its competition with the disfavor that prompted the building of the Los Angeles mill.

In 1889 northern Texas was beginning to be aware that its soil was

123

good for something beside grazing and cowboys, that indeed it was quite as well qualified as was Oklahoma to produce excellent wheat.

In the early 1880s the town of Wichita Falls existed to serve the cattlemen as a transfer point. Herds were driven constantly through the townsite either to be trailed west or to be shipped east to market. The thunder of their protest filled the air and so did the dust of their hooves. To escape from these hardships to nerves and throats herders had only to make their way to the nearest saloon. That was never difficult, for the one highway of Wichita Falls boasted fifteen of them.

Life as uninterrupted melodrama began to disappear from the Texas communities in the late 1880s when sober settlers moved in from Sweden, Germany, and Bohemia. They were not impressed by the grandiose notion, prevalent among ranchers, that one man's property to be of respectable size must stretch across the equivalent of several counties. They were ready to devote themselves to the less spectacular occupation of growing wheat.

In the early days of this new activity, grain was shipped by rail directly to Fort Worth or to Galveston for export. But in 1890 the first really adequate mill was erected at Wichita Falls with a daily capacity of 500 barrels; it had as an additional asset an elevator that could store 500,000 bushels. This enterprise passed, in 1896, into the hands of a gifted latecomer to the tradition of the pioneer builder.

For thirty years and more Frank Kell dominated a business realm in which he had a different role for every day in the week. He was, all at once, cattleman, miller, banker, hotel owner, oil operator, official of a glass factory, and railroad tycoon. But the most substantial of his many contributions to the economy of the Southwest was the creation of the "Kell group" of mills which processed a large part of the hard winter wheat grown in Oklahoma and Texas. "The man who made milling in Texas" became the tag attached to his name.

The story of wheat and flour added a dramatic chapter to its record in the Southwest during the first quarter of the twentieth century. Edging its way modestly into the economy of Oklahoma, between the thunderous interests of cattle and the often luridly exciting interests of oil, wheat became steadily more and more significant, contributing in 1926 nearly 74 million bushels to the agricultural wealth of the country. Texas produced only half as much fine winter wheat but the state's typical drive toward achievement was expressed in the building of mills. Of these it

124

had half again as many as Oklahoma and Frank Kell continued to buy a large share of his neighbor's raw material.

The vast increase in production of wheat gave the Southwest an important advantage in competition with other parts of the country. (Kell once boasted to a fellow miller that he could stand on one of his elevators and see more wheat than was raised in all the state of Iowa.) Flour made from the hard winter wheat of the region became an important factor in the market between 1905 and 1910. Bakers began to accept it because it worked well in operations where machines were used. More and more of it came into family use as well because the quality was such that only experts could distinguish between it and flour made from spring wheat.

The Southwest was already a leading contender for high place among producers of flour. In 1899 the region had turned out only 9 million barrels as compared with the 30 million barrels from the Midwest. In 1914, the Southwest produced 20 million; the Midwest still 30 million. And the time was not far ahead when the Southwest would overtake and pass the Midwest.

To manage his many undertakings Kell was constantly in need of strong lieutenants. In 1913 he found such a man in T. C. Thatcher, a young Iowa-born giant who had migrated to Texas in 1890. With the gargantuan appetite of the young, and particularly the breed that thrives in Texas, Thatcher had worked at many pioneering tasks, saved a fortune of $1600 out of a salary of $60 a month, and set himself up as a small town banker before Frank Kell drafted him for service in the milling industry.

Thatcher was at first reluctant to change careers still another time. He knew nothing about milling, he said, beyond the hearsay report that flour was made from wheat. It made no difference, Kell answered. An executive needed chiefly to know three things: the general workings of finance, the art of hiring men who knew more than he did, and the technique of merchandising. With these as his only instructions, Thatcher started for Oklahoma City to manage Kell properties.

In the favorable climate of Kell's enthusiasm and trust Thatcher did exceptionally well. Sometimes looking over his account books he would become concerned about Kell's indifference to his rapidly growing share in this abundance. Didn't he want some money? Thatcher would ask his employer. Oh no, Kell would say: Keep it turning.

It was with the watchful eye of the canny trader that Kell observed the spectacle of national growth. But he understood, also, the thought concern of the theorist and he wished to keep one move ahead of circumstance that he might plan for the good of his industry.

There were many who saw Kell merely as the shrewd operator who could, as an acquaintance said of him in his youth, go into a trading session "owning only a jackknife and come out with a mule." Such stories did not in the least displease their subject, and he added many to them. It had cost him nothing, he once boasted, to attend the great spectacle of the opening of the Cherokee strip. He had simply bought up a block of tickets on the train that prospective settlers must ride and, as competition grew sharp for places in the coach, he discreetly advanced the price. Tickets for which he paid sixty cents he sold for a dollar and had his own excursion free.

But the fact was that Kell took a great deal more interest in what money could do than in a growing bank account. He had no difficulty throughout his lifetime in turning an honest million, now and again, in one or another of his projects, but a major share of his resources went back into his projects. In Texas and Oklahoma he followed the drama of progress, not with a desire to exploit it, but rather with a determination to discipline the region's young strength that it might not be wasted.

The period during and after World War I was exhilarating in the Southwest. The earth seemed to be unable to withhold its riches, pouring forth wheat in greater and greater abundance with every harvest. But the offspring of exhilaration threatened to be overabundance. Economists talked gloomily of the growing surplus of grain and in their own sessions the members of the Southwestern Millers' League rebuked each other for producing an embarrassment of riches in the form of flour. It was folly to allow the supply so far to exceed domestic demand. Tense competition among manufacturers had created a buyers' market "of which," one speaker said, "we all bitterly complain." An end must be made of trying to conduct business on a basis of survival of the fittest. After listening to thoughtful speeches in this vein millers returned to their homes to make more flour than ever and to brood with secret, unregenerate satisfaction over this triumph of business.

In Kell's particular realm, Oklahoma's activities kept him strenuously occupied. Between 1906 and 1926 the wheat crop there had increased from 18 million bushels to 74 million. In the same period milling capacity increased 240 per cent. But after the first spurt of energy the industry within the borders could do no more and the rest of the wheat crop had to be shipped out of the state. Kell had done his best to boost capacity. In 1917 he had increased facilities at Wichita Falls, bought mills at Waco and Vernon, and finally in 1920 built a plant at Amarillo. Yet he realized that the limits of profitable expansion were well in sight, and that the millers of the Southwest must turn to cooperation and caution, rather than to continue individual policies of reckless and greedy "Beggar my neighbor."

As perennial vice president of the Southwestern Millers' League he reiterated his plea for common sense. In November 1923 he warned his fellow members that overproduction was robbing them of the profits to which they "felt entitled." At the spring session half a year later he insisted that milling conditions would not improve until the facts of the situation had been faced candidly. Two ways of dealing with it were possible.

"One is the old brutal procedure of survival of the fittest which would possibly mean the elimination of 40 to 60 per cent of our milling capacity. The other is the modern one of cooperation in our effort to meet problems in a businesslike way. We must get rid of distrust of each other and of selfishness."

Even when matters began to mend in 1924 Kell foresaw that the good fortune brought back by rising prices of wheat and flour could not be expected to last. The "present prosperity" was based on world shortage, a circumstance which had enabled the United States to become once more a leading exporter. But to hold this advantage a program of mutual support must be put into effect quickly to get long overdue concessions in the matter of freight rates. Only by cooperation could they thrive or even survive.

For years the Southwestern Millers' League had complained that the railroads were unduly sympathetic toward the wishes of rival enterprises in Minneapolis. Again and again they applied to the Interstate Commerce Commission for reductions in their rates. A famous decision handed down in 1908 had established the principle that the railroad men must be allowed to make the lower rate from Minneapolis because their lines faced competition from the Great Lakes shipping route.

But the matter was by no means settled in the minds of the southwestern millers. They entered one plea after another and in the course of these controversies gained many concessions. When at last, in 1927,

127

the Interstate Commerce Commission reversed the principle of 1908 and gave the Southwest equality with Minneapolis in the Central Freight Association territory, T. C. Thatcher, then president of the league, announced the news to the members as conclusive evidence that there was, after all, a Santa Claus.

In all these causes Kell took active part. As a railroad man himself he had helped other millers as well as himself by maintaining low freight rates to the Gulf ports. He drew up a schedule of charges which had helped significantly to make large-scale milling possible. Even after the victory with the Interstate Commerce Commission he continued to preach the doctrine of cooperation. What he hoped for chiefly was the painless retirement of excessive milling capacity. Economic pressures had begun already to do it painfully, eliminating the unfit so ruthlessly that the number of flour mills fell from 63 in 1906 to 26 in 1926. The battle was harsh and victory was going only to those few large modern mills that were strategically placed and efficiently operated. These were able to produce more flour, less expensively, than the many scattered units of an earlier day.

Impelled by his faith in cooperation Kell began in the mid 1920s a vigorous, indefatigable one-man war against further expansion of an industry that was already "overextended." In 1925 he said to the Southwestern Millers' League: "It might be advantageous if millers operated in a few large companies as is the tendency among bakers. Perhaps that will come."

Soon after that meeting another Minneapolis miller, J. F. Bell, began to talk to him informally about large milling problems. After their first meeting Bell commented in his diary: "How he runs all the things in which he is interested I cannot tell . . . but they embrace oil wells, land developments, hotels, cement mills, glass works, railroads, a traction company and a bus line. His command of detail and his knowledge are startling."

(This is a little like an awe-stricken tribute from one natural phenomenon to another. It is as though Niagara Falls were to say to the Colorado River: "I don't see how you do it.")

The minds of the two men were converging upon the same objective. This proved to be the formation of General Mills.

9

Toward Consolidation

THE BIRTH OF GENERAL MILLS

T HE years 1926 to 1928 might well be described as the period in which everyone in America was trying to buy everyone else out. Fantasy seemed to take possession of the native intelligence and, in a kind of mass hysteria, citizens with or without capital went investment mad. Underwriting houses, of course, did not hesitate to take advantage of this high degree of receptivity or to stimulate it; it seemed virtually to demand to be exploited.

This spectacle appalled the sober. In his diary, J. F. Bell recorded the impressions of a visit made to New York during the feverish excitement in January 1926: "I learned more of what is going on in banking circles. The technique is to grab off a few companies, wrap them together in a combination and throw them into the waiting maw of the public. How long this can continue is a matter of conjecture. It looks as though it were near the bursting point. There is neither heart nor soul in any of it. I was never in such a depressing atmosphere in my life."

The "cup of opportunity," as Bell said, was filled to the brim with heady intoxicants. American financiers were draining it recklessly. In that moment he earned a modest reputation as a prophet by pointing out, three years before the stock market crash, that such maneuvers could not "come to good."

These often quite arbitrary combinations of interests to which Bell referred had the attraction only of promising quick profits, but the sly expedients of the promoters managed to reserve all real profits to themselves. Owners of a successful enterprise were persuaded to allow the formation of a new company under a new capital structure. Often they agreed to take paper gains as the total recompense for their surrender of independence and they continued dutifully to manage the business; meanwhile, the promoters sold stock in the new organization and pocketed the rewards. Prospectuses of the newborn companies were largely works of imagination based on the beguiling notions that the sky was the limit, that expansion was infinitely possible, and that profits would multiply automatically at the will of the promoter. The underwriting houses were inspired also by a kind of imaginative frenzy in the manipulation of values. Stocks sold to the public were guaranteed to return enormous profits but the original owners found themselves with nothing to say about how these profits were to be produced. Control of the business remained with the new owners through the "voting stock" for which they paid nothing. The former owners, faced with orders to produce a volume of business as little related to reality as was the volume of water produced by the sorcerer's apprentice in the fairy story, had lost all regulation of their own affairs.

Bell had no intention of being lured into any such melodrama. He might conceivably sell outright if bankers insisted on letting their cup of opportunity splash in his direction. But the fairy-tale predicament of a manager who must produce flour from wheat that did not exist and find customers to buy that flour from population statistics that were completely imaginary — this he was determined to avoid.

There was, however, a design for combining the forces of the milling industry that seemed to him not only realistic but absolutely necessary to the continuing health of the business. He had begun to labor with the formulation of a plan in the early spring of 1928, fitting the pieces together with the absorbed fascination that had led him at other times to the construction of gasoline engines, household gadgets, and laboratory instruments. Now, at last, all the elements of his variable nature had come to focus on a single major problem: his love of mechanical precision, his preoccupation with the theoretical approach to a practical issue, his devotion to analysis. He set himself the task of putting on paper an orderly analysis of the milling industry.

It was by no means easy for a man who sat on a dozen boards and whose office was the clearinghouse for a vast multiplicity of business details to find time for such an exhaustive analysis. Nor did Bell's house offer a secure retreat, for his children were all interested in making music

and from morning to night the halls rang with the competitive and conflicting rhythms of a conservatory. In humorous desperation Bell retired
to a bathroom and wrote what his associates called jocularly his "magnum
opus."

The magnum opus, actually a confidential report to the directors of
Washburn Crosby, took a clear-eyed and candid view of the situation
confronting the miller. It was intended to show that the past was dead or
dying and could not be revived. A new age had begun for industry and
only those who followed its inexorable dictates could hope to survive.

A major difficulty, he suggested, was that unusual circumstances had
caused the simultaneous rise of wages and fall of commodity prices.
Profits squeezed between the two movements had shrunk dangerously.
This downward trend had begun in 1926–27 after "a period of prosperity
and industrial activity." But now the nation had become engaged in "a
gigantic struggle" and "a period of elimination" had begun. The inefficient were "falling by the way" and business was rapidly becoming concentrated in the hands of the few.

The tendency toward consolidation was to be observed everywhere.
A "horizontal integration" of closely related interests had given huge
buying power to new elements in industry. The chain stores, for example,
had begun to control outlets to the ultimate consumer and their power
appeared to be almost unlimited. Their impetuous movement in going
out to greet destiny had strewn the path of business with crippled inter-
mediaries, the wholesalers and the jobbers. Against the drive of this impulse all arbitrary legislation had proved to be ineffective. The income
tax reports for the year 1925, "a notably prosperous year," indicated that
"one-fourth of one per cent of all corporations had earned 65 per cent of
all net profits." That the tendency had continued steadily a statement
issued by the Treasury Department revealed unmistakably. In the year
1927, 40 per cent of all funds collected by the government as income tax
had been paid by some 200 concerns.

Yet despite all the disadvantages that he knew to be massed against
him, the miller still tried to battle his way through problems as an
individual operator. The decline in the per capita consumption of flour
and the overextension of milling capacity — his classic difficulties — now
had major aggravations in the newly acquired bargaining power of the
forces with which he must deal. He had seen his family flour business
grow increasingly susceptible to the whims of the great chain retailers

of those days. Similarly his bakery flour business was influenced more and more by the larger commercial operators. It was plainly a case of a small enterprise in the milling industry having to match strength with groups having tremendous and often concentrated buying power.

If he took no active account of the economic process that was moving steadily against his advantage, the miller might, like the wholesaler and the jobber, find himself overwhelmed by an avalanche. It was even possible that the milling industry would be pushed from its "essential position in the economic scheme" by a new combination of forces that would take over the processing of wheat as part of its vast operation.

"The handwriting is on the wall," Bell said. "The process of concentration moves forward steadily. Bargaining power of the buyer is growing. There is no denying its effect on trade conditions. No legerdemain, no high pressure sales method, no intensive merchandising practice can restore the old order. The question is how to deal with it."

Bell's discussion paused at this moment and turned back to survey the various distribution outlets of the milling industry and the part that each had played in the conduct of the Washburn Crosby business. He began with a quotation from Dr. Julius Klein, director of the Bureau of Foreign and Domestic Commerce of the United States Department of Commerce, who had pointed out that, in the great bustle and stir of modern business, "it profits us nothing in the long run if we waste on distribution what we save in production." This was the central problem that had haunted the great producers from Andrew Carnegie on down the line.

It needed to be studied closely in the milling industry, Bell pointed out, to determine where future advantage lay. He identified five chief outlets for flour, each with its own price level: the export trade; trade with large bakers; service to institutions; trade with small bakers; and trade with the great American family.

Each classification presented problems that needed to be reexamined. The value of each as a contributor of profits to the company must be reappraised.

The export business long had been an important factor in the Washburn Crosby operation, bulking too large, in J. S. Bell's opinion, even in the period of World War I. Yet it had risen since — from 14.5 per cent of the company's total business in 1912–13 to 24.6 per cent in 1927. For Washburn Crosby the gross income on a barrel of flour in the export trade, before provision for costs of production, selling, and taxes, was 81 cents in the least productive of recent years and $1.04 in the best. Bell argued that "we should direct our efforts toward more remunerative fields."

Business with the large bakers was essential as a contributor of volume in a heavy production program. It constituted, in the last months of the year 1927, 16.7 per cent of the total business. The bargaining power of the bakers had forced the rate of recovery on a barrel of flour lower than in the export field. The problem was to maintain a desirable balance between the need of this outlet and the burden that it sometimes put upon other kinds of trade.

Institutional business, difficult to separate from other classifications, particularly that of the bakers, was not of great significance except for its service aspect. Business with small bakers, constituting 30.1 per cent of the total, provided gross income that varied from 99 cents per barrel in 1925–26 to $1.12 in 1926–27. These were valuable customers for the present and they would probably continue to be in the immediate future. "Naturally we desire the greatest number of buyers," Bell continued, "and this field does present possibilities for future development."

The business in flour for "household use" offered the most rewarding opportunity. In the seven months ending January 31, 1928, Washburn Crosby sold 1,444,000 barrels of hard wheat family flour. The addition of 87,000 barrels of soft wheat flour brought the total to 1,531,000, making up 20 per cent of the total business (25.4 per cent of the volume from which export flour was excluded). Bell warned his colleagues that various forms of competition and pressure might make it difficult to keep to current price levels. The great objective must be to reduce expenses in order that the margin of profit might be maintained.

These, then, were the facts determining the outlook for the immediate future if the company continued to do business in the familiar way. He realized that his report would not be considered encouraging, but he was sure that it was necessary to look closely at the realities of the situation. "It is," he wrote, "clearly impossible to go ahead without the truth or to revert to former conditions or traditions existing in an atmosphere that no longer prevails today. The methods of the past are not applicable to the present and any attempt to fit them into a modern setting would be suicidal. The first thing to do is to put our house in order."

Toward Consolidation

His examination of fundamental problems then took another close look at the Washburn Crosby Company's past, present, and possible future. In the course of its development the firm had passed through successive phases, achieving first regional, then national, and finally international distribution. The prestige of flour made from hard spring wheat had given impetus to this gratifying advance. Now the movement threatened to go into reverse. Southwest wheat was good; it was abundant; bakers no longer showed any preference between the two varieties. The certainty was that a company the major part of whose manufacturing facilities were concentrated in an area that now produced only 25 per cent of the wheat available must either relocate these facilities at more strategic points or accept the doom with which Bell threatened those who showed lack of foresight. In the circumstances the Minneapolis mills could not expand. Dwindling was inevitable and the whole effort might be forced to shrink back within regional limits.

Bell was, of course, unwilling to accept for Washburn Crosby the possibility of shrinking. He wanted no compromise with the tradition of leadership. The company must take the lead by moving with the times toward consolidation.

He knew precisely what sort of combination of elements within the milling industry he would like to bring about. It would not be a union of the large milling firms at Minneapolis, for that might alarm crusading believers in the principles of the Sherman-Clayton antitrust acts. Rather it would be a "horizontal integration" with broad geographical representation covering the entire country. This would be in perfect sympathy with the trend toward concentration which in the years between 1914 and 1925 had seen a reduction in the number of mills from 5055 to 2606 and at the same time an increase in the number of large plants from 218 in 1914 to 247 in 1925. By the latter year the large mills produced 76 per cent of the entire output. Concentration, as Bell saw it, was inevitable.

So, at last, he offered his plan, one which he believed would meet the demand for consolidation of effort and yet preserve the "element of individuality and a certain freedom in operation." In his own words the proposal was as follows:

"Form a central company. Purchase in stock of the central company the assets of the selected mills on the basis of ten times their average five year earnings. The stock would be non-transferable stock, allocated

134

to the mill and linked to it in ownership. There would be but one form of issue, seven per cent cumulative stock. The central company would have the right to the earnings of all its units up to the amount of the stock issue and, if any individual unit failed to furnish its proportionate share the amount would be charged as a lien against the stock holdings of that mill in the central company. Beyond the amount required to meet this seven per cent dividend, each unit would be entitled to its own earnings to be distributed among its own stockholders. Each company would operate as a separate unit with its own President, Board of Directors and stockholders. The present outstanding stock in each of these companies could be issued, not against the assets of the mill, but against the equity represented by that company's stockholdings in the central company. Trading would be permitted in the stock of the individual companies but the stock of the central company could not be traded because it would be identified with the mill and would pass only with the ownership of the mill. The affairs of the central company would be administered by a Board composed of Directors of the operating units with a permanent Chairman. It would be the intent of the Board to permit the units to operate individually; nevertheless general policies would be laid down. It would consolidate such parts of its buying as proved to be desirable. It would establish a raw material price basis and by-products price basis. It might stabilize production among its members. Its powers in general would include taking measures to eliminate price cutting, vicious trade practices and over-lapping efforts."

The magnum opus was not regarded as a cheerful document, but Bell insisted that truth must be served. To a critic of his attitudes he once retorted: "I'd rather be a constructive pessimist than a theoretical optimist." His own opinion was that the temper of what he had set down was entirely hopeful. The Washburn Crosby enterprise always had been highly profitable and it could continue to be, not by waiting for revocation of the law of diminishing returns, but simply by going where new opportunities were to be found.

The purpose of the report was to persuade his fellow directors that the only way to stake out a claim on the future was to organize a proper combination and then to command it. In this Bell did not immediately succeed. One of his partners wrote a long memorandum on the report which completely ignored the bold, innovative plan. Instead it dilated with discreet favor on an alternative suggestion which Bell had offered, as an interpreter must suspect, with his tongue lodged firmly in his cheek. This second plan was to shrink back contentedly to a regional basis of operation with facilities expanded here and curtailed there to suit the situation.

The difficulty was that the owners of the company still felt shadowed by the memory of the debt they had carried so long in the process of buying in the stock belonging to the estates of Dunwoody and Martin. There had been many times, as one of the partners remembered ruefully, when, despite the company's great success, he "hardly had a free dollar to rub against another." Now that they were free of that load they were reluctant – the elder ones among them – to accept commitments that might once more mean anxiety and sacrifice. No matter what that very positive man, Bell, said about the necessity of responding to a challenge, the truth was that he proposed to lead them into a speculative adventure.

So the confidential report, delivered in March 1928, was filed but not forgotten – at least not by Bell. In stubborn and determined pursuit of his idea he set out presently on a journey in search of allies. At Wichita Falls he found Frank Kell ready to turn a sympathetic ear toward any plan that proposed more efficient and better disciplined use of existing facilities rather than a reckless snatching at prosperity through further overexpansion.

A month after Bell's first pilgrimage, he himself was momentarily deflected. This interruption, dangling an illusory promise of escape from all the burdens of business, served, finally, to make a determined man all the more determined to embark on the great adventure of his life as organizer. But for the moment it seemed to have ended his career.

En route to the East for a vacation with his family, Bell received an urgent telegram from the head of the great underwriting firm of Blair and Company urging him to proceed immediately to New York. A telephone conversation, made from a way station, assured him, further, that something was hot on the fire if he would go at once.

The tasty dish put before him was an offer for his business, cash on the barrelhead with no entangling managerial alliances. Such an offer he had always said he would consider. Now, when a group of important financiers asked him to name his price, he temporized. But only for a moment, because he was given no time even to reach a telephone that he might talk to his associates. At last, in a state of mind that suggested that of the sleepwalker he reached into the blue for a figure. Forty million dollars, he said solemnly. The partners of Blair and Company moved toward him en masse and shook his hand, each in turn. It was, they said, a deal.

Bell's first thought was to reach John Crosby, still the astute and reticent chairman of the board, and confess what he had done. "I've sold the company," he said bluntly as soon as the telephone connection had been made. This directness seemed, as he remembers, to be the only possible approach but his voice vibrated between exultation and trepidation. After a pause during which Crosby lost and recovered his own hold upon the real world, a crisp voice, made crisper by asperity, said: "You had no authority to do that." But Bell was not in a mood to be easily deflated. "What would you say," he asked, "if I were to tell you that I'd got forty million dollars?" There was another pause and then the crisp voice, suddenly softened by Yankee drollery said: "You had the authority."

For purposes of drama the episode should end here, on a note of triumph. But this was a stutter, not a forthright utterance, and the drama went on to a depressing anticlimax. Officials of the Washburn Crosby Company — Bullis and Davis together with their Minneapolis attorney, Frank Morley — joined Bell in New York, loaded with substantiating documents. The client, never named but supposed by everyone involved to be of the milling fraternity, remained in the background while for weeks negotiations proceeded ceremoniously through Blair and Company. Bullis struggled with accountants and Morley with lawyers until the final "t" on "agreement" seemed to have been crossed.

At last all the documents were ready; proofs were corrected and sent to the printer; the protocol of ceremonial dinners preliminary to signing was satisfied. Then, on a morning when all details had been completed and the Washburn Crosby representatives had assembled en masse for the signing, the stutter reached the point of absolute suspension of breath. The clients, unable as it appeared to win the final approval of a dissenting director, had withdrawn. A fantasy of high finance had faded. The deal was off.

When he realized that the comedy was over, Bell remembers having felt "so low" that he "could have walked under a caterpillar with a high hat on."

Toward Consolidation

But such moods were short-lived with him. It was presently evident that he felt nothing but relief. To retire when he was not yet fifty years old was the last thing he wanted to do. To fill the odd moments of a crowded life with hobbies of a dozen different kinds was one thing, but to make a lifework of them was another. Relieved that the threat of leisure had been removed, he reached out for what was to him the real cup of opportunity — the chance to do a new, creative job.

The near sale of the company had had the effect of exposing the minds even of the die-hards among Bell's fellow directors to the idea of change. Some of them, as he once reported, had taken it as "a bitter blow to have our whole plan break up." Capitalizing on the new adventurous spirit with which the other officers of the company now regarded the future, Bell set out again in vigorous pursuit of his own vision.

He knew now where he was going and the way led first to the patriarch of banking, George F. Baker, Sr. In 1928 Mr. Baker was eighty-eight years old and though illness occasionally made him miss a day or two from his office (he was absent at the time of Bell's first call) he was still in full command of a perennially youthful philosophy. It seemed never to have occurred to him that, as an octogenarian, he might not have fifty years before him in which to watch the development of the new enterprises in which he interested himself. He and Bell had served together on the board of the Lehigh Valley Railroad and they spoke the same language of enthusiasm and expectancy. For Baker's benefit, Bell outlined the story of what had happened to him and how narrowly he had escaped having millions of dollars' worth of idleness forced upon him. What he wished really to do, he said, was to form a company based on sound values of capitalization, one that would show, over the years, "substantial development and justify reasonable expectations of profit." He knew precisely how he could put such a company together out of units already in existence in the Southwest, in the central region, and on the Pacific Coast.

Baker listened with the serene courtesy of an old man and the eagerness of a young one. "I like your language," he said at last. "Go out and see what you can do."

"May I take your blessing?" Bell asked, "Not, of course, as a commitment, but just as a suggestion that if the pattern can be worked out the First National Bank would be interested?"

"You may," Baker said.

138

The scene had a significance greater than appeared on the surface. This was not simply the consummation of a business agreement. Baker, a pioneer of business, had helped America to come of age in furthering the development of electrical power by speeding up production of steel. Now at a patriarchal age he sent a younger man on the pilgrimage to find new solutions for the old problem of feeding a great continental nation. The tradition of service in American enterprise was implicitly restated in the understanding between Baker and Bell.

To start negotiations one of the Washburn Crosby Company's ablest young men, Harry A. Bullis, took to the road as prophet of the idea. He went first to Wichita Falls to talk to Kell and his chief associate, T. P. Duncan. Out of his intimate knowledge of figures, Bullis brought questions so searching that not even owner and administrator of the properties concerned were able immediately to answer them. Duncan returned to the mill to get the assistance of his chief accountant. It had been the hope of all the negotiators that Bullis' identity might, for the moment, remain a secret so that gossip should not disturb the day's work. However, the accountant recognized his name as that of a recent speaker at a Federation meeting. "He's with the Washburn Crosby Company," the undeluded accountant said. "Are they going to take over our mills?" A grasshopper plague of rumors settled immediately on the consolidation plan.

Bullis shook them off and proceeded on his fact-finding expedition. With his expert grain man, Ralph Stiles, he went twice through the Kell properties at Wichita Falls, at Oklahoma City, and at Amarillo. Then, having hacked his way through a jungle of figures during forty-eight hours of sleepless concentration, he made his final report to a full-scale gathering of possible participants called at Kansas City.

These included Bell, John Crosby, Franklin Crosby, Bullis, and Davis – all of the Washburn Crosby group; Kell, Thatcher, and Duncan of the Kell group; and Roger Hurd, with his lieutenants from the Red Star Milling Company of Wichita, Kansas. Bullis' report was thoroughly examined and discussed. Every aspect of the proposed merger was turned over thoroughly. There appeared to be general agreement that consolidation was inevitable. The difficult matter of comparative evaluation of properties was boldly begun. Bell evolved a mathematical formula to be applied to each group of plants in turn and this resulted in a considerable shrinkage in the theoretical evaluation of his own properties. But he stuck to his formula and it appeared that the consolidation was virtually a *fait accompli*.

Then, quite suddenly and unexpectedly, Kell and Thatcher withdrew. Though the basic plan for the exchange of stock (buying fixed assets with stock in the new corporation) had met with their enthusiastic endorsement, "something came o'er the spirit" of Kell's dream and he made a stately exit from the conference, wrapped in his own secrets and abstractions.

There was actually no mystery to this curious maneuver. The impulse of the old trade had taken possession of his mind at the last moment. It seemed likely to him, as a close associate later interpreted the matter, that a momentary retreat into independence might get him a better price for his jackknife. Kell had hoped to have some of his outlying mills (at St. Louis and Arkansas City) included in the consolidation, but Bell was convinced that only those concentrated in the Southwest would be useful to the over-all design. Negotiation had reached an impasse between two very positive forces.

There remained only Roger Hurd of the Red Star Milling Company. That young man's resolution was subject to no such wavering. He had been reluctant to accept the idea of consolidation, but having become convinced by Bell's arguments that new forces were driving the industry inexorably in a new direction, he did not try to resist.

If Bell was disappointed by the retreat of Kell he concealed the fact even from his diary, which continued through the first weeks of June 1928 to be characterized by a kind of bland and happy contentiousness. In his negotiations with the other participants in the merger, he yielded no point lightly; a rein was held tight on the idea so that no one else might escape full commitment to its principle.

The corporation in this first phase of its new life wove into its design milling interests from three sources. There was, first, the business and property of the Washburn Crosby Company in Minneapolis, together with its other mills in Buffalo, Kansas City, and Louisville. There was, second, the group of associate companies of which the Washburn Crosby directors were also directors: the Royal Milling Company of Great Falls, Montana; the Rocky Mountain Elevator Company, also at Great Falls; and the Kalispell Flour Mill Company at Kalispell. There was, finally, the one previously quite independent company, the Red Star Milling Company of Wichita, Kansas.

On the longest day of the year, June 21, millers and bankers interested in the formation of General Mills made a very long day of it in the Ritz-Carlton Hotel in New York. Each group was supported by a small standing army of lawyers. Behind the lawyers stood the accountants. And all about stretched, not mountains of papers, but rather a Sahara of legal documents spread out on long tables with all the bleached bones of contention exposed to view.

Tension threatened to flare into crisis over certain last-minute demands for reevaluation of facilities, but at last after many grueling hours of argument the final papers were ready to be executed. Bell came in from his bed, wearing pajamas, to sign as president of the new company, and Bullis, who seems never to have gone to bed at any time throughout the negotiations, signed as its secretary. John Crosby interrupted a lifetime habit of reticence to offer jovial salutes to the occasion. On June 22 General Mills had come into existence. The official date of incorporation, June 20, refers to the drawing up of papers and ignores the wrangle before final signing.

It was actually only a frail shadowing forth of what Bell had meant it to be and of what it was actually to become. But the philosophy that had prompted the creation of the new company had impressed American bankers and the prestige that its name seemed immediately to evoke impressed the American public. Newspapers saluted "the new $50,000,000 corporation with respect." The response of buyers to the stock offered through brokers was so spontaneous and eager that, in Chicago, all allotments had been disposed of through telephone calls from unsolicited customers before any selling campaign could be made. Bell recorded in his diary the notations that "the Washburn Crosby personnel would have taken the whole issue" and bankers in New York were "much impressed by the response to our organization."

The authorized capitalization of General Mills, Incorporated, consisted of 500,000 shares of preferred stock at a par value of $100 and 1,000,000 shares of common stock with no par value. By action of the incorporators at their first meeting in June 1928, the Board of Directors "was authorized to issue the Capital Stock of the Corporation from time to time for money, property, labor done, or services rendered as the Board should determine." The same meeting authorized the issuance of $17,000,000 par value stock and 350,000 shares of common stock to acquire the assets of the five companies of the original merger. Comparative values of the units are indicated by the numbers of shares of preferred stock that went to each: 135,418 to the Washburn Crosby Company; 20,152 to the Red Star Milling Company; 8122 to the Royal Milling Company; 3671 to the Kalispell Flour Mills Company; and 2637 to the Rocky Mountain Elevator Company.

Of the 6 per cent cumulative preferred stock, $3,400,000 was offered to the public in the belief, as expressed by Bell, that investment seekers had begun to demand "participation in the important enterprises of the country"; General Mills, he said, wished to give full recognition to that right. At the same time 70,000 shares of common stock were issued at a price of $65. All went so promptly that the advertisements announcing their availability carried also the statement that the issues were exhausted.

Little had been added in the way of physical facilities to those which the Washburn Crosby Company previously had owned or controlled. Of the ten mills concerned only one was new; the 63,500-barrel capacity named by General Mills had been increased only by the 4700 barrel capacity of the Red Star Mill. But investors believed in the idea and they believed that it would grow. As Bell said in his public announcement of the birth of General Mills:

"The trend toward growth in size of well-organized and successful industries has been seen clearly in the last two years. Economies achieved by mass production have made additional capital available to business and this capital has been used to accommodate the demands of the consuming public for better, more efficient service. We must eliminate overlapping and duplicating processes, expensive and wasteful sales methods, unnecessary duplications in transportation. Our present standards of living demand these savings. The organization of General Mills should prove to be a forward step in this direction."

The idea of General Mills was to grow impressively within six months of the original merger. But there was no need to wait patiently for justification of the idea. Like a royal infant, laden with titles in its cradle, the newborn General crowed in lusty triumph.

10

Idea in Action

THE LARGEST MILLER IN THE WORLD

T H E new corporation's stock kept rising. Issued at 65, it reached 86 in the first spirited trading. But Bell and his associates were not satisfied with these glittering signs of success. They wanted its solid substance. If the original idea of General Mills were really to be fulfilled, companies in the Southwest and Pacific Northwest must be brought in.

It was more than ever necessary to follow the wheat. A report made by Bell soon after the birth of General Mills showed that better representation in the Southwest was essential to the company's "national program of manufacture." Supplies of winter wheat were far ahead of those of spring wheat. The season 1927–28 produced approximately 550,000,000 bushels of the former and 320,000,000 of the latter. Even in its own mills at Minneapolis, Buffalo, and Chicago, the Washburn Crosby Company had been using a large percentage of winter wheat — 42 per cent in 1927–28.

As Bell later wrote: "The milling units of the Washburn Crosby Company were not favorably situated for grinding a larger proportion of winter wheat and it was, therefore, imperative that facilities should be secured which would allow a great proportion of flour to be made from the southwestern wheat and to be distributed without freight penalty. To secure such capacity was one motive in the organization of General Mills."

In December 1928, with the first steps toward reorganization taken successfully, Bell looked hopefully once more toward the Texas-Oklahoma region.

Idea in Action

Other still unfulfilled reasons for creating General Mills were stirring in his mind. One was expressed in the very name of the corporation. Despite the doubts of several associates Bell had insisted on designation that would be simple, dramatic, and suggestive of breadth. He wanted, he said, to feel free to manufacture anything from flour to locomotives. For the name General Mills, Bell had the support of Tracy Vought, whose firm of merger experts, White and Case, had presided over the consolidation. Bell, Davis, Bullis, Morley, and Vought had sat all one afternoon in a New York hotel room checking all suggested names with the catalogue of existing firms in a New York telephone book. Gradually all competitors were eliminated for their too great similarity to names already well established in the folklore of American capitalism. General Mills still held the field. It remained only to get the approval of John Crosby, at home in Minneapolis. When he was informed by telephone of the decision, he commented dryly: "Well, I'm glad you didn't name it General Miles because General Miles didn't have much of a record in the Civil War."

As though to justify its name General Mills continued with each day's trading to augment its prestige in the stock market. From the stronghold to which, in June, he had retired with his jackknife, Frank Kell watched developments. At seventy, he had begun to weary of juggling many enterprises. Once the acquisitive impulse had worked in him so automatically that friends, seeing him already in possession of nearly every other kind of institution, used to ask him jocularly: "When are you going to take over the post office?" But he knew, along with Ecclesiastes, that "There is a time to keep and a time to cast away." So he knocked once more at the gates of General Mills.

It was Bullis who went to answer. Adept at the conference table, after a rugged initiation in the sessions that preceded the original merger, he knew how to anticipate the probing of any Wall Street financier. Day after day, and often until midnight, he had been subjected to the most exhaustive and exhausting examination. But he knew all the answers because as comptroller he had long since established the practice of putting together at the end of each fiscal year a full report containing the substantial facts of the business. Bullis' flair for figures together with his striking ability to interpret them had made him extremely useful to Bell in the preparation of the "magnum opus." The same combination of talents was later to make him a brilliant top executive. Figures con-

144

tain the law and gospel by which a corporation lives and the ability to interpret their text is essential to modern business leadership.

Bullis, accompanied by a Kansas City representative of the company, made the rounds of the Kell plants playing the role of innocent sightseers. But each time one or the other would make a revealingly professional gesture in handling flour and the sharp eye of a miller would penetrate the pretense. Rumors were air-borne halfway across the continent and again the story went out that General Mills was on the march.

The campaign did not have to be conducted long in secrecy. On October 24, Kell and his son, Joseph, arrived in Minneapolis for further negotiation. Kell, Jr. — a familiar paradox of the machine age — liked to drive his car at ninety miles an hour through the heaviest traffic of great cities but followed his father's lead in all other matters, dutifully calling him "Papa." The poker game of matching assets went on but this time with the confidence in everyone's mind that it would reach a showdown. General Mills, though it had not yet absorbed the Texas-Oklahoma group of properties, had surrounded them with the strength of an idea in which Kell also believed implicitly.

A team of Minneapolis men — Davis, McMillan, Morley, and Bullis — went to Wichita Falls, Texas, and began final negotiations with Frank Kell and his associates. Bullis put a member of his own staff in each plant to make the kind of thorough survey of operations that he had made in the Minneapolis plant and general office a half-dozen years earlier, the purpose of which had been to coordinate activities and to eliminate waste. Davis supervised the public relations aspects of consolidation, Morley the legal aspects, McMillan those having to do with operations in grain, and Bullis the over-all plan.

Presently the team moved on to El Reno, Oklahoma, where Bell had persuaded Karl Humphrey to think well of the idea of consolidation. Much much more than a mill was wanted in this instance. Karl Humphrey, like Bell himself, had belonged to the "ancient and honorable" tradition of milling through two generations of broad and original effort. His father, Edwin Humphrey, may be said to have helped create the state of Oklahoma out of little to begin with besides handsome scenery and a favorable climate. By building the El Reno mill in the mid-1880s to process local wheat, he had given a strong impetus to settlement.

Karl Humphrey had followed the pattern established for sons of the pioneers by exploring fully the region's opportunities for specialized education. He had been graduated from the University of Kansas in 1907, entered his father's company as bookkeeper, become general manager in 1909, and president eight years later. Bell had recognized Humphrey as a kindred spirit, recording in his diary the opinion that, though El Reno as a milling point was not particularly "advantageous" and the mill itself was merely "a nice piece of property," it had one great asset — Karl Humphrey himself.

The plans to absorb El Reno went forward uneventfully. So the team prepared to converge once more upon Kell for final settlement. But before the group could leave El Reno, Davis fell ill of "flu" and the rest had to go on without him.

Bullis became captain of the team and again the contests in adjustment required of him all the show of strength that he had learned as comptroller and perfected in Wall Street. With a kind of amiable pugnacity each side clung to the letter of the law in point after point. The formal, stylized love of controversy still was in control and resolution came slowly. At last every detail seemed to be settled. Then crisis flared again. The price of flour, being a variable factor, did not lend itself to easy translation into exact terms of sale. On an item of this kind buyers and sellers were $25,000 apart. As Thatcher later said of the episode with a kind of urchin glee, it seemed to be his job and that of Duncan and young Kell to outtrade "the gentlemen from Minneapolis." "We thought," he said, "that we had put them to sleep. And our chests swelled so that we couldn't see our feet."

But they reckoned without Bullis who could also be resolute. He would not yield the point. Nor would he, as he said, "go back to Minneapolis and admit failure to Mr. Bell." Deadlock! "Shall we go and see Mr. Kell?" someone asked. And they all moved across the street to the modest office where this curious genius presided over his empire.

Kell received the delegation in the mood that had become habitual with him over the years. Circumstance and the broad extent of his interests had required him to become a blend of oracle, idealist, and trader. He asked each of the contestants to tell his story. "Bullis, what have you to say?" "Duncan, you?" "And you, Thatcher?" He turned finally to his son. "What do you think, Joe?" "Well, Papa . . ." the younger Kell began. But his father cut him short. "The General Mills boys are right," Kell said.

It was as though he had snapped his jackknife shut and handed it over for good. The fate of the industry was what really mattered to him as it had mattered from the day when he first told the Southwest Millers' League that consolidation and salvation were synonymous.

So, on December 18, 1928, the merger was made complete. The mills of the Kell group at Wichita Falls, Amarillo, Vernon, and Waco, Texas, and at Oklahoma City and Perry, Oklahoma, added to the total daily capacity of General Mills another 9500 barrels. It added also grain storage capacity of 3,500,000 bushels.

For these properties General Mills agreed to pay in preferred and common stock of the corporation. For the "net current assets" of the four Texas mills, the original owners were to receive under the terms of the contract stocks "equally the full value thereof not exceeding $949,000"; for "all other assets," stocks worth $2,475,000. The preferred stock was to be valued at par; the common stock at $70 a share. The balance between preferred and common stock was to be preserved throughout all these negotiations on the basis of issuing, for every $400 of preferred, shares of common having an aggregate value of not more than $1100.

Figures for the Oklahoma City mill called for payment in preferred stock of $267,000 and in common stock, $975,000. The Perry mill was valued at $83,200 in preferred and $300,000 in common stock.

The basis for acquisition of Humphrey's El Reno mill was in every detail the same. This "nice little property" had a daily milling capacity of 1100 barrels and storage capacity of 900,000 bushels of grain. For the absorption of these facilities the corporation agreed to issue stock to a total of $1,095,000 of which $800,000 was to be common stock and the rest preferred.

The over-all transaction in the Southwest involved a total net value of "not less than $6,000,000" and to cover these obligations the Board of Directors ordered the issuance of 61,286 shares of common stock and 15,000 of preferred.

The scene of the expansion movement shifted now to California. Bell went there in November, a fortunate moment for negotiation. Hoover had just been elected President of the United States and the temper of his adherents was hopeful. The President-elect himself was there resting after the campaign at his home in Palo Alto. He was, as Bell's diary reports with an almost startling devotion to understatement, "in a fine frame of mind." Present also was Dr. Alonzo Taylor, at that time head of the Food Research Institute at Stanford University. The three associates of the wartime Food Administration had an enthusiastic reunion, which presently resolved itself into an informal, private forum on problems of farm relief.

Reviewing his own recent experience and decisions, Bell pointed out that the power of the buying public had become supreme in establishing commodity prices, at least in the realm of wheat products. If they wished to revolt against the price of a particular commodity, buyers had only to start using other commodities. The result inevitably had been that "lower types of wheat" had begun to claim an increased share of the business. Such considerations must be taken into account in all future legislation affecting farm products.

Dr. Taylor, who as impersonal analyst also believed in the necessity of finding new ways to distribute food supplies more efficiently and cheaply, had prepared the way for a meeting between Bell and Bishop of the Sperry interests. At the first session the three men agreed that consolidation was essential, because only by unified action could millers regain a favorable bargaining position. Since there was need of less, rather than more, milling capacity, new adjustments must be made by merging facilities already in existence. Bishop already had done much work in that direction, consolidating useful mills and eliminating submarginal properties. As president of the Sperry Flour Company he had been quite frankly engaged in the task of making it ready for sale and, though the opportunity had come a little earlier than he had anticipated, he was nonetheless ready to meet it.

Again a team — Davis, Bullis, and McMillan of Minneapolis and Vought of New York — went to San Francisco to negotiate with Bishop and his associates. After a ten-day session, agreement was finally reached in February 1929. The Sperry Flour Company of California had, at the time of its acquisition by General Mills, capital stock of $9,000,000 of which 36,000 shares of preferred and 54,000 of common were outstanding. In payment for its assets, the absorbing corporation issued 27,000 shares of its 6 per cent cumulative preferred stock and 31,765 of common. It paid, in addition, $3,000,000 for "retirement by calling for redemption" of the 7 per cent preferred stock of the old company. A further cash payment was made of a little more than $1,000,000 for income tax indebtedness.

Having fulfilled the essential design of General Mills by drawing into a cooperative enterprise a group of mills in the Southwest and another scattered along the Pacific Coast from Seattle to Los Angeles, with a total daily capacity of 86,000 barrels, Bell was ready to take thought for integration having to do with the by-products of milling. For almost as long as the "formula-feed" business had existed, an argument had gone doggedly on about its place in the strategy of selling. This kind of operation, said its adherents, could not be used simply as a prop to flour. If it were not handled by specialists, it would sicken and serve no one well. Purists of the flour tradition retorted that "commercial feed departments must not be allowed to run loose." Above all they must not "interfere" with flour accounts. In the opinion of such men, formula feed must be content to be forever flour's humble brother. Bell, listening impatiently to this unending wrangle, liked to shock his associates by speaking out loud and clear saying: "I look on flour as an adjunct of the feed business."

With the formation of General Mills he began to look for a high-grade formula-feed business to fill out the pattern of a well-rounded enterprise. A month after agreement with Sperry had been reached, negotiations were begun with the Larrowe Milling Company. Larrowe and his younger partner, Searle Mowat, had known the Washburn Crosby Company well and done much business with its representatives. On one of his routine visits to Minneapolis, Mowat was urged to see Bell, who outlined his plans and suggested the possibility of a merger. Mowat was quick to appreciate the advantages that such a combine of forces would give. Its size alone would offer both protection and opportunity. Its strategic position in relation to markets would assure the availability of all the raw materials the Larrowe Company needed. Mowat went home to Detroit, impressed but cautious, to discuss the prospect with Larrowe.

During the past half-dozen years Larrowe had been led by his scientific curiosity into many adventures in subsidization. He had backed one enterprise in particular which had led toward a blind alley where threats of bankruptcy lurked. Assuming all financial responsibility for the initial mistake, he had wrenched the venture out of its difficulties and continued his experiments until the enterprise turned the corner and in the end made a comfortable fortune. But the practice of bringing off small miracles had tired him and he was ready to relinquish his tasks

149

a little at a time. Even the stock of his central organization, the Larrowe Milling Company, which he had kept almost entirely to himself, was put on the market. These symptoms of a readiness to retire brought him many offers during the months when reorganizations were the vogue. He had five such offers before him from various underwriting firms at the very moment when Mowat returned from Minneapolis with the suggestion that a merger with General Mills might be the most profitable move of all.

Larrowe hesitated. This man who had never touched anything that did not eventually prosper was haunted, as his partner Mowat once observed, by the fear of ending his life in penury. At the prospect of relinquishing firm hold on his most successful venture he was "blown out of shape." Still he began to sort through the possibilities with a kind of resentful resolution. Several went into the discard because Larrowe saw no point in combining with other feed manufacturers. This might well be to multiply problems without finding the protection to one's interests that only an organization with diversified interests could ensure. A merger with General Mills did offer that kind of insurance. Larrowe contemplated half-eagerly, half-doubtfully, the outlook of dominating the formula-feed world from the vantage point offered by a large organization.

Negotiations made halting progress. Frank Henry of Buffalo went to Detroit to present his credentials as a long-time representative of the Washburn Crosby Company and one who had profited greatly by its readiness to follow new leads and take new ground. Bullis, whom Larrowe found to be a perfect kindred spirit of enterprise, once more unpacked his bags of figures. An over-all price was agreed upon; differences of detail melted away one by one. And still Larrowe hesitated.

Finally, he turned to his partner with the impatience of a man who was unused to indecision and disliked it in himself more than he had disliked it in anyone else. "Mowat," he said, "you'll be the one to live with it. You decide."

Mowat was helped to reach his decision by the outcome of a conference in Chicago with Bell and Henry at which a representative of the First National Bank was also present. There Mowat made the suggestion that what the formula-feed business needed most was "to control a certain number of retail outlets." Warming to his theme he pointed out that it was often necessary, in order to sell one's product, to do most of the retailer's work for him, often even against his will. Why not, therefore, become the retailer oneself? A great merchandising organization should have enough farm stores to ensure its prosperity.

"I believe in retail stores," Bell said. Then turning to the banker he asked: "What about it? If we decide to expand can we have $10,000,00?"

"Mr. Bell, the banker answered, "you can have $10,000,000 or $50,000,000."

This prospect was irresistible to Mowat. "We have no choice but to join up," he told Larrowe.

Negotiators had agreed that the assets of the Larrowe Milling Company were worth 26,000 shares of General Mills preferred and 61,176 shares of common stock. But to speed up Larrowe's cautious processes, the offer was changed to $6,511,008 cash, plus 6308 shares of preferred and 7900 shares of common stock.

The design was now complete. General Mills, not yet an operating, but simply a holding company, kept the original names of the associated companies and, in theory, these subsidiaries were autonomous. Each had as its own president a man who had long been identified with the original companies. C. C. Bovey became president of the Washburn Crosby Company, Inc., of Minneapolis; Frank Henry of the Washburn Crosby Company of Buffalo; J. W. Sherwood of the Royal Milling Company. In the Southwest Roger Hurd continued to be president of the Red Star Milling Company at Wichita, Kansas; Karl Humphrey moved for a time into the presidency of the Oklahoma City Mill and Elevator Company; T. C. Thatcher retained his sturdy hold on the activities of the Wichita Mill and Elevator Company at Wichita Falls, Texas. On the West Coast, Roy Bishop stayed on, a little restively, as president of the Sperry Flour Company.

The old "team" of the Washburn Crosby Company supplied the chief officers of General Mills, Inc.: Bell, as president; Franklin Crosby, vice president; Davis, vice president and treasurer; McMillan, vice president; Bullis, secretary and comptroller.

Within five months of coming to be, General Mills had accomplished these campaigns of reorganization for efficiency to which Bell's will was dedicated. By consolidating operations and getting rid of unneeded facilities the corporation emerged in trim condition, ready for action. It

151

had twenty-seven associated operating companies in sixteen states. Of these units, seventeen were engaged in milling operations, the others in buying and storing grain and in merchandising products. Total daily productive capacity was fixed at 81,700 barrels of flour including bread wheat, durum wheat, rye, and corn; 5950 tons of commercial feeds; and 720,000 pounds of other cereal products. The total terminal and mill elevator storage capacity was 36,424,000 bushels, with 10,498,000 additional storage capacity at 212 country stations. General Mills had become the largest miller in the world.

Since "efficiency" and "economy" were the two favorite bywords of this giant, "organization" had quickly to become a third. In 1928 and during the first decade of the corporation's life the broad supporting principle of operation was that the various units would get on with the business of producing things to sell while the central company would devote itself to the task of integrating the processes of advertising and selling those products on a national scale. Bell himself once outlined the program in these words:

"Our associates can be trusted for products; we in General Mills are selling results rather than products. Our primary functions are merchandising and advertising; on one side we act as a sales agency for wheat farmers and on the other side as a service agency for our customers — the grocers, bakers and housewives of the nation. None of these groups is interested in flour as such, but only in what flour will do for them and theirs. The grocer wants turnover, goods that will sell. The baker wants flour which will give results pleasing to his customers. The housewife wants the utmost in nutrition and tasty diet for her family. Our job isn't finished when flour is sold but rather only when it is consumed; consequently, we maintain a continuous drive to get the flour out of the grocer's stock and the baker's bins and off the kitchen shelves to the table in forms appealing to the appetite. To do this efficiently, at a low cost, and to the general satisfaction of the consuming public, requires a large organization because the United States is a tremendous market. General Mills limits itself to those functions which have a national aspect, but even those functions are constantly subject to review by the men in the field who are making and selling our products. Our aim is to give the maximum of help to our associates with the minimum of interference."

On this theory General Mills assumed responsibility for administrative functions of broad scope. The central company, from the beginning, managed the financial transactions of the corporation, paid national taxes, handled insurance programs, and kept corporate records. It was the agency through which funds were borrowed for the use of the associate companies in its purchases of raw materials. Because General Mills was a big borrower, with an enviable reputation among bankers, it received credit at lower rates than would have been available to any of its units in their comparatively small operations covering restricted districts. This, of course, was one of the great services that the central organization was able to contribute.

However, in the earlier phase of operation each of the associate companies had its own profit-and-loss system, did its own buying of wheat, maintained its own hedge, and made its own requests for loans from the general treasury to conduct its market operations.

Another function named by Bell in the early outline of organization, advertising, was managed from the beginning out of the central headquarters. The logic here, too, was obvious, for there were savings to be made by placing contracts on a national basis. Various service functions — research, work on nutrition programs, design of sales programs, assistance to bakers — were also centered in Minneapolis as a clearinghouse for ideas that might contribute to the good of each of the units.

These contributions to the "idea in action" constituted the maximum of help that Bell had said General Mills wished to give its associates. In this economic federation the purpose of the central government was to coordinate the activities of the member units. Initiative remained with the associate company whose executives were responsible for sales and for the success of effort in every branch. The central staff originated ideas but did not impose them arbitrarily upon the president of the unit in the field. It was the latter's privilege to accept or to reject the suggestion. Similarly, over-all responsibility for operating policy was reposed in a General Operating Board made up of sixteen representatives of the associate companies. In the beginning, and for many years after, the elder statesman of the company, Frank Henry of Buffalo, was chairman of this administrative body with Bullis as secretary. He and his board received suggestions, gave each a proper hearing, and perfected any plan for presentation to the Executive Committee of General Mills, which in turn presented it to the Board of Directors. It was Bell's belief that a new idea should begin at the bottom and work its way to the top, as many a well-disciplined executive had done in the pioneer days of enterprise.

Later years were to see significant modifications of this pattern. A search for the perfect balance of authority between the forces that favor centralization and those that favor decentralization went on inevitably, as in any large corporation, through many changes. But as Bell observed a few years after the formation of General Mills: "So far this plan has worked excellently, during bad years as well as good. Under it earnings have been stable and our progress steady."

The miracle was that this should have been so from the beginning. For only a little more than a year after its debut, the new corporation faced the crisis of world-wide depression. The 1929 stock market collapse brought down many institutions that had seemed to be solid and indestructible. A kind of affinity with disintegration gave the economic life of the 1930s its dreary unity of tone. Yet in this time of "change and decay" General Mills managed to change and grow.

11

"Breakfast of Champions"

THE STORY OF WHEATIES

T H E steady progress of General Mills through the early 1930s, a period that was for American industry as a whole one of violent stress and distress, may be attributed in part to its own faith in a program of diversification. As partner to flour there must, Bell had always felt, be other products, particularly ones that explored further the infinite resources of the wheat berry. He was still not ready to manufacture anything resembling those locomotives which he had said General Mills must be free to make if it wished to do so. But he had provided himself with other foods to sell, ones whose popularity made them the most reliable of assets in the days of the depression.

It was by no means easy to establish these new products in a highly competitive market. The story of the development of Wheaties offers an illustration of the patience, the thoroughness, the unwavering confidence in a plan which are needed to capture a public for any new commodity.

The account begins with an experiment that was almost literally dropped in Bell's lap in 1921 just at the moment when he was looking for "a line of specialties with which to supplement staples." There came to him one day the legal representative of a Minneapolis theorist of diet who, between bouts of putting the obese and lazy through physical exercises and Turkish baths, had brooded a little angrily about the need of bulk in human food. Neither of these requirements was adequately satisfied, he believed, by prevailing habits of the table. Bran, in his opinion, was the ideal disciplinarian of the digestive tracts. His lawyer

155

had secured a patent on a process for making bran flakes and he asked the Washburn Crosby Company to interest itself in producing them commercially. Bell agreed to try to develop the process and to provide quarters in the mill for experimentation with methods suitable to large-scale production.

The discovery of the bran flakes had been completely accidental. The health clinician, in mixing up morning gruel for patients, had spattered a few drops on the hot stove where they had taken the form of thin, round wafers. They seemed crisp and tasty; he had made more by dropping his bran gruel on a griddle. He prepared at the Washburn Crosby mill to proceed in much the same way and his fondest desires seemed to be satisfied when he was provided with mixing bowls and a hot plate as his entire laboratory equipment.

George Cormack, long Washburn Crosby's head miller with whom, as Bell once said, his job was not a profession but a passion, watched these amateur efforts in his plant with the doubt and distaste of a practical man. Difficulties immediately presented themselves as he had known they would. The bran-flake man proved to be unstable and his product even more so. The flat discs, when tumbled about in a package, settled to the bottom and "formed a very small volume in the package itself." They tended also to crumble into powder and nothing that anyone was inspired to do could make them less friable.

The prospect of a new food faded and the creator went back to his Turkish baths and the stubborn patients who refused to eat bran. The Washburn Crosby Company had invested months in the experiment, and, despite the simplicity of the equipment, a considerable amount of money. Something had to be salvaged from the effort and it was George Cormack who managed to do so.

The idea of a flake lodged in his mind. This, of course, belonged legally to anyone who had the imagination and the skill to discipline it into something tangible (in this instance, edible) and in 1924 Cormack received Bell's ready permission to start all over again with an experiment of his own.

He collected samples of thirty-six different varieties of wheat from every growing area and tested them for responsiveness to treatment. His equipment, considerably more complicated than that of the bran-man, was still simple enough. It consisted of an obsolete pair of rolls, a retired wheat steamer, a pressure cooker, and an electric oven. The wheat was tempered, steamed, and cracked, then put into the pressure cooker after it had been exposed to the benign influences of syrup, sugar, and salt. The cooked product was spread on boards that the flakes might be separated from one another. These were passed through rolls to make them as flat and thin as possible and, finally, they were put into the electric oven for drying. The first batch of wheat flakes was ceremoniously served up for the Board of Directors of the Washburn Crosby Company. From their headquarters a few blocks away they trooped down to the C mill as though for an unveiling and when they had tasted the new product they agreed that George Cormack's passion for milling had never served him better. The wheat flakes were good.

A sample of the first batch was sealed and preserved as a master model. The first run of the commercial product matched it in quality and the ready-to-eat cereal was ready for the market in November 1924. It needed only "a local habitation and a name." The home was found in the plant at Chicago built especially for the manufacture of packaged foods and equipped with heavy duty flaking rolls, revolving gas ovens, and maturing tanks.

The name was presently provided, too. A contest held among employees, their wives, and husbands, was won by Jane Bausman, wife of R. F. Bausman, the company's New York authority on the export market. She was the first person to say "Wheaties," knowing that nothing endears a man, an institution, or a thing to the American heart quite so surely as does a diminutive nickname. ("Teddy" for Roosevelt; the "movies" for moving pictures; "Wheaties" for a new adventure of the breakfast table.) It was her understanding of the native love of casualness which told Mrs. Bausman at a glance that these wheat flakes were "Wheaties." She was right as James Thurber once commented in one of the essays of his volume *The Beast in Me.* "Wheaties," he said, in a discussion of the cereal's contribution to the history of radio advertising, "became a household word."

But household words do not get about until someone takes the trouble to give them circulation. The new product was introduced a little tentatively first in the territory near its place of manufacture — the Illinois towns of Peoria, Danville, and Joliet. There was little organized sales effort on its behalf. Indeed, it even met with a certain amount of discreet sabotage within the organization from salesmen who felt that they already had quite enough to peddle.

"Breakfast of Champions"

It was at this moment that Donald Davis took a hand. He had always been acutely aware of the customer not as a unit in a sales report but as a human being with needs to be satisfied and tastes to be pleased. He had gone about the study of this individual with characteristic detachment and thoroughness. To him, every problem, even one involving the whims of customers, was an engineering problem. A colleague once said of him, half in admiration, half in irritation: "He is always eager to reduce policy to exact black and white terms." Again, it was the engineer's faith in specifications that guided him, as merchandiser, and he rejected the idea that there was anything unknowable, or mystic, about markets, tastes, or public response to a promotion program.

Davis' way of finding out what housewives wanted in his own field of service was simple and direct: he asked them by the thousands what they liked and what they did not like. He asked them what they wanted in a food product, what appealed to them in the way of household advice, what newspapers and magazines they read. He did this by sending out survey crews to look into typical homes in every corner of America, to ring doorbells, to get interviews. He communicated with America through telephone calls and questionnaires. His salesmen were trained to act as polite sleuths, observing, gathering data, making reports. Out of all this precise information there was assembled a portrait of the housewife in America, one that revealed everything Davis needed to know.

One thing that he learned from these excursions into the home life of his customers was that they liked to be spoken to directly, frequently, and intimately where matters of food were concerned. With this awareness in mind, he appeared at his office one day with a new and, as some of his associates thought, staggering proposal for promotion. "Let's walk around the idea," Davis frequently said when other people suggested audacities. The hint of leisureliness was characteristic of him, for he seemed never to hurry even when he was going forward most resolutely. But he circulated around this particular idea in a high-powered vehicle dragging not only his own company but the whole of the community at his wheels. His idea was to buy and operate a radio station.

A suggestion the wisdom of which seems self-evident today struck many in the early 1920s as being fantastic. People who had watched their young sons putting together strange little gadgets that they called crystal sets, and who remembered how those hypnotized boys had sat for

158

hours, crowned with earphones, looking rapt and withdrawn as though they had found a short cut to nirvana, were sure that radio would never be anything but a toy for children or a hobby for cranks. The fact, as Davis foresaw, was that this toy was to wield the most tremendous power in all the history of organized communication. He was determined to make his company a pioneer in the new field.

There was plenty of groundwork still to be done even though Minnesota had taken an early lead in radio's development. The experiments of C. L. Jansky, Jr., an electrical engineer of the University of Minnesota, made in 1920 and 1921, had occurred simultaneously with the earliest efforts of eastern pioneers. Various enterprising men and business firms had followed his lead and in the years 1923 and 1924 several small stations began to speak to the wide midwestern area. One of the most ambitious of these was station WLAG, the "Call of the North," operated by the *Minneapolis Journal*. But the audience of even this struggling candidate for attention was small and scattered. One by one the other midwestern pioneers of radio gave up. All, that is, except the University of Minnesota station WLB and Donald Davis.

At the moment when station WLAG was about to utter its last gasp, Davis called together a group of men representing the civic agencies of Minneapolis and St. Paul and offered to advance money with which to buy the broadcasting equipment. He suggested further that his company might buy and install the latest apparatus to strengthen the station's voice and would pay half of the cost of operation if the two cities would assume, through their official organizations, responsibility for the other half.

The proposal was accepted and instead of being fatally stricken, the station rose strengthened and renewed. Its new call letters were WCCO, initials that stood for Washburn Crosby Company. Its debut occurred on September 1, 1924. Seven months later WCCO made history in the Midwest by using its new 5000-watt voice to broadcast the inauguration ceremonies that sent Calvin Coolidge back to the White House.

Meanwhile the history of Wheaties had paralleled the history of radio itself. The virtues of both were presently to become known to gratified millions but for the moment the public of each was still small, too small to provide a profitable market for a ready-to-eat cereal. Washburn Crosby salesmen were still unpersuaded and through every conference there ran a leitmotiv of doom gathering Wagnerian volume as supply continued to run far ahead of demand. Executives, too, began to lose faith. It was no one's idea to manufacture Wheaties in the strictest confidence but the means had not yet been found of spreading what Bell, Davis, and other enthusiasts considered to be the good news about them. America went on unconcernedly eating oats and corn for breakfast despite the fact that wheat was actually the country's favorite grain.

Late in 1926 Davis grew tired of this indecisive struggle between believers and doubters. He called in the manager of WCCO and suggested making a special radio campaign for Wheaties. The station had been used continuously, of course, to present the Washburn Crosby merchandising program. Now Davis wanted to make a specific test to "find out what that radio station of ours is good for."

He spoke to a sympathetic ear. Earl Gammons, who had lately succeeded Henry Adams Bellows, first manager of the station, had previously been editor of the Washburn Crosby Company's house organ, the *Eventually News*. As a lover of innovation and an experienced newsman, Gammons was pleased with an opportunity to explore the potentialities of the new medium.

What he offered was the first "singing commercial," an appeal on behalf of Wheaties that seems a model of decorum, courtesy, and effectiveness. The Wheaties song did not threaten, intimidate, whisper to the snob, urge conspicuous waste, or commit any of the offenses against taste or truth of which many a later contribution to the literature has been guilty. It simply put a sensible suggestion before the public:

> Have you tried Wheaties?
> They're whole wheat with all of the bran.
> Won't you try Wheaties?
> For wheat is the best food of man.

The popular tune to which the commercial was set had as its original title, "She's a Jazz Baby." Provocative as this theme may be considered to be, the melody itself was not of the frenetic sort loved in the tension-conscious 1920s. Rather it was gentle, reflective, and pleasantly cajoling. The words "tried" and "try" which replaced the word "jazz" in the first and third lines of the quatrain quoted were sung on a lingeringly persuasive note: "tr-r-ried" and "tr-r-r-y."

This innovation was presented first in the mellow mood of the Christmas season, on Christmas Eve in fact. The singers were members of a male quartet, men who had a variety of daytime jobs but who liked to

160

sing and were quite willing to offer half-hour programs for a grand total of $24 a performance, once each week. There were those who considered such an expenditure reckless extravagance but, in that simple time before radio fees had reached high into the thousands for single performances, it was thought to be "not too much if it worked."

And it did work. But this was not immediately apparent. In 1929, a year after the formation of General Mills, Wheaties was still in trouble as a product seeking national distribution. At a session of the Operating Board, called in August to decide what the future of the product would be (indeed whether or not it would have a future of any kind), Frank Henry pointed out that sales were falling — from 105,000 cases in 1927 to 53,000 in 1929. The liveliness of other products — Gold Medal Flour itself and Gold Medal Cake Flour — seemed to some observers to be threatened by having a laggard at their heels. Wheaties, the most audacious of the rebels protested, dragged its fellow commodities down.

It was a moment of critical decision, for to have discarded Wheaties would have been a blow to the diversification program. The consensus was strong that five years of exploitation were enough to test the value of a product. Though there had been no special sales force for Wheaties, it should by now have made its way. Wheaties seemed about to be voted out of existence.

Then, with something of the sensational effect of a last-minute rescue in the movies, a champion of Wheaties appeared — Samuel Chester Gale of the Advertising Department.

This man believed in his profession with the zest of a creative intelligence and with the disciplined outlook of an unusual background. He came justly by originality of mind. His father, Harlow Gale, trained in Germany, was an early exponent of the laboratory method in psychology. The curious rhyming of family interests is reflected in the fact that the elder Gale was author of a study called *The Psychology of Advertising*, written long before the American public had become aware that it was in the grip of the one or that it was deeply influenced by the other.

On James Ford Bell's team of young executives Sam Gale has played a significant part. He may be said to embody and to personify that stanch and sensible idealism in the development of "services of worth to the American people" which Bell himself has insisted must be the goal of General Mills. This small dynamo, standing five feet six inches high, had demonstrated the positiveness of this idealism many times over before his professional career began. He interrupted his college career at the University of Minnesota to go, in 1916, with the National Guard to the border during the Mexican incident. After taking his degree with honors in organic chemistry and economics, he went straight into World War I and, serving as a lieutenant on the Meuse-Argonne front, he was wounded and gassed.

His debut as an advertising expert gave him an opportunity to formulate his private principles into a professional code by which he himself has lived steadfastly and which has been borrowed widely throughout industry. If advertising was to serve a positive set of values, he pointed out, copy must satisfy three tests: first, it must be truthful, informative, educational; second, it must be based on the concept of service; third, it must be designed to expand markets rather than to snatch business away from competitors.

So, in this moment of need, Gale brought his gift of insight and his belief in advertising to the service of Wheaties. It was true, he told that Operating Board at its decisive meeting, that national distribution had been limited to 53,000 cases. But a fact worth noticing was that of that number 30,000 cases had been delivered in the area of Minneapolis and St. Paul. Had a special sales campaign been made in this region? No. What was the difference between the Twin City territory and other territories? Only the existence of station WCCO and the steady, consistent advertising by the Wheaties quartet over a period of three years. This had been the only special advertising effort but it had had the effect of persuading people actually to "try Wheaties." Once the trial had been made, the cereal found its own way into favor. "I believe," Gale said, "that if the use of radio were extended to other territories these figures would be duplicated and that Wheaties need not be dropped."

His judgment prevailed and within six weeks the Operating Board, already encouraged by a new prospect of prosperity, created a Package Foods Division to further the interests of Gold Medal Flour and Wheaties.

Chosen to head it was Walter Barry. If he and General Mills could have known what was presently in store for the American economy they might not have decided upon this particular moment to launch a new project. But they were committed to expansion in the early fall of 1929 and there was no turning back even when events took their formidable turn. As Barry, a living monument to the salesman's endurance, once observed: "All in one week in October 1929, I got a new job, I got married, and the stock market crashed."

Drawing heavily upon his Irish gift of adaptability, Barry invented new campaigns daily. He had about him "a group of lively youngsters" who, as one of them, Raymond L. Brang, once said, "believed intensely in each other." The new division thrived and Wheaties shared in the general well-being.

The problem that Barry faced was still that of putting a clear awareness of the quality of his products before a public to whose eyes, ears, and sensibilities constant appeals were being made by the owners of other products. It was, in short, a merchandising task. And now everyone was persuaded that radio advertising must be broadly extended. The Wheaties quartet received for its early missionary work the highest accolade in the gift of radio: it was put on a coast to coast hookup, the first of half-hour programs of ballads and folk songs to be created by the newly formed Columbia Broadcasting System. The quartet had now become the Gold Medal Fast Freight, complete with fireman (first tenor), brakeman (second tenor), conductor (baritone), and engineer (bass). Weekly, the Fast Freight made its way, under the stimulus of appropriate music, to the various communities of the Wheaties market: "Shuffle Off to Buffalo," "Chicago, Chicago, It's a Wonderful Town." The movement in Wheaties stepped up its tempo commercially in pace with sprightly tunes.

A striking development occurred a year later with the debut of the Skippy program. This was of significance both to the shaping of radio tradition and to the formulation of new merchandising methods. It was not, therefore, lacking in significance as an item in the social history of the United States. This was the first well-planned effort to speak directly to the child as the ultimate consumer of a ready-to-eat cereal, to create a child bloc among customers. Previously the Wheaties appeal, as it emerged out of advertising copy printed in the *Saturday Evening Post* and others of the national magazines, was addressed to adults. Recurring themes were, first, the wholesome wholeness of the wheat in Wheaties, second, the attractiveness of the product ("Gay as a French confection"), and finally, a blend of the two ("Eat Whole Wheat This Alluring Way"). Adults were addressed also as parents but the image of the mother in the advertising writer's mind was obviously that of dictator of the child's

163

tastes. ("Make Your Child Love Whole Wheat," "It's Worth Anything a Mother Could Pay But It Costs You 5 Cents Extra a Week.")

Presently it became clear that if the parent was only the penultimate consumer and the child himself must finally be won, then it would be well to speak to him directly. After months of consultation General Mills found a way of doing so. Through his comic strip "Skippy," Percy Crosby was already speaking to young Americans by the millions. This widely syndicated newspaper feature was a favorite with Donald Davis himself. He knew that it was, at the moment, contributing as much as any one influence to the mores of preadolescents. An astonishing number of men, known to their intimates as Skippy — or still more strenuously as Skip — lately reached legal age in this country; their company rivals in size the groups of men who have matured as "Bud," "Junior," "Sonny," or under any of the other amiable shadows of parental fatuity. This is cited merely as evidence of the power once wielded by the very name. In mass appeal it must greatly have exceeded that exercised by Mark Twain through Tom Sawyer, or by Booth Tarkington through Willie Baxter. Tastes in adventure, idiom, humor, and dress were under the virtual dictatorship of Percy Crosby for one crowded hour.

It was Frank Hummert, a member of the Chicago advertising firm of Blackett-Sample-Hummert, who pointed out to General Mills the desirability of having Skippy dictate also the taste in breakfast food of his many namesakes. To introduce him as a figure in the new medium of entertainment, Hummert chose a fabulous man of the writing world, Robert Andrews. This phenomenon of energy, lately graduated from the University of Minnesota, had, as a cub reporter on the *Minneapolis Journal*, written his way through the assignments of three or four men daily and then pleaded with his city editor for more. Proceeding to Chicago and the *Daily News* he had once made a bet that he could produce a full-length novel in a week, performing his usual stint as reporter at the same time. He had won the bet and his newspaper had been glad to print the result serially. The success of the story had precipitated Andrews into radio work. During the next few years, this midwestern equivalent of Dumas the father and Dumas the son combined had operated a busy fiction mill (capacity: 1,000,000 words a year), producing highly marketable goods in the form of radio scripts, moving picture scenarios, and novels.

Andrews promptly got Skippy under the relaxed and friendly discipline of his own still boyish imagination. In Skippy's name he organized a secret-society-of-the-air to all the rights of which listeners were entitled upon payment of a modest number of box tops. Members became possessors of the key to a code which Andrews had had the deftness to lift from Edgar Allan Poe's early detective story, "The Gold Bug," and also of a secret grip. All the second-string Skippys from Portland, Maine, to La Jolla, California, were extremely happy and the sales of Wheaties climbed from a million and a quarter cases in the crop year of 1931–32 to more than a million and a half in the crop year of 1932–33.

A new and important trend in merchandising had been clarified. The "avenue to the home" of which Bell had always made so much in his discussions of service had been pushed beyond the goal that once had seemed ultimate: the housewife's kitchen. Through radio it had penetrated into the nursery where so often the tastes of the family are actually shaped by the most powerful of dictators, the housewife's adored children.

The young having been captured securely by the excitement of the Skippy program, General Mills undertook to seize the lateral ground of battle still occupied by parents. Advertising copy was once more addressed to them, but with a difference of tone. Percy Crosby himself provided appropriate drawings of Skippy to illustrate such appealing legends as "No More Arguments at Breakfast." These, of course, were well designed to pluck up the flagging spirit of the average mother and to send her scurrying to the nearest store for a package of Wheaties. The new approach was supported by the most powerfully persuasive of statements about the product itself: "Get the whole wheat in all the marvelous, energy-giving, body-building elements."

But not all the parents were won. The sort of earnest observer who discovers periodically that the fairy stories of Grimm are certain to induce neuroses and that *Treasure Island* displays an unfortunate preoccupation with violence made objection to the very features of the Skippy program that the exuberant young liked best. The suggestion that life holds the threat of danger was not unwelcome to the listeners for whom Andrews intended his tales, but it shocked those who feel that the natural taste of the child for rugged events should be drugged with discreet doses of paregoric in fiction form. Andrews bravely tried to satisfy the protests of a handful of complainers by changing the story line. To do so and keep pace with the program he once had to produce twenty-five

165

scripts in a single day. Hummert, in an effort to clear his client, Skippy, called in a battery of psychologists who testified in favor of living dangerously and made sharp objections of their own to the influences in American life that tend to coddle the young in tender lies.

But in Gale's, and any realistic, advertising code it is unwise to try to browbeat when the real intention is to woo. General Mills refused to force *Skippy* on a reluctant group no matter how small its minority might be. The program was canceled in favor of another, *Jack Armstrong, All-American Boy.* Andrews moved readily over into the new environment as creator of the new hero and author of the first scripts celebrating his spotless adventures. Meanwhile, the irrepressibility of the young writer had virtually forced him to find outlet in still another series. For another General Mills product, he created the first of those studies in human relations to which the descriptive phrase "soap opera" so closely adheres. The designation "cereal opera" would have reflected the social history of radio more accurately, for General Mills had pioneered indefatigably in the development of the new form. Andrews' *Betty and Bob* established the classic pattern for the many dramatic interpretations of domestic life which have placed the stubborn "himness" of him in sprightly contrast to the sly, whimsical, undefeated "herness" of her. The program later reverted to Wheaties in recognition of a natural affinity between domesticity and breakfast cereals.

With *Jack Armstrong* General Mills was determined that there should be no tactical false turns. The program was the company's own. Problems of sensibility in authors had persuaded General Mills, for the moment, that a central point of strategy in building up radio as an avenue into the home was to have the right to control the whole thoroughfare out of the central office. Further, the program must be kept innocent of sophistication. As a name for the young hero who supplanted Skippy the advertising agency offered "Red Jones." Sam Gale tried the nickname on his own private indicator of responses and found it wanting. "Red" might identify any sort of boy from an eccentric to a juvenile delinquent; what was needed, Gale said, was a name that would somehow suggest courage, resourcefulness, ambition, and imagination. Jack Armstrong he became, named by Gale for a boy whom he had known as a young neighbor in Minneapolis.

(A succession of minor problems took shape out of this circumstance. The real Jack Armstrong had sometimes to accept long-distance telephone calls — once with the charges reversed — from disciples of the radio character. More serious was the episode in which the post office in a rare moment of abstractedness delivered to General Mills an important letter which offered the real Jack Armstrong a job. The latter was not pleased when the letter reached him after the job had gone to someone else. He was mollified only when a better job presently came to him.)

Jack Armstrong, all-American boy, had a long and honorable history before he passed finally into Valhalla, Radio Division. His interests were of an appropriate virility, but the story line was kept free of entanglements such as had tripped up Skippy. Psychoanalysts were summoned as consultants to guide him wisely through the mazes of adolescence. A succession of able writers helped him to mature sensibly until he emerged as a young scientist with a genuinely creative turn of mind. Indeed, Jack Armstrong of the air managed during World War II to anticipate so many advances in the science of weapons that the United States government felt obliged, finally, to step in for security reasons and censor the program.

In the early days the temperament of Jack Armstrong had been kept to a kind of boiling point of energy and of boyish absorption in projects. This gave General Mills an opportunity to build up sales by the use of premiums. Many of them were inspired selections which added a certain solid worth to the charm that any gadget holds for the very young. Such, for example, was the Explorer Telescope which went out to all Jack Armstrong admirers and which encouraged in many of them an interest in nature lore. Later, when Jack Armstrong was allowed to grow up with the years, he lost the designation "all-American boy," and became the dignified Armstrong of the SBI, the initials of which stood for an imaginary but plausible Scientific Bureau of Investigation. More than ever his followers were encouraged to develop sober interests.

The importance of the Armstrong story is simply that it helped to formulate a new technique in merchandising. This was to use a mass medium of entertainment to reach and not so much capture as enrapture inescapably a quite new group of customers.

With the audience of women and the audience of children brought successfully to attention for Wheaties, General Mills began a roundup of the third important section of the population. There seemed to be no valid reason why men, too, should not be enrolled among lovers of a substantial breakfast. But if the traditional love of ham and eggs was to be challenged on behalf of Wheaties, then a special appeal must be made to masculine imagination. Gale, who had made a habit of defying convention in the choice of advertising method, decided once more to try something entirely new. He persuaded General Mills to sponsor the broadcasts of local baseball games.

Nothing in the history of merchandising more brilliantly dramatizes the possibility of summoning customers out of limbo by an appropriate appeal than does the record of the baseball broadcasts for Wheaties. Radio's "avenue to the home" sought out men and boys sitting together in the afternoon before the loud-speaker. The responsive mood thus induced proved to be far more effective than anyone had dared to hope. Experts had once suggested that the ceiling for sales of Wheaties would undoubtedly be 1,500,000 cases a year. Enthusiasm for baseball and Wheaties, in happy combination, blew this appraisal sky-high and in the late 1930s sales tripled that figure.

Simply to have sponsored a baseball broadcast would not have accomplished this result even when the coverage of games was extended to 67 stations. A neat and unforgettable verbalization was needed to link sport and Wheaties inseparably so that, in the minds of devotees, a home run should somehow seem to be an eloquent endorsement of a General Mills product. A witty and discerning man, Knox Reeves, head of one of the advertising agencies used by General Mills, supplied precisely the right words. Adept at what may be called the profane poetry of the trade, Reeves knew that an advertising slogan, though it unlocks no mystery as real poetry may be expected to do, still shares with true art the attribute of epitomizing drama in a phrase resonant with meaning. He invented such a phrase: "Breakfast of Champions."

It came to him, according to legend, one day when a representative of the ballpark arrived in his office to say that as sponsor of the broadcasts, General Mills was entitled to a sign in full view of the grandstand. What was to be painted on it? the ballpark manager wanted to know. Without a moment's thought, but apparently under the prompting of an unconscious mind that had been brooding for a long time about the problem, Reeves wrote out the evocative declaration. Boys by the millions were to repeat it with awe in the next few years. Indeed, testimony to its aptness had been gathered in abundance before the General Mills officials left the ballpark on the first day when the sign went up. Gale heard many a man, as well as many a boy, saying "Breakfast of champions" over and over again as though it were some kind of incantation to the goddess of health.

Certainly the slogan served. The powerful names of the moment in boxing, swimming, tennis — Dempsey, Weissmuller, Budge — appeared in advertisements as witnesses to its truth and the sale of Wheaties soared. The great witnesses have continued to appear on the Wheaties box ever since.

The love affair between Wheaties and the public was endorsed by the sober and reflective approval of the American Medical Association. In 1933 Gale won the right for Wheaties to wear the seal of acceptance of the Association's Council on Foods. A few years later General Mills made a large investment in a new technique for incorporating into Wheaties all the virtue in vitamins contained in the natural berry. With this improvement Wheaties went on the preferred list of cereals prepared by the Council on Foods.

The product had gone long since on the preferred list of buyers. In November 1941, figures for Wheaties had climbed to a new high, claiming 12 per cent of the United States cereal market and drawing General Mills close to the top of the class in cereal business. (Only one well-entrenched manufacturer with a long history in the enterprise surpassed its total sales in this field.) Nothing exceeded Wheaties sales, first among cereals in dollar volume according to an impartial survey made in 1939 by a national market research organization. As Bell had predicted they would do, "the sensitive little nerves that fringe the tongue" had carried their "message from the human tongue to the human pocket book" and Wheaties had profited accordingly.

And the new product had justified, too, the faith of Donald Davis, Walter Barry, and Sam Gale in new advertising methods which made the air resound with their enthusiasm. Wheaties and radio had grown up together.

12

First Lady of Food

THE LIFE AND TIMES OF BETTY CROCKER

IT WAS the amusing and original discovery of J. S. Bell that advertising was as old as the Egyptian monuments on which kings and queens carved testimonials to themselves. As master merchandiser he was well aware that the man with something to sell must persuade the world that his brand stands for quality.

The men who followed him brought that principle down to date by the use of new mediums of communication. They also gave a modern slant to an ancient method of dramatizing the idea of quality. This is to call into being a high priestess who presides over a cult of excellence and whose every word endorses the idealism of a particular human effort.

General Mills' Betty Crocker is such a high priestess and she belongs to the great tradition of symbolic figures. Though she is no more than life-size, she is somehow just a little more than human, the apotheosis of the positive attitude in homemaking, of benevolence and grace in human relations. Yet, at the same time, her success has been so great in a purely commercial way that she has sometimes been called "General Mills' best salesman." A study of the life and times of Betty Crocker throws significant light on the recent social history of the United States.

The story of her evolution begins with the death of Benjamin Bull. He had been in his time a pioneer of advertising principle. His succinct and challenging query "Eventually — Why Not Now?" had been painted in red and green letters on billboards and blank walls throughout the territory that Washburn Crosby then claimed as its own, north of the Ohio

170

River and east of the Mississippi. It vied for the buyer's attention with the cleanliness of Ivory Soap, the pick-up value of Uneeda Biscuit, and the manly gratifications of Bull Durham tobacco.

In addition to this outdoor advertising, Bull covered the back pages of several national magazines with statements that were similarly simple, dogmatic, and unsearching.

Beyond these appeals Bull would not consent to go. Involved in many duties (so inclusive that once, when a letter came bearing the address "To the God Almighty of the Washburn Crosby Company," everyone knew immediately for whom it was intended), Bull had been content to sit on the lid of advertising. But at the time of his death, in 1920, the lid was shaken violently by the impulse of America's industrial energy. Fred Atkinson, who assumed responsibility for some of Bull's many tasks, delegated the duties having to do with advertising and sales promotion to younger men. These executives were in cordial communication with the spirit of the time and, under their influence, sprightly new developments occurred almost daily.

In the spring of 1921 the seething under the advertising lid seemed somehow to communicate its ferment to other departments. Appropriately enough the laboratory came first of all. James Ford Bell's innovation at the turn of the century, this unit had multiplied its activities many times over. A complete bakery had been installed in 1910, and, as the baking industry grew rapidly during the war decade, this division developed correspondingly.

The idea of promoting sales through service to bakers was expanded by the new young men to include service to housewives. Two young women trained in home economics — Ina Rowe and Agnes White — were engaged to go into communities near the Twin Cities, there to meet with church groups, school groups, indeed with any organization that was concerned with the two universals of human interest: homemaking and money-making. Any such company of earnest souls, if it would undertake to sell Gold Medal Flour at its meetings, would receive the usual commission to be used for its cause. Demonstrations of the uses of Gold Medal Flour gave to sessions of this kind the flavor of social life seasoned by self-improvement. They proved to be immediately and overwhelmingly successful.

Surcharged with energy by this encouragement, the sales promotion department prepared to organize similar campaigns beyond the

171

borders of the state. Into Wisconsin went a new recruit of the advertising department, the same Sam Gale who was presently to be useful to the company in so many ways.

Gale was the right man to send on such a mission. In his meetings with school groups and church groups he was able to put all his theories to work. He believed that if industry were to develop new markets, it must be by offering wider service to customers. The idealism that lay at the warm center of his temperament found one of its chief expressions in a passion for education. He believed with Thomas Jefferson that in a democracy it is the function of leadership "to inform the discretion of the people." When he went into Wisconsin to inform the discretion of women's clubs and also to sell Gold Medal Flour, it was with the perfect confidence that the new spirit of industry spoke through him.

He did not linger long on that first excursion, for a crisis arose at home and he was summoned back to cope with it. In place of its familiar kind of Benjamin Bull advertisement, the Washburn Crosby Company had printed in a national magazine a picture puzzle, which when fitted together showed a village scene with customers carrying sacks of Gold Medal Flour out of the grocery store to their trucks. The prize for completing the puzzle was a miniature sack suitably stuffed for use as a pin cushion and, of course, bearing the Gold Medal label. The puzzle was so easy that thirty thousand contestants sent in correct solutions. This almost calamitous success of the experiment left the company stunned and baffled. It had had no experience in handling such an avalanche of mail. There was no office in which it could be received; there was no crew; there were, in truth, far from enough little sacks to go around. Gale was called home like a diplomat on a foreign mission to deal with a major State Department crisis. For weeks an augmented staff, set up in a transformed corner of the mill, did the equivalent of a rushing mail-order business.

Among the 30,000 responses to the challenge of the picture puzzle there were several hundred letters in which isolated housewives, feeling obviously that a cordial rapport had been established with a sympathetic spirit of some kind, asked questions that might in more neighborly communities have been asked over the back fence: How do you make a one-crust cherry pie? What is a good recipe for apple dumplings? No organization existed for handling this mail either. But Gale, with characteristic conscientiousness, was determined to keep faith with the customers. The letters must be answered to strengthen the personal link between merchant and housewife.

From laboratory personnel and from the home economists he collected recipes. Then in a conference of the new young brains of the advertising department it was decided that answers would achieve a more spontaneous tone if they were signed with a woman's name. The surname Crocker was chosen because it had belonged to the enormously popular secretary and director of the Washburn Crosby Company, William G. Crocker, who had lately died in service after a career of thirty years. The new figure was christened Betty because this is one of the most familiar and somehow one of the most companionable of all family nicknames.

They did not, of course, realize what an extraordinary thing they had done in that moment of the day's routine. But as the years were to show they had created one of the most trusted and liked of American public characters. Betty Crocker became the eternal and supreme housewife, all-wise, generous of time, advice, sympathy.

This essential woman shares the proper interests of all creators of domestic comfort and harmony. The table is her particular province and its graces are her delight; but she is a woman of large mind and imagination and her interest in grace rays out into every corner of the household. It illuminates the practice of hospitality, taste in decoration, even the discipline of children. Her experience is normal but not narrow; it touches as well the ways of life of Park Avenue, Broadway, Hollywood, and official Washington. But for all her social adaptability, she is not a superior being. Rather she is the stalwart, reliable essence of the maternal. There need be no wonder at the fact that Betty Crocker was once voted the second best known woman in America. The first was, of course, Eleanor Roosevelt. They occupy their conspicuous positions for the same reason. Each is in complete control of the art of being maternal; Mrs. Roosevelt, at the height of her career, merely developed the art to its ultimate refinement as an instrument of social betterment and international diplomacy.

What might be called the mortalization of Betty Crocker has been the work of many minds. To the concept Gale unquestionably contributed the idea of making her a kind of preceptress-without-pain. When it became necessary for her to have a signature to fix her identity in the eyes of letter readers, all the young women in the Washburn Crosby office were invited to participate in an informal contest to see which could produce the most Crocker-like of hands. (It was won by Florence Lindeberg, long important among Betty Crocker's subdivided selves.) Over the years there developed a Betty Crocker literary style, written and spoken, a Betty Crocker idiom, a Betty Crocker set of values. Everyone who used her name was indoctrinated in the Betty Crocker philosophic system, simpler and narrower in range, to be sure, than that of Kant or Kierkegaard, but quite as carefully formulated.

It was decided finally that she must have a physical image and that, too, was planned discreetly. She sat for her portrait to the one woman in America who could do her justice, Neysa M. McMein. At the moment when the picture was made, Miss McMein was herself a kind of American demigoddess: the most courted of commercial artists, hostess in her New York studio to all the "Algonquin wits" — Benchley, Parker, Franklin P. Adams — a wit herself. Sophistication lay rouge-deep upon the personalities of her cover girls; beneath lay reassuring testimonials to health and wholesomeness.

To Betty Crocker, Neysa McMein gave a fine Nordic brow and shape of skull, a jaw of slightly Slavic resolution, and features that might be claimed contentedly by various European groups (eyes, Irish; nose, classic Roman) — the perfect composite of the twentieth-century American woman. Direct, forceful, candid, and completely in control of her world, she looked out of advertisements with reassuring seriousness ready to face any emergency of hospitality.

Her enormous usefulness did not become fully apparent even to her creators during the first years of Betty Crocker. Other interests predominated and Betty Crocker was quiescent during the period when the Washburn Crosby cooking schools multiplied. These were carefully organized to make the most of the double opportunity for service and for sales promotion. A staff which grew at last to twenty sent its representatives into every regional territory. Under the sponsorship of a local newspaper in each community these sessions provided the Washburn Crosby home economists with a chance to give the news of late discoveries and improvements in the technique of cookery. Before and during these conferences in commercial clubs, churches, and schools, the special advantages of using Gold Medal Flour were not, of course, neglected.

During this period there grew up in industry a new concept of the relationship between merchant and customer. Among millers, tradition had always favored the idea of intimacy; but the cozy picture of the farmer bringing his grain to the gristmill and passing the time of day while it was ground had passed, long, long since, into the exclusive possession of the Currier and Ives print imitators. With its letter-writing program and its cooking schools, the Washburn Crosby Company set out to establish a modern equivalent of the old homely temper. Under the direction of an expert in organization work, Ruth Haynes Carpenter, the newly created "educational division" of the Advertising Department grew and became at last a department on its own. "Home Service" it was called and to it came several women who were later to have an important share in the development of the ideas and attitudes that entered into and matured the character of Betty Crocker. One of these was Marjorie Child Husted, who managed, for twenty years, at the start of each day's work in the Home Service Department to transform herself into the very personification of the philosophy of Betty Crocker.

Mrs. Husted was unusually well equipped to explore the world of women. She had been graduated, shortly before World War I, from the University of Minnesota with degrees in both home economics and education. Inevitably she was caught up into the service of the Red Cross during 1917–18 and, after the Armistice, she took back to peacetime assignments the preoccupation with the problems of the helpless that her war experience had induced. For a succession of welfare agencies she examined many of the crucial problems of community life today: malnutrition in infants, juvenile delinquency, breakdowns of public health, threats to the family unit. There was little in the way of challenge to the success of the home that she did not encounter during her period of service to these clinics in human relations. This background, crowded with emergency yet one that was full of testimony to the curability of social ills, Mrs. Husted presently put at the service of business.

She had several different kinds of adventure with the Washburn Crosby Company in the field before she settled to the task of being Betty Crocker's other self. For a time, as representative of the distaff side in the Kansas City region, she very energetically covered the whole midwestern territory, from Iowa to Texas, in the interest of Gold Medal Flour, not merely conducting cooking schools but working closely with salesmen on promotion programs.

Another recruit of the early years was Janette Kelley who, when Mrs. Husted retired to become food consultant to General Mills and other companies, became her successor as head of the department. Miss Kelley, a graduate of the University of Montana, brought to the Washburn Crosby Company the entirely original idea of establishing her own private "bureau of standards" to determine precisely what a loaf of bread should be. She believed that housewives would welcome the chance to measure the product of their own ovens against an absolute standard. Her system of appraisal was set forth in a leaflet which proved to be so popular that it had to be reprinted again and again. Clinging tenaciously to a place in women's affections long after they had forgotten everything else on the season's list of best loved books, the pamphlet showed more clearly than ever that the idea of service had solid value as merchandising method. Not only housewives but teachers of home economics and leaders of 4-H clubs used Miss Kelley's study gratefully. Her conscientiousness cast reflected glory on Gold Medal Flour.

After several years as a member of the field service group under Mrs. Carpenter, Miss Kelley resigned to serve another industrial organization in the East. She later returned after the organization of General Mills.

By 1924 radio had begun to replace the regional cooking school as the best means of reaching a large audience of women. Marjorie Husted returned to Minneapolis to assume responsibility for the Betty Crocker mail while another young woman, Blanche Ingersoll, took up the assignment of being Betty Crocker's voice.

Every Friday morning the Betty Crocker Cooking School of the Air was broadcast and in these sessions, Miss Ingersoll undertook to make the philosophy of homemaking as fresh — and as specific — as a breakfast muffin. Listeners might enroll by asking for cards on which recipes were printed, making the advertised product themselves, and filling out reports on their success. Those who completed all the lessons and prepared all the dishes were graduated at a ceremony broadcast from the station studio. At the first of these sessions 238 women received diplomas. An indication of the truth that age cannot wither a proper interest in eating was offered by the presence at these ceremonies of one graduate aged eighty-two.

One radio enterprise on Betty Crocker's behalf inevitably led to another and, in 1925, Miss Ingersoll went to Buffalo to indoctrinate a local Betty Crocker in the correct presentation, over station WGR, of material sent out from what can only be called the mother-kitchen at

Minneapolis. To the substitute Betty Crocker Miss Ingersoll offered advice which indicates clearly what the basic concept of this apostle of domesticity was from the very beginning. Miss Ingersoll urged the Buffalo interpreter to be "chatty" and "offhand." What she wanted was the tone of the "friendly visit." And, she added crisply, "for goodness' sake avoid the sickening, sweet tones affected by some women broadcasters. Betty Crocker is a sensible sort of person."

A lively correspondence sprang up between Miss Ingersoll and G. S. Kennedy, who assumed, along with scores of other duties, the job of supervising the Buffalo broadcasts. The "Dean of Betty Crocker University," as he called himself, passed on such research questions as that of a worried customer who wanted to know if it could be considered permissible in any circumstances to serve tea at night. It was the Dean's private opinion that "tea should never be served as long as the prewar stuff can be had by merely crossing Niagara." The pleasant frivolity that sparked back and forth between the Dean and the first Betty Crocker of the Air helped to wither away pretension from the concept and to leave a completely human creature who claimed to be in possession of no realm broader than that of common sense.

The experiment at Buffalo brought letters by the tens of thousands and it became obvious that there was need of still more Betty Crockers to speak in the several regions to local audiences. By October 1925, thirteen of them passed on the messages sent out from the mother-kitchen. When in 1926 WCCO became affiliated with the National Broadcasting Company (later it switched to Columbia) Betty Crocker could speak once more with one actual voice to large sections of the mid-continent. Betty Bucholtz spoke for her on the western network. But out of the headquarters at Minneapolis, Marjorie Husted had now become her interpreter in the fullest sense. She took over the task of preparing the Betty Crocker scripts and for ten years, in the midwestern section, she also spoke them before the microphone.

It was she who established the primary tenet of the faith on which the whole concept is based. Homemaking, Mrs. Husted believed with the earnestness of a zealot, is a career equal in dignity and significance to any career a woman might have in the arts, in the professions, or in industry. Her intention in every broadcast was to underscore the conviction that a sense of personal worth is the reward to which any housewife is entitled for the proper discharge of her duties in the kitchen.

First Lady of Food

Obviously no merchant would spend millions of dollars over a period of three decades to build up such a figure simply for the creative satisfaction of doing so. Betty Crocker has had, throughout the years, her own intrinsic worth and it is great indeed. Her mission, as Gale has pointed out, has been to perform first for the Washburn Crosby Company and later for General Mills "its major consumer selling job." By offering service of the kind that Betty Crocker epitomizes, General Mills has enormously enlarged the company of housewives using her products.

The function of General Mills' Home Service Department has been to convince the buyer that she was being introduced, through its literature, to "tangible ways of using the product more effectively in carrying out her basic job." The modern housewife was susceptible to such suggestion for two reasons: first, because the advanced education many of her kind had received made them all sympathetic to the new approach (planning a meal with reference to proper dietary balance; measuring in calories); second, because as a busy college student she had not had time to serve the apprenticeship of the stove that had given her mother and grandmother their training.

Realizing what an enormous asset Betty Crocker had become, General Mills nourished the concept with even greater eagerness than the Washburn Crosby Company had shown. Her name continued to be signed to the letters that now reached the Home Service Department at the rate of 4000 a day. Printed material emphasized her authority. Service advertisements in magazines developed her philosophy in relation to all matters of essential interest to women as wives, as mothers, and as conservers of American principle and belief. And, of course, she continued to speak directly to her following day by day over the air. No campaign to establish such an individuality has ever before been conducted with such thoroughness, consistency, and continuity.

But mere reiteration of promises would in the end have served no useful purpose if Betty Crocker had not been able to offer a persuasive answer to the customer's tacit question: "What can you do for me?"

In her sphere Betty Crocker had the most satisfactory of all possible answers. In response to the cry for help, she said, in effect: "I can show you how to bake a cake (pie, loaf of bread, biscuit) with never a failure if you will simply follow my instructions."

She arrived at this confidence through a technique of triple testing that ensured results as far as flood, spontaneous combustion, or unpredictable cataclysm of nature would allow. The basic test was, and is, simply that of baking again and again in the Home Service kitchens until the perfect formula seems to have been achieved. It is followed by tests made by selected housewives in their own stoves to determine whether or not the less perfectly controlled conditions of the family kitchen will produce the same satisfactory results. And there is finally a test conducted by the Market Analysis Department in a cross section of homes from the Atlantic to the Pacific. The cumulative value of this experimentation is significant because the Betty Crocker testing programs accomplish what it would take generation upon generation of housewives to learn in the old trial-and-error way. A Betty Crocker recipe has all the merit of a treasure inherited from an ancestor who once fed George Washington. At the same time it has the merit of being a laboratory-tested, modern formula. Betty Crocker's prestige has risen with the success of her recipes and she has remained long at the head of the country's list of home service personalities.

It was wise, of course, to support this prestige with every sort of incidental attraction. The radio programs offered a fine opportunity to present the great lady winningly. Betty Crocker has been to Hollywood and interviewed leading members of America's substitute for a titled aristocracy. It was characteristic of her touch that she found there exactly what the average housewife would like to believe is to be found in any royal neighborhood: beauty and high spirit and wit, springing out of sensible habits, particularly out of sensible eating habits. In another series of broadcasts, Betty Crocker explored the history of American cookery. She and her staff turned over hundreds of volumes to discover the mysteries of such oddly named delicacies as New England's apple pan dowdy and Philadelphia scrapple. A pilgrimage to the famous American eating places took her from East 52nd Street, New York, through the Vieux Carré of New Orleans, and on to Chinatown in San Francisco, digesting quietly and happily all the way and inviting America to share the tour with her vicariously.

But Betty Crocker's best service came not in sharing these worldly pleasures but rather in seizing upon the opportunity, presented ungenerously by the depression, to demonstrate her real gift of maternal wisdom. Even before the brilliant aspects of her temperament had been revealed she had shown her solid worth by giving the kind of service to which there is none superior, in an hour of crisis — that of helping to balance the budget. In the depth of the depression housewives whose husbands had brought home the news of a third or fourth wage cut filled Betty Crocker's mailbag with pleas of desperation. The economy move was on but, as they might have said had they not been too frightened for frivolity, the budget refused to budge. Many a young woman was caught for the first time, in that moment, under the terrifying shadow of economic disaster.

Betty Crocker did not fail her. She put a member of her staff at the task of developing recipes for low-cost dishes. She planned entire meals for families on drastically reduced income. But always she avoided the lugubrious tone of reluctant benefaction in making these suggestions. The possible attractiveness of these diets was emphasized so that those who felt unfortunate need not also feel squalid. For two weeks Betty Crocker even addressed herself to the job of brightening the food prospects for families on relief. These were actually pioneer efforts to solve the problem of feeding the nation cheaply yet without sacrifice of essential standards of nutrition. The leaflet in which all these suggestions were brought together won immediate recognition among social workers and nutritionists as an authoritative treatment of the subject. It should be pointed out, as a comment on the character of Betty Crocker as citizen, that her response to the public plea for help was spontaneous and unselfish. The use made of her skills to advertise General Mills and to serve the miller's enlightened self-interest was of secondary importance. In her mind — the collective mind of the Home Service Department — it was almost an afterthought.

In all Betty Crocker's service to the public, the Friday cooking school continued to be the constant item. The kitchen was her shrine and she issued her chief messages out of it by radio. But the spoken word was steadily supported by the printed recipe made available in various ways. The first cookbook issued in the 1890s under the Washburn Crosby name had been picked up by the wife of J. S. Bell in a Boston department store. The shrewd merchandiser had seen the possibility of using it as an advertising item and had bought a large edition to be stamped with his own company's name and brand identification. Bell the younger as a boy had spent part of his apprentice time, on Saturday mornings, wielding this green rubber stamp.

The cover of this volume was decorated with a picture in muddy colors that aimed a mild joke at connubiality. A frock-coated gentleman, wearing the handle-bar mustache of the period, sprawled over a newspaper at the dining table while his neglected wife sighed out her boredom. As a contribution to food research the book was almost as inept as its cover would suggest and presently it was replaced by another, prepared especially for the Washburn Crosby Company under the direction of a nationally known authority. A succession of such books appeared under the company name at intervals for three decades.

In 1928, to celebrate the formation of General Mills, recipes were for the first time put into sacks of Gold Medal Flour. With a certain number of coupons, also to be found in sacks of flour, a housewife could acquire a neat little oak box in which to file her recipes. In 1932 the container underwent streamlining treatment and emerged trimmed in green or ivory-colored metal.

The cookbook idea was revived a year later when Betty Crocker invited the great chefs of the world to contribute $25,000 worth of recipes to a handsome brochure which was printed in France and brought home to subscribers on the maiden voyage of the Normandie.

In 1934 a use for the cookbook as an educational device was discovered. Fear had set the suggestible to whispering that bread was "fattening." Another handsome brochure launched Betty Crocker's counterrevolution with the wary cry "Vitality Demands Energy." The subtitle of the pamphlet was "109 Smart New Ways to Serve Bread — Our Outstanding Energy Food."

Attacking the subject with vigor and even with a little aggressiveness, Betty Crocker pointed out that the world's "disgrace of malnutrition could be wiped out tomorrow" if only the well-established truths of diet were heeded. "Our bodies are machines," the collective intelligence of Betty Crocker observed, "ones that are in use continuously, whether in repose or at work. The biggest contribution of the diet is energy. This energy is secured in large part from carbohydrate foods such as bread."

Wishing perhaps to avoid patronage, Betty Crocker refrained from pointing out that bread could not possibly be more fattening than any other food containing a similar number of calories. She was content to address women with the reminder that "beauty and the capacity to enjoy life are not possible without abundant energy. Instead of being avoided bread should be the prominent energy food of the woman who would enhance her own charm."

To the support of this basic contention Betty Crocker brought two of the most distinguished physiological chemists in America — Dr. Lafayette Mendel of Yale and Dr. E. V. McCollom of Johns Hopkins. They were in agreement that breadstuffs should constitute the principal source of energy in the American diet.

Having established her point, Betty Crocker went on to show the great adaptability of bread. It could be all things to all men and to all tastes. From the toast melba served with soup at a formal dinner or as the foundation of a canapé preceding a smart supper on down to the sturdy reliability of its daily life as sandwich, bread continued to be something that man could not do without. Sober of text but lush in illustrative material Betty Crocker's book set "the little nerves that fringe the tongue" to quivering.

To encourage the graces of life, as a proper mother should, Betty Crocker began in 1932 to put in flour containers coupons redeemable in silverware. The pattern was first called Friendship. Later a contest presided over by outside judges produced the name Medality. This sidelong salute to the familiar name Gold Medal, though it made no important contribution to the language from a semantic point of view, had a noble ring that pleased owners of the silverware.

So, during the 1930s, the individuality of Betty Crocker crystallized and took on clarity and a kind of brilliance. She was a merchandising triumph in large part because she had become so nearly human that her followers, in their own imaginations, insisted on clothing her in flesh.

The essence of Betty Crocker was — and is — reassurance. She became to many women the personification of the "giving" impulse, the one to whom the infant turns instinctively and after whom the mature individual still yearns. Food is her métier; comfort, grace, and security the extensions of her realm. This image has been carefully studied and scrupulously preserved and none of her followers has ever wanted to challenge her reality. She has fulfilled too deep a need.

To keep the identity of Betty Crocker clear and untainted by any impulse at exploitation, General Mills has often consulted experts about her development. One psychologist offered, as model, the concept of the "mother figure" to whom normal men and women turn all their lives to find the springs of confidence. For many a woman Betty Crocker has become, at the twist of the radio dial, the complete evocation of that figure.

She has used her power wisely. The enclosing philosophy of the

Betty Crocker broadcasts has suggested always that a woman is at her best when she is consciously proud of being a woman, when she realizes that her job has the deepest kind of significance, when she respects her own dependence on a man, knowing that only the magic of her femininity can release her husband's gift of leadership.

Down the years Betty Crocker has presided over a world of fantasy. The soap operas sponsored by General Mills on behalf of its products — *Valiant Lady, The Guiding Light,* and the rest — all have been designed to provide an escape from humdrum reality. But the Betty Crocker contribution to these exercises has been designed to make the correction that must finally be made by all mature people after the flight into fantasy. She recalls her listeners to the real world with the reassurance that it is, after all, a good world in which to live. It is, she says to her housewife follower, a world in which there are duties that only she can fulfill. This power to serve endorses her work and crowns her life with dignity.

These were the stages in the evolution of Betty Crocker, the means by which she became essential woman, essential mother, at once teacher and source of inspiration. This comforting concept of security Betty Crocker translated into the dependability, practicality, and simplicity of her recipes. Because she understood the whole person that she existed to serve, Betty Crocker understood also, as her analyst once wrote, that women "live largely in anticipation."

It is as high priestess of anticipation that she has attracted her audience. It is as America's first lady of food that she has held it.

13

Island of Security

GENERAL MILLS IN THE DEPRESSION

O<small>N</small> October 29, 1929, the frenzy of speculation among American investors reached the "bursting point" that Bell, in his private diary, had predicted for it three years earlier. On that day a first crack appeared in the façade of finance and presently the great inevitable explosion followed. Smaller detonations of tragedy filled the air for years, resounding fearfully through the lives of men and institutions.

Yet catastrophe was no means universal throughout the business world. There were islands of security that felt the effects of cataclysm only indirectly, as though they received on their shores some of the debris of wrecks from distant storms on other stretches of sea.

Within the organization of General Mills individual men had succumbed to the speculative fever. Their bills for long-distance calls to New York brokers bore impressive witness to resourcefulness, however misguided. Some of these had, in the crisis, to be "bailed out" by generous-minded and provident associates. But the company itself had never clung with more disciplined fixity of purpose to its conservative philosophy and its cautious program. Bell, rejecting the all but universal impulse to gamble, insisted more firmly than ever that the cost card must dictate price. Adherence to this principle, in the wild moment when plausible substitutes for logic promoted fantastic schemes of operation, kept earnings stable. During the bleakest period of the depression, between 1931 and 1933, consolidated net income steadily rose. Average earnings for the first five years slightly exceeded three times the preferred dividend requirements. Dividends on common stock, initiated on

184

November 18, 1928, at the rate of $3 per annum, were paid regularly from that moment on. No sensitive plant, General Mills thrived, if not on adversity, at least in defiance of hardship.

Not all buyers of General Mills stock had, however, quite the same conservative approach to the conduct of their affairs as did the company itself. The panic in Wall Street had the effect of throwing on the market some of the General Mills securities which had found such a responsive public when they were first offered for sale. It was a moment, of course, when "dumped stocks" looked anything but appetizing and the financial world suffered a severe attack of investment anemia.

In this time of tension Bell, as the father of General Mills, did not forget the man who might be considered the foster father of the corporation, George F. Baker, Sr. The chairman of the board of the First National Bank of New York was no longer active, but two of his associates, Jackson Reynolds and Henry S. Sturgis, took a lively interest in the company that they had helped to create. Both were bankers of the best twentieth-century design, with solid academic training, and they found themselves in sympathy with Bell's theoretical approach to the solution of industrial problems. Reynolds, a graduate of Stanford University and a graduate in law of Columbia, had been an associate professor of law and general attorney for a railroad line before Baker had drawn him into the banking business. He took over the problem of General Mills' stock with the absorbed interest of a man who liked to see big business and big banking properly paired.

To work on the case, Reynolds called in a young man, S. Marshall Kempner, who had been graduated from Harvard with a brilliant record not long before. He and a partner had established themselves as members of the New York Stock Exchange and they were well equipped to stand as sponsors at the debut of a company that was, despite some small previous experiences in offering stock, really new to the investment world. An analysis of the long unbroken record of success that General Mills had inherited from the Washburn Crosby Company impressed the experts, especially at a time when so many corporations could only mourn their lost innocence and their lost leadership.

"Get their stock around," Reynolds urged Kempner. "Get it stabilized."

Kempner's first campaign was to acquaint the business world with the story of General Mills' success which in a day of panic must, as he

185

reflected, seem beautifully serene to harassed investors. Oddly enough, it was not perfectly easy to do this. There were plenty of sympathetic listeners, but among General Mills' own executives some doubted stubbornly that they wanted their story told quite so openly. Reared in the atmosphere of Dunwoody's habitual caution about "letting the figures out," of Bull's determination to keep details of his system so secret that only he understood them, and of the prevailing philosophy "Addition, division and silence," they resisted the idea of revealing the data of the company's operation. But it was characteristic of the flexibility of Bell's mind that he became a leader in the development of new techniques for taking the public into the business executive's confidence.

United States Steel already had made a start in this new direction. Its leaders had seen the benefit of free publicity that might be derived from the public discussion of its statistics by editors of financial sections in the newspapers. Kempner followed this lead by putting accounts of the rapid growth of General Mills in the hands of important commentators. He helped them to explore the even tenor of the corporation's way as it moved from one unspectacular success to another and built up its business by finding new products to sell.

The result of this favorable attention was that the available stock in General Mills was gathered up, not in large part by individuals, but by investors on the grand scale — insurance companies, schools, and investment trusts many of which bought in blocks of 15,000 shares. Banking firms became interested and put the stock high on their lists of items recommended for fiduciary accounts. An almost completely unknown stock became one with a triple A rating for widows and orphans. The reward of forty years of conservative, yet imaginative, management came with the admiring acknowledgment of the business world that General Mills' securities — symbols of integrity and shrewdness in the conduct of affairs — were rocks on which an investment program could be substantially and reliably built.

As public ownership of General Mills gradually grew broader and broader over the years, trading still was not heavy. Large holders were also steady holders and they became, finally, *old* holders with no inclination to relinquish their grasp upon something that was confortingly solid.

The storm in Wall Street was not the only one that gave General Mills an opportunity to demonstrate its stanchness in the first years of its existence. The closest ties of sympathy linked the miller to the American farmer who was still wrestling with a tempest of maladjustment. Year after year conscientious leaders in the realms of finance, industry, education, and legislation looked for some permanent solution to agricultural discontent and distress. Year after year there was presented to Congress one or another version of a legislative nostrum, the McNary Haugen Bill. Though each revision added new complications the essential principle remained the same. This purpose was to maintain a fair price to producers of basic crops like wheat so that circumstance might not force the farmer to sell his crop in the world market at a figure below the actual cost of growing the grain. It was the old difficulty of the surplus that constantly threatened wheat with this drastic devaluation. What the McNary Haugen Bill proposed was that the surplus be impounded by the government and sold abroad at the world price. Then "an equalization fee," collected from those who had benefited by the higher home market price, was paid to exporters to make up the difference and ensure their profit. Congress, weary of debate, finally passed the McNary Haugen Bill at the 1927 session. But President Coolidge was more resolute. He vetoed the measure on the ground that it would not provide "a practical method of controlling the agricultural surplus which lies at the heart of the problem."

The hand of Herbert Hoover, Coolidge's secretary of commerce, was detected by experts in the President's veto message. Two years later the problem, appropriately enough, became Hoover's own. As Coolidge's successor in the White House he had to face the storm that still raged over the wheat fields.

His solution was to secure the passage of the Agricultural Marketing Act which retrieved from the old McNary Haugen Bill the idea of creating a Federal Farm Board whose function would be to "bring about" the "orderly marketing" and price stabilization of farm products. Hoover's message to Congress on the subject of "systematic relief" for agriculture emphasized his belief in the desirability of building up the farmer's own marketing organizations. To that end Congress provided a capital of $500,000,000 and once more there began an adventure in altruism to which many high-minded men gave spirited, if sometimes anguished, effort.

Even before the Farm Board could take its first official step, the stock market had collapsed and the price of grain had gone hurtling down along with that of stocks. But Hoover insisted stoutly and stubbornly that the Wall Street incident was minor, that the effects would be fleeting and insignificant. Under this hopeful influence the board proceeded to set up a Grain Stabilization Corporation called for by the terms of the Marketing Act. Its function as commercial agent for the board was to buy huge quantities of wheat, corn, and cotton to be stored in the elevators of farm cooperatives against the day when it could be sold advantageously.

The milling industry, disciplined by such experiences as that of the cooperative effort led by Bell in World War I, offered no official criticism of a plan to which most of its individual members were opposed. Indeed, following an impulse of adaptability that had become habitual in the community life of millers, the National Federation, meeting in November 1929, passed a resolution creating a special committee to work with the Farm Board in carrying out the provisions of the Marketing Act.

"It would be hypocritical," the *Northwestern Miller* commented, "to pretend that millers believe the Farm Board can succeed in influencing the price of wheat, exercising any considerable measure of control over world values or effecting any substantial saving in marketing costs." Yet, despite theoretical doubts, the millers were ready to see the experiment through. Their sympathy with agriculture, together with a certain degree of self-interest, made them wish to be adaptable. As the editor of the *Northwestern Miller* concluded: "All that a miller needs from the grain market is a supply of wheat, available when and where he wants it, and everything accomplished toward price stabilization is directly to the benefit of milling which suffers constantly from violent market changes and varying spreads between cash and future prices."

For two years wheat piled up alarmingly in the elevators and the "advantageous moment" for its disposal seemed to be indefinitely postponed. The whole prospect so discouraged the chairman of the board, Alexander Legge, that he resigned, leaving behind him, as Harold Brubaker pointed out in the *New Yorker*, "a fragrant memory and an awful lot of wheat."

By 1931 Bell had watched this struggle in silence as long as it was possible for so analytical and articulate a man to do. He was reminded of an episode that had occurred several years before, in 1926, when his old chief of the Food Administration, Herbert Hoover, had been Coolidge's secretary of commerce. With his characteristic passion for exploring a problem to its roots, Bell had reexamined the old hazard of the surplus and reached the conclusion that it sprang out of the stubborn cultivation of marginal lands. Why not, then, get rid of the two simultaneously by the retirement of the unneeded acreage of inferior farm land? He was easily able to persuade certain grain men and railroad men of the soundness of his plan for a permanent solution of the difficulty that had plagued agriculture so long. It was his duty, Bell's friends told him, to put this proposal before the government along with the suggestion that the government find a means of eliminating the marginal lands from cultivation.

"But I'm no evangelist," Bell protested.

Since he would not push his proposal singlehanded, a delegation was formed to wait on Hoover and put it before him. The then secretary of commerce, in the very heart of whose realm such a broad-scale plan lay, listened attentively and with sympathy. But in the end he shook his head and rejected it. The suggestion was, he said, "economically sound" but it "lacked political appeal." The delegation retired, puzzled by the evidence that political pressure could smother an idea that seemed so neatly to fit an acute and immediate need.

Now, five years later, with the problem more than ever in the foreground of the public mind, Bell thought of his proposal again. He retired briefly into his ivory tower (which he managed always to maintain just two leaps away from the center of his business activity) and presently emerged with a complete formulation of his proposal for easing the farm crisis.

His article appeared in the *Saturday Evening Post* on December 5, 1931, under the title "The Public Attitude toward Agriculture." It began with a quotation from Will Rogers, who had once made the characteristically witty and disturbing suggestion that "farm relief" seemed to mean "relieving" the farmer of everything that he had. It was time, Bell urged, for relief to take a rather more generous and at the same time more practical form.

If it was true, as he had argued before, that the most crucial part of the surplus came from "too much land under cultivation" then it was the job of government to seek a fundamental cure. Why should the United States not draw upon its experience in stabilizing money and credit, through the influence of the Federal Reserve banking system, to create a similar institution, a Federal Farm Reserve? Such a "corporate body with stock ownership resting in the Federal government" might well be entrusted with the responsibility of "expanding or contracting the value of the agricultural plant through open transactions in these lands." One of the chief duties would be to purchase "marginal lands the very existence and cultivation of which imperil and depress the efforts of the whole agricultural community." These "retired lands" could be turned over possibly to reforestation projects or to the development of "commodities other than those in which a surplus now exists."

The applicability of this treatment to the actual disease was more evident to many than it had been when Bell first presented it. But to an administration headed by the same man who had doubted its political appeal and which faced the daily trials of the depression, it had not gained in charm. Meanwhile the erratic plunging descent of the price of wheat continued. It had gone to 55¼ cents a bushel in early 1932 and was to fall to 35 cents a bushel in the bleak days of the marketing season in the same year. Once more, the problem was allowed to falter on without any attempt being made at an over-all solution.

In December 1932 the Farm Board in its annual report to Congress mixed an admirable brand of dignity with masochistic candor in the acknowledgment that its own solution of the problem had done much more harm than good. "It is futile," the report said, "to engage in stabilization purchases over a period of years in the face of a constantly accumulating surplus of the product."

It was a moment for similar soul searching in almost every corner of the economy of the United States. But in the gathering gloom of that portentous year, General Mills still managed to elude fear. Bullis, advancing rapidly through this period (secretary and comptroller in 1928, elected director in January 1930, and vice president in May 1931) spoke the company's mind in a statement of faith made for a special issue of a business publication:

"General Mills, Inc. under the enthusiastic leadership of its President, Mr. James Ford Bell, has not succumbed to the pessimistic point of view which has been so general during recent months. The management is confidently preparing for the best rather than the worse."

The company might well be optimistic. The annual report of 1932 again showed increased earnings over the previous year — a miracle of affirmative drive in a time when business had fallen into the way of

190

thinking that it had done admirably if it managed to hold off bankruptcy and liquidation.

This miracle had been accomplished by a strict acknowledgment of the authority of common sense. Bell had, in the midst of the universal crisis of fear, fought the wholesale slashing of wages, pointing out that would be simply to "reduce the buying power of the community and to lessen the proceeds going back to industry." His sincerity was not to be questioned, for his own company at that moment restored a temporary 10 per cent cut in salaries. The central point of Bell's philosophy of common sense was expressed in an open letter to the editor of the *Northwestern Miller.*

"The question is," he wrote, "are we going to be overwhelmed by false promises or are we going to FACE THE FACTS, take command of ourselves and in an attitude of good judgment and common horse sense perform the service we are obliged to do? Are we going to continue the policy of trying to grab all the business we can for the sake of keeping our wheels running, or are we going to be content with the volume of business we can secure at a price that will keep us in a profitable state over this period of temporary distress?

"The difference in the purchase of a barrel of flour at a profit and one at a loss is not going to impede the purchase of the flour, but a losing price is a blow at the national structure of this country at a time when it needs the confidence that comes through successful and profitable operation of its industries."

Out of the fortitude and patience with which Bell himself faced the facts in the formative years of General Mills' existence, the company's own success grew undeterred by the shadow of the depression. Indeed, the figures for the annual report of 1931–32 amazed the economic world (nearly $4,000,000 consolidated net income) and delighted directors and stockholders. As William Morris of Buffalo exclaimed with the ardor of an infatuated lover, it was "one sweet report."

But the shadow of the depression constantly deepened. On Friday, March 3, 1933, Bell was returning to Minneapolis from a business trip which had taken him to Washington for conferences with officials of the incoming Roosevelt administration and also to other cities on various private matters. At Macon, Mississippi, he stopped to conduct personal business. Entries in his diary for the next ten days offer a curious, oblique glimpse of a momentous period in recent American history.

191

March 3: Talked with Farmers and Merchants Bank. Fine little institution. Excellent position. Directors increased bank deposits by $350,000.

March 4: Bank holiday declared. Getting back home.

March 5: (Sunday) Chicago. Can't get much information.

March 6: Arrived home. Everything at a standstill. Regulations coming hourly out of Washington.

March 8: Regular bank meeting. Jitters. Working with Washington to permit us to move sales by purchase of futures from the Grain Stabilization Corporation.

March 9: President delivered message to Congress. First National Bank of New York moved promptly to transfer money to Minneapolis.

March 13: Left for Washington at request of General Johnson.

From the moment of false serenity in the stout little bank at Macon, Mississippi, through the jitters and adjustments of the most spectacular event in the nation's banking history, one man had passed to a full realization of the fact that life had, for the moment, resolved itself into a progression of major crises.

The mission to Washington was, of course, concerned with the new administration's program for agriculture and with the milling industry's stake in its future. The chief concern of Bell and his colleagues was with a proposal that recurred again and again in every theoretical approach to the problem of farm relief. The basic idea, as outlined by M. L. Wilson of the University of Montana in one version of the plan, was that a tax be imposed at the processing point in every branch of manufacture. Thus, the miller would pay for the privilege of making flour from wheat, the textile manufacturer for making goods from cotton, the packer for making processed meat from farm animals. Funds collected in this way would be paid back on a pro rata basis to the wheat grower, the cotton grower, and the stock raiser in return for his promise to support the government's program. The government itself would then be in a position to control, or rather to eliminate, surpluses, to tell the farmer when, for example, he must curtail a crop. It was this fundamental suggestion which Roosevelt's New Dealers were eying with approval and which Bell had been called to Washington to consider once more.

He had been consulted regularly in the past as a leader of his branch of industry. At the time of President Harding's big agricultural

192

conference in 1922 he had been a delegate. A conspicuous fellow member was Bernard Baruch, one of whose clamorous mouthpieces in his research organization was General Hugh Johnson. En route to Washington, Bell, traveling with the Minneapolis grain man Frederick B. Welles, had read at Johnson's request an exposition of "equality for agriculture" done with the General's characteristic emphasis and conviction. This was, in fact, the first statement of a theme which had several variations in the successive versions of the McNary Haugen Bill. Both Bell and Welles were impressed with its clever economic reasoning and when Baruch met them in Washington with an eager request for a comment on it, Bell risked the "horse back opinion" that the millers might support it. Later, Sydney Anderson, an authority on agriculture representing Minnesota in the House of Representatives at Washington, had torn the proposal apart before Johnson's eyes and left all its flaws exposed to full view. Bell and Welles had withdrawn their hasty endorsement, but failure to notify Baruch of their change of heart had left relations among these men of good will a little strained. Coolidge vetoed the McNary Haugen Bill in 1927 and the crack widened enough for General Johnson to shout through it the maledictions for which he was famous.

When Hoover was voted out of office and Roosevelt was about to take over the administration of affairs in Washington, Bell accepted the philosophy of the "good loser" and went to see Baruch. He had begun to regard the "processing tax" not as an economic inspiration but as a psychological necessity in a time of tension. He urged now that a tax be put not simply on wheat and a few basic commodities but on all commodities. Called by Baruch into this conference, Johnson was at first unforgiving. "Why should we have anything to do with you?" he asked Bell crisply. But after a twelve-hour session over Bell's proposal he agreed that there was "something in it." The President was asked to call a conference of forty leaders of industry to consider a proposed bill for agricultural relief. It was to this session that Bell had been summoned on March 13.

Meanwhile Baruch had discussed the theory publicly. A one-cent tax here and a one-cent tax there, he suggested, would be comparatively painless to those who were asked to bear them, yet would still add up to a tremendous sum in total. At White Sulphur Springs, just before his inauguration, Roosevelt had heard Baruch's analysis of the proposal and endorsed it.

Island of Security

The first conference on the legislation that was to become the Agricultural Adjustment Act was held on Wednesday, March 15, and lasted for eight clamorous hours. It promptly became evident there were to be other losers beside the former adherents of Hoover. The conservative element of the New Deal, represented in this issue by Baruch and Johnson, and also by George Peek who became administrator of the A.A.A., had powerful opposition to face. From the start two entirely different attitudes toward government and toward control of social problems were represented in the shaping of the measure. This conflict over design permitted the A.A.A. to become an omnibus provision into which two unlike philosophies were deposited by stubborn men. Among the doctrinaire liberals who wished to see the New Deal take major steps toward the redistribution of wealth were Rexford Guy Tugwell, Mordecai Ezekiel, and Jerome Frank. The evidence of their hands in the writing of the original bill disturbed Baruch. "It won't do," he said and set about an effort to get it redrafted.

For two weeks after his summons from General Johnson, Bell vibrated between Washington and New York trying to get such modifications of the measure as would satisfy its necessary social aims without assigning too great powers to its administrator. Baruch kept urging the appointment of a three-man committee from industry to redraft the bill. It was to consist of Bell as the representative of milling, T. E. Wilson to speak for the packers, and Robert T. Stevens for the cotton millers. But Tugwell was reluctant even to let anyone see the bill and the secretary of agriculture, Henry Wallace, showed a disposition at first to stand aloof from the conflicts of his assistants. But Bell managed to see him at last in a private interview. The secretary struck him as being "an earnest, honest young man."

"I told him," Bell's diary records, "that he was the victim of too much partisanship and was torn by the farmers on one side and the processors on the other. I said that the thing for him to do was to shake clear and pick his own man to do the job. The administrator should be able to command the confidence of the public and that Baruch was the ideal man."

But this effort to snatch victory from defeat was foredoomed, in part because Baruch had refused to make himself available. Powerful momentum, Bell saw, was bound to carry the bill through all obstacles. He returned to Minneapolis at the end of March, there to receive a wire

194

from Sydney Anderson, reading: "It looks like sundown," which being interpreted meant that the bill was sure of passage.

On May 10 it was rushed through both houses of Congress and ten days later the President's signature made it law. By its terms processing taxes were imposed on only seven basic commodities — wheat, cotton, corn, tobacco, rice, hogs, and milk. Tugwell was author of a statement which fixed 30 cents a bushel as the proper tax to be levied on wheat. This rate, he announced, in a fine, authoritative clatter of legal phrases, "equals the difference between the current average farm price for wheat and the fair exchange value of wheat which price and value as defined in said act have been ascertained by me from available statistics of the Department of Agriculture." To General Mills the payment of this tax meant, according to the figures of an impartial observer, turning over to the government $110,000 daily.

Before it could be put into operation the A.A.A. was subjected to a barrage of criticism from left, right, and center simultaneously. *Business Week* summed up the objections by saying editorially that it had the look "of a document hastily drawn to the specifications of divergent and conflicting groups."

During the late summer and fall, Bell once more assumed the burdens of a commuter, plying between Minneapolis and Washington as a member of the National Advisory Board on Food. The close study of experiments in which he had always delighted made him a cool, detached, but thorough, anatomist of the A.A.A. in action. In answer to challenges from Baruch he offered his ideas.

The measure had, he told Baruch, betrayed the philosophy of those who had talked about "farm relief." Leftists in the Agricultural Department had in operation steered it deliberately toward social planning of a bold, innovative sort. At best its methods were artificial. The purpose was to stimulate commodity prices. But, as General Johnson had pointed out in the first place, the theory of the A.A.A. would be vitiated unless "industrial employment and earning power moved forward step by step with any advance made by agriculture." Even under the controls which the government was supposed to be exercising, the two groups were being forced to work against each other. Industrial workers had benefited slightly perhaps; in some plants wages had risen as much as 50 per cent. But, in the end, their interests would not be served if the philosophy were allowed to develop of making one group comfortable at the expense of another. Farmers had profited little by the A.A.A. They had "experienced some money advance" but in real returns they had suffered losses and were "going backward at a very rapid rate." Wheat prices had risen slowly as compared with prices of goods the farmers had to buy. These costs had climbed on an average of 17 per cent during the first year of the A.A.A. Agriculture still was lagging. Little had been accomplished toward wiping out the disparity between agricultural and nonagricultural prices.

But despite these "complications" (as Bell mildly described the effects of the processing tax in his report to stockholders), General Mills continued to enjoy the effects of its success in applying principles of economy and efficiency to problems of manufacture, selling, and distribution. For the crucially bad year 1933–34 net consolidated earnings were more than $3,700,000. Exclusive of the wheat processing charges, the company had paid in taxes to federal, state, and local governments the equivalent of $2.12 on every share of common stock held by its investors. Yet it had earned and paid the usual common dividends of three dollars a share and the preferred dividend of six dollars a share and in addition had increased its capital modestly by a retention of earnings.

Millers continued to fight the processing tax but with the courtesy to be expected of a "loyal opposition." They conducted their campaign on a level of dignified statesmanship. Addressing the Millers' National Federation as its president, Fred Lingham said: "We have considered the legislation unsound and we have believed that it would not bring about the desired effect. But every problem of life must be measured on the basis of existing conditions rather than on what they might have been. We may say that the law is based on untried theories. But the law actually exists. That must be our starting point for consideration and action concerning our problem."

The perfectly disciplined democrat spoke when Lingham urged millers to remember that "any rule must be for the welfare of the general public" and that the men in Washington who have sponsored the new ideas are "of an exceptionally high type personally."

The *Northwestern Miller* adopted, as item number one of its policy, a demand for repeal of the processing tax, saying in a statement reprinted in each issue: "Whether it be paid by the producer or the consumer it is a tax on productive labor or on hunger. The excise now being collected on bread is inequitable, unfair and a gross abuse of the taxing power granted to the federal government by the states. It is a heavy addition to the burden of millions who are struggling for a means of existence and of doubtful or negative value to the chosen few. It should be repealed."

There, midway of 1934, the struggle stood undecided. But, to anticipate, the millers presently found relief. By the year 1935 a strong tide of unfavorable opinion had gathered against the A.A.A. In an impartial study of the act prepared for the Brookings Institution, Joseph Stancliffe Davis of Stanford University offered the opinion that the A.A.A. showed in its influence several tendencies that were "contrary to the aims or principles of A.A.A. leaders." These perverse and unexpected tendencies were (1) to keep inefficient farmers in wheat production; (2) to give millers a poorer selection of wheats; (3) to interfere in the ordinary course of wheat marketing; (4) to restrict commercial exports of wheat and flour; and (5) to accentuate a drift toward economic nationalism. Strengthened in their own protest by such adverse testimony from academic experts, millers began, in 1935, to institute suits intended to test the constitutionality of the act. Federal injunctions were obtained to restrain the government from collecting the tax on processors and on January 6, 1936, the Supreme Court held the production control activities of the A.A.A. to be unconstitutional. In its verdict on the Hoosac Mills case, the court declared the processing tax invalid and the funds deposited in escrow were returned to the milling companies. The story of what became, finally, of General Mills' share belongs to another chapter.

Approaching a significant moment in his own career, Bell surveyed the events of the depression and of government control. In his personal diary he recorded judgments that were to have a significant effect on his own action and on the future development of General Mills. The industrial world, he wrote, was changing at a greatly accelerated rate. It was changing not merely in pace but also in principle. Theories of the New Deal implied the belief that "the day of industrial earnings has passed; that the necessities of life are rightfully the property of the people and that the production and distribution of these necessities should rest in the people."

What, then, remained in this changing world for an industrialist who wished still to claim a place for himself? Bell answered his own question.

197

Island of Security

"Our biggest assets rest in our Good Will, our merchandising ability and our efficiency in the use of publicity. These must be carried into new fields of profit opportunity.

"Our line of thinking and experience fits us to exploit projects that have their roots in the soil that grows wheat. We may follow the trunk of the tree to its utmost tip, but also we should not be averse to grafting new branches upon it."

The diary recalled the central argument of the "magnum opus" that if the company wished to grow it must not be content with a local position but seek a national and international prestige of ever broader reach. The argument was extended now to show that "we must create new fields of opportunity that will utilize our organization and the non-capital assets we possess."

The future, then, lay in research. "We must look afield to enhance this department bringing into it a stronger note of commercial interest to harmonize with its note of purely academic interest."

In this mood Bell decided on August 14, 1934, to resign from the presidency of General Mills. His letter to the Board of Directors said that the moment had come to lay aside "the activities that have engaged my time for the past thirty years." He reminded his fellow directors that "We have enjoyed a surprising immunity from the variations in earnings that have marked most businesses through the changing cycles." In the contemporary world of social upheaval he could only be grateful that the spirit of the organization he headed was the spirit "of youth, of change, of adjustment, of adaptation."

The type of organization under which General Mills had passed its formative years had enabled each man of initiative in its ranks to become "an essential factor in framing policies." The Operating Board served the function of the legislative body of democratic government; the president the executive branch; the Board of Directors the judicial. "We have circumscribed each with checks and balances that bid fair to perpetuate the spirit that now rests in the organization."

So, as he surveyed the past and glanced toward the future, Bell saw that, "Beginning with the simple milling of flour, we have grown through numerous stages until we are now essentially advertisers and merchandisers." Flour, he reflected, was still "the medium through which we express these abilities" and it was still essential. But through research new aptitudes must be discovered.

198

When he wrote his farewell letter Bell at fifty-five was trying dutifully to feel old. He anesthetized his spirit with the phrases of resignation in order to persuade himself that he was ready to assume the role of elder statesman who would be content from now on to observe and to advise from a distance. Fortunately for General Mills he was to serve for another fourteen years as chairman of the board during a period of expansion that followed exactly the design he had outlined in his diary and in his farewell letter.

The twilight tone of his valedictory belied both his energies and his outlook. It was to be high noon with him for many years to come.

14

Research Thinks Big

VITAMINS, BISQUICK, AND CHEERIOS

Think it big and keep it simple" was a characteristically succinct dictum of J. F. Bell and in his basic philosophy of research he showed clearly what he meant.

A miller could not, in his opinion, afford to waste time brooding over the decline of potential production at one point (Minneapolis) from 36,000 barrels of flour a day to less than half that figure. General Mills had been created to enable Bell to plan on a national and international scale, keeping many centers in operation simultaneously to the full advantage of the trade and of the company. Only research could properly support planning and thinking on this scale; only by close study of soils, markets, transportation problems, economic needs, cultural trends, world conditions could a great corporation hope to serve the whole community of mankind. This was what Bell meant by "thinking big."

Again, a merchant could not allow himself to become baffled by the complexities and irregularities of his market, especially when he worked with a raw material that was subject to many changes from season to season and from soil to soil. Only research could enable him to cut through the perplexities, solve mysteries, eliminate hazards, and reduce his operation to a reliable, predictable course. This was what Bell meant by keeping his interests "simple."

From the beginning of his career he had been dedicated to the faith that research must be one's master and that one must follow where it leads. General Mills had been in existence only a year when he committed himself completely and permanently to this faith by creating a Research Department with a long-range, large-scale program under the guidance of a highly trained academic expert. In 1929 Bell was able to attract as its first head Dr. C. H. Bailey, one of the leading cereal chemists of the world, recipient of both the Thomas Burr Osborne and the Nicholas Appert medals in acknowledgment of the breadth and significance of his work in food technology. Continuing as part-time professor of biochemistry at the University of Minnesota, Bailey presided over the debut of a plan for organized research that was, at the time, unique in the milling industry.

In 1930 Bailey designed and supervised the construction of a new research laboratory at Minneapolis. Built to allow for expansion, the laboratory grew prodigiously through the years with major additions to its facilities in 1938 and 1939.

Bell insisted upon having a research staff that was well trained to pick up wisdom's often elusive track. Appointments were given not to young men who were primarily interested in milling but to high-grade young Ph.D.'s. It was the theory on which General Mills' program was based that it was more effective to teach a theorist all that he need know about milling than to try to teach a miller all that he need know about theory. At one moment in its formative years, the Research Department startled the academic world by announcing that it had a place for the best young physicist that could be found. Rejecting the limitations of emphasis on a narrow field of study, the program literally followed where research led, even over the artificial barriers betweens areas of knowledge.

From various sources, all sound in academic background, General Mills brought together a staff that originally included R. C. Sherwood, J. S. Andrews, C. G. Ferrari, and W. B. Wade, in addition to Dr. Bailey. L. F. Borchardt joined the group in 1933 and F. C. Hildebrand in 1935. All of them remained long in the service of the company, making significant contributions not merely to the efficiency of its own procedures but to the permanent store of knowledge in the field of engineering chemistry.

At approximately the same time — the late 1920s and early 1930s — another closely related innovation was taking shape under the guidance of Bell's faith in the scientific approach to any problem. The name that this effort came to bear, Products Control, was the creation of General

Mills' men. It has passed since into the possession of all industry and become part of the language of technology.

This innovation was a typical product of necessity. In an earlier day when audacity rather than aptitude had been the salesman's chief attribute, a prevailing policy — as formulated by a wit of the fraternity — had been to "sell and repent." But in the merchandising era it had become evident that it was no longer wise to allow "salesmanship" and "sin" to be virtually synonymous terms.

A vigorous reformer among the young executives of General Mills was G. Cullen Thomas, who had lived all his professional life in the immaculate atmosphere of the laboratory. When he was still an undergraduate at Butler University in Indianapolis, he had been employed in the laboratories of the Indiana State Board of Health, actually assuming charge for a time of the food and water divisions. His superior there had been Dr. Harry Everett Barnard, a major figure in the crusade for the protection of health. Barnard's own predecessor in this tradition was Dr. Harvey Wiley, onetime state chemist of Indiana who had gone to Washington to become author of the first Pure Food and Drug Law (1906). Devotion to the idea of protecting standards of quality in food sold to the American people seemed to pass, among these men of Indiana, by direct inheritance from Wiley to Barnard to Thomas.

In 1919 Barnard left state work to become the first director of the American Institute of Baking which, before taking up permanent headquarters in Chicago, had the first year of its life under the roof of the Dunwoody Institute in Minneapolis. Thomas followed his old chief, enrolled in the course, and, after graduation, entered the baking business in Minneapolis. Later professional training followed at Milwaukee where it was his job to direct the change-over from handicraft method to the method of the machine age in the plant of the largest wholesale bakery west of New York. The schooling was unusually complete, for a brother of the wholesale baker operated a large mill nearby. Close cooperation between the two institutions offered Thomas intimate insight into all the problems, all the perils, and all the opportunities of the baking trade.

From this experience he learned that bakers are bitterly out of sympathy with the variables that affect the behavior of flour. They want uniformity. They will not use a flour that "jumps all over the place." Such a foolish athletic inclination reminds them of the random movements of the infant and they wish to see it put under the discipline of an orderly and mature technique.

For five years at Milwaukee Thomas undertook to control the mill from the bakery, looking for ways to circumvent irregularities of action and to ensure uniformity of response in commercial baking. The daily headache involved in this exacting chore offered in the end the benediction of any complete experience. It amounted to a liberal education in the problems of baking. When Thomas was invited to join the staff of the Washburn Crosby Company in 1924, he found himself equipped with the intimate and detailed knowledge needed to perform the creative task to which he was presently assigned.

This was to create an entirely new department within the company. His panorama survey of milling operations showed that actually there were three large divisions to the over-all design: that of procurement (the Grain Department), that of manufacturing, and that of sales. The problem of quality could not be solved, Thomas thought, until a fourth department had been established which would be responsible to none of the others but which would be dedicated to the all-important values of product quality and uniformity. Under its watchful eye, production standards must be maintained at the highest possible levels, protecting the interests of the customer and at the same time building the good reputation of the company.

The Products Control Department — the beautifully apt name was coined by Thomas — became the stronghold of the idea of quality. It had Bell's enthusiastic and unreserved backing. Indeed, at the very start, he clothed Thomas with authority to close down the mills at any time should the quality of the grain offered him fail to measure up to established standards. This was done to anticipate any possible recalcitrance on the part of the wheat department. But the very existence of the Products Control had the effect for which Bell and Thomas had hoped; the kind of wheat they wanted was promptly provided.

It did not take the new department long to establish its prestige. Milling, as all responsible men could understand readily, was no opportunist business in which it was safe to sell and repent or sell and run. Rather it must be based on the idea of bringing together a company of customers who would buy and be content, buy and buy again. As the significance of the work of the new department became increasingly clear, salesmen above all others became grateful for its existence. For it was easier on return visits to face completely satisfied customers. The salesman's own security depended on the dependability of his product.

To be sure not all the problems associated with the milling of wheat could be solved by persuading grain men to supply the best quality available. In certain bad seasons even the best grades of wheat developed eccentricities. These were transmitted to flour and its unanticipated whims made bakers extremely unhappy. In 1930 there was such a crisis and millers had all the baking fraternity on their doorsteps, demanding to know what, in the name of fermentation, had been done to their flour.

General Mills, with a reputation for service to support and two departments to help in the task, immediately put the laboratories of Products Control and Research to work looking for a solution. At first its scientists were also at a loss to understand. The wheat seemed to be of superior rather than inferior quality, plump and healthy-looking in the kernel. But Bailey and his associates followed every possible lead and finally found the right one.

Involved in the sudden breakdown of the wheat's performance was the fact that the grain, as it approaches maturity, undergoes a sequence of physiological changes that are designed by nature to bring it into a dormant stage. It is rather like a bear in hibernation, with all processes reduced to a minimum that the living organism may be preserved during a nongrowing period.

The 1930 wheat, as Bailey discovered, had developed a high level of this kind of dormancy. To bakers this condition was intolerable because they required, rather than sluggish unresponsiveness, a high degree of activity in the ingredients with which they worked.

While Bailey and his associates in the Minneapolis research laboratories worked on this problem, A. A. Towner, head of the Products Control laboratory at Wichita, was engaged in an independent investigation. By a remarkable coincidence an important discovery was made at almost exactly the same time by two groups of scientists working at two different places within the General Mills system.

This discovery had to do with the fact that the finest quality of bread resulted when the fermentable sugar content of the dough remained fairly constant during the process of fermentation. This can occur only when sugars are being produced from starch at approximately the same rate as sugar is being converted into carbon dioxide and alcohol by action of the yeast present. The conversion of starch into a fermentable sugar (maltose) can be effected in the dough by active agents, or enzymes, known to the chemist as amylases. Not all natural wheat flours have enough of these amylases to ensure perfect performance. What the General Mills research men learned was that this deficiency can be corrected by the addition of flour made from malted or sprouted wheat. The addition must be carefully adjusted to the properties of the flour and special techniques were developed by the General Mills staff that proved to be triumphantly successful.

What the layman need understand is that a method had been found, through the agency of a beneficent and busy enzyme, to control and to accelerate the bread-making process. "There are more things in heaven and earth than are dreamed of" in any processor's philosophy. Once more science had cut through a cluster to these unknown factors to find a simple solution of the baker's problem, one that absolutely ensures the proper fermentation of his dough.

For this process Thomas of Products Control thought up the ingenious identification Ferm-A-Sured, a trade nickname for "fermentation assured." It was a discovery of more than casual importance to biochemistry. To General Mills its immediate importance was great indeed. An official statement of progress during the first five years of the corporation reported that "Despite the downward trend of dollar volume of sales [during the depression] the development of new products and new processes such as Ferm-A-Sured have helped to sustain profits."

It is a matter of incidental interest that the jealousy with which General Mills protected names selected for its processes sometimes prompted surprising action. In 1933 the corporation purchased outright all the assets of the Red Band Company, Inc., with headquarters at Johnson City, Tennessee, simply so that there might be no doubt as to its own right to use the trademark "kitchen-tested" for flour. The Red Band Company had held exclusive right to the trademark in five southeastern states. It seemed only right that Betty Crocker, the universal housewife, should gather into her brood any product that was in any way related to her own kitchen-proved product.

Out of the Research laboratory there came, in the first year of its existence, an entirely new product, Embo. Its appearance anticipated the impulse that Bell once described as "hitting the vitamin trail." Derived from embryo, the name offered a kind of lisping acknowledgment of its parenthood. Each morsel of this product was, in fact, the embryo of a kernel of wheat, removed uncrushed from the wheat berry. Rich in vitamin B_1, a good source of B_2, and further supplied with valuable proteins, carbohydrates, iron, phosphorus, and many factors of the vitamin B complex, it was presented as a "storehouse of nutrients." Looking and tasting much like tiny nuts, these fragments of wheat could be eaten as a cereal or, advertising copy suggested, sprinkled over fruit, salad, pudding, ice cream. A vivid repertory of gastronomic acts was suggested for Embo.

From this beginning there developed during the 1930s a strenuous second career for General Mills. Plans for other new products multiplied so rapidly it was necessary to create a new corporation to perfect processes and sell the results. Looking back fondly on Ferm-A-Sured, the directors decided first on the name Sun-A-Sured, Inc., for its vitamin-selling vehicle. In the interest of scientific rigor and exactitude this was changed successively to American Research Products, Inc., Research Products Division, and finally, in 1941, to Special Commodities Division.

There were added to the highly trained staff of the laboratory several graduate nutrition scientists who worked with a vast army of white rats to determine the exact dietary effects of various vitamins. Among the new offerings that resulted from this original effort were a wheat-germ oil called Merit, intended for human consumption; another to which the trade name Arpro was given, a veterinary preparation designed for feed dealers and large breeders; and several concentrates of vitamin A and vitamin D.

Perhaps the most important contribution made by General Mills to the work of exploiting vitamins was the evolution in its laboratories of a process (known as ARPI, after American Research Products, Inc.) for producing vitamin D, the sunshine vitamin, efficiently, cheaply, and in enormous supply. Nature collaborates in the idea of storing sunshine by transforming ergosterol into vitamin D when it is subjected to ultraviolet light. Ergosterol may be obtained by isolation from yeast or ergot. It is activated in the ARPI process by placing the pure crystalline chemical compound in a vacuum chamber and subjecting it to the action of electrons that are produced by a high-frequency electrical discharge.

The discovery of this method made the Special Commodities Division of General Mills a large producer of vitamin D. Its supply is used chiefly for the fortification of milk but it is sold also, in other concentrates, to makers of vitamin tablets, oleomargarine, and malted milk.

These successes stimulated other studies. Starting with the conviction that wheat-eating peoples are the most vigorous in the human family, Bell wished to learn the source of the grain's superiority as food. The laboratories of General Mills were urged to explore still farther that storehouse of energy, the wheat germ. The devious route of this exploration led through some previously unexplored country of the mind and resulted in a long collaboration between two companies whose interests would have seemed not to meet at any point. For more than a decade General Mills and the Eastman Kodak Company worked closely together on a joint project to produce vitamins by distillation under high vacuum.

The story goes back to 1933 when Bell became aware that the Eastman laboratories had done experimental work in the field. Their investigator, Dr. K. C. D. Hickman, had interested himself in the subject as a "pure" scientist and also as a student who must apply any new knowledge he could acquire to the problems of photography. It was important to him to know, among other things, the exact melting point of certain substances and here the high-vacuum process was useful. But after taking out certain patents, Eastman reached the conclusion that the immediate applicability was not great enough to justify further research and Hickman shelved his experiments.

Meanwhile there had come to General Mills, as an associate in Sun-A-Sured, Inc., M. H. Wodlinger, a man with an infinite capacity for seeking out elusive ideas. The one that Eastman had dropped inevitably attracted him. Bell, more than ever determined to explore his own field broadly at this moment when vitamins were just beginning to be talked about, sent Wodlinger to Rochester to obtain a license to use Hickman's apparatus with vegetable oils.

Eastman not only granted the license but built a still for General Mills' experiments and sent Hickman to Minneapolis to install the equipment. Everyone was in such a hurry to begin that Hickman proposed to travel by train sharing his Pullman drawing room with the still. But the bulky apparatus could not be moved down the narrow corridor. While Hickman sat all night worrying about his delicate giant, the still was banged about in a rear baggage car.

Despite the injuries it had received there, it was put promptly to work in the Minneapolis laboratories. It did not, however, produce the hoped-for results. Having failed to make the high-vacuum still yield vitamins from vegetable oils, General Mills became anxious to try fish oils. There was presently another trip to Rochester to ask Eastman for a broadening of the license. This time enthusiasm for the Hickman process had revived under the stimulus of General Mills' interest. Why not join forces? Eastman suggested. Once more Bell followed where research led. His diary reflects the high excitement of an adventure in intercompany cooperation. "They outlined a plan for a jointly owned company. Fine people: show very generous attitude. Plant is model of efficiency."

In this harmonious atmosphere the "Joint Project," as it was first called informally, began the operation of distilling vitamins from fish oils brought from Australia, Brazil, and other South American countries. A miller and a manufacturer of cameras became the biggest customers of the important fisheries of the world. Building 44 at Eastman's Kodak Park in Rochester was the home of the experiment. Eastman supplied apparatus, overhead, and research supervision; General Mills, two thirds of all expenses and capital investment. Products derived from vacuum distillation were to be sold by General Mills and receipts from sales were divided on the basis of two thirds to General Mills, one third to Eastman.

The genuine scientific importance of the Joint Project, at the time, was that it showed the practicability of a new method of molecular distillation. By the new technique it was possible to extract whole molecules of vitamin A, along with its natural protectives (natural ester form). Previous methods of producing concentrates had broken up the molecule, separated it from its protectives, leaving the A ingredient vulnerable to the effects of light and air.

The Joint Project did not escape the confusions that threaten all such enterprise. At one moment it became involved in a great international drama of finance. An Englishman, Cecil Reginald Burch, held a patent, protected in the United States, which was possibly in conflict with that held by Eastman. Burch had assigned the commanding patent to Metropolitan Vickers in England and the Imperial Chemical Company was also concerned. A further complication was that E. I. du Pont de Nemours and Company held license rights under the Burch patents. Bell was successful in getting du Pont to relinquish its rights and a complicated international agreement with the British interests freed the Joint Project to proceed with its own plans.

The most important of the Joint Project's contributions to the basic science of molecular distillation was the substitution for the "falling film" still of the centrifugal still. In the first procedure the film of hot oil fell under gravity in a high vacuum and could not be made to spread even over a distilling surface. The result was that where the film was thick the vitamins could not be properly distilled and where it was thin the oil charred and the vitamins were lost. In 1935 in the Eastman plant a rotating disc replaced the falling film devices. It improved techniques and greatly increased productive capacity.

The Joint Project achieved full-scale operation in 1938 and, still owned in partnership between Eastman Kodak and General Mills, Distillation Products, Inc., was formed in June 1939. Another large financial investment was made by General Mills at that time.

For another ten years the collaboration continued profitably. In 1941 there were twenty-two large stills in operation at Rochester, producing vitamin A esters and a concentrate of vitamin E, called Vegel. The Special Commodities Division of General Mills served as sales agent. In 1942 Karl Humphrey, then vice president and treasurer of General Mills, became also president and general manager of Distillation Products. There matters rested comfortably until 1949 when new discoveries rewrote completely the vitamin chapter of scientific advancement and corresponding adjustments had to be made. General Mills sold out its interest to Eastman and, still later, Eastman disposed of its commitments to others.

But while it lasted, this cooperative experiment between two major companies offered a model of mutual understanding in a project to employ facilities to the best interests of the public.

From the moment of the establishment of its formalized program, research in the laboratories of General Mills was of two different kinds. The first began simply with the idea of the superiority of wheat as food and explored the close-packed kernel for new possibilities. The second began with a new product that was already a possibility in a miller's creative intelligence and put all of the resources of the laboratory at the disposal of those who hoped to perfect its commercial practicability. Both were long-range affairs requiring a great deal of patience on the part of experimenters and ingenuity on the part of merchandisers before a successful product finally was introduced to the market. But both efforts proved to be eminently worth while, tending, happily, to offset the declining per capita consumption of flour by making people want wheat in forms that had not existed before.

In a report of progress to fellow millers, Bell made this statement about General Mills' program of the 1930s: "We set to work to demonstrate what could be done toward increasing the use of wheat products. We did it. How? By beginning with the consumer, by making him or her actively want a great variety of wheat products. We didn't set out to sell flour; we set out to sell result. We brought the baker and the grocer into the picture as partners; we gave them an active interest in stimulating demand. Up went consumption, and people were glad to pay the slightly increased prices because they were getting so much more real value and satisfaction for their money."

Perhaps the most dramatic evidence of this approach to the problem of merchandising is to be found in the story of Bisquick, a new product which revolutionized American eating habits, provided a new adventure of the table, and in the depth of the depression kept the financial picture of General Mills a cheerful one indeed.

Like many another idea that has affected human life attractively, the inspiration for Bisquick might easily have been missed. But a shrewdly observant man happened to be on the alert at precisely the right moment. Carl Smith, a sales executive for Sperry, traveling home to San Francisco by train on a November day in 1930, entered the diner late and hungry. He was not hopeful about what he would get for luncheon at such an hour and his delight was correspondingly great when he found himself facing, among other things, a plateful of oven-hot biscuits, produced as though by magic only a very short time after he had sat down.

A salesman's professional curiosity led him to the galley where the chef was pleased to tell him how it had been possible to offer such biscuits. Just before leaving Portland on the trip to San Francisco he had blended together lard, flour, baking powder, and salt. From this mixture stored in the ice chest, he had made biscuits to order.

To have conceived this idea demonstrated in the Negro chef of the Southern Pacific lines possession of the kind of creative skill that gives human character its distinction. To have recognized the commercial

Left, Harry A. Bullis took over a "third shift" when he became president of General Mills in 1942. Right, Charles H. Bell brought a familiar name to the presidency in 1952

Colleagues in the Food Administration of World War I, J. F. Bell and Donald D. Davis worked together at General Mills as chairman of the board and president, respectively, from 1934 until 1942

John Crosby II and Charles C. Bovey, lifetime associates in both
Washburn Crosby and General Mills

During the presidency of Leslie N. Perrin (left), T. A. Erickson, 4-H
consultant to General Mills, celebrated his eightieth birthday with the help
of J. F. Bell and Harry A. Bullis

Harry A. Bullis, Leslie N. Perrin, Walter H. Barry, and Samuel C. Gale
bake a cake in the Home Service kitchen

General Mills executives "at work" — for the photographer

J. F. Bell sells a package of Wheaties to a housewife
during one of General Mills' baseball contests

Two views of the Minneapolis mills, home of Gold Medal Flour

Loading wheat into a Great Lakes freighter, destined for the Buffalo mills

Ten-pound flour sacks coming off the conveyor belt at the
rate of twenty per minute

The Mechanical Division produces industrial instruments
and special equipment

During World War II military guard stood watch day and night while
the Mechanical Division manufactured fire control
instruments for the armed forces

From the beginning of his career, J. F. Bell was "dedicated to the faith that research must be one's master"

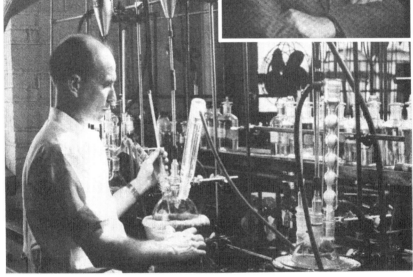

The Research Department follows Bell's dictum to "think it big and keep it simple"

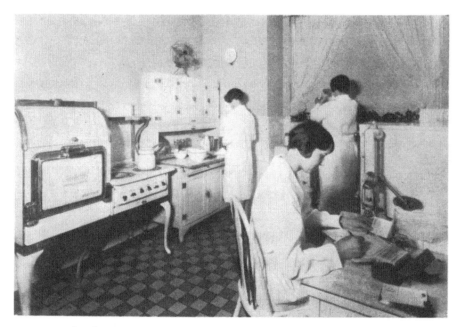

The first Home Service staff worked in this Betty Crocker
kitchen of the 1920s

In the 1950s one kitchen had grown to five and a dining room for
company entertaining had been added

Sponges, a product of the
O-Cel-O Division

Bulk flour, a commodity transported in king-size containers

"By his goods do you know him"

Packaged breakfast cereals being
inspected at the Chicago plant

The Brown 'n Serve process,
a gift to the bakers of America

The Wheaties quartet sent the first "singing commercial" over the airwaves in 1926

On behalf of Cheerios, the Lone Ranger has entertained the young and not so young on radio since 1941, on television since 1949

The animal circus displays the intelligence of properly reared animals to Larro customers

Advertising with imagination

Educational booklets and posters from the Department of Public
Relations aid the schools

A regional stockholders' meeting gives two San Franciscans an
opportunity to chat with J. F. Bell

General Mills employees relax — in the 1890s and the 1950s

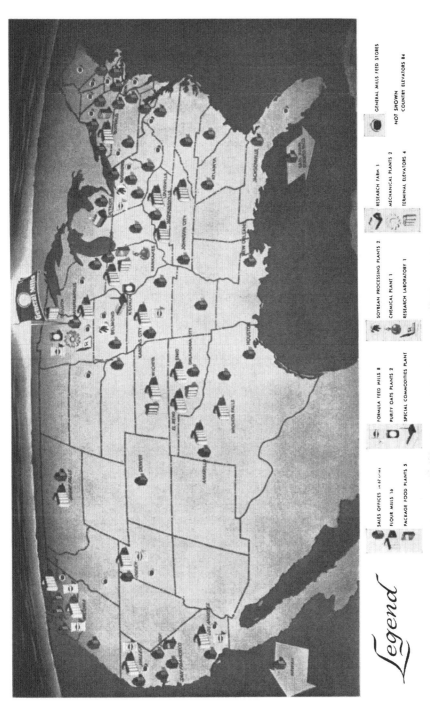

Legend

SALES OFFICES in 27 cities
FLOUR MILLS 16
PACKAGE FOOD PLANTS 5

FORMULA FEED MILLS 8
PURITY OATS PLANTS 2
SPECIAL COMMODITIES PLANT

SOYBEAN PROCESSING PLANTS 2
CHEMICAL PLANT 1
RESEARCH LABORATORY 1

RESEARCH FARM 1
MECHANICAL PLANTS 2
TERMINAL ELEVATORS 4

GENERAL MILLS FEED STORES

NOT SHOWN
COUNTRY ELEVATORS 84

General Mills plant and facilities in the United States

The mills at Buffalo, New York, largest in the world

General Mills, east and west . . .

The new plant at Lodi, California

The chemoil plant at Kankakee, Illinois

. . . north and south

Grain elevators at Enid, Oklahoma

Operation Skyhook, a research project by General Mills for the United States navy, took the "jolly miller" to the stratosphere

possibilities of the idea demonstrated in Carl Smith a similar kind of insight. For it was an entirely new idea. In 1930 there were none of the short cuts to comfort in cooking with which the present generation of housewives has grown up — no cake mixes, no hot roll mixes, no muffin mixes. It is probably as difficult for the modern woman to conceive of the rudimentary demands that were made on the creativity of the cook twenty years ago as it would be for modern man to conceive of what the problem of transportation would be if he had first to invent and construct the wheel. But in that distant day of the old-fashioned kitchen the housewife had to start any experiment in baking with her own inconveniently large containers of flour and lard. Smith knew that an incident in a minor revolution had taken place. If this idea could be exploited commercially, baking would never again be quite the same. He took the exciting word back to Sperry.

Specifically, he took it to Charles Kress, head chemist. This highly trained man (graduate of the University of Michigan, postgraduate student at the University of California) once wrote that "milling is both an art and a science, but very largely an art." It was his lifelong preoccupation to search out "the secret hidden away in the heart of the wheat kernel."

But, in this instance, his responsibility was less dramatic and more exacting. He had to arrange a chemical meeting between flour and shortening in an alliance that could be counted upon to endure and not turn sour on the grocer's shelf. The leavening agent, too, must be of the kind that would retain its power through weeks of inactivity in the package. To ensure the "shelf life" of the product was all important to the success of Bisquick.

Kress solved the problem. His intimate knowledge of the behavior of wheat and flour made him sure that they possessed a special affinity for a little known fat, called sesame oil, pressed from imported Indian benne beans. The great virtue of sesame oil was that it kept its sweetness under the stress of difficult circumstances. Kress made a deep secret of the existence of what he called "Ingredient S——." Had he not done so, the imitations of the new product which were sure to follow its appearance on the market would have had equal advantage with the original. But without sesame oil rivals would soon be in trouble and Kress could count on maintaining a comfortable lead. (More recent discoveries have retired sesame oil to a place among the footnotes to the science of baking.

211

But in its time it was almost literally the "Open Sesame" to a new world of discovery.)

When Kress was sure that he had a workable formula for the new product, Sperry made plans for its manufacture and exploitation. "Martha Meade," the West Coast company's equivalent of Betty Crocker, announced its debut to her radio following and trial packages were accepted eagerly by hundreds of her listeners.

Until this time the new product had continued to be a comparatively small family affair at Sperry. With the name of the West Coast branch of General Mills displayed prominently on the proposed package, the plan was simply to add it to the list of commodities offered in the local market. But the unique quality of this innovation could not escape the shrewd, appraising eye of Donald Davis. Like a new kind of exploring conqueror, he claimed it for Betty Crocker, for General Mills, and for the nation. To signalize the occasion properly, Davis himself rechristened the product — bis, for biscuit, quick, to give the tongue a twist around a second syllable that resulted, all at once, in a pun, a tribute, and an absolutely unforgettable trade name. Gold Medal replaced Sperry as sponsor on the package.

Meanwhile, further work to perfect the technique of making Bisquick had begun in the Products Control and Research laboratories in Minneapolis. One helpful discovery was that the interests of baking were served best if the ingredients of Bisquick were not stirred into complete homogeneity. What was needed was a laminated constitution — a layer of flour, a lump of fat, a layer of flour, a lump of fat. Such mixing could be counted upon to produce invariably a crisp, completely treated article. To this characteristic, the new product owed something of its generally accepted reputation of being "failure proof."

At the same time the firm and steady discipline of Products Control was applied to the problem of maintaining this reputation through the hazards of distribution and sale. It might be weeks before a particular package was taken from the shelf and put into the hands of a customer. Escape must be found for Bisquick from the dismal threat of rancidity. Products Control discovered that where a lump of fat lay next to the wrapping the part of the ingredient that was absorbed by the paper became rancid quickly. The live fiber of the paper was exposed, of course, to air and so the fat, too, was exposed to spoiling. Solution: wrap Bisquick in parchment like that in which butter and oleomargarine are wrapped. It was this kind of thoughtful treatment in advance of and in preparation for its debut that gave Bisquick its enormous success.

There was also the delighted championship that Bisquick received from its salesmen. The subtle prompting that tells an expert when he has something superlatively good on his hands — a sweepstakes winner, a long-run hit on Broadway, or a new product — spoke to the men of General Mills when they looked at Bisquick. In particular, it spoke to Raymond L. Brang, later to be a vice president of General Mills. He loved selling with the ardor of an artist and he made a sharp distinction between this and the automatic kind which he called "pattern cutting." But the task of selling Bisquick could not, in the first year of its existence, be considered a challenge to anyone's gifts. The immediate delight of customers made it, as Brang once reported, "as easy as shooting fish in a barrel." It was necessary only to say to a new customer: "Take a package and try it." When the salesman returned, the trial itself had done all his work for him. In the first seven months after its debut, Bisquick sold more than half a million cases, a record which the trade regarded as phenomenal.

The success of Bisquick became so great a challenge to competitors that within a year a big parade of imitations entered the market, some with enormous fanfare, some in the sly hope of being mistaken for their better. But so conspicuous was the prestige of Bisquick and so great its head start that, within another year, the rivals had fallen away one by one and only six continued to struggle on. Bisquick, in its turn, became a household word, a word of such authority as to capture approximately 75 per cent of all prepared biscuit mix sales in America. In a time when the art of salesmanship tended of necessity to become a toe-to-toe slugging match among its practitioners, the very existence of Bisquick kept the men of General Mills serene and secure. It was, as Bullis once remarked, "a real morale-builder."

For one new product that seemed to float fortuitously into the collective consciousness of the manufacturers, needing only to be perfected for the market, there were many derivatives of grains that had to be coaxed into existence by the most patient experimentation of scientists. The success of Wheaties and Bisquick had made Bell wish to look still farther for a diversity of products. His eye wandered in fact into the fields where corn, oats, and rice were grown.

Research Thinks Big

Between the Research branch and that of Products Control there was a complete segregation but there was also an effective working arrangement for the development of new commodities and new methods. A close personal affiliation existed as well in the 1930s, for Dr. F. A. Collatz of the Products Control laboratory had done his work for the Ph.D. degree under Dr. Bailey of Research.

Collatz himself was a research-minded man and when Cullen Thomas suggested that the future for an ambitious young man lay through the development of new products, his laboratory soon began to steam with experiments.

With Wheaties established as an aristocrat of the ready-to-eat cereal market, General Mills had been eager for several years to find another such product with which to capture still more of the trade. To attract the attention of buyers Collatz wanted something different from the flake form of Wheaties. To woo novelty he thought well of the idea of offering a puffed cereal. He tried a variety of grains, cooking each of them first and then puffing the dough.

The puffing process had been invented by Professor Alexander Pierce Anderson, who had gone out from the University of Minnesota to take his Ph.D. at the University of Munich and then returned to his alma mater to teach botany. Later as curator of the herbarium at Columbia he had settled to his lifework which was the study of cereal grains. It was Anderson's discovery that cornstarch when placed in a tube and subjected to intense heat expanded to ten times the original volume. When the tube was cracked open there was an instantaneous noisy explosion. This was caused by the escape, as steam, of the condensed water of the starch nucleus which, by the same process, had shattered the starch granule. The very dangerous operation of cracking the tube presently was eliminated by the development of a "puffing gun" which actually looks and behaves like a competent and determined cannon.

Food shot from guns took possession of the imagination of the American public by virtue of its unexpectedness much as the circus idea of shooting women from cannons has pleased customers of all ages. By the year 1929 patents on the Anderson process had had their legal life and the field was open for developments such as Collatz had in mind.

He experimented tirelessly until he had achieved at last a method that was essentially different from any that had been used before. Instead of working with raw grain, he prepared a mixture of cooked grain

214

products seasoned appropriately and fortified with protective ingredients.

Two ready-to-eat cereals were developed out of this ingenious method — Kix from corn and Cheerios from oats. In each instance cooked dough was pressed through a die and then expanded in a puffing gun.

Four years of study and experimentation went into the adaptation and further elaboration of this technique before Cheerios went on the market. A research team produced in the end a genuinely original product. It looked like a miniature doughnut and made an immediate appeal both to the eye and to the taste bud. Customers upon whom this latest addition to the General Mills family of products was tested in May 1941 found it greatly to their liking for a variety of reasons — taste, crispness, digestibility. All were united in the opinion that its form was a delightful surprise. Cheerios in the course of its career has grown steadily in popularity, paralleling the triumph of Wheaties.

For the new product the delightfully inspired name Cheerioats was originally chosen. "He's feeling his Cheerioats," punned the cartoon advertisements which showed a fine fellow in the display of some attractive if not quite believable prowess like juggling anvils. But the bright tag was relinquished when a rival merchant suggested that he held some moral right to the exclusive use of the word "oats" in a commercial name. Three years after its debut, Cheerioats became Cheerios, which also is a jaunty trade name, one that has proved to be worthy of the product's popularity.

Besides a threatened lawsuit, Cheerios' life had been seriously marred at the start by another touch of melodrama. The cereal plant at Buffalo which was eventually to become its home was having the final touches put to its exterior on a day in February 1940 when suddenly it burst into flames. Twelve men at work on the seventh floor were trapped and rescued dramatically when firemen anchored a rope ladder to the roof down which the victims lowered themselves to safety. But the completely new structure in which the sprinkling apparatus had not yet been installed could only be allowed to burn out. A long delay resulted, but at last Cheerios assumed occupancy in October 1941.

One of the hazards of a diversified operation may have caused the Buffalo fire. General Mills claimed at one time to be the world's largest distributor of airplanes, but these were of the kind that may be given away as premiums to right-thinking sons of the age of flight who were

215

also right-living users of General Mills' products. The Buffalo blaze is thought to have started in a room where these flimsy souvenirs had been stored temporarily.

The debut of new products demonstrated again that the folk culture of our civilization is bound up forever with its commercial life. To exploit Cheerios General Mills employed one of its most successful radio serials, *The Lone Ranger*. This Robin Hood of the frontier, minus "merrie men," operates a kind of one-man Community Chest, producing, in his own rugged and romantic way, help for the needy and hard-pressed. A reticent righter of wrongs and blighter of wrongdoers, the Lone Ranger wears a mask. He rides a white horse (nowadays on television), calls out the summons "Hi-ho, Silver" to this companion, and in moments of great extremity shoots a silver bullet. The audience of American children has seldom been offered an entertainment in any form that is more completely to its taste.

The history of Cheerios dramatizes the complexity of the operation involved in getting a new product to market. The developmental stage was long and patient. The relatively high cost of the raw materials made it necessary to plan with the utmost care, yet the high nutritional value of oats made the experimenters persist until they had achieved a unique product.

The ingenious tests devised to determine whether or not Cheerios would fill an economic need were such as only a modern corporation could afford to apply. An astonishing number of man-hours had been exhausted before the first package of Cheerios could be put on the shelf in the neighborhood store. More surprising still is the thought of the army of highly trained people drafted for the campaign: scientists, laboratory technicians, experts in market analysis, conductors of surveys, psychologists, radio entertainers. All had a share in carrying Cheerios to market.

But whether the Research laboratories were engaged in developing new cereal products for manufacture in the home plants or collaborating with other laboratories like those of Eastman in the development and distribution of new supports to human well-being, General Mills worked actively during the 1930s and 1940s to fulfill the principle enunciated by Bell in his address before the Millers' National Federation at the annual convention in May 1939. "The ancient and honorable profession," he had said, must not try to live on its reputation, indeed, could not survive in

216

the tradition of the past. Instead, it must "look steadily at the task ahead, that of creating new values for our industry — new values based on products possessing the attributes which, in turn, create increased demand, improved methods of manufacture and service of greater worth to the American people."

15

Toward Centralization

GENERAL MILLS BECOMES AN OPERATING COMPANY

W HEN Bell became chairman of the board of General Mills in August 1934, he found himself faced by a major task, that of reorganizing the corporation so that its essential design might more exactly suit the needs of a greatly changed economic program. At his side, in the president's chair, was a sympathetic ally, that engineer of business, Donald Davis, who fed on facts and took his chief delight in surveys, graphs, and blueprints.

The principle of diversification upon which Bell had insisted in shaping the original pattern of General Mills had paid off handsomely. The company had shown a consolidated net profit throughout the depression of approximately $4,000,000 each year. It had done so, despite the falling per capita consumption of flour, by making a great variety of products all the way from vitamins to packaging machinery (though not yet the locomotives of which Bell had spoken whimsically and perhaps a little wistfully). But the diversification program had created problems of distribution and sale that had not been foreseen in the original pattern of organization.

Percentage figures revealed clearly the shift of emphasis within the company's operation. Beginning in 1932 sales from flour began to account for a smaller share of the company's total income. During the next two decades it dropped from 72 per cent to 55. This did not mean, of course, that General Mills sold less flour; its activity in this field was as great as ever. But though flour was the first-born and continued to be the heir to the milling tradition, it was no longer an only child to be petted and worried over. Sales from packaged foods lately had contributed an ever greater share to General Mills' total income — 6 per cent in 1932, 17 per cent twenty years later.

Adaptations and adjustments to the realities of the situation had brought about many changes during the years just after the formation of General Mills. As the competition of the chain store began to be more acute it became evident that the only way to cope with this great national force was to summon all one's own strength as a national force. This meant, above all else, the maintenance of a well-organized merchandising program on a national scale.

The old order was indeed gone forever, as Bell had observed. Many analysts within the company supported this view by pointing out that, even when they had only flour to sell, millers could no longer expect the jobbers to do the task because the jobber–independent grocer field was being encroached upon by the multiply owned retailers. For its own part the chain store would be interested in a particular flour like Gold Medal only if its prestige were maintained by vigorous, effective advertising and by an energetic search for all possible outlets that promotion could uncover.

If this was true of flour it was even more true of packaged foods. The chains not merely controlled many of the channels of distribution in this area but they were themselves manufacturers, too, with products of their own to enter in direct competition with the products of General Mills. As Walter Barry once expressed the issue: "In choosing between a food product of a national manufacturer and a food product of their own, these distributors will lend support to the manufacturer's brand only when they see that it is being promoted to the consumers by the manufacturer."

The only conclusion to be drawn was that the man with something to sell must take his story directly to the buyer, using a loud-speaker of national strength to do so. A gratifying respect for one's product, shown in the form of orders, could be expected of the trade only if a demand were created first in the mind of that busy figure, the woman shopper.

The arts of advertising and merchandising — cornerstones of modern business — were, of course, intimately familiar to the men of General Mills, and the Board of Directors did not hesitate, even as the depression deepened, to vote in January 1930 for a great expansion program calling for a substantial investment in promotion and advertising.

Still they tried to work through the original design of General Mills which undermined a little of its force as a national organization by giving virtual autonomy to the associated companies. The terms of the 1930 program made each of these operating units a jobber of the packaged food items with exclusive rights in a specified territory. The price of the product to these companies allowed a margin for selling expense and for profit. Advertising expense was assumed by the central company.

But almost immediately an agitation began for still greater recognition of the rights of grocery products. There must be, the experts agreed, a complete segregation of the company's quite different interests. Into one category they believed should go bakers' flour and feed; into another family flour and grocery products. As the chain stores steadily expanded their outlets it became vitally necessary to preserve and to extend the distribution of Gold Medal Kitchen-Tested Flour and no less important to make a full-time project of exploiting the grocery store items. The techniques of selling Wheaties, Bisquick, and Gold Medal Flour all were similar and should be the province of one salesman. The handling of "general" flour and feed was a different sort of operation and should be developed by a different group.

In the minds of several of these experts the question was implicit of whether or not the original organization plan of General Mills was right for present conditions. The supposedly autonomous operating companies, linked under the guidance of a holding company, might not have the power to act in the unity called for by the national campaigns now proposed. The old regional divisions seemed to have lost significance in the need for selling programs on the national scale. The "avenue to the home," about which Bell had talked as the one along which the wise merchandiser would send his diversity of products, must be a broad one covering the country from end to end, not a complicated network of little country roads.

During the depression it became unpleasantly evident that there was need for the greatest possible unity of action in other fields. The high prestige of Gold Medal Flour and the speed shown by Bisquick and Wheaties in taking the lead away from competitors had been chiefly responsible for the comforting figures of the General Mills' annual reports. Yet the corporation had not entirely escaped some of the minor symptoms of the economic illness of the time. The chief of these was experienced in the formula-feeds branch of the business which the diagnosticians did not hesitate to describe as very sick indeed.

The reasons were obvious. In the early 1930s when the farmer's bravest hope was simply to survive, dairymen and poultry raisers among them were in a peculiarly bad way. Even with rough feeds selling at absurdly low prices it was impossible to make a profit. The revenue from eggs was not enough to justify keeping a flock. The whole operation had moved into the realm of dreary fantasy. A man could indulge himself in the luxury of being industrious if it pleased his vanity. But he must not expect to make a profit from his effort. Profits had, for the moment, entirely disappeared in the withering face of hardship.

It can be readily understood that such men were not in the market for formula feeds of the superior type that General Mills had to sell. The government offered no help in this crisis. Its authoritative word to farmers was that animals did not require grains and that pasturage served their needs quite well enough.

At this threat to all that his painstaking records had been designed to prove, Charles Staff treadled his feet in his wastebasket, as was his habit, in an ecstasy of excitement and finally removed them to go to the research farm and start a new set of experiments. From the herd he selected the three best cows and subjected them to a dietary program in which the volume of grain-formulated feed was steadily diminished, finally to nothing at all. They were then put on straight pasturage as the government had recommended that all cows should be. Within a pathetically short time the productivity of each of these choice animals had dropped from approximately seventy pounds of milk a day to approximately thirty.

Zealot that he was for proof, and very nearly mystic in his belief in statistics, Staff kept account of his animals' behavior for two years more. During this time he reinstated the grain formula feeds and saw his cows return to the level of productivity that had been theirs before the experiment began.

But the task of persuading the farmer that he was a businessman who must make a reasonable investment in order to earn a satisfactory return was one calling for patient, educational fervor. The devotees of Larro religion had such patience.

Meanwhile James Larrowe was determined to have nothing to do with red-ink accounts. He was never at a loss either for ideas or for energy. When he found it impossible to make a profit in his own business, he simply deflected his attention to one in which there were immediate opportunities. People who would not buy formula feeds for their cattle still bought sugar for themselves. During the depression Larrowe was interested in several sugar factories and he managed these interests so effectively that he emerged from the experience to find that he had become, much to his own incredulous annoyance, a hero in the industry. He managed, also, to offset the losses of feed operations and to keep his affairs "in the black."

The rural stores, the acquisition of which Mowat had urged at the time of the formation of General Mills, were, in the same period of universal doubt, wavering down the wrong side of the ledger. Theoretically and actually they provided outlets for the products of the company. More than a hundred of them had been strategically placed about the country. Many were in New England; another large group covered Minnesota and the adjacent territory; still others were scattered through Ohio, Florida, and (in a later period) along the Pacific Coast. But such access to the farm as the rural stores provided could hardly be considered an asset if it cost more money than it produced in sales.

It was characteristic of the approach to this problem made by the men of General Mills that they all remained incorruptibly hopeful. Since the time when the benignity of J. S. Bell presided over the affairs of Washburn Crosby, this attitude had had an almost ritualistic authority that was seldom forsaken or betrayed. Even in the dismal year when the stores were suffering their most serious blight, the tone of reports and discussions was never permitted to become resentful or impatient. Few organizations, perhaps, have managed to maintain through various changes of leadership so consistent an attitude of faith in the bright prospect of tomorrow.

Bell's solution of the immediate problem was to turn it over to the most flexibly enthusiastic of all General Mills' executives, Bullis. This, he said in the idiom of the day, was Bullis' baby. At Chicago when the operating executives of the Farm Service Stores were brought together to look at "figures that are not pleasant" no one seems to have thought of making threats or presenting challenges that wore black, commanding brows. Rather, Bullis reminded his team that Knute Rockne had once said of one of his players that though the boy was a great runner, he seemed to run too long in the same place. Under the exacting conditions of the depression, he suggested, that kind of running could be improved upon.

Result: the Farm Service Stores showed only a very small loss in the year when the depression reached its lowest point and within two years had become "a bright spot" of the annual report, showing a reasonable profit.

In the same year the formula-feed salesmen completed the missionary work for which Larro religion called. The story of Staff's cows reached enough farmers so that the volume of sales increased impressively. These products were launched upon a new career and eventually they became the second largest contributor in all the family of General Mills' commodities to the profits of the company. The volume of this fast-growing industry is divided among many comparatively small operators. Even the giant of the business, Ralston Purina, has captured only 6 per cent of the country's total volume and General Mills only 2 per cent. But it is precisely the sort of enterprise in which General Mills takes especial interest because its increasing authority in the agricultural world offers an opportunity for indefinite expansion through service.

The need to distinguish clearly between types of operation and to bring about a close consolidation of effort within the province of each had been in the background of Bell's mind all through the adroit campaigns to fight off the ill effects of the depression. Late in 1933 he had noted in his diary that the effect of A.A.A. regulations had been further to emphasize these differences of procedure. He wrote: "Already the government is recognizing the difference between flour manufacturing and packaged foods, something I have long advocated doing within. Now the windows are broken from without and we are forced to a procedure we should have initiated."

In May 1936 he decided that, no matter what immediate crisis might urge delay, it would be unwise to temporize longer. He went before the Board of Directors, armored in data and carrying as shield another "magnum opus" similar in design to the one with which he had gone before the directors of the Washburn Crosby Company to urge the formation of General Mills. Change was again his theme and, again, it seemed necessary to him that he and his associates must seize the initiative in warding off its ill effects. Obsolescence, he pointed out, "is the inevitable result of time and progress." New goods and services constantly push old

223

goods and services aside. "Industrial enterprises justify themselves through the performance of economic services in an efficient and economical manner. Progress is measured in terms of the betterment of old goods and services and the production of new goods and services at decreasing costs and prices." It was time for General Mills to review its situation and determine how it might best serve this exacting principle of progress. A simplification of its basic structure seemed to be essential.

General Mills had been created in the image of an ideal decentralization of authority. The theory on which the organizers had proceeded was that of providing "checks and balances to prevent the tendency toward centralized control" and to encourage the initiative of individuals. "That these measures were well devised," Bell wrote, "is demonstrated by accomplishment. The spirit, interest and morale which exist within the organization are a matter of comment in the business world. We all know what we have done through these difficult years, how closely we have been brought together in a common cause."

But now the form had become top-heavy. It was beginning to cost too much to perform essential services. "From the outset I have urged that we see the thing big but keep it simple," Bell echoed a favorite dictum. He was in no doubt that General Mills had been seeing big; the thing to do now was to look steadily and without sentimental regard for tradition at the problem of achieving simplicity.

His program resolved itself into these suggestions: creation of a convenient number of sales territories and the concentration of all bulk flour and feed activities (except for those of Larrowe) within them; centralization of all wheat operations under a wheat executive; segregation of Gold Medal Kitchen-Tested Flour from other flour interests and its addition to the responsibilities of a centralized packaged goods division.

These items covered the part of Bell's definition of progress that referred to the improvement of old goods and services. Looking toward the introduction of new goods and services he urged "continuing research into diversified uses of flour . . . study of new grocery-shelf items of related character and also of unrelated character . . . further research in by-products whether of related or unrelated character."

The advantages to be gained from this program of simplification he expected to be several. Properly administered the new units could do what could not be demanded of organization under the old form: elimination of the overlapping of sales effort, elimination of the evil of intercompany competition, elimination of the difficulties and uncertainties of intercompany transactions in the same fields, economies in the organization of staffs.

There was still another reason for suggesting these changes. Bell believed that the effect of new tax legislation would be to penalize the holding company. The general effect of the prevailing philosophy was virtually to compel "the segregation of operating companies and, still more, the consolidation of these into fewer units or a single unit." Bell found this "a compelling force and one in which our discretion will not be the determining factor." It was, however, a force that happened to move powerfully in the same direction as the force of the impulse, which Bell found most compelling of all, to put his house in order.

The effect of this second "magnum opus" was much like the effect of the first. His associates were used, by now, to having the even tenor of their ways suddenly shaken by Bell's determination to anticipate change. As one such man once observed with a kind of amused and affectionate awe, "He was forever bringing in a nice, competent little volcano and setting it in operation on my desk." But everyone faced the volcano gallantly. Conferences about the proposed change went on all summer with Bell, Davis, and Bullis going from one regional headquarters to another taking the opinions of the executives concerned. Though there was wide divergence of opinion among them about matters of detail, the over-all judgment of the great majority was that a simplified program was desirable.

The matter was finally decided on June 1, 1937, when by action of the Board of Directors plans were adopted "for the complete liquidation and dissolution of all subsidiary companies." (Excepted from this sweeping decision were three — the Washburn Crosby Company, Ltd., of Port Colborne, Ontario; the Frontier Elevator Company of Buffalo; and the Pacific Coast Elevator Company of Portland, Oregon — all of whose functions reached outside the close design now planned for General Mills.) Beginning on the day of the board's action "all business heretofore conducted by the discontinued subsidiary companies will be conducted by General Mills which becomes an operating company."

The essential purposes of Bell's proposal were accomplished in another feature of the plan of reorganization. This created two distinct divisions of company operations, that of Flour and Feed and that of Grocery Products. All manufacturing and merchandising activities associated with each of these great consolidations were to be in charge of the executive chosen to head it. For Flour and Feed this was Bullis, for Grocery Products, Barry.

To Bullis' realm belonged all bulk flour and feed activities throughout the company, including the flour and feed plants. To Barry belonged Wheaties, Softasilk Cake Flour, Bisquick, Gold Medal Kitchen-Tested Flour (all originally of the Washburn Crosby family of products); Drifted Snow Flour, La Pina Flour, Wheat Hearts, Pancake Flour (all from Sperry); and Red Band Flour (from the Southeast). Regardless of regional origin, Barry became foster father to the merchandising of them all, in the interest of a unified program of exploitation.

The purpose of the reorganization was to increase efficiency, not simply to augment the prestige of General Mills. It was decided, therefore, not to toss away the valuable good will that had accumulated over the years around the names of the individual companies now dissolved. Those having lost their significance as separate entities reclaimed a compensatory importance as sales territories. The old trade names were clearly retained to identify old units in the minds of old customers. What was officially the Eastern Division of General Mills was, for the men who had long done business over its counters, the Washburn Crosby Company, Buffalo, branch of General Mills. The Central Division — headquarters Chicago — conducted its business under the old trade names of Washburn Crosby, Royal Milling Company, and Rocky Mountain Elevator Company. The Southwestern and Southeastern divisions listed all the old familiar firms associated with their beginnings. The fifth division, the Western as it was called in the plans for reorganization, was particularly jealous of its old fame. West Coast executives were convinced that the name Sperry had a very special significance. General Mills, having no desire to be doctrinaire in such matters, voted presently to acknowledge a moral right and the Western Division became the Sperry Division.

Men with long careers of service to their credit headed each of these divisions as chief executives, retaining at the time of the 1937 reorganization the title president. These were William Morris at Buffalo; H. R. McLaughlin at Chicago; James Hargett at Oklahoma City; Frank Burke at San Francisco; and James Selvage at Atlanta.

Four other units were to function as integral parts of General Mills but under their own names. There was, first, the Larrowe Division, which already satisfied Bell's principle of organization. Its manufacturing and merchandising activities were consolidated and its program was national in scope. There was, second, the Farm Service Division, also already unified in its organization at Minneapolis, while its activities through the rural stores covered the nation. The Star Grain Division still served as jobber in Chicago and its program was not changed. The American Research Products Division had been organized from the beginning on a unified basis for national service.

The movement toward centralization, represented by the reorganization of 1937, went only a very small part of the way as a still later change was to demonstrate. Though it seemed revolutionary because it insisted on the importance of over-all planning from headquarters, it did not wipe out the authority of the executive in the field — at San Francisco, or Chicago, or Oklahoma City. The all-important profit-and-loss responsibility remained with him to provide its stimulus to effective management. To be sure, the headquarters vice president in charge of Flour and Feed, or Grocery Products, shared the profit-and-loss responsibility. But the executive in the field kept his own figures and was able to interpret their significance in the day-by-day operations.

With him there remained also freedom to make the brisk decision and to take the quick action involved in trading activities. What the geographical divisions had forgone chiefly was the right to initiate policies that might be in conflict with the policies of other units, tending to create the overlapping of effort, duplication of service, or intramural warfare against which Bell's report had protested. General Mills, as the operating company, was now much more securely in possession of certain administrative rights. It could protect quality; regulate selling programs; supervise milling construction and renovation; make suggestions regarding prices to be used on cost cards; call upon mills that lacked adequate orders to supply flour for mills that were operating on expensive overtime; even, in pressing circumstances, direct that flour be sold for export rather than in the domestic market. Bell had urged in his 1937 challenge that changes must undertake to retain those advantages of the old form that led "to the creation of opportunities and to the building of big men to be identified with operations." And, in fact, the reorganized corporation managed to cling to many of the fundamental principles of the original design and it moved toward centralization only so far as to claim the advantages of unified action in manufacturing and selling.

Toward Centralization

The new program seemed to have a blessing to offer. Only two years after it had been put into effect, the annual report (1938–39) happily called attention to its belief that credit for the record of this, "the most successful year in the company's history," belonged to "thousands of individuals who had loyally and intelligently played their parts with an ever-broadening perception of the relationship of each one of them to the company as a whole." Between them, management and workers had lifted consolidated net income from a little more than four million dollars in the year before to six and a half million in the year that ended May 31, 1939.

In a report made at the same time to all the "men and women of General Mills," Bell offered his own summing up of the first decade. The company, he pointed out once more, was the "largest miller of grain in the United States, virtually twice the size of the next largest operator." This did not mean that General Mills possessed a monopoly; indeed, it produced only 11 per cent of the grain products consumed in the United States. Size did, however, indicate an aptitude and opportunity for leadership. One fact that testified most strongly to the honesty of that leadership was that General Mills, alone among milling operators, had "earned and paid an annual dividend on common stock without diminution right through the depression." And again leadership was reflected in the company's record of progress.

"Progress in every phase of our business — improved methods in milling and packaging, improved practices of distribution, improved conditions of employment, new and improved products resulting from our ceaseless research — all have brought us profit and leadership."

But it has brought obligation, too.

"Because the organization of General Mills is necessarily diffuse and complex it is all the more important that unity in action, recognition of individual responsibility and the spirit of cooperation prevail. This spirit, securing the welfare of all, has been responsible for the company's success, progress and growth throughout a decade marked by depression and uncertainty."

16

Corporate Citizen

WORLD WAR II AND AFTER

WHEN Harry Amos Bullis became president of General Mills in 1942 just a year after Pearl Harbor, his inaugural gesture seemed to be that of creating a third shift to be held down by himself as entire staff. The second shift for which he had long had the habit of "sticking around" no longer exhausted his sense of responsibility. In wartime, the third shift was the essential one. Bullis made reference to it in an article, "Industry Masses Its Power for Victory," written just after he had taken office. Quoting Kipling's "Epitaph for a Battery Out of Ammunition," he observed that the American workers must never face the same tragic indictment:

> "If any mourn us in the workshop, say
> We died because the shift kept holiday."

Bullis had succeeded Donald Davis when the latter resigned in December 1942 to go into active war work as a member of the War Production Board. In the early days of the war Davis had felt that as a leader in an essential industry which actually produced war material, he served the armed forces directly and faithfully. Later, he had changed his mind and volunteered for service in Washington. Bell's diary commented, "I am sad to see him go." But the break had to be final because, as Bell said, a permanent appointment must be made immediately from among the men who had long been his close allies. Bullis, who had been executive vice president for two years and acting president for three months, was, of course, the inevitable choice.

A series of fortunate circumstances, each with its significant place in the essential development of General Mills, made the company able and willing to go, almost as one might say at the drop of a bomb, into war work. Bell had said at the time of the formation that he must feel free to make anything from flour to locomotives and he had been, in the years just before Pearl Harbor, edging ever closer and closer to the locomotives. General Mills always had been concerned with the task of making machinery to perform its own chores. One mechanical genius in particular, Thomas James, had performed brilliant services in the development of such things as puffing guns and packaging equipment. But the stern economic fact still remained that the capital investment required for this work could not be justified by doing only these limited tasks. Additional work must be found or the effort could not be continued.

Because it was always Bell's preference to expand rather than to contract, the company began to look for other assignments in the mechanical field. Shortly before Pearl Harbor, when the Northern Pump Company of Minneapolis turned to the manufacture of big barrel guns, a new plant was required. The old one stood empty and in 1940 General Mills bought it with the intention of broadening the scope of its activities in sympathy with the flexibility of Bell's original plan.

The moment of decision that followed Pearl Harbor presented crucial problems to every citizen, public and private. To the men of General Mills it meant among other things that they must get into war work or lose both the mechanical experts and the modern machine tools that they had been developing.

But it was less easy to get war assignments than might be supposed. In the mechanical field one must demonstrate fitness as well as willingness. As soon as war broke out Bell and Davis (then still president of General Mills) went to Washington, seeking advice more than immediate employment. Should they put in money and expand in the expectation of being useful to the government in the manufacture of munitions; would the possibilities justify this investment of the stockholders' money? Frank Knox, secretary of the navy, was dubious. When he called in an admiral for further consultation, that defender of the standards of his service was openly indignant. Why should flour manufacturers imagine that they were capable of doing the kind of delicate precision work required by the navy?

The most that anyone was willing to do was to toss the British, still *in extremis* in their need of weapons, in Bell's way. The British Admiralty permitted General Mills to work on breechblock equipment with the particular hope of developing a "roll corrector." When the task was done and its success demonstrated, the Admiralty still asked for a reexamination, expressing its frank disbelief that a satisfactory job could have been done so quickly. But in the end its representatives offered full acknowledgment that the "roll corrector" was a success. They offered also extravagant compliments for the accuracy of its working.

And now at last the American navy was persuaded. Its first request of General Mills was for an eight-inch gun sight. In an atmosphere of haste and impatience the project went forward. No one could wait for such matters as that of having tolerances checked. Suddenly in the midst of a tense effort the designer confessed that he himself had never made one of these instruments complete. Scarcely remarkable, thought the men of General Mills, that the parts called for by a theoretical design did not immediately fit. James, of the Mechanical Division, redesigned the whole thing and made it work. Assignments followed to make torpedo directors and torpedo indicators for the navy, which now demonstrated its gratitude by offering the Army-Navy E Award on several different occasions. As a commander of the navy said in making one such award, "You started from scratch in a new field of production in response to your country's great need for weapons and the results in only two years have been outstanding."

General Mills, fortunate as always in the selection of men, had found exactly the right chief for its greatly expanded mechanical activities. Arthur Hyde, born in Minnesota and resident of Joliet, Ill., who had traveled to the University of Illinois and to Columbia for his bachelor of arts degree and his degree as bachelor of science in engineering, had come to Bell's attention as a classmate of his own son. Bell straightway marked the young man as his own. Hyde was persuaded to travel to Minneapolis and begin an apprenticeship under the dean of practical millers, George Cormack. He joined General Mills in the very year of its formation and advanced rapidly, becoming in 1935 director of the manufacturing department.

The wartime growth of the Mechanical Division plant producing war equipment was prodigious. At first 1000 new employees had been audaciously added to the staff; within a few months 1000 more were required. The first torpedo director made by General Mills was delivered to the navy in time to give gratifying service at Guadalcanal in October

1942. During that struggle the United States destroyer Duncan took off in pursuit of a Japanese cruiser. In a brilliantly executed maneuver the American vessel sent a torpedo toward the enemy ship lunging, as a picturesque report had it, "like a crazed whale." Chiefly because of the precision of the director machined by General Mills to a tolerance of one ten-thousandth of an inch, the missile reached its goal and the Japanese cruiser was neatly dispatched to the bottom of the sea.

This was only the beginning. There were many significant modifications of the original design, complicated enough at the start with its thousand parts and its need to be virtually indestructible in all kinds of weather and battle conditions. With designs adapted and perfected by General Mills' technicians, the instruments became more subtle and complicated with each phase of the war. By 1943 General Mills was producing weapons that were strangely and wonderfully made to outwit the enemy. Among them was a "jitterbug" torpedo that could run in one direction as though its goal had been lost and then, with the target ship lulled into false security, suddenly swerved at a right angle and found its mark. The jitterbug torpedo could do a U-turn or even describe a figure 8, all in the interest of baffling the Japanese by following what the scientists called, with admirable detachment, "an unusual trajectory pattern."

An unusual trajectory pattern, certainly, was the one into which Bell and Bullis, with the assistance of all the major men of their staff, directed the drive of the company. The activities of the newly created Mechanical Division, with Arthur Hyde as its indefatigable head, represented only one of the striking departures made by General Mills from its ordinary routine. All the other departments were similarly involved in war work. At Rochester, New York, Distillation Products made coating for lenses and high-precision instruments. At Buffalo the company's fine mechanical equipment was put at the task of packaging dehydrated eggs for lend-lease shipment. At Vallejo, California, bags were produced suitable for conversion into sandbags. Granular flour, from which came the vast supply of alcohol needed for the production of smokeless powder by the armed services, was another by-product that went to war.

These wartime activities floated on the surface of the company's flow of energy. The stream itself carried the established products, many put into wartime uniform, to be distributed to the service and among America's lend-lease customers. These included flour, vitamin concen-

trates, ready-to-eat breakfast foods, mill feeds in new abundance, and —
a new variation on an old theme — oat flour for D-rations.

When anyone said to Bullis that the bypaths up which he was leading his troops must be exhausting, and even a little confusing, he replied
that he found the changes stimulating. "The beaten path is for beaten
men," he would say.

What had been happening within the circle of American industry
in those years just before and just after Pearl Harbor was a really momentous event — the debut, no less, of a new kind of creature in a new kind of
democratic life. The impulse that had brought this good genius into
existence had been gathering strength for a long time. Indeed, J. F. Bell
may be said to have called upon industry in World War I to bring this
entity to life. The idea behind his operation of the Milling Division of
the Food Administration was simply that industry had a duty, exactly
like that of a private individual, to sacrifice personal advantage, in wartime, to the public advantage and to work wholeheartedly for the
common good. Law already had made the corporation a legal person,
an economic man. Now, that man shouldered the obligations of a citizen,
a corporate citizen. He, too, enlisted "for the duration" and took on jobs
well outside his normal range just as the private citizen was required
to do.

It is, perhaps, not too much to suggest that in this moment of industry's rebirth as corporate citizen the issue was settled between Hitler
and the world he challenged. The Nazis could demand only that their
followers choose between guns and butter, the foregone conclusion of a
dictatorship being that its adherents would choose guns. Democracy,
however, was able to do much better, once its energies were roused. With
resolution unparalleled in human history, it supplied both guns and
butter. General Mills had, in this time, the gratifying experience of being
able to pour from its crowded cornucopia a noble welter of seemingly
unrelated objects — gun sights, breakfast foods, alcohol, dehydrated
eggs, dehydrated soups, vitamins, and sandbags. It was the early consciousness of emergency on the part of its leaders that made this possible;
it was a long history of disciplined adaptability that made the program
possible.

In the midst of the war Bell made his own public statement of faith
about what the duties of a corporate citizen should be. Already looking
toward the postwar world, in an article written for the *Atlantic Monthly*

233

in July 1943 and called "Can We Finance the Future," Bell suggested what two fundamental concepts must underlie all planning. First, "that the increased welfare of the common man as world citizen is the only true and workable basis for a prosperous future" and, second, "that we must urge economic democracy to sustain the common man in his struggle toward his goal."

Surveying the formidable prospect of rehabilitation that must follow the war, Bell offered the guiding principle that "government and free industry must achieve in the new world a proper coordination of authority and responsibility." Any project for the restoration of the good life in countries where war had corrupted or destroyed it, any proposal to develop backward countries must, Bell urged, call for the cooperative participation of national governments and private capital.

Industry, as corporate citizen, had developed not merely an increased sense of responsibility but a philosophy with which to control its drive and an objective toward which to direct it.

Long before the end of the war seemed to be remotely in prospect, Bullis began to plan for the future, determined that there should be, for General Mills, no postwar slump. All divisions and activities, he reported, showed "fortunate" increases for the immediate past. Flour production was up 31 per cent over the figure for 1940–41; commercial feed totals had increased enormously, approximately doubling those of 1940–41; and even packaged foods, the advances of which had been steady and impressive for a decade, had shot forward for a 40 per cent gain.

The purpose of Bell and Bullis was to find a means of maintaining this stride when the impetus supplied by the war should slacken. Bullis, ever an inexhaustible explorer of figures and factual data, appointed a thirteen-man committee, with himself as chairman, to find out precisely where the company stood with regard to existing facilities, to the efficiency of its services, and to the prospect of finding new ways of being active in the postwar world. That fantastic changes were taking place no one doubted. Everything from the means of transporting goods to the tastes of people who would consume these goods had undergone startling alteration. The vastly increased use of electric power, the discoveries of new uses for old commodities, the growing ease of communication, the tightening of the world into economic interdependence — all of these influences needed study if one were to know how to lay confident hands on a segment of tomorrow and make it one's own.

234

Bullis, of course, was determined to expand and this impulse was entirely in sympathy with the philosophy that always had animated Bell's imagination. The "avenue to the home" about which the chairman of the board had had so much to say in the contemplative discussions of the past was now, he saw, broader than ever before. Facilities for moving along it were more powerful and faster than they had been. There were more kinds of goods to carry. The only question that remained was what new goods could be produced most profitably.

These had to be chosen wisely that they might fit appropriately into the general merchandising program. Bullis had a figure of speech that he liked to repeat because it was so neatly apposite. The obelisks of ancient Egypt, he reminded his audiences, had crumbled to the ground because they stood alone and unsupported. The pyramids built upon broad indestructible bases must stand forever. "We must broaden the base," Bullis would say.

Two stout documents appeared as a result of the work of Bullis' committee — first, the *Postwar Planning Report* and, second, the *Current and Future Planning Report*. The temper of the two studies, both of which range widely, impartially, illuminatingly over every aspect of commercial production, was expressed by Bullis in one paragraph in particular:

"We know that the source of more jobs for the postwar period is more production. To secure more production, we must offer better and cheaper products for sale to the American people. In order to manufacture more and cheaper products, we must develop new products and have modern efficient plants in which to manufacture them as well as our present products."

The men of this modern corporation knew well that times had changed and that new ways must be found of financing the strenuous future for which they planned. Bell in particular remembered that in the old days of Dunwoody and Bell, Senior, the affairs of the Washburn Crosby Company had been operated on the most conservative possible basis with working capital kept, like a well-cared-for but hard-worked plow horse, to a strict regime. This draft animal was given the special nourishment of borrowing only in moments of great crisis like that of buying out the Washburn heirs. He knew also that though tradition in business is never sacred, it is still true that fathers cast long shadows over the minds of their sons.

Corporate Citizen

The story is told of Andrew Mellon that shortly after he had accepted the appointment as secretary of the treasury, in President Harding's cabinet, he was visited in Washington by his brother. The latter availed himself of a fraternal privilege to ask what rent the secretary was paying for his apartment. Andrew Mellon named the figure. "And what is your salary in government service?" Andrew Mellon named that figure, too. It did not equal the cost per year of his apartment. The more frugal of the Mellons clucked his tongue reproachfully. "What would father say?" he mourned.

There was never a man who asked himself more often "What would father say?" than did J. F. Bell. But there is evidence in this instance that he put away his father's caution regretfully. An item in his diary refers to the "Martin-Dunwoody-Bell tradition of ownership management." But to that tradition he made a respectful gesture of farewell. In the modern world of finance, he wrote, such stern self-sufficiency was neither possible nor desirable.

Still essentially conservative in operation General Mills was jealous of its reputation for paying all bills at the end of the year. Borrowing for expansion was, therefore, not part of its program. The company grew by ploughing back profits into new fields. Its theory of operation as far as facilities were concerned was that it was "cheaper to build them than to buy them." If a corporation grew from within there was no need to put out capital for good will; its money could go for something of immediate practical value.

But there was still need to borrow in order to apply the principles of insurance to the capital market and have more money available with which to do business. At the annual meeting of the year 1943–44, preferred stockholders were asked to authorize (and did so authorize) borrowing up to $20,000,000. Of this only $10,000,000 actually was issued in January 1944, in 2½ per cent debentures. These were sold at par to nine of General Mills' depository banks and the proceeds added to the corporate funds. The low rate of interest for debentures, together with the favorable tax effect of this form of financing, made it one to which even the shade of Dunwoody would have given cautious approval.

Though the over-all plan for expansion dictated the principle of building rather than buying additional facilities, Bullis did not hesitate, under the pressure of war conditions, to purchase certain plants that became available for immediate use. A first step toward the future made under his presidency was the acquisition of the Purity Oats property at Keokuk, Iowa. This was needed to provide oat flour for use in the ready-to-eat cereal Cheerios. During the war, however, it served chiefly to make army K-rations. Clarence Hidding, who allowed himself to be acquired along with the Keokuk property, became manager for General Mills. He developed another wartime commodity, a dehydrated soup mix of which UNRRA ordered millions of pounds. After World War II, he and his associates explored the South American and Far Eastern markets where their products earned a fine reputation. Large five-and-a-half-inch tin containers of Quick Cooking Oats went out under labels in eighteen languages to carry the message of democratic plenty to a half-starved world.

Also in the midst of the war, General Mills demonstrated its faith in the future by acquiring properties at Lake Superior for the further broadening of its strategic base. The Duluth Elevator Division, as this new branch was called, served the Eastern, Central, and Purity Oats divisions as storage place for goods in transit.

Shortly before V-J day, Bell wrote in his diary: "Victory will prove to be not an end but a beginning. Problems will loom larger than ever."

In setting down this comment, Bell experienced, of course, a generous-minded man's awareness of the pity as well as the grandeur of victory. Yet something indefatigable in him welcomed the new crisis, the fresh start. In the course of a single crowded day during this time he met with the staff of the General Mills Research laboratory to consider new projects; met with the ever stimulatingly contentious Elizabeth Kenny to consider major problems of her institute for polio treatment in Minneapolis; consulted with public-spirited citizens about the possibility of establishing a navy school at the University of Minnesota; lunched with the director of the Minneapolis Institute of Arts to listen to the report of a young friend who had worked with the OSS in the French underground; and went into a huddle with the chief executive of General Mills, Bullis, on the further extension of the diversification program.

Bell had communicated to Bullis the same enthusiasm for the fresh start. As Bullis said with a characteristic air of having just heard the shot announcing the start of a marathon race:

"We are confronted with the greatest challenge ever to face mankind. We must achieve, in a rapid and orderly manner, a level of production and distribution of goods and services in this country at least

237

half again as high as has ever been achieved in peacetime in the past. To us at General Mills the surrender of Japan is a signal to begin putting our postwar plans into action."

The first step of this action was, of course, once more to increase the working capital with which to nourish the growth of many new projects — proposed or already begun. The moment was propitious for inviting investment. The annual report for the year 1944–45 produced comforting evidence that the period just past had been the best in the company's history, showing a net income of nearly $6,500,000. Investors offered enthusiastic endorsement by trading in General Mills' stock so vigorously that it went to a new high. Shares of what the *Wall Street Journal* called "this blue chip stock of the food industry," which had been issued at $60 at the time of the formation of General Mills, were selling at approximately $130 during 1945 and they reached a peak price of $139 in June of that year.

At the annual meeting held in August 1945, stockholders were asked to authorize an increase in the number of shares of common stock from 1,000,000 to 3,000,000 and to exchange their old stocks on the basis of one old share for three of the new. The practice was familiar at the moment among companies that had enjoyed rapid growth and prosperity. Stockholders agreed, the more cheerfully for the fact that in place of the original share on which they had received $4 a year as dividend, they now received on each of the three new shares dividends of $1.50. The purpose of General Mills was simply to get its stock into wider distribution, since 3,000,000 shares were more likely to move about freely than were 1,000,000. The new shares proved to be popular with investors, too. No sooner had the three-for-one split taken place than the offspring by partition went energetically forward on their own and climbed to $50 each (and more) in the brisk August trading.

Simultaneously, the Board of Directors asked for and received permission to issue a new series of convertible preferred stock, 99,758 shares of which were to be sold to the public at a par value of $100. Again, the public owners of General Mills, when they were offered an opportunity to subscribe on a basis of buying one share of preferred stock for every twenty shares of common stock held after the three-for-one split, were both obliging and prompt. By September 25 the stock sale had been completed and Bell was able to call on representatives of Dillon Reed in New York to thank them for "the splendid job done."

No niggard when prospects for enterprise were at stake, General Mills decided in 1946 to spend a total of $22,000,000 on improvements of fixed facilities, of which $9,000,000 was to be spent on new units or on the remodeling of ones already in existence. A year and a half later the physical manifestations of the postwar planning program began to dot the American landscape from the state of Washington to Kentucky. In May 1948 the new packaged food plant in the pretty town of Lodi, California, began operations. This completely modern structure, standing in the midst of the serene rich glory of the grape-growing country and wearing, in season, plumes of cherry blossom about its windows, offers a kind of approach to the unimaginative who have seen no possibility of beauty in industrial architecture. Artists always have understood the dignity of the silhouette presented against the sky by a milling center. Joseph Pennell long ago had urged the subject upon fellow etchers, saying that the handsomeness of the Minneapolis milling district was comparable to that of any Gothic cathedral. Franklin Crosby had thought the elevators too beautiful to be defaced by advertising. At Lodi a new attraction was revealed in the contrast between white towers and the green plants growing all about.

In February 1949 the Los Angeles flour mill was completed after nearly two years of planning. It occupies a spacious area in a kind of Olympian center of American industry. The fabulous growth of southern California has inspired all the "immortal names" among manufacturers to establish branches in this close-packed district. A tour of the neighborhood is like examining a capsule history of enterprise in the United States.

The mill itself, intended to be a kind of pilot plant for testing innovations, has provided for the industry the equivalent of a postgraduate education in engineering and technology. The four-story structure of reinforced concrete uses every original improvement of recent years. The enclosed Redler conveyor replaces the belt on which in the old-fashioned mill grain moves, exposed to dust. The pneumatic method (suction by air) has been used throughout. Storage tanks are of airtight welded steel; they can be blanketed with inert gas to prevent fire or explosion. Weighing statistics are recorded automatically. Because of the benignity of the California climate it has been possible to conserve space by mounting equipment for dust collecting outside of the building. This equipment tops the fourth story and the mill has become known

239

to the jocular as "the one without a roof." California, birthplace of many innovations, is leader in the development of new methods for the bulk handling of products. Feed goes to many a large operator loaded, directly from the mill, into tank trucks.

The Los Angeles experiment with the techniques of tomorrow has not been free of hardships. As with anything previously untried, there has been the inevitable need to redesign, to modify, and to adapt. But it has become in the end an effective unit, capable of performing any kind of milling operation — a model of sanitation and of safety. It has been built, as its designers have the great satisfaction of knowing, on the threshold of the twenty-first century instead of in the back country of the nineteenth.

Along with these shining new ornaments to its system, General Mills acquired in the postwar years of expansion already existing mills to balance its representation in various regions. Purchase of a plant in Hopkinsville, Kentucky, supported the merchandising campaigns in the Southeast, while expansion of the "A" mill in Tacoma, Washington, protected the position in the Northwest. The empire expanded, but always with the purpose of achieving a tighter pattern of operation.

In the postwar years preoccupation with research dominated the planning of General Mills as never before. Its leaders pointed out that their quarters had become cramped once more and that they needed room in which to swing their imaginations. Its facilities were greatly expanded.

Not least important the home office at Minneapolis needed a place of its own. Expansion had gone on so fast and so many crises had intruded needing immediate attention that General Mills had outgrown its old quarters in the Chamber of Commerce Building without being quite aware that interdepartment traffic had become intense and departments themselves as congested as the grounds of any American state fair on opening day. The former Hodgson Building, renamed for its new owner, supplied twelve floors in the heart of the Minneapolis business district where most of the executive departments could be concentrated along with a whole floor of dream kitchens for Betty Crocker, a library, recreational areas, lunch room, medical department — all the adjuncts of a commercial institution whose business it is to be more than a little like a home.

On the twelfth floor, handsome offices survey the city on all four

240

sides above the roofs of lower neighboring structures. Here in beautifully paneled rooms are the quarters of the chairman of the board, the
president, the vice presidents, known inevitably to the irreverent as the
"twelve apostles." Already outgrown because of the continuing expansion of activities, the General Mills Building presents a pleasant face
to the public and supports that appearance of cordiality in the home
kitchen where every day Betty Crocker receives scores of visitors. Not
infrequently they are entertained in the Betty Crocker dining room,
a replica of an early American room, the very walls of which were
brought piece by piece from a New England house. It is appropriate
that Betty Crocker, first lady of food, should have drawn so liberally
and with such perfect taste from the best of native tradition in homemaking.

The war and its aftermath of adjustment brought to all industry
a moment of sober appraisal not unlike that which marked the end of
the depression. In 1939 it had been the boast of certain industries that
they had, throughout the crises of the previous decade, managed to
earn and pay each regular dividend without diminution on common
stock. There had been eighteen of these stalwart business houses whose
stock was registered on the New York Stock Exchange. But the crises
went on and on. During the 1940s the challenges of war brought unexpected problems and as one critical situation developed after another,
ten of the rugged companies fell from grace.

But in 1953 there were still eight companies listed on the New York
Exchange that could repeat the proud statement that not once in these
crucial years had they failed to earn and pay these dividends. The
"golden eight" they came to be called in financial circles.

No fact of company history gives the men of General Mills more
satisfaction than that of knowing that their corporation is one of these
golden eight.

17

Paths of Tomorrow

RESEARCH, NEW STYLE

T H E theme that took possession of Bell's mind in the development of General Mills after World War II was that of the obligation to
find higher uses for the by-products of flour manufacture. This, as he
saw it, was a duty not merely toward one's own organization but toward
the whole economy of the country (and, of course, of the world as
well). Only by the development of commercial uses for the annual
harvest of grains could a sound and vigorous approach be made to the
problem which Bell had accepted as the first duty of civilized society:
that of securing "the welfare of the common man as world citizen." Here,
too, lay hope for solving the old problem of what to do with surplus
grains.

During World War II a significant development had taken place
which opened up new opportunities for service. The big new soybean
crop provided a wealth of elements needed for the making of superior
animal feeds. Bell, acting as always on the principle that the public was
his boss, responded promptly to the order of the day which was to
"upgrade" the products of milling by the full use of new resources.

The story of the soybean industry is one of dramatic growth. In the
year 1929, shortly after the formation of General Mills, the entire soybean crop in the United States amounted to no more than 12,000,000
bushels. In 1942 it had risen to 240,000,000 bushels. In the period between these two dates research had begun to spread the news that this
was perhaps the most versatile of all earth's plants.

Even so the word did not travel as fast as it should have done. It was

242

not many years ago that the *New Yorker* magazine arched its flexible eyebrow with provocative disesteem to announce that the soybean might be used "with aplomb" in bean bags. The editors reckoned, however, without the aplomb of research chemists who showed presently that products of the soybean crop might be used in a fascinating diversity of goods: stock feed, fertilizer, glue, plastics, enamels, lacquers, protective coverings for various kinds of surfaces like those of refrigerators, protective coverings of another sort (cosmetics), wallboard, mayonnaise, bread, crackers, printing ink, soap, paint, ice cream, varnish, infant and invalid foods, condiments, and candy. Indeed, like its old rival, coal tar, the soybean may be said to be "all things to all men."

Its virtue was first discovered in China where, according to legend, the Emperor Shen-nung (in 2838 B.C.) established himself as the good genius of agriculture by giving this product to his people. Laborers, working for fourteen hours a day, virtually lived on it, submitting with oriental docility to the monotony of a diet that consisted of soybean cake for breakfast, dinner, and supper. Whatever may have been the lack of charm of this edible, its utility as fuel for the human machine cannot be called into question.

The soybean made an inconspicuous appearance in the American economy a century and a half ago but it gained real importance only during World War I when the United States was cut off from its overseas sources of coconut, palm, and peanut oils. In 1918 millions of pounds of soybean oil were imported from the Orient to meet the critical need. Four years later, the American farmer had gone into production on his own and produced a million pounds of oil. Over the years production has multiplied fantastically and has reached now an annual figure of a billion and a half pounds.

In 1942 when General Mills decided to enter the soybean industry, Leslie Perrin, shortly to be elected executive vice president, brought into the company a man well trained to head the new experiment. Whitney Eastman had behind him thirty years of experience in the field. He and Perrin between them were responsible for the striking success of the soybean development.

Eastman offers a good example of the American pioneer, Type III. The original representative of the native species was a pioneer of space who conquered the land and made it give up its natural riches. The second was a pioneer of method who conquered the problem of utilizing natural wealth, of manufacturing it into various kinds of commodities, and of giving wide distribution to these goods. The third pioneer is the pioneer of knowledge who undertakes to conquer the secrets of science and so to unlock the door on new riches.

Pioneer Number One had been admirable for his brawn, courage, adaptability, and natural understanding. Pioneer Number Two was an educated man, self-made more often than not, but familiar with books either as college graduate or as self-guided explorer of theoretical knowledge. Pioneer Number Three knows the vital importance of academic training and usually has more than one degree to his name.

Eastman, born on a New York State farm, was graduated from Dartmouth in 1910 with a degree of bachelor of science; a year later at the same institution, he earned a degree in civil engineering. From the moment of his graduation from college and for the forty years and more of his subsequent career he has been concerned with the oil-seed industry. His first professional assignments were with a succession of linseed oil companies, and he became at last an associate of the Archer-Daniels-Midland Company, vegetable oil manufacturers in Minneapolis. He retired temporarily from business (as he once observed, a man needs a respite after thirty years of running a business "with his hat on, standing up") and it was out of this seclusion that General Mills drew him to manage its soybean operations (offering the positive guarantee that he could take his hat off and even sit down occasionally).

Not that he availed himself frequently of that privilege. The creative opportunity before him was too stimulating to allow of much relaxation. His appointment coincided with the appointment of Arthur Hyde as director of research. That vigorous and forthright young man had set himself ambitious goals with regard to new operations. He was determined to explore fully what Bell had called the "paths of tomorrow" up which research beckons and at the same time to help broaden the base of the corporation's commercial enterprise so as to stabilize its earnings in the postwar world and ensure employment to its workers.

The first project which Hyde and Eastman made their own, under the supervisory guidance of Bell, Bullis, and Perrin, was the creation in 1943 of the Chemical Division. It was not given this name to begin with because even the directors were not immediately clear as to where emphasis should fall. The original name, Vegetable Oil and Protein Division, gave way to the other, more proper, designation when the general principle took shape that the Food Division of the company must be supported on one side by a Mechanical Division and on the other by a Chemical Division.

Eastman knew his way about in administrative as well as in research affairs. In the 1920s and 1930s he had worked with Henry Ford on every aspect of the problem of developing a soybean protein that might be used to make plastic parts for motor cars. He had processed soybeans, produced at the Ford Dearborn farms, in a project to evolve an oil for car finishes. At the same time he had collaborated with I. F. Laucks in developing a special soybean protein for the manufacture of plywood glue.

In 1934 he built, after a design imported from Germany, the first continuous soybean solvent equipment to be used in this country. As one of the original (now one of the few surviving) pioneers of the soybean adventure, he knew exactly what he wanted when he set out, in the employ of General Mills, to build a new plant.

America knew what it wanted, too. Soybean meal was badly needed for animal feeds, because of the war crisis, and the government offered priorities to companies that could get into immediate production.

Eastman went straight into the heart of the soybean country and, at Belmond, Iowa, found a set of buildings that suited his requirements well. These had belonged to a sugar refinery, property of a cooperative that had recently failed. Its collapse had left the entire community without reason for existence. There it stood at a crossroads all dressed up for normal life but with no place to go to work. One of the incidental romances of industry is that its vitality, given in transfusions to such sick towns, restores them to life. Thanks to General Mills, Belmond was transformed from an abandoned waif of enterprise into one of the state's healthiest and best-cared-for towns, one in which men are employed twelve months a year, in which neat, modern homes have sprung up everywhere and in which a vigorous community spirit thrives.

The Belmond plant was an improvised emergency affair to begin with. Since the war it has been completely modernized. Its output has been increased by more than 50 per cent with no major increase in capital investment and almost no increase in manpower. All these miracles have come to what was once called "agriculture's Cinderella" through technological improvements.

With the close of World War II, when government restrictions were lifted, the soybean crop came spectacularly into its own. Its refined oil produces an enamel so superior that it is in demand by all the distinguished customers referred to by the trade as "Tiffany accounts," among them the leading makers of refrigerators. To the whole protective covering trade soybean oil has made a welcome contribution in the form of durability.

The next project of the expansion program in the Chemical Division was to develop from polyamide resins a great army of products to be sent into the commercial field. Credit for the first experimentation belongs to Wallace H. Carothers of the Du Pont Company whose discoveries led to the creation of nylon. But the extraordinary versatility of the chemical was still to be explored fully and in 1941 the task of developing it from vegetable oil was undertaken by the Northern Regional Research Laboratory of the United States Department of Agriculture. Dr. Ralph Manley, Dr. Robert Foster, and Dr. Donald H. Wheeler discovered a chemical cousin to nylon which they called Norelac. This tough, translucent, amber-colored resin had many unusual and valuable properties, ones that could be commercialized effectively and profitably.

General Mills undertook to do so and caught up as its own team of specialists the originators, Manley, Foster, and Wheeler. Manley eventually became director of research for General Mills when Hyde's title was changed to vice president in charge of research.

The great virtue of polyamide resin is its own combination of adaptability and resistance. Melted and spread on paper, foil, or plastic film, it can be counted upon to endure almost any kind of attack from heat or from the organic solvents that defeat the purpose of other protective coverings. It went to war in the 1940s, protecting guns and mechanical parts from corrosion during shipment overseas. Since 1947 three chief polyamides have assumed important roles in the paper industry and the packaging business. They have served as heat-sealing adhesives and as coatings resistant to water vapor, to grease, and to oil; they have collaborated with cellophane wallboard and plastic film to make each of these products more effective and reliable in all its uses; they have added something of brightness to the kitchen shelf by helping to preserve the gay colors of the modern package.

The third project of the Chemical Division, which Eastman and his associates had under study and consideration for five years before it was inaugurated successfully, was the development of new careers for

246

fatty acids. The usefulness of these substances has been known from the day of the tallow candle. In new form this "little candle" was to throw its beam into surprising corners of human enterprise before all its potentialities were discovered.

In the days of ancient Rome the fuel of lamps was whale or vegetable oil. But, as an essay by Dr. Manley has pointed out, the difficulty with burning such oils for light was that they were "tear gas generators."

"Happily," Dr. Manley goes on to report, "the French chemist, Chevreul, discovered in 1815 that tallow could be chemically treated to yield glycerine and a hard, high melting waxy fat acid. Since candles from Chevreul's substance burned without giving off tear gas, many a pretty face was saved from the scourge of tears — and the fatty acid industry was born."

Industry continues to split off glycerine to recover fatty acids, but it knows today that there are many different kinds of these substances and that they vary greatly in character. It has become one of the tasks of General Mills to provide makers of a wide variety of products with precisely the fatty acid that each needs.

In accordance with the principle of spreading its base of operations over the surface of the United States, the company established its Chem-oil Plant in Kankakee, Illinois. There was sound reason for doing so because Kankakee stands in the very center of the region from which come many of the needed raw materials — notably corn and soybeans. Also, many of the industries that would be General Mills' best customers for fatty acids had their plants within easy shipping distance. There was the further reason that Kankakee is a tidy community in which a tidy industry could feel at home. The commercial growth of the fatty acid operation has been steady and orderly. Without upsetting the labor market of a small community, its small force fit comfortably into the local economy, offering regular employment and fine opportunity to whatever might prove to be the Kankakee group of chemists, engineers, and pipefitters. These are among the considerations that enter into the deliberations of a responsible corporate citizen of today.

The Kankakee enterprise has thrived. In its program of producing and selling to other formulators the organic derivatives of fatty acids, the Chemoil Plant has been steadily useful to a wide variety of industrial buyers, among them makers of soap, synthetic rubber, varnish, chocolate candy, and lipstick. But this carries the story of the development of the fatty acid industry only to the threshold of today. Just across the threshold lie brilliant, important, and dramatic programs for the future.

The expansion program of the 1940s which led many of General Mills' explorers up surprising bypaths led others back to a reconsideration of the possibilities for enterprise within the mill itself. The search for higher uses for by-products led to the discovery that new tricks could be turned by wheat starch and wheat gluten. Chemurgy, as this branch of applied chemistry is somewhat sternly called, turned up new opportunities in many fields.

Wheat starch had been used in the earliest times for such purposes as giving stanchness to paper documents. It had stiffened Queen Elizabeth's ruff and powdered George Washington's wig. Pre-Victorian laundresses liked it for the treatment of detachable collars and cuffs. But by 1850 it was largely supplanted in all such roles by a less expensive rival, cornstarch.

However, it still had its special virtues and in the starch-gluten plant at Keokuk, Iowa, General Mills began to experiment with new tasks for old faithful — for warp sizing, as textile finisher (making materials smooth and soil resistant), for high-speed coating jobs (these compounds contain less water than others commonly used and so dry faster), for protective coverings of the lacquer family.

Starches began also to play secondary roles in various food dramas. One compound holds more sugar in water solution than other starches and is, therefore, an artful ally in the making of candy. Another "produces emulsions that remain stable under the agitation of shipping," a characteristic that is of the greatest comfort to manufacturers of commercial salad dressing. A third comforts the life of the baker. Added to pie filling, wheat starch serves to make the material gel and so prevents the "weeping" that sometimes makes pastry look depressed and depressing.

Wheat gluten, the mixture of proteins left when starch is washed from wheat flour, is the best source material for the manufacture of glutamic acid and its compounds. When wheat gluten is converted by acid hydrolysis, it gives glutamic acid hydrochloride, used to compensate for hydrochloric acid deficiency in the digestive tract.

Most dramatic of gluten derivatives is monosodium glutamate, one of the most effective of all flavoring agents. Its appeal to the "little nerves that fringe the tongue" is so great that one part dissolved in

3000 parts of water can be detected; salt loses its savor in any combination less than seven times as strong.

In the Orient, monosodium glutamate has been in vogue these many centuries to give a meatlike flavor to vegetarian dishes. It made its entry into the American diet through processed foods, particularly soups and sauces. But since World War II the American housewife has become aware of the strong and subtle enticements of this flavor intensifier. She has begun to depend upon it as an important household condiment.

The long, winding route upon which research sometimes lures the susceptible manufacturer runs its full course through the story of General Mills' interest in the growing of guar and the processing of its seeds into flour. This drought-resistant, pod-bearing legume, indigenous to India, has had a curious record in the United States, marked by many vicissitudes. It was first introduced in 1903 but, though the Department of Agriculture sponsored its start in America, farmers seemed to want none of it. It was, oddly enough, the paper industry that next drew attention to the qualities of guar. Essential to its operation is a kind of mucilaginous gum produced by certain seeds. To procure it, paper chemists had long imported locust bean seeds. They knew that guar seeds also contained this gum and they were eager to experiment with what might prove to be a better source of raw material.

Arthur Hyde of General Mills, ready always for any new attempt to broaden the interests of his company, became interested and built an experimental mill for the purpose of studying guar seeds. His staff became enthusiastic about new possibilities and General Mills had gone so far as to enter into primary producer contracts and to arrange for the subsidization of growers of guar when more cautious judgment prevailed. The position of guar in the economy seemed too precarious. Later, however, it did catch on as an interim crop in the Southwest, where it thrives uncomplainingly on irrigated lands. The long growing season essential to its full development is available in that region and guar now has claimed a solid place among native crops.

Since 1943, General Mills has been a processor of flour made from guar seeds. The chemical Svengalis have developed its versatility and made it reveal many of the same gifts as wheat starch. But it has also advantages of its own in that its thickening power is eight times that of its rival. The interest of General Mills lies in the long-term chemurgic possibilities that may still be latent in the guar seed. Already it has proved its usefulness as ally to a curious assortment of products: cosmetics, ice cream mixes, rubber latex, pharmaceuticals, cheese spreads, and printing pastes.

It is a strangely devious road that leads from Cadwallader Washburn's mill at the Falls of St. Anthony to a guar field in Texas, to a breakfast food plant in Chicago, to a fatty acid operation in Kankakee. But the expansion program of the 1940s, presided over by the triumvirate of Bell, Bullis, and Hyde was an inevitable development of the foresight shared by these leaders. The evolution of the company from a unit concerned with the simple conversion of a primary product into a complex organization of many closely integrated parts, all dependent for success upon an intimate acquaintance with science and technology, was inspired by an impulse to serve the American housewife ever more faithfully. It was still down Bell's "avenue to the home" that the General Mills products moved. Though these have become many, though they have different kinds of histories, characters, uses, still it is toward the kitchen shelf, or the medicine cabinet, or some repository of home needs that they are directed.

A central drama of the early postwar years was the retirement of J. F. Bell. He had decided in his sixty-eighth year that he must make full acknowledgment of his own belief that "new and young blood must flow steadily through the veins of any successful company." Time, as he once observed slyly, was "still up to its old geriatrics," and he could not expect to be spared. "I've seen too many old men linger on to block the way of the new generation," he said. "It is the spirit of our organization to keep the way to the top open and to keep the young men alert to opportunity by developing their sense of responsibility."

On November 25, 1947, he asked permission of the board to withdraw. Bullis was elected to his place as chairman after serving five years as president and Leslie Perrin followed Bullis into the presidency. These changes occurred as of January 1, 1948.

But in the very moment of making the uncharacteristic gesture of putting burdens away, Bell made the entirely characteristic one of catching up a new set of responsibilities of his own. He accepted appointment to chairmanship of a new General Mills committee on "finance and technological progress." To an interviewer who asked him the significance of the new appointment, he answered hopefully that "a job is what a man makes of it."

Within a month, it had become clear that Bell's retirement would bear the same cheerful resemblance to a five-ring circus that his previous career had shown. During one week in the autumn of 1947, when he made what he imagined to be the great renunciation, Bell flew over Manitoba to inspect the bird and game situation; flew to New York for a succession of board meetings; arranged there for the completion of a great authoritative work on the history of milling (since published under the title *Flour for Man's Bread*); arranged for a thorough analysis of the company's operation by a committee of disinterested experts; flew back to Minneapolis for a cluster of meetings in each of which he was a driving force, meetings on advertising budgets, nutrition programs, plans for new mills, prospects for new products.

Leslie Perrin, who had been responsible for expansion through research in such operations as development of the soybean interests of General Mills, devoted the four-year term of his presidency to research of another kind which led to the improvement of existing products and to the invention of new processes to make their use easier and more dramatically successful. There were many of these advances during the late 1940s and early 1950s.

No one ever occupied the center stage of a business drama more modestly than did Perrin. Requests for biographical material brought from him the merest rudiments of fact, but these somehow shadowed forth an unusual fullness and completeness of character. Throughout his administration the president's door stood open to all comers and his patience covered even the importunity of the few who came on pointless errands. A secret warmth eluded the control of his modesty and enveloped those who stood in the relation to him of students or of lieutenants. He towered above them physically, his height matching that of the other giants, Bell and Bullis. But an unobtrusive geniality enclosed all his activities and it is not surprising that the incidents of his regime have chiefly to do with the offering of new services to the public.

General Mills gathered these up wherever they were to be found all the way from California to Florida. Typical was the adventure of Harry Baker, a round-eyed, intense little man of sixty-four who for many years had made a career of baking for the great ladies of Hollywood. One of his specialties was a miracle of the oven that combined the richness of

251

butter cake with the lightness of sponge cake. How he achieved this triumph remained Harry Baker's closely held secret. (In Hollywood homes he had always insisted on being allowed to operate behind a screen. His determination to keep his special knowledge to himself required Baker to make the sacrifice — extreme, in a man, to the point of fanaticism — of washing his own dishes when he was through baking.) But the proper guardian of his secret, Baker thought, would be the first lady of food, Betty Crocker. His price to General Mills, just for the privilege of seeing him bake his cake, was $5000. Marjorie Husted, now on a special cookbook writing assignment, and Ralph Gaylord of Products Control watched the miracle performed, and when the demonstration was over General Mills thought the results so satisfactory that the company was willing to pay Baker's full price (never disclosed) that the formula might be passed on to the world.

The mysterious ingredient had proved to be salad oil. The staff of Janette Kelley, now head of the Home Service Department, perfected the recipe, made its operation failure proof, and named the result Betty Crocker Chiffon Cake.

The next innovation was Betty Crocker Ginger Cake Mix. This was no improvised affair for a culinary Cinderella. Created by the Research Department, it was thoroughly pretested in Home Service and in the field where a panel of home testers is maintained for that purpose. Because the new product was to be made of Softasilk Cake Flour it seemed appropriate to call it not Ginger*bread*, but Ginger *Cake*. This break with the honorable tradition of a favorite American dish did a kind of psychological violence to the housewife's loyalties and presently the name Gingerbread was restored.

In 1948 the gallery of Betty Crocker's highly photogenic products was brightened by the image of Crustquick. This was the lineal descendant of an earlier offering, Apple Pyequick. After the war when General Mills dropped all its interest in dehydrated foods, the idea of offering, in one package, all the ingredients of an apple pie was also scrapped. But the crust mix survived to become a natural sister product to Bisquick and one of ever growing prestige.

Out of the "home kitchen" there came in 1949 two more handsome additions to Betty Crocker's family of products, the twins Party Cake Mix and Devils Food Cake Mix. Betty Crocker Yellow Cake Mix, Honey Spice Cake Mix, and Angel Food Cake Mix are still later additions.

It was, of course, no mere restless search for novelty that prompted General Mills to prepare this pageant of products. Unlike the pedestrian lyricist of whom it was said that he had "just gone out of his way to write a poem," Betty Crocker had not gone out of her way to invent new cakes. Rather she was inspired by warnings from the Board of Directors to whom it seemed "reasonable to believe that the higher standards of living established during the war will include larger quantities of dairy, poultry and animal products." This meant that there would be a tendency to eat less of the bread foods. General Mills was determined to offset this tendency by making such appeals to appetite and to convenience as could not be resisted. The fact that its fine flours kept pace with its packaged foods in establishing new highs in total volume of sales showed the wisdom and the effectiveness of this policy.

One of the ways in which General Mills managed to stimulate the sale of its flours is illustrated by the adventure which culminated in the presentation to the baking industry of the process known as Brown 'n Serve.

This was the accidental discovery of two young men who ran a small bakery at Avon Park, Florida. One of them, Joseph Gregor, a former mess sergeant, had been stationed in the community during the war and to it he had returned after his discharge. His study of southern taste in foods had made him aware that hot rolls were very nearly sacred to the local cuisine. But these were hard for the commercial baker to provide. Gregor could discover no trick for keeping rolls hot during the long interval between the time when they left the oven and the time when they reached the customer.

If the baker had not been a member of the volunteer fire department he might never have solved the problem. One day when his rolls had been half-baked the siren sounded. There was nothing to do but pull the trays of dough out of the oven. Later, Gregor noticed that though the white masses were not a particularly appetizing sight, they had kept their form. On impulse he returned the half-baked product to the oven and seven minutes later removed the freshest tasting Parker House rolls he had ever made. The principle of interrupted baking had been accidentally discovered.

Gregor tried the new delicacy on his customers. What he called Pop-N-Oven rolls began to sell even more spiritedly than the hot cakes of tradition.

Paths of Tomorrow

Word got about in the trade. It reached an alert salesman for General Mills, James Taggart, and was passed on to Gaylord, assistant director of Products Control. The company helped the developers perfect their patent on the process and presently Number 2,549,595 was purchased and presented as an act of fellowship and good will to the baking industry.

Altruism, however, also had "method in it." As Perrin observed at the unveiling of the renamed Brown 'n Serve process: "What is good for the baking industry is good for the milling industry. By relieving homemakers of the measuring, kneading and raising steps of breadmaking, we may open up vast new markets."

Modest as were General Mills' own claims to offering bounty, others — the bakers in particular — were exuberant in praise. The *Northwestern Miller* called this an act of "industrial statesmanship."

Despite a proper absorption in its own problems, General Mills did not forgo, in the postwar period, its willingness to take on any assignment in research of which its government had need and for which its experts had the training. Such was the project to which the name Operation Skyhook was given. What the "jolly miller" is doing in the stratosphere is a story that authenticates beyond any possible doubt the sincerity of his desire to diversify. It even improves upon the locomotives of which Bell spoke wistfully at the time of the formation of General Mills.

It was soon after V-J day in 1946 that General Mills, an old hand now at special assignments for the armed forces, created its aeronautical research laboratories. Its chief assignment from the Office of Naval Research has been to develop plastic balloons capable of carrying the instruments of scientific investigation to heights above the earth never reached before.

Made of polyethylene, a plastic film derived from petroleum, the balloons are capable of soaring more than twenty miles high, penetrating to the very top of the earth's atmosphere. They carry as much as 250 pounds of equipment which automatically records data about such matters as the nature of cosmic rays which for forty years have engaged and frustrated the interest of physicists. Certain important new clues to the sources of atomic energy have been caught by these instruments, which are returned, via parachute, to earth and to the hands of investigating scientists.

Operation Skyhook has provided many moments of incidental drama and performed many an incidental service. Each balloon trails from its head a great shimmering shroud of unfamiliar material. To the properly trained reader of weird stories it may look very like an authentic ghost. The balloons also look like gigantic tears. And on one occasion they looked to hundreds of worried citizens like visitors from another planet.

On October 21, 1947, the first of these apparitions revealed itself over Minneapolis. "It hung," said a newspaper account, "almost motionless burning a bright hole in the evening dusk." And as the same writer added: "Reflecting the sun's rays, it glowed an angry red."

Minneapolis paused on its way home from work that evening to catch its breath in momentary apprehension and some residents wondered if they were destined ever to reach their own thresholds. Another such panic as Orson Welles once precipitated with his radio broadcast about an assault by armies from Mars might have followed except for the obvious fact that in a decade the American people had had every kind of chance to grow up. A plane from the Minneapolis airport took off in pursuit of the object only to radio back that from a height of 10,000 feet the strange thing seemed to be as far away as ever. So the commuters went home to dinner and awaited an explanation. Because of security reasons this gave General Mills not a little trouble.

The adaptability of Operation Skyhook inevitably suggested to leaders of the Crusade for Freedom another possibility. A series of pillow-shaped balloons were loosed in Europe to drift beyond the Iron Curtain and drop propaganda literature behind the lines of Communist-held countries.

The decade of the 1940s was for General Mills, through good times and bad, a period of continuous growth and prosperity. This fortunate result of effort may be attributed in part to diversification, in part to new products, in part to selling skill. But in research and in all other branches one word suggests the reason for success. In the development of such assets as Bisquick, a secret ingredient was thought to have brought off the miracle. But the really animating ingredient of each project was imagination.

Research, new style, has enabled General Mills to follow the "paths of tomorrow" even when these led into the great highway of the sky.

18

Age of Responsibility

THE COMPANY AND THE GOVERNMENT

TH E story of General Mills is, in part, the story of a steady and sturdy growth in a sense of social responsibility. The old-time miller who earned a fortune in a year or two and then retired because he could no longer make as much as a dollar's profit on a barrel of flour has had no counterpart for many years. A craftsman does not put aside his task at will; his awareness of its importance would not permit him to do so.

Proof that this sense of social responsibility is an animating force in the minds of millers may be found in the number of projects of large-scale significance in which its members have engaged, working often — though not always — in collaboration with the government. General Mills' own tacitly acknowledged philosophy of deserving well by serving well has made it a conspicuous leader in all such projects. Down the years, especially from the time of World War I onward, its record has been honorably marked by the vigorous initiative it has taken in protecting the public good.

The first of these efforts occurred before the formation of General Mills. The occasion was the black stem rust crisis of the early 1920s. A serious threat to the prosperity of midwestern farmers was averted by a well-organized, well-disciplined campaign against an enemy of agriculture capable of making a sudden, subtly destructive attack anywhere on the continent. A tremendous cooperative effort brought together farmers, grain men, railroad men, millers, teachers, scientists, and government representatives in a long-range fight for the welfare of the wheat crop. Financed at first by voluntary private contributions, the undertaking earned and finally received the support of both the state and federal governments.

There had been a dismal preview of trouble in 1916 when the Midwest experienced a bad epidemic of wheat rust. Almost at the end of what had seemed to be the most ideal of growing seasons, the disease appeared, leaving a shriveled product which robbed the farmer of his income and made unexpected problems for millers. The Washburn Crosby Company, in order to maintain normal operations, had to bring in wheat from Kansas. In 1919 the same kind of crisis occurred. The crop was seriously infected with rust and the whole agricultural world began to ask anxiously what could be done to control a savage whim of nature that threatened its livelihood.

The answer was literally at the farmer's doorstep. It lay with the barberry bush which early settlers had brought with them from New England — a souvenir of the homeland. They used the berries of the plant to make jelly, its sturdy stem for rake handles, and its pleasing contour for decoration of yard or garden. John Lee Coulter, once president of the North Dakota Agricultural College, recalled with mild chagrin that, as an undergraduate earning his way through school in the employ of a nursery, he had given away scores of barberry bushes, as premiums to substantial buyers. Disaster was spread in the name of beauty.

What the New England settlers did not know was that the barberry bush was host to rust races the spores of which infected their grain. They should have known with what a dangerous enemy they were dallying. The bad news had been familiar in Europe for more than two centuries. The first barberry eradication law had been passed in Rouen in 1660. A hundred years later the farm experts of England rediscovered the mischief-making propensity of the barberry bush, and the agricultural publications of the time were full of warnings. Danish scientists knew the story so well that, in 1903, they headed a successful drive to rid their country of barberry bushes, root and branch.

It is the tragic habit of mankind to mislay its wisdom so that it has to be learned again and again. In the first decade of the century a group of Minnesota scientists began piling up evidence against the barberry bush. The distinguished plant pathologist Edward Monroe Freeman, of the University of Minnesota, put his best students to work on the problem. E. C. Stakman, even before the 1916 epidemic, had been trying to overcome the stubborn ignorance to which even notable authorities clung. A reference work of the time declared that the barberry bush could not be held responsible for wheat rust and offered as proof the fact that Australian wheat suffered from the blight though there wasn't a barberry bush on the continent. Even harder to combat was the glib misinformation of the popularizer of science. A lady writer who loved *Our Northern Shrubs* not wisely but too well communicated to her readers the happy news that the vile canard against the barberry bush had been "laid to rest by the microscope," an interesting feat in itself. "The two rusts," she wrote, evidently with the mounting excitement of a champion of a cause, "are entirely different — one has nothing to do with the other. That one should follow the other is mere coincidence."

In 1918 the sentimental view of the barberry bush, entertained by lady botanists, was sharply reversed by the plant pathologists. In that year the federal Department of Agriculture persuaded the thirteen northern grain-growing states to join in an eradication campaign. Stakman became a leader of the movement in Minnesota. This most articulate, dedicated, and serene of crusaders had no difficulty in putting a light to J. F. Bell's enthusiasm. Bell's love of a large, exacting project had already caught fire from his own study of the Danish program.

The Conference for the Prevention of Grain Rust (later, simply the Rust Prevention Association) began its work on a volunteer basis. The finance committee, made up of representatives of business groups (Ralph Budd, then of the Great Northern Railroad, C. C. Webber of the Deere and Webber Company, Frank Heffelfinger of the Peavey Elevator Company), raised a fund of $85,000 for educational and publicity work. There were, in 1921, no known varieties of bread wheat that were resistant to rust. So with an eagerness that happily was unaware of the vastness of its task, the Conference set out to kill off the barberry bush.

The representative of the milling industry in the Minnesota program was Franklin Crosby, who brought such enthusiasm to the task that his contributions to rust eradication became one of the great monuments to his career. Crosby was an inveterate experimenter who, on his own 800-acre farm, tried out all the suggestions for enriching soil, improving crops, and caring for stock that agricultural experts had to offer.

The younger brother of John Crosby offered an interesting variation in the family pattern. After many years in Minnesota the mood of Maine still enveloped both men. They were essentially of New England in their self-sufficiency, their dignity, their distaste for display of any kind, particularly a display of personal integrity, the preservation of which they took to be the simple duty of any decent man. There, conspicuous similarity ended. Franklin Crosby liked the battle line of business as much as John Crosby liked its withdrawn stronghold of study and investigation. Humor, which seemed to seep secretly through the temperament of John Crosby, flooded the nature of his brother, finding expression in a quizzical, almost roguish smile, a lively tongue, an exuberance of manner. Trading, as practiced by Franklin Crosby, was not merely an occupation but an art and a delight. His flair was like a high talent for a musical instrument and he played upon it with a sure touch, making himself one of the best informed of grain men.

Out of Yale, his own college, he brought as chief assistant Walter Mills of Boston, who became heir to his skills, his responsibilities, and his enthusiasms. Later a vice president of General Mills, Crosby's protégé made a distinguished contribution to many aspects of the company's cooperation with government.

The work of these men may be said to constitute a major contribution to a major effort. In the moment when they undertook to implement the wheat rust program with a workable tool, in the form of organization supported by voluntary contributions of money and time, the midwestern community faced the future with unrelieved hopelessness. Buyers of wheat were operating in a bleak, unfamiliar climate of scarcity. To keep one step ahead of nature, protecting the quality of the flour that must be made from wheat shriveled by rust, demanded more ingenuity and adaptability than any professional problem of recent years. Crosby and Mills as directors of the financial campaign gave significant help to Stakman who, as scientist, undertook to reverse what seemed to be an inevitable downward trend for men whose livelihoods depended on wheat. The three transformed the most cheerless of prospects into one of hope.

It was because he declared his integrity so simply yet so unchallengeably that Crosby exercised great influence in the republic of business. Almost at the sound of his voice, when he spoke of public need, purse strings opened.

The creative contribution of the scientists offers even more striking evidence of how effective an influence in a cooperative enterprise the faith of the laboratory may be.

259

Age of Responsibility

The wheat situation had become crucial. When even Marquis, the aristocrat among hard spring wheats, betrayed the confidence of the community by proving to be highly susceptible to black stem rust, farmers, in panic, began to grow a grain that they knew they could bring safely to maturity. Durum, the macaroni wheat, took a steadily more and more important place in the agricultural economy. Before 1910 comparatively little of it had been produced in the United States and 98 per cent of all macaroni needed to gratify the nostalgic palates of Italian Americans had to be imported. In the desperate teens of the century and in the 1920s, a new American activity came into existence and wider awareness of macaroni brightened the prospect for good eating.

But macaroni wheat could not displace bread wheat because flour made from it does not produce good bread. Accordingly, the agricultural stations of the Midwest went briskly about the task of producing rust-resistant types of grain. At the University of North Dakota, L. R. Waldron developed Ceres, which justified its noble name by proving to be the first commercial variety to be really resistant. At Minnesota, H. K. Hayes produced, first, Marquille and, later, Thatcher, named for Roscoe Thatcher, long a brilliant figure of the midwestern agricultural community. The result of the introduction of these types was that, in the next decades, loss of wheat from black stem rust was cut virtually in half.

Stakman's studies demonstrated that the disease, black stem rust, was no simple morbid condition of the plant but rather that it resulted from the attack of many different races of organisms. These look alike to the eye and even to the microscope but their identities may be discovered by their individual ways of attack. Stakman gave these criminals numbers and explored the habits of each.

To knowledge of the subject he added the disquieting news that the barberry bush acts not merely as host to the spores of rust, but serves as a laboratory for the hybridization of new races. Types of wheat that were regarded as resistant to the old races may be susceptible to the attack of the new. So the struggle must go on.

The fight in which eighteen states are now enrolled became international when Stakman made it clear that the infection may be wind-borne all the way from northern Mexico. The Rust Prevention Project of the Department of Agriculture now derives funds for its continuing war from the federal government as well as from the state government. But business may claim credit for seizing the initiative in the matter.

One of the first criminals to be identified, 15B, still gives major trouble. A large-scale effort to wipe out this public enemy now involves the whole Rust Prevention Association (of which Walter Mills is a trustee), the Rockefeller Foundation, and the government of Mexico. In this great task General Mills has had an honorable and a conspicuous share.

Quite as striking was the campaign for human welfare in which General Mills collaborated with the government during the early years of the 1940s. Chief actors for the company in this drama, along with Bell and Bullis who appeared side by side in nearly every event of the period, were G. Cullen Thomas and Dr. Alonzo Taylor. The intimate knowledge of flour that Thomas had acquired as creator and head of the Products Control operation made him an enormously useful leader of a great dietary revolution that swept over the United States in 1941. Dr. Taylor's encyclopedic grasp, as food economist, of the importance of wheat to the health of humankind ensured him a hearing whenever and wherever these matters were discussed. After booming cheerfully and authoritatively all down the years in every crisis of Bell's career, Dr. Taylor had finally joined his staff, becoming director of research for General Mills in 1936.

As scientists, idealists, and statesmen of business these representatives of a great modern corporation were able to make a significant contribution to a program which has been called the greatest ever to undertake the improvement of public health.

The atmosphere was right in 1941 for such a revolution. Ever since the turn of the century scientists in various corners of the world had been preoccupied with the problem of making available food supplies serve the human body more adequately. Evidence existed everywhere that eating habits were failing to maintain a high level of well-being. In Java a Dutch hygienist, Christian Eijkman, discovered that a diet limited to polished rice caused beriberi. Even in a land of abundance like the United States deficiencies were alarmingly apparent. Professor E. V. McCollum of Johns Hopkins contributed to the process of reeducating the American public about its basic needs by identifying as "protective foods" those having certain elements necessary to good health.

261

Age of Responsibility

Professor Henry Sherman of Columbia explored the important subject of man's requirements in mineral form. Presently Casimir Funk coined the word "vitamin," and science was straightway launched on another adventure of discovery to recognize and to evaluate the potential benefits that were to be derived from each of these constituents of natural foods.

As citizens, with a fully awakened awareness of a special responsibility toward public health, the miller and the baker wished also to make a contribution to the nation's welfare. But even in the early 1930s scientists still knew little about the nutritional values of wheat beyond the fact that the grain offered a good source of vitamins, particularly thiamine. They knew, further, that while wheat germ was relatively high in thiamine, white flour as it was then milled and marketed must be considered low in this important factor.

The problem was to produce a flour which would offer the advantages of the natural grain and still have wide public acceptance. Clearly the solution could not be to limit production to whole-wheat flour. This product had been available, but less than 3 per cent of buyers had ever found it acceptable. Scientists believed that there were factors in the whole grain that tended to repel appetite appeal and that this distaste sprang from an unconscious and instinctual awareness of unadvantageous qualities in whole-wheat flour and bread: a tendency to irritate the intestinal tract, a tendency to inhibit the absorption of minerals.

From the miller's point of view there were other objections to whole-wheat flour. It did not keep well; in warm climates its behavior had proved to be completely unsatisfactory; a system of refrigeration which no one was prepared to provide would be needed to preserve it while in transit to the housewife and it would need unavailable space in the housewife's own ice chest. Still the commanding consideration was that the American market has shown always an overwhelming preference for products baked from white flour.

Research men in the General Mills laboratories had followed all developments in their field with the keenest concern. At a time when the group was relatively small and only half a dozen men were assigned to specific types of work, one of its experts made a full-time job of exploring the problem of how to make a refined flour that would offer the nutrients of the whole grain.

The year 1936 was significant in the history of the movement to enrich flour. It was then that Dr. R. R. Williams first managed to synthesize vitamin B_1. An attractive exemplar of the scientific spirit at its most dedicated, Williams had reserved the right when he became chemical director of the Bell Telephone laboratories in New York to continue his work in pure research. To his seminars at Teachers College, Columbia, he made frequent reports of progress in the isolation of B_1. His success in synthesization accomplished three things: first, it made a vitally important contribution to understanding of the chemistry of vitamins; second, as a result of his work, it became possible to determine quantitatively the presence of vitamins in foods; and, third, the establishment of human needs, in the form of vitamins, promptly followed.

The development of these analytical processes inevitably stimulated research everywhere. In the year of innovation, 1936, John Andrews returned to the General Mills laboratories, after earning his Ph.D. degree at Johns Hopkins, and it became his task to seek techniques for making flour enrichment practicable. The wheat kernel was explored, as Cullen Thomas has said, "to its remotest corner. The amount of vitamin and iron in each tissue of the wheat berry was determined; we found how vitamin content varied in wheats grown in different places and in wheats of different varieties. We discovered how much thiamine, riboflavin, niacin, and iron went into each of the milling fractions — patent flour, shorts, bran. The country's great chemical and pharmaceutical companies perfected large-scale production of these important vitamins in synthetic form."

Among the important discoveries of the research men was the fact that the distribution of these nutrients is spread throughout the wheat berry, not concentrated — as is widely but quite erroneously believed even today — in the wheat germ. The highest portion of thiamine was found to be in the tissues immediately surrounding the germ, and niacin is largely to be found in the bran layers.

The basic problem which Dr. Andrews faced was to make a flour that would somehow retain the feed portion of the grist. His distinguished success was presently to be revealed and to become a model for the further guidance of the entire industry.

Meanwhile another important development in the history of the enrichment program had brought together three men who occupied strategic positions in the field: Dr. Russell Wilder, then head of the department of medicine of the Mayo Foundation and member of the Mayo Clinic at Rochester, Minnesota; J. F. Bell of General Mills; and Dr. Taylor of Bell's research staff.

Dr. Wilder had been, since 1930, a member of the Council on Foods and Nutrition of the American Medical Association. His sense of the fitness of things and his belief in the rights of all humankind had been outraged by the way in which makers of luxury foods were exploiting vitamins. Even manufacturers of chewing gum were attempting to "hit the vitamin trail," as Bell once said, by fortifying their product. But, Dr. Wilder argued, if vitamins were essential to well-being, they should be made available to everyone in simple, everyday foods.

As a student of diet, Wilder had made his own experiments with deficiency problems. When his experimental subjects were put on a diet severely restricted in B_1 they soon displayed significant symptoms — loss of appetite, loss of weight, weakness, vomiting. Even much less severely restricted diets induced disturbances of the central nervous system — neuroses, anxiety patterns, irritability. These studies were supported by many others in which vitamin deficiency appeared as villain in the drama of disease. Experimenters in state hospitals had induced symptomatic beriberi simply by removal of vitamin B from the diet of patients.

Eager for the support of leaders in the industry Wilder went to see Bell. But he found that his purpose had been anticipated. "Doctor," Bell said even before his visitor had had a chance to state his errand, "for ten years and more I have been telling my associates that we must give wheat users what nature intended them to have. Our purpose in refining flour was to give the public what it wanted, a pure white product, the best and cheapest source of energy food. But now other values have come to be understood. Why not make white flour the vehicle for conveying to the American people the vitamins they need?"

"That," replied the surprised and delighted Wilder, "is what I've come to see you about."

With Bell's enthusiastic support and with the aid of Dr. Taylor who preached enrichment eloquently in many forums of science, Wilder proceeded to outline a campaign for a dietary revolution. A first important step was the adoption in March 1939 by the Council on Foods and Nutrition of a resolution stating the position of science. In that early form the principle of "restoration" was stressed. It urged that any food which in its processing lost certain vitamins and minerals should be permitted to

264

add these nutrients once more so that the levels of the natural materials should be reached.

While this process of reeducating the American public was carried forward with conscientious zeal by Wilder, Taylor, Williams, and their many brilliant confreres in the world of science, General Mills seized the initiative by making a practical demonstration of what could be done to improve the vitamin content of "the staff of life." In June 1940, Vibic Flour, the formula for which was largely Dr. Andrews' work, made its appearance on the list of products. Laboratory investigation had shown that in the floury particles adjacent to the aleurone cells of the wheat berry enough vitamin B_1 content existed so that when these fractions were isolated and added to patent flour the finished product completely satisfied the recommendations of the Council on Foods. Also added were vitamin B_2 and calcium and iron. Once more General Mills had given itself the satisfaction of taking the lead in a public issue. The American Medical Association acknowledged this cooperative gesture by putting its valued seal of acceptance on Vibic Flour.

In the summer of the same year, interest in the subject of fortification was quickened by the events that were leading America toward war. Wilder had gone to Washington to head the committee on medicine appointed by the National Research Council. He had insisted that his group must have a subcommittee on food and, very firmly, he made himself chairman of this inner group. The next step in his campaign was to get a resolution passed recommending that all white flour bought for the armed services be fortified with thiamine. Happily, at almost the same moment in September 1940, the Food and Drug Administration at last set dates for a public hearing, scheduled long before, to establish "standards for the identity of foods." The most recent federal Food, Drug, and Cosmetic Act had ordered that such an effort be made in order to remove from the realm of conjecture or of whim the concept of basic requirements. Every buyer, the law insisted, had a right to know what was in every article he purchased and also to be assured that it satisfied fixed standards.

To these hearings Cullen Thomas of General Mills went as representative of the food industry. It was at his suggestion that Dr. Clyde Bailey, no longer associated with the company's Research Department, was called to Washington to present technical aspects of the problem to government officials. As nonexperts these conscientious advocates of human welfare were bewildered by the intricacies of the subject until Dr. Bailey offered the illuminating experience of dissecting the wheat berry before their eyes. Standing at his blackboard, enclosing within his small person all the attributes of teacher and statesman, Bailey was able to clear away many of the confusions. Though the early inclination of the government had been to close the door on the improvement of white flour by insisting on whole-wheat flour as the standard, the hearing ended with government, science, and industry in complete accord on an adaptable program. In November of 1940 the Committee on Food and Nutrition, established as a result of the hearings, offered general endorsement for the program of improving flour by the addition of thiamine, nicotinic acid, and other important nutrients present in the wheat berry.

The theory which the committee espoused was still that of restoration as opposed to that of fortification. It asked only that essential ingredients be added once more to the milled product of wheat and that they be added only "to the amounts that were found in the entire wheat berry."

It is the fate of the public agency to operate under many aliases in the course of its career. The Committee on Food and Nutrition had not been long in existence when it became the Food and Nutrition Board, but its program remained the same. This board continues today as an authoritative body made up of scientists who advise our own government, as well as the Food and Agricultural Organization of the United Nations, on all matters having to do with nutrition.

Wilder resigned from all other committees to serve as the first chairman of this board. Because its recommendations were concerned with the improvement of public health through food, it was important that the food-processing industry should cooperate with science and government toward this goal. Wilder chose Cullen Thomas of General Mills as one of the original members of this group to serve as technologist representing all food industries. Thomas demonstrated his enormous usefulness by securing the close cooperation of the whole milling and baking fraternity.

A cereal subcommittee of the Food and Nutrition Board was established under the chairmanship of Dr. R. R. Williams. Other members — Dr. Henry Sebrell, Dr. Elmer Nelson, Dr. Charles Frey, Dr. George Cowgill, Dr. Conrad Elvehjem — all were recognized as distinguished leaders in the fields of chemistry, biochemistry, and nutrition. Wilder has called the record of their work for the improvement of public health as one of "beautiful cooperation." They constituted one of those superb councils of the aristocrats of learning whose accomplishments do much to restore faith in the wisdom of the race and in the philosophy of idealism. With Wilder and Thomas these men made up the guiding force that brought the program for the enrichment of flour and bread to practical reality.

In May 1941, President Roosevelt was persuaded to call a great National Nutrition Conference for Defense. The government had been deeply disturbed by the very great number of rejections among men called for duty in the draft army. Statistics showed that some 37 per cent of the American public suffered from inadequate diet. Here was another powerful argument for a close reconsideration of nutrition problems. Defense itself required that it be done.

In this atmosphere the arguments of restoration versus fortification were rehearsed again. Conducted in a mood of stanch patriotism, these discussions inevitably ended by taking account of the immediate emergency. Under the strain of war which the whole world was obliged to endure it seemed wise to use certain foods as vehicles for carrying to the people the protective attributes of diet needed to combat disease. This, of course, was the theory of fortification, differing from that of restoration in that it made certain foods specially built-up agents of health.

A first draft of the resolution adopted by the Food and Nutrition Board, written in pencil on the back of an envelope in the hand of Cullen Thomas, remains in his possession today as a valued souvenir of this campaign. In its final form the position of the board was stated in these opening paragraphs:

"Whereas there exist deficiencies of vitamins and minerals in the diets of significant segments of the population of the United States which cannot be corrected by public education in the proper choice of foods, be it resolved in order to correct and prevent such deficiencies:

"That the committee endorsed the addition of specific nutrients to staple foods which are effective vehicles for correcting the above deficiencies of the general population . . ."

In general, the group favored "whenever practicable" the choice of vehicles for the corrective distribution of vitamins and minerals which had suffered loss in the refining process and urged that vitamins added should be of the kind native to the food in its unrefined state. The addition of "other than natural levels" might be sanctioned "when more natural routes were practically unavailable." As for flour and bread, the group favored "appropriate enrichment."

By the close of the year 1942, there were few who held out against the policy which General Mills actually had inaugurated with its Vibic Flour. The company also had been the first to order the enrichment of all its family brands. This was done by Bullis, as president, against the advice of some of his associates. Some rival companies did not immediately put themselves to this expense, but Bullis, acting on principle, insisted that General Mills must do so voluntarily. And, in the end, 75 to 80 per cent of all family flour was being enriched throughout the industry. The purpose of the program was protected in its first years, as far as baker's white flour was concerned, by allowing bakers the option of using enriched flour or of adding enrichment ingredients themselves to unenriched flour.

The enrichment program has been called "the greatest contribution ever made to the program of public health." Powerful evidence has been assembled to show that the addition of vitamins and other accessory elements has led to enormous improvement in the American diet. Dr. Norman Jolliffe of the New York University College of Medicine wrote in 1943: "I attribute to bread enrichment a marked and unmistakable decrease in the evidence of florid beriberi and pellagra in my wards in Bellevue Hospital." A Chicago doctor, who had opposed the enrichment program was won round when he discovered that alcoholic neuritis had ceased suddenly to exist within the city limits. There were no fewer alcoholics, to be sure, nor were there fewer evidences of bad eating habits among them. The explanation, obvious even to a doubter, was that the change had come about because all the bread in Chicago lately had been enriched; its beneficial effect had eliminated one stubborn deficiency disease.

Newfoundland, in 1944, offered a perfect laboratory for another experiment with the effects of enrichment. The population had showed throughout its recorded medical history a marked deficiency of vitamin B. The government was persuaded to try enrichment and, only four years later, impartial witnesses were ready to testify to great improvement. This was due to no increase of prosperity as a result of wartime activity. Examinations showed that though lesions from thiamine deficiency had improved, lesions from other deficiencies were worse rather than better.

Unmistakably evident were other facts: infant mortality had fallen dramatically; the incidence of tuberculosis was far below what had been regarded as inevitable; the incidence of childbed death had been greatly modified. Newfoundland, neatly isolated for observation under peculiarly revealing circumstances, seemed to have proved once for all that there was tremendous virtue in enrichment.

The less spectacular benefits are less easy to demonstrate, but Wilder believes that a general improvement in the American community's sense of well-being may be expected to follow the consistent use of enriched foods. In the "age of anxiety" this is in itself a far from negligible consideration.

More than half the states have adopted a uniform law requiring the enrichment of flour. But whether its customers belong to communities that may claim enrichment as a right or to communities that can make no such claim, General Mills has continued its program, begun on a voluntary basis long before the public program existed.

In the words of Cullen Thomas "the milling and baking industries are so closely allied as to be almost one." This was no less true in the support lent by each to the enrichment program. The wholehearted cooperation of bakers in producing enriched bread complemented and fulfilled the miller's role. Indeed, E. L. Henderson, past president of the American Medical Association, in summing up the story of this "modest miracle," found all contributors to its success equally distinguished. "Our nation," he said, "owes a debt of gratitude to the scientists, the doctors, the millers and the bakers of America who voluntarily brought to the people one of the most significant contributions to better health in our generation."

The entry of the United States into World War II brought about between the milling industry and government a relationship as comfortable as circumstance could ever make it. Bullis commented: "We are in the hands of our government. Our policy is to be as helpful as possible for the duration." His reference was to the effect that under war conditions the parity price support program was bound to run into difficulties unforeseen at the time the history-making Agricultural Adjustment Act of 1938 had been passed by Congress. It had been designed to retrieve for the benefit of the farmer the workable features of the A.A.A. of 1933. Fundamental to the program was that of government price support in a direct relation to "parity" as might be determined from time to time by the Congress, but in general supposed to rest on the golden moment between 1909 and 1914. This program had as an important feature the creation of an "ever normal granary," a national storehouse of products to be filled in good times against need in periods of drought and shortage. The Commodity Credit Corporation was the purchaser for this storehouse.

Now that war had come the government needed to use these assets of its program to the full. Overnight the vocabulary of economics underwent a significant change. There was no longer any such thing as a surplus. All goods were needed for prosecution of immediate aims, and this was true to a striking extent of the versatile wheat berry.

On October 4, 1943, Leon Henderson of the Office of Price Administration froze flour prices. For a moment the faces of millers, too, were frozen with consternation. But as the *Northwestern Miller* pointed out patiently the industry was used to "the endless efforts of government to supervise the production and marketing of wheat." There was no protest until suddenly the price of wheat began to rise.

Presumably even economists and legislators had got out of the habit of thinking that this could happen. No ceiling had been placed on the price of wheat. The flour ceiling had been based on wheat price at a specified level (89 per cent of parity), and now the natural relationship between purchase price of raw material and selling price of processed product no longer existed. Wheat rose, the flour ceiling stayed where it had been, and the miller, squeezed between, developed first claustrophobia and then, at the prospect of seeing his profit disappear, complete panic.

The fantastic world of wheels within wheels into which war had transformed the economy prompted the government to strange maneuvers that involved the simultaneous application of accelerator and brake. In normal times the mill was the destination of the great part of the wheat crop. But now the Commodity Credit Corporation was selling large quantities of its purchases for purposes other than those of flour manufacture — 40,000,000 bushels each month for feed and another 10,000,000 for the making of alcohol. Business was lively with the usual result that prices rose. Wheat went far beyond that dreamed of by the writers of regulations.

To make the wheels mesh neatly once more there were two things that government could do: it could raise the ceiling on flour or it could reimburse millers for the unexpected increase in the cost of wheat. Talk of subsidy began.

The very word had an alarming sound to the miller's ear. Its power of seduction was great, obviously, but like all such enticement it must be studied carefully for hidden commitments. To accept a subsidy would be to accept government control of operations. That was uncomfortable enough. But if subsidy were to be tied to dictation of what constituted a proper profit that, from the miller's point of view, was worse still.

Bell at first thought the position quite untenable. He wished to see the adoption of a plan by which government would buy up wheat and sell it to millers at 89 per cent of parity. Existing regulations made that impossible. Still Bell protested: "If our profits are confined to that which falls within the Excess Profits Tax credit, when the normal tax is raised from 40 to 45 per cent, we will be in rather sorry straits."

It was with the greatest reluctance that General Mills permitted its representatives even to participate in discussions of subsidy. In the end, however, two executives went to Washington. They were Sydney Anderson, long General Mills' legal adviser and expert in legislative matters, and G. S. Kennedy, whom Bullis had transferred from Buffalo to Minneapolis in 1939 as director of Operations Control. Washington became virtually Kennedy's place of residence for the duration of the war. Deeply involved in the task of serving on advisory committees, he deserves credit for making the subsidy program work smoothly through the regulations of which he was chief author. With his help, Jesse Jones of the Reconstruction Finance Corporation and Fred M. Vinson, then director of the Office of Economic Stabilization, were able to arrive at a theoretical formula that satisfied the consciences of millers in accepting a subsidy and a practical formula that satisfied the miller's cost card.

The representatives of government and industry cooperated well to the important end of getting wheat to the places where it was needed most to serve a nation at war. The subsidy, they agreed, was in reality a flour production payment designed to adjust conflicting regulations with as little confusion as possible. It permitted the miller to pay a higher price for wheat than the flour ceiling permitted him to pay. If anyone received a real subsidy it was the consumer who bought wheat products at prices lower than would have been possible had normal conditions of competition prevailed, with the market "open" and with no ceiling on flour. The miller was chosen as the "vehicle of subsidization" chiefly because there were only 3000 members of his group, whereas there were 135,000,000 consumers.

But of subsidy in the ordinary sense — direct aid by government designed to stimulate activity in a time of emergency — there was none. The alcohol program might be said to have been subsidized and so might certain mining operations in which the government offered attractions to get "all-out" production in fields that had few attractions in themselves. The milling fraternity, as a group of corporate citizens, received from government only the payment of a just obligation.

The subsidies, paid on the basis of the number of bushels of wheat ground during each monthly period, were subject to complex procedures with rates changing frequently. To the formidable task of making these regulations work General Mills made a significant contribution in the patience and the administrative skill of its representative, Kennedy. One of his striking gifts was the ability to translate professional jargon into English and another was the sly art of lending a humorous tone to discussion of stern matters. His writing of regulations was austere enough to ensure intelligibility. But Kennedy became a kind of ambassador at large serving the entire industry, and his business letters to colleagues gleam with witty shrewdness. To the biddable he offered wise counsel; to the stubborn he offered perhaps the best advice of all: "Why don't you just go ahead and do what you're going to do anyway."

The subsidy program expired on June 30, 1946, when a congressional measure intended to continue operations of the Office of Price Control was killed by veto. During the two and a half years of its life government and the corporate citizen had worked together in an atmosphere of mutual concern for a common cause. As a result, flour was always available in the domestic market, wherever our armed forces were fighting, and wherever the government needed it for the feeding of liberated peoples.

The next great occasion, in 1946, for close collaboration between the milling industry and government had in its background a grim crisis, the fear of world famine. Grain crops in the southern hemisphere were almost complete failures, and the only place in the food economy of the globe where savings could be made was in America. Evidence gathered by Herbert Hoover in the course of a world survey of threatened areas indicated that unless effective steps were taken millions of men, women, and children would be condemned to diets hideously like those of the Nazi prison camps. It was, Hoover reported, "the grimmest spectre of famine in all the history of the world."

Millers were, of course, concerned with their responsibility to help feed a tired, frightened, war-shattered world. Bell, who had so recently announced the principle that the welfare of the common man must be the chief objective of the peace, had the support of Bullis, always an advocate of high production, and of Alonzo Taylor, still active, still the best informed and most conscientious of food economists.

But these three differed sharply with the government in Washington on the question of how the necessary saving could be brought about. James Byrnes, then Truman's secretary of state, had returned from the London conference to make the suggestion that England's experiment with "high-extraction flour" be imitated in the United States. After a cabinet meeting held in February 1946, the announcement was made that the possibility was being "explored." Never was an expedition into the heart of a complex matter conducted with such dispatch. Less than a week later a high-extraction program had become the administration's official policy. No consultation had taken place meanwhile with the men of the industry who would be required to carry out the blunt instructions.

To produce the flour from which the familiar white bread of the American table was made, millers used the most highly refined 68 to 72 per cent of the original wheat berry. In England the percentage of extraction had been raised to 85 and it was this percentage that Byrnes had suggested for American mills. Clinton Anderson, secretary of agriculture, realizing that less than 2 per cent of buyers in the United States had ever been in the market for whole-wheat bread (the close equivalent of bread made from high-extraction flour) protested. Finally, in one of those curious compromises the fine impartiality of which is demonstrated in that it pleases no one, the figure 80 per cent was written in. As War Food Order Number 144, this directive was issued to millers.

Before it was put finally into effect, on February 15, 1946, millers protested vigorously. Bell believed that the government's program of saving flour for stricken regions could be met but not by the method suggested. Millers experienced in dealing with crisis situations should be allowed to work out their own solution, one that would not destroy their economy. Bullis pointed out that, during World War I, dark breads had been tried and they had failed to satisfy the American people. In tacit indignation the public had turned to other foods, and it seemed probable that, in the new situation, they might do so again. The final result to American agriculture might well be serious.

In a telegram to the President, Bullis subscribed enthusiastically to the objective of feeding Europe but urged reconsideration of method. The goal could be reached by limiting mill production for domestic use to 85 per cent for the year before and by putting the same limitation on the baker's output. The difference could be saved for the stricken areas.

Since both hunger and the government were moving fast in this crisis, the millers, too, must show all possible speed. Bullis went to Washington as official representative of the flour millers of America with an appointment to talk to the President. At his request, Bell joined him there and together they developed a detailed plan of their own. Its chief guarantee was that, if industry were permitted to continue its habitual method of extraction, it would agree to a "set aside" order binding all millers to deliver for export to needy countries a higher percentage of its production. Further, industry would follow a voluntary system of allocation of the remaining production based on deliveries to each class of trade during the last quarter of the year 1945.

Across the smooth surface of his desk, swept clean of the souvenirs that had covered it in Roosevelt's time, President Truman faced Bell and Bullis with a courtesy no less smooth. If the mills had a plan which was better than that of the administration, he would be glad to consider it, he said. Bell returned to Georgia where he was on vacation but Bullis, before he returned to Minneapolis, soon ascertained that the President's statement had been merely a concession to politeness. All the while the high-extraction plan was moving forward inexorably. While Truman had talked to Bell and Bullis, Secretary Anderson was telling a group of millers and bakers that the matter was quite settled. He suggested crisply that nothing remained for them to do except to go home and start producing 80 per cent extraction flour.

This the millers proceeded loyally to do. As president of General Mills, Bullis issued an order on February 16, 1946, to stop the production of Gold Medal Kitchen-Tested Flour. The "All America" brand took its place while "King Wheat" took the place of General Mills' bakery flour. Into temporary eclipse went also Softasilk Flour and Bisquick. The purpose was, of course, to preserve the prestige which had been built up so conscientiously. Until the authentic product could be offered once more, no substitute was to be allowed to wear the old name.

But Bell and Bullis were determined to produce, even in these circumstances, a flour that "would approach the quality" of Gold Medal Kitchen-Tested. All departments concentrated on that purpose. Products Control and Research were quick to devise new techniques for bridging the distance between familiar and unfamiliar ways. Home Service produced new recipes for the effective use of the new flour. Within two weeks of the change Bell and Bullis were able to make a tour of the plant congratulating heads of departments "on the fine job done in adjusting to the new order."

Meanwhile Bullis argued patiently but persistently with Secretary Anderson to get War Food Order Number 144 modified. To his own associates he said: "One of the sources of strength of General Mills is that we do not cry over spilled milk but we endeavor to learn the rules of the game and then, as operating officials, work night and day to satisfy the operation of those rules." But to the government, he presented day by day the rapidly gathering evidence that the program would not and could not work.

Indeed, the six-month period when War Food Order Number 144 was in effect proved to be one of uninterrupted nightmare. As Bell had predicted, it became a kind of "relief in reverse" since it seemed to back awkwardly away from its own objective. The wheat which the program was supposed to save for Europe went to fatten hogs on the farms. Hoover, serving on Truman's Famine Emergency Committee, continued to plead for a generous flow of wheat from the farms into the export market. But his speeches were wintry with threats and they did not bring out the grain. At last the government offered a bonus of thirty cents a bushel to persuade farmers to support the program. This created still more problems for millers who were required by law to store raw material for no more than twenty-one days at a time. When farmers attracted by the bonus began at last to direct the flow of wheat into the export market, the mills found it almost impossible to replenish their supplies. Seriously crippled in all their operations, many small millers and bakers faced the fear of actual extinction.

In the midst of these chaotic conditions General Mills managed to maintain not merely its poise but also its profits. The annual report, released in July 1946, showed that, even in this time of high prices and comparatively low productivity, a new peak in total income had been achieved along with comfortably increased net earnings and with reasonably satisfactory production.

"General Mills has been fortunate," Bullis observed modestly, "in performing services for the public which the people consider necessary."

Once more that policy of audacity in enterprise and conservatism in management had justified itself.

On August 26, 1946, an end came to one of the crippling restrictions put upon millers. Secretary Anderson announced that prospects for an excellent crop made it possible simultaneously to raise "export targets" and to modify limitations on domestic use. The 80 per cent extraction order ended its short but highly dramatic career on September 1. Two months later, "as though in answer to prayer," said the *Hook-Up*, publication of the Millers' National Federation, Secretary Anderson signed an order ending the regulation that millers limit production for domestic use to 85 per cent of that of the sacred "base period" in 1945. This signalized the last gasp of War Food Order Number 144. "Hic jacet," wrote the *Northwestern Miller*, adding with a touch of urchin humor, "and may the imps of Hell have their pitchforks hot."

But hunger is a problem that, at no time in human history, has stayed solved long. Within a year, during the autumn of 1947, another crisis existed. Some 200,000,000 people in Western Europe faced undernourishment once more unless American citizens could add, by their savings, at least 100,000,000 bushels of wheat to the exportable surplus of 470,000,000 bushels. Again there was no possible turning away from the problem because the struggle resolved itself into one of bread as the champion of freedom. In the words of Secretary of State George Marshall:

"Food is a vital factor in our foreign policy. The attitude of Americans can make or break our efforts to secure peace and security throughout the world. The connection between the individual American and world affairs is unmistakably clear — our foreign policy has entered the American home and taken a seat at the family table."

This time, however, government had learned to trust the food industry as a willing and skillful collaborator in its humanitarian plans. On September 28, 1947, President Truman appointed a Citizen's Food

Committee to act with the Food Committee of the cabinet to determine what voluntary effort could do. Charles Luckman, then of Lever Brothers, became its chairman and Bullis of General Mills was named chairman of a subcommittee representing industry.

A brilliant campaign was launched overnight in which all advertising intelligences of the country were enlisted. Their slogan, Save Meat, Save Wheat, Save the Peace, became familiar to the entire American world, spoken as it was by all the great voices of government, industry, diplomacy, and the entertainment world. The program, endorsed with equal eloquence by religion and labor, press and government, caught public attention and public support instantly.

More than sentiment was involved, however, and the wits of men with economic insight were needed to keep the values clear. At the first of the three sessions of the Citizen's Food Committee, held in the White House, Bullis put the issues straight before the zealots who were clamoring once more for "gray bread," as the product of 80 per cent extraction has come to be called. Even its advocates seemed to acknowledge in that phrase a morbid impulse on their part to mortify the flesh by feeding it poorly.

High grinding of wheat, Bullis pointed out, would serve no purpose. It would merely aggravate a shortage of feed stuffs and it was precisely the shortage of feed grains that had created the crisis in the first place. There would be plenty of wheat to carry out the program of the President and Secretary Marshall and also to fulfill domestic needs were it not for the insufficiency of other crops, particularly of corn. The proper solution, as D. A. Stevens and G. S. Kennedy of General Mills pointed out to the Department of Agriculture, was efficient utilization of existing supplies. It was essential also to use the prod of price incentive "to move wheat off the farms." Their reports had emphatic things to say about the disastrously wasteful effect of price controls.

The program which made allies of distillers, brewers, bakers, millers, poultry and livestock raisers, restaurateurs, and the public was conducted from first to last on a voluntary basis. It reached a climax in the progress across the country of the Freedom Train. The idea, originated by columnist Drew Pearson, was sponsored by the Association of American Railroads. Not one but many trains, numbering in all 481 cars, were filled by the gift of the people with wheat flour, condensed milk, and mixed foods of all kinds.

Age of Responsibility

The lesson that modern industry had learned in coming to regard itself as a corporate citizen could, as the example of the Citizen's Food Committee showed, be applied in reverse. When the situation called for such action, the head of a great corporation could resolve himself into a private citizen once more to lend his experience in the management of complex affairs to the most immediate of human problems. Neighborliness on a vast international scale was the aim of the Citizen's Food Committee. And this purpose was aided greatly by the fact that it was directed by men like Bullis who, as purveyors of food, always had been familiar with the business of being neighborly.

This has been called the "age of responsibility." Amplification of the meaning of the phrase might well suggest that, in the world of today, the more essential one's occupation may be, the greater becomes one's duty to serve it with scrupulous devotion. Few industries have come so frequently under the eye and the direct control of government, because of their essential character, as has the milling industry. Few have shown so generous a willingness to cooperate even when they disagreed with the methods pursued by government. And few, indeed, have so often anticipated the action of government in voluntary improvement of their services. General Mills' record of leadership in all these ways testifies eloquently to the maturity of its temper as a servant of humanity and the delicacy of its conscience as corporate citizen.

19

Owners of General Mills

THE COMPANY AND THE PUBLIC

In the days of Dunwoody when the motto of the Washburn Crosby Company was said to be Addition, division, and silence, the Quaker capitalist had never dismissed a session of fellow executives without a warning that "the figure must be kept confidential."

He would have shaken his head with the decorous disapproval appropriate to his temper if he could have returned to earth on September 12, 1939, to observe what the son of his old partner was up to. At the door of a suite in a Detroit hotel stood James Ford Bell receiving as honored guests the local stockholders of General Mills. He was there to offer hospitality, to answer questions, above all to reveal the figures of his company's operations and to analyze their significance.

The first "regional stockholders' meeting" was held as an experiment to test Bell's theory that the (then) ten thousand owners of General Mills could be and should be persuaded to take more interest in the business. It had struck him as significant that at an annual meeting of the corporation in Wilmington, Delaware, few stockholders outside of those active in the company had appeared to participate. He was conscious of the fact that many small investors fail to answer proxy requests.

But it was not difficult to discern that this might be largely the fault of circumstance. Suppose General Mills, instead of expecting the stockholder to come to the corporation, were to go to the stockholder? Suppose the enclosing conditions of the meeting, instead of being allowed to seem formidable and unfamiliar, were allowed to have the tone and atmosphere of an informal get-together? Might industry not avail itself of a common interest in dividends which would be at least as great as a common interest in a game of bridge?

This, according to the unsolicited testimony of Henry R. Trumbower, professor of economics at the University of Wisconsin, was "a wholly new idea and departure in corporation management, something which every large corporation might do well to imitate."

The experimental session was so successful that others followed in Los Angeles, San Francisco, Chicago, New York, Boston, Buffalo, and, finally, Minneapolis. The pattern was everywhere the same. Bell, then still chairman of the board, and — in his own interpretation of the role — representative extraordinary of both management and ownership, greeted the gathering, introduced fellow officers, and finally invited questioners into active participation by examining plans and prospects with them.

Gordon Ballhorn (comptroller of the corporation in 1939, now a vice president as well) presently explored the complexities of assets, liabilities, taxes, and profits, using all the visual aids of the screen to make his analysis clear. Both Bell and Ballhorn answered questions directly and frankly, satisfying every legitimate interest in the details of management.

Bell's principle in creating the regional stockholders' meeting was essentially that of assuring the public that "business had nothing to hide." These owners of General Mills should be persuaded to interest themselves more actively in shaping the public attitudes that affect commerce. "Politics," Bell pointed out, "in its effect on business is not a proper concern of management but it is very much the concern of the owners of American industry." This large group of men and women represented "a potential force that must be awakened to an understanding of what business is trying to accomplish."

For the art of host who must greet men and women whom he had never seen before Bell showed an expansive gift and the word "jovial" followed him everywhere. His lifelong concern with "building men," a responsibility which he felt he had inherited from his father, seemed to enable him to build men on the spot. Reticent questioners felt confidence and importance communicated to them by his graciousness. In the atmosphere created by this "gentle kindly man," as the financial editor of the *Chicago Daily News* called him, small stockholders who had come to the meeting feeling like audacious interlopers left it full of the confidence of partners in a successful enterprise.

280

The tradition was carried on in the same spirited style when Bullis became chairman of the board. Only during the years of World War II was the tradition of the regional stockholders' meeting allowed to lapse. Before and after that period, a "troupe" of General Mills employees took to the road every other year to dramatize the news of the corporation before stockholders and other guests in some ten or twelve major cities of the country. Bullis, with Ballhorn, headed the company of hosts in 1948, 1950, and 1952.

Under Bullis' dynamic leadership, the potentialities of the tradition were expanded. It is his opinion that the regional stockholders' meeting offers a special opportunity "to bridge the gap between education and industry." To present the purposes and prospects of business sympathetically before students, Bullis arranged for simulated sessions of this kind in half a dozen important educational institutions. Such "stockholder meetings" were held at schools of business at Michigan, Harvard, Pennsylvania, Minnesota, Cornell, and Massachusetts Institute of Technology.

Still another new development of the regional stockholders' meeting idea was that of taking the facts of a corporation's daily life before sessions of experts. In the years between 1948 and 1953 Bullis and Ballhorn have broadened the program of the stockholder tours by speaking at sessions of the Society of Security Analysts at New York, Boston, Cleveland, and San Francisco.

The regional stockholders' meetings have been called many things. Sober observers of the press have saluted the idea as a pioneer effort "in a new field of social responsibility." Candid men within the General Mills organization have called them "super sales meetings." But the unmistakable fact is that they represent an honest and spontaneous desire to establish a close link with the public.

Bell's preoccupation with the "avenue to the home" made him unusually conscientious in interpreting his duty toward the customer. The buyer of a package of Wheaties has never been to him a mere unit of consumption but an individual who lived on his broad highway and whose daily experience deserved to be made as rich and complete as possible. In 1936, before the practice had become usual, General Mills created a department of public relations. Henry Adams Bellows became its head.

Bellows was an altogether remarkable man with a creative gift that enabled him to give definition to the "public relation" idea at a moment when it was tantalizing, but largely eluding, many other intelligences.

The broad measure of Bellows' interest may be taken from the span covered by his publications. These included a *Treatise on Riot Duty for National Guards,* a volume of poems, *Highland Light,* and a *Short History of Flour Milling.*

In his maturity he managed to suggest in personal appearance the several very different kinds of careers he had had. After taking his Ph.D. at Harvard he had taught English; in the period of World War I he had been a soldier, serving as a colonel of the Minnesota National Guard; later he had edited the *Bellman* and the *Northwestern Miller* and written music criticism for the *Minneapolis Daily News;* and at last when Donald Davis created station WCCO in the year 1925, Bellows had been its manager. For a decade during which the pattern of radio entertainment took definite design, traditions of radio education were established, and forms of radio advertising were devised, Bellows sat on every important council. He was for a time vice president of CBS.

A man with so sweeping a view of human interests, one who was no more afraid of setting foot on the slopes of Parnassus than of slugging out an issue with rugged business competitors (and who knew how to quell a riot if necessary) had exactly the kind of vigor and imagination needed to create a Department of Relations with the Public, as the General Mills unit was first called. Humanist and humanitarian, Bellows gave character, purpose, and plan to the project. A new company publication, the *Modern Millwheel,* created in 1936 to give expression to his ideas, had no difficulty in establishing a new high standard for such house organs. To the advantage of being edited by a poet it added that of having as chief editorial writer Bell himself, a man who had fallen in his youth under the spell of the King James version of the Bible. Bell brought to any consideration of the responsibilities and opportunities of business the powerful rhythmic swing of the purposeful verb, the sudden, brilliant illumination of the homely image.

Bellows seemed, all his life, to be under a compulsion to change profession every third year. Exactly three years after he had established the Department of Relations with the Public, Bellows' life — as though it were under the control of the same restless compulsion — came to an end. He died in 1939 of cancer of the lung. "The spirit that dwelt in Henry A. Bellows," wrote Bell, "was the spirit of a simple faith in mankind." And it was this faith that he translated into the positive terms of a public relations program.

Belief in mankind had need of emphatic reaffirmation in 1939. In that year Hitler invaded Poland, Russia overran Finland, and the "phoney war" dragged on. In September 1940 the United States pushed through the Selective Service Act to conscript a great army to be on the alert and the American people began to be aware that there was no escape from the job of preparing for "total defense."

It was in this period that the Department of Relations with the Public (later the Department of Public Services and still later the Department of Public Relations) assumed complete design. Fulfilling the purposes outlined by Bell and Bellows, it took up an active part in furthering the government's program of home defense.

The collaboration was appropriate because General Mills always had been in intimate communication with the housewife, urging her interest in its products. Now the company addressed the same housewife on behalf of national welfare. But the terms of communication were the same. As the president of the company pointed out, women had been unofficially drafted for defense. Since they had always been active in community service, they could now be asked confidently to assume responsibility for morale.

The first contribution to the effort to safeguard health had been, of course, the part played by General Mills in the enrichment of flour. "The ever generous support of General Mills" had been credited by Paul L. Cornell, of the enrichment enthusiasts, with a large share in the success of the campaign.

To pursue the subject of nutrition was the inevitable next development in the company's private war against fear. A kit of seven pamphlets was issued and distributed through women's organizations. They presented, in easily understood language, the latest findings of the social scientist concerning all matters affecting the stability of the family unit under stress. There were discussions of homemaking, nutrition, health, buying, recreation, community education — everything that might strengthen the housewife's hold upon her more-than-ever-before scattered tasks.

General Mills widened its audience next by addressing teachers and leaders of groups. The first edition of a new Nutrition Study Kit went to 20,000 such workers. This set of pamphlets included discussions of *Meal Planning on a Limited Budget, The Wheat Kernel and Its Elements,* and the whole subject of enrichment of flour and bread. The matters in which General Mills was expert were submitted to reexamination by specialists in diet and presented, without commercial pressure of any kind, to the public as information essential to its own well-being in this time of anxiety.

The year's end brought Pearl Harbor and the sharp turn of events that made the United States a combatant nation. General Mills stepped up its own program correspondingly, issuing 1,000,000 copies of *War Work — a Daybook for the Home* and within six months, when the first edition was exhausted, another appeared, nearly as large. This study was designed to show each housewife how her own domestic routine might become an effective instrument of war. The climax of this effort came when the distribution of still another pamphlet, *Your Share,* reached some 7,000,000 copies. *Your Share* offered a complete account of what the housewife had a right to expect as the dietary due of her family and of how, even in a time of emergency, she might make available foods stretch to cover her needs.

Bell's affinity all down the years with the agricultural community made him deeply sympathetic with such tasks as the extension divisions of the land grant colleges of America had undertaken in carrying to the farmer news of late improvements in growing crops. He had watched from the beginning the development of the 4-H clubs. These organizations had come into existence at the turn of the century in an effort to reverse the tendency of youth to run away from the farm the first time the gate was left open. American leaders, Theodore Roosevelt among them, felt that some means must be found of making rural life more attractive to the young. The projects sponsored by the 4-H clubs, the prizes offered by their leaders, and above all the eloquent persuasions of zealots among them, had proved to be enormously effective in making farm life seem to offer one of the most dignified and satisfying of careers. Indeed the 4-H adventure may be credited with a significant share in helping to make a business and a science of agriculture.

The finest contributor to the program in Minnesota was T. A. Erickson. As a superintendent of schools in a rural community he had launched the movement locally by digging into his own pocket for money with which to buy seed for competitive projects among boys and girls. "Dad" Erickson had grown venerable, though he remained perennially young, with this youth movement. In 1940 it was time for him to retire from the

University of Minnesota where the 4-H clubs of the state were now under the supervision of the Agricultural Extension Division. Bell, as regent of the university, was intimately acquainted with the qualifications of all its important men. He invited Erickson to become, upon his retirement, a consultant to General Mills on rural relations.

The suggestion startled Erickson. To what extent, he wanted to know, would he be expected to commercialize his 4-H work in the service of General Mills?

"To no extent at all," Bell answered. "I shouldn't want you to exploit your position."

Erickson looked incredulous. "You don't ask me to advertise General Mills' products?"

"Certainly not," Bell laughed.

"But then, what do you get out of it?"

"Mr. Erickson," Bell said, "General Mills expects to be in business a hundred years from now. We think that by supporting the finest citizen-building movement in recent social history we will earn all the good will our effort may deserve."

On that basis an agreement was made. This tall, gaunt man took a desk in the General Mills offices. Looking like a Don Quixote in modern dress, Erickson tilted at no windmills but drove straight at eminently practical projects. One of these was to supply the 4-H movement with the printed literature which had been a conspicuous lack. His first assignment to himself was to produce a pamphlet called *Guide Posts for Local 4-H Leaders*. He had no way of knowing whether or not other states, each jealous of its own prestige, would be willing to use it. Feeling that he made an audacious suggestion, he asked that 10,000 copies be printed. "How many local leaders are there?" Bell wanted to know when the matter came to his attention. There were approximately 150,000, he was told. "Then that's the number of copies we'll print," he said. Erickson went home oppressed by the thought of the mountain of paper General Mills would have on its hands.

But he was wrong. The pamphlet was an immediate success. All the local leaders wanted copies for themselves and for their assistants. Up to 1953, 425,000 copies had been distributed on request in four successive editions. And the flow of pamphlets continued: *The Parent's Part in 4-H Work, Older Rural Youth, The Church and the 4-H Clubs, Safety Guide for Farm and Home*. In 1950 it was estimated that more than 2,000,000 copies of ten pamphlets published by General Mills had been distributed from coast to coast, all of them upon request. With the pamphlet distribution went intimate counseling on the multifarious problems of organizing and maintaining rural youth groups. Sometimes curious challenges were presented to Erickson. On one occasion readers in Florida acknowledged receipt of the pamphlet containing instructions for organizing 4-H Clubs in rural churches. Their spokesman wrote to say that they had the 4-H club, right enough, but no church. And so, how about a little help in organizing a church!

In 1952 Erickson, seeming more stalwart and knightly than ever, paused long enough on his eightieth birthday to receive congratulations from fellow workers including Bell, Bullis, Perrin, and Gale and to eat a slice of Betty Crocker birthday cake. Then once more he turned briskly to his task. That it is a significant one an impersonal observer of the Department of Agriculture has suggested by saying that food produced and conserved annually by 4-H workers is enough to feed 1,000,000 men of the armed services for a year.

Erickson's long and distinguished career was recognized by Epsilon Sigma Phi, national honorary extension fraternity, in 1953 when it awarded him the Distinguished Service Ruby for service to rural youth. Erickson was the first Minnesotan and the first representative of industry to receive this honor. In December of that year, after thirteen years with General Mills, he retired at the age of eighty-two to write his autobiography and memoirs.

The intimacy of General Mills' relationship to the public has increased with each year of its history. Indicative of the company's deep preoccupation with community welfare has been its active concern with matters of theoretical education. Americans always have been shrewd enough to realize and candid enough to admit that one of the uses of education is that of a tool, an aid to success in business. Within the last decade business itself has become increasingly aware of the role it may play as educator and has accepted, as a social responsibility, a share in certain kinds of instruction related to its own activities. General Mills was one of the first large corporations to feel that responsibility.

The company had been concerned for many years with the idea that a business institution whose job it is to sell food must undertake to teach people what food they need. This impulse had revealed itself in the daily activities of the organization: in the cooking schools established in the teens of the century, in the radio programs of the 1920s, in the nutrition pamphlets of the depression and of the war years. In the 1940s, General Mills pushed its program one step farther by going outside its own walls to undertake the role of consultant to schools and to the various educational agencies of the country.

The appointment in 1943 of Dr. Lela Booher as chief nutritionist launched the company's full and consistent program of urging attention to nutritional problems on the public. For eight years, Dr. Booher directed public concern toward the problem of maintaining absolute standards of nutrition. Her pamphlet *A Nutrition Guide* discussed such matters as the seven basic foods groups, the quantities of each required by workers of various kinds, calorie content, vitamin sources, and thrift in the preparation, serving, and storing of food. Her booklet *The Story of Cereal Grains* carried to the general audience all the fundamental information about the nutritive contributions of grains.

This approach to the task of persuading people to eat better still was too passive to satisfy the company's compulsive drive toward achievement. It was not enough to supply science with a loud-speaker, for there were still many who would avail themselves of what Woodrow Wilson once described as humanity's infinite capacity for avoiding knowledge. The thing to do was to take this kind of information to the center established in a democratic society for the distribution of knowledge, for its forced feeding if necessary — the public school.

Bell once observed: "The basic convictions, prejudices, and opinions of adult life are formed in the mind of the preadolescent and adolescent child. In later life it is possible to rearrange these convictions and opinions, but they are seldom changed."

In 1945 General Mills embarked on a study of the eating habits of American children. What it found supported all too well the suspicion that there was need of missionary work. Fewer than 40 per cent of the children examined in the first survey reported good diets. Breakfast was the most neglected meal of the day and it tended to be snubbed more and more as children grew older. The young in rural districts were fed worse, not better, than children in urban communities.

Cross-section surveys of nine schools in Minnesota showed that undernourishment in children seemed to have nothing to do with the

287

income of parents. Lack of information, rather than lack of money, had permitted the eating habits of America to deteriorate seriously.

To get another look at the American table, from a quite different angle, a group of schools in Georgia were added to the demonstration program. Today such surveys have been conducted in many states. Food patterns, before and after special training, have been studied and evaluated revealingly.

Having estimated that two out of every five of the Tom Sawyers and Becky Thatchers of the American schoolroom suffer from eating problems, the General Mills experts were aware of the seriousness of the task before them in undertaking to improve traditions of the table. They set about it, first, by creating a new literature of instructions: handbooks for teachers, guides for parents, charts and posters designed to catch the child's own eye and imagination. In the summer of 1945 at the University of Minnesota, there came together a great company of educators to consider these materials. General Mills served simply as sponsoring host; teachers of elementary grades, administrators, curriculum advisers were given free hands to tear the suggested program apart and put it together again. The final result satisfied the professionals; at last, an effective approach had been made to the vitally important task of teaching children to eat. It was, in fact, the teachers' own program.

General Mills, under advice from other experts in visual aids to education, put these materials of instruction into printed form. The persuasive subtlety of their design was so attractive that happy teachers found their children were being seduced into learning to read as well as into learning to eat. Many of these booklets have received the endorsement of college teachers as model materials. Again the only identification claimed by General Mills is the appearance of its seal on the back cover. No commercial products are mentioned in them. Yet some of these pamphlets have been called the best salesmen on General Mills' payroll because of the great improvement in eating habits that have become evident since the program began.

These gratifying results were recorded for the stimulation of educators and parents in a film called *The School That Learned to Eat*. At an international film festival, held in Edinburgh, Scotland, this unpretentious but curiously moving little study was judged to be an outstanding documentary film in the field of education.

In the hope of improving the materials for use in the public schools

288

in the nation, General Mills has cooperated with many educational institutions in their research studies. It helped to finance an undertaking of the Iowa State College, at Ames, to appraise the effects of school lunch programs. It lent assistance to Teachers College, Columbia, in its study of nutrition in the elementary schools, designed to improve methods of instruction. It gave funds to the University of Georgia for another project of a similar kind. As many as forty-five summer workshops in nutrition study have received help in a single season.

All these activities are under the management of the Department of Public Relations, now a unit with a large staff ultimately responsible to the chairman of the board. Its interests range widely over every aspect of public interest in General Mills and of General Mills' special interest, as host and instructor, in the public. It supervises the preparation of "institutional advertising" in which General Mills sets forth its philosophy of service. It is the semiofficial diner-out, the accepter of public invitations and fulfiller of engagements to speak. It makes arrangements for such occasions as the regional stockholders' meetings. For the sessions held in 1952 it prepared an ingenious film, done in the style of the cartoon comedy in which a symbolic figure, the genial little General, explained to "Mr. and Mrs. Stockholder" the workings of the company. Briskly he dramatized the need to return profits, as "working dollars," to the corporation's activities that these might grow with the growing needs of a dynamic America. The film established a new high standard of excellence in developing General Mills' favorite theme: the public is our boss.

As manager of the Department of Public Relations, Abbott Washburn was the initiator of many of these programs in the interest of general education. And even while he was strenuously engaged in organizing the nutrition project and in launching the "basic economics" experiment, he found time for activities of still broader significance. One of these, the Crusade for Freedom, finally demanded his full attention. Drafted, in a sense, by General Lucius Clay, then head of the National Committee for Free Europe, Washburn resigned from General Mills in 1951 to become director of the committee's first financial campaign. Later he entered the Eisenhower administration as director of informational activities. His experience parallels that of many another executive of General Mills who has put himself on loan to the government in time of emergency.

Owners of General Mills

There is, under heaven, no zeal to equal that of the educator once he has set out on a mission. The latest development of the task of General Mills' Department of Public Relations has taken the company into a field where it is likely to double the number of young minds its programs will reach. It has been estimated that the nutrition materials have reached 25,000,000 young people in some 120,000 schools. The new effort seems likely to prove even more effective.

The genesis of the new program was in the mind of J. F. Bell. Far too little, he thought, was being done to present democratic principles of government to those same preadolescent children whose attitudes were destined to become the controlling factors in the minds of tomorrow's voters. In a world surcharged with propaganda, some of which was deliberately damaging to faith in democracy, it was time for the businessman to say a word for himself and for the economic system under which he hoped to continue to operate.

The techniques learned in the process of developing the nutrition program were applied again. A study of available materials for the teaching of basic economics in the elementary schools revealed that almost none existed. The subject of economics was regarded as one belonging to the rarified upper reaches of the educational system. Only within recent years had it appeared, in homeopathic doses, as "social studies" in the curriculum of secondary schools. General Mills undertook to make a start toward the production of proper materials for the teaching of basic economics, undisguised as anything else, in the midgrades of the public schools.

An advisory committee made up of educators from the University of Minnesota, the public school systems of Des Moines, Iowa, and Duluth and Austin, Minnesota, was asked to suggest themes. These were developed in terms of the industry that General Mills understands best — the story of making flour for bread. A series of picture panels, suitable for display on blackboard chalk trays, traced the development of technological methods in everything from planting to marketing. Later, more ambitious efforts — two filmstrips called *Specialization* and *We Depend on Each Other* — presented concepts important to a basic understanding of the pattern of free enterprise. More recently still, a picture booklet, *Freedom of Choice*, has used the ever fascinating figures of Robinson Crusoe and the Swiss Family to show that man alone, men together, men in simple economies, and men in complex ones must exercise freedom in choosing their fundamental values. Only if these values are chosen freely, the booklet suggests, can they be permanently rewarding.

In January 1951 General Mills took the initiative in inviting to a conference at Des Moines, Iowa, representatives of twenty-two corporations, each concerned with a different basic industry, to consider the further development of such efforts. S. C. Gale of General Mills pointed out to the gathering that the program which his company had sponsored was in no sense a private possession. "Educators," he said, "conducted the major portion of the experimental work. Our company has worked with educators and endeavored to cooperate fully. But educators did the job."

There was, Gale suggested, need for this experiment to have companions.

"Every basic industry has a story to tell — chemicals, transportation, communications, banking. We have not sought, and do not recommend now, a new association for group action. We seek no collective effort. But we say, with utter candor, that the job is too big for any one company or for any one industry. It is clearly a task for all to do, each going his own way and on his own initiative."

Endorsement of these purposes has come to General Mills on more than one occasion from high sources. In June 1950, Chairman of the Board Bullis breakfasted at 60 Morningside Heights with Dwight D. Eisenhower, then president of Columbia University, and invited him to visit Minneapolis to discuss problems of education as they impinge upon the problems of industry. A month later Eisenhower was able to accept the invitation and Bullis presided at a large dinner meeting given in his honor at the Minneapolis Club. On Eisenhower's return to New York, he set down in a letter to Bullis the principles and purposes that had been discussed. He offered the suggestion that "It is the responsibility of our educational system to establish a sharper understanding of the American system, a sharper appreciation of its values and a more intense devotion to its fundamental purposes."

He suggested also "the establishment of a great center where business and professional men can meet in forums to design new ways of putting American objectives clearly before the people."

From this second suggestion grew the creation of the American Assembly which has held four sessions in Arden House at Harriman,

New York, to discuss foreign relations, inflation and monetary policies, and social security problems. Bullis serves as one of the nine members of the National Policy Board of the American Assembly.

The initiative seized by General Mills, half a dozen years ago, in starting its own educational program may be said to have anticipated a significant development in national policy. General Mills has put printing presses and facilities for film making at the disposal of teachers to help them implant in young minds an awareness of the responsibilities and opportunities of the way of life to which they were born.

In the estimation of Bell, these activities are essential to the proper performance of his job. He believes, with Disraeli, that "the health of the people is really the foundation upon which all their happiness and all their powers as a State depend."

20

The Humanities of Business

THE COMPANY AND ITS EMPLOYEES

THE humanities of business today are more important than the techniques of business."

This was the statement of faith made by Bullis at a conference on business theory held at the University of Buffalo in December 1951. Human relations are, in his opinion, "the most important element in business because of the necessity to secure more efficiency and greater productivity from the men on the job."

A significant aspect of a change that the century has brought about in the relationship between employer and employee may be glimpsed in this judgment. It acknowledges the priority of human rights in the development of human society just as Bell once had done when he said that the welfare of the common man must be the goal of future effort. At the same time it testifies to the sincerity of the attitude by suggesting that the well-being of the worker is a measurable and a valuable asset of enterprise.

The story of conflict between owner and worker has had its most vivid scenes in the industrial realms of mining, steel, railroads, and shipyards. The flour-milling industry offers no comparable challenge to the imagination. Its plant has a small staff and the tone of its daily life has always been intimate, almost familial. Milling seems, also, to have attracted the kind of entrepreneur who has stayed close to his enterprise, known its personnel — each man by his first name — and felt the kind of responsibility not shared by the distant overseer of a vast industrial undertaking. Horace Davis in California, Cadwallader

Washburn in Minnesota, Frank Kell in Texas, all were men of the same type. They disciplined their love of opportunity with an awareness of obligation.

General Mills has managed to grow huge without losing that tradition. Closeness to an essential and universal concern of humankind, the production of man's daily bread, has preserved the common touch and given this corporation a prevailing sense of responsibility both toward its craft and toward the workers in it.

From the beginning of his management of the mills at Minneapolis Cadwallader Washburn followed a generous policy. In 1884 a local newspaper called attention to the fact that "the Washburn mills pay double time for Sunday work, the only milling concern in the city to be so liberal."

If the Washburn Crosby mills at Minneapolis are taken as representative of the character of the whole enterprise, it is of importance to notice that, in the whole history of their independent existence before the formation of General Mills, there were only two strikes against management — one in 1894 and one in 1903. The first was a small abortive affair, soon ended; the second, involving the seventeen mills of the three major milling companies, lasted longer but produced no violence. An indirect result was the establishment, as the fixed rule in the industry, of the eight-hour workday. In this matter millers anticipated the rest of American business by more than a decade. It took many strikes and all the combined pressures of World War I to get general recognition for the principle of the eight-hour day.

In 1918 the Washburn Crosby Company, without accepting the still distasteful idea of unionism, voluntarily took a decisive step toward employee representation in the discussion of wages and conditions of work. The War Labor Board, meeting at Minneapolis in December of that year, held a hearing on wages and offered recommendations concerning requests for increases made by Washburn Crosby employees. The company invited mill workers to choose representatives to sit with management in joint discussion of these terms. The session was a complete success and advances for workers were put into immediate effect. Out of this experience grew the committee system which remained in effect for many years.

This consisted of a neat dovetailing of elected representatives of various departments into a counseling body. Each department named a committee of three members; the forty-four chairmen of these groups constituted the Employees' General Committee; this group in turn named seven of its number to the Employees' Executive Committee. The latter met twice a month with management to discuss questions of broad concern to owners and workers. The employees' committees were the only recognized bargaining agencies.

Meanwhile various acknowledgments were made of the humanities of business by the Washburn Crosby Company. In 1915 a health department was created; in 1919 a group insurance plan was adopted covering 3000 mill workers. More important than these arrangements from the standpoint of the development of an independent philosophy of industrial relations was the Guarantee Plan.

When Bell returned to Minneapolis after his service to the government in World War I, he brought the idea, inspired perhaps by his recent experience in bringing harmony out of disparate interests and impulses, that security in the possession of his job is a chief prerequisite for the worker's success. In August 1918, Bell outlined a proposal whereby the mill employee, previously subject to all the hazards of layoffs and shutdowns, could be given that security. It suggested that employees who had been in service for two years, but less than three, should be guaranteed 2080 hours of work each year, and that employees of three years' standing or more should be guaranteed 2400 hours. If it is assumed that there are 300 possible working days in the year, then the Washburn Crosby Company guaranteed its two-year men 260 eight-hour days and its three-year men 300 eight-hour days. This virtually full, regular employment was a genuine innovation at a time when many industries operated on a much more seasonal basis. The only reservations made by the company were that overtime allowance must be applied against the guarantee and that if the mills stood idle because of "fire, strike, riot or disaster," the number of guaranteed hours would be reduced.

With various minor modifications, rising out of changing economic situations, this plan remained in effect for twelve years. The favorable psychology of the joint conference made the mill employees generously responsive to every suggestion of change which seemed essential to management. When, for example, it was found that the number of men graduated from the two-year to the three-year class imposed a burden on the company, the workers, because they had found conditions of employment generally comfortable, agreed readily to a reduction in the number of guaranteed hours. (The slice was comparatively insignificant — less than 5 per cent.)

In his report for the year 1922–23, the assistant superintendent of the Washburn Crosby mills pointed out that "open expressions of approval" testified to the success of the plan in the estimation of employees. They all agreed that an "oversupply of labor elsewhere" had threatened the welfare of the workers but that "this company, in an unmistakable manner, has refused to take advantage of the circumstance."

"The impression is a deep one," the report continued. "Another effect has already been seen in recent increases by other milling companies in this district. Their employees have given this company credit for maintaining and improving their wages. The prestige of this company is a thing to be proud of."

It was the tremendous change that came about within the industry that brought an end to the plan at last. The inevitable decline of the milling center at Minneapolis and the growth in strategic importance of other places in the system, particularly Buffalo, required that the number of guaranteed hours be reduced. Even after abandonment of the system so long in effect, the employee committees continued to be the point of contact between the men in the mills and management. But an arrangement that had been comfortable and orderly in the comparatively uncomplicated predepression days, when the family relationship between owner and worker was enough to assure harmony, proved to be less satisfactory when industry itself became far more complex. With the confusion of economic distress tending to unravel all that had seemed well knit in the old pattern, new designs for the humanities of business began to take form.

In 1932, when the pinch of fear was undermining the morale of America, Bell made emphatic declaration of his loyalty to labor. A statement of policy addressed to his associates made this central point:

"It is unthinkable that anyone would wish to exploit labor under the present conditions that handicap it. Such methods are unfair, unethical, un-American and destructive. The prevalent state of employment demands the utilization of all methods to give work to the greatest number of people consistent with maintaining the efficient operation of our plants."

The twelve-year history of the guarantee plan testified to the sincerity of Bell's desire to treat workers generously and "to protect them in the security of adequate work and adequate pay at all times."

As Arthur Hyde observed in a report on labor relations: "Our wage scales, hours of work and provisions covering overtime, holidays and vacations are equal to the best prevailing in this country. Our employees' annual earnings are among the highest, their costs among the lowest. We provide and maintain good conditions. We provide protection against risks by old age pensions, disability compensation, hospitalization and death benefits. We have always recognized that employees have clear right to organize and to select their representatives for collective bargaining purposes."

General Mills became the first member of the milling fraternity to create a pension plan for workers. The story of how this came about goes back to the time when the Supreme Court declared the processing tax, a feature of the A.A.A., to be unconstitutional. When the claim of the last customer had been satisfied, under the terms established by the Treasury Department, there remained, as "a credit to Surplus" on the books of General Mills, a tidy item of $1,650,000. The problem of what to do with it was resolved at last by matching it with a question of where money could be found with which to discharge a responsibility that had been troubling Bullis for some eighteen years, ever since his own young days in the company's service.

At frequent intervals, Bullis had called the attention of officers and directors to the need for a formal pension system to replace the informal and inadequate one then in existence. No policy had ever been set down to guide those who administered these donations. Each case was examined presumably on its merits. The "means test" was applied loosely, trailing its fringe of inequalities through the corporation's affairs. Men who had provided frugally for their own old age were allowed to do so. Sometimes the improvident by the very nature of the plan were condoned in their heedlessness.

Now it was possible to provide a just and generous system. Pensions, Bullis always had insisted, must be regarded "as an element of cost, a form of depreciation on men." The $1,650,000 could be used legitimately to defray that cost. Matching the sum, dollar for dollar, the directors deposited a total of $3,300,000 with the Bankers Trust Company of New York, "pending the execution by the company of the Pension Trust."

The Humanities of Business

What resulted finally was a system the general idea of which has become familiar: retirement at 65; provisions for pensions ranging up to 50 per cent of an employee's average annual wage, depending upon the individual's earnings and the years of service; provisions for disability; provision in case of death for benefits to be paid to survivors.

Fortunately for the fate of the human race, theory runs far ahead of practice in all such social efforts as that of providing for the "too old" worker. New plans for the protection of his security, his dignity, and his sense of well-being are under discussion today in industry. Specialists wish to determine what is the limit of "functional age" for each individual instead of being satisfied with automatic retirement from full productive life at the age of 65. There is talk of needs that are not met by mere financial support during retirement. Above all, there is talk of the need to avoid complacency in dealing with the over-all problem that progress in the field may not be blocked. A company like General Mills, which under the driving and determined leadership of Bullis seized initiative in the matter before any of its competitors had created pension systems, may be trusted to continue its interest in theory and to endorse, as they appear, new ideas for contributing to the welfare of the worker. The company is committed to the belief that one of its chief sources of strength has been the stanch character of its employees.

The passage in 1935 of the National Labor Relations Act put another aspect of the workers' collective need clearly before General Mills. Notice was served that the federal government would aid labor in pushing its organized effort and would compel employers to bargain collectively with unions. The tremendous power of labor had received full acknowledgment. There were, in certain quarters, deep-throated grumblings against this sudden access of strength. General Mills, however, drawing again upon its long experience under government regulation, found that it need endure no inner struggle in accepting the new dispensation. When in 1936 the National Labor Relations Board ruled, in effect, that collective bargaining was improper unless it was conducted through a labor union, the old system of employee committees was scrapped. The president of General Mills announced that its policy would be to negotiate "under such procedures and methods as might be determined by the employees themselves or through representatives of their own choosing certified to be such by the National Labor Relations Board." There was no reluctant hanging back from honest commitment to the new program.

In 1937 the constitutionality of the National Labor Relations Act (popularly known as the Wagner Act) was challenged and the law sustained. This wrote finis to any doubt that might have been entertained lingeringly about the status of the legislation. The position of labor had become fixed in the new mold, and an end had come to an era of conflict. General Mills reached an agreement with the American Federation of Labor applicable throughout its system whereby the fundamentals of employer-employee relationship were written in contract form leaving to local unions and plant officials the task of wrestling with the perennial question of wages. The agreement was unique at the time in that it protected the company and the union from jurisdictional disputes initiated by any affiliate of the A. F. of L.

The period between 1937 and 1941 was one of peaceful negotiation during which Arthur Hyde, representing General Mills, and Meyer Lewis, representing the union, conducted all matters of labor relations in an atmosphere of mutual understanding.

General Mills is proud of its labor record. As Arthur Hyde wrote in 1940: "In the past three years, with contracts in effect at 17 plants, we have never had a difficulty that has not been adjusted without reference to arbitration machinery provided in the contract."

After Pearl Harbor there began a new phase in the recent history of industrial relations. The War Labor Dispute (Smith-Connelly) Act required labor to give a no-strike pledge and offered in exchange the guarantee of impartial arbitration of differences through the War Labor Board. These procedures for the peaceful solution of disputes created a great deal of work for the government because all contracts tended to gravitate toward the desk of the board. But the relation of General Mills to the WLB never lost its cordiality. Many cases involving its affairs were put before the board. On occasion the decisions were favorable to the company. Sometimes the vote of the board went against its interests. (For example, the company protested vigorously against a decision of the New York War Labor Board that the union contract should require each worker not merely to take out membership in the union but to maintain that membership.) But always General Mills accepted the board's judgment and none of its cases was taken to court.

In 1944 the company joined forces with a union from the Mechanical Division at Minneapolis to ask authorization from the Wage Stabilization Board of an increase for workers in that division. Both management and the union knew that the board had recently granted to another company engaged in ordnance production an exception from its wage-ceiling policy. Bullis took a troupe of thirteen men from the plant to appear before the Chicago branch of the board. Of the eighteen members on the official panel, six represented industry, six labor, and six the public. It was clear immediately that the labor members were well disposed toward the company's suggestion. The job was to persuade the members representing industry and the public to think well of the proposal. Armed with charts and other "visual education" aids, the Minneapolis troupe put on a lively and impressive drama. At the end of the session everyone — industry and public, as well as labor — was impressed by the eloquence with which a company had pleaded for the right to increase its employees' wages. The board voted unanimously in favor of the request.

With the end of the war and the removal of controls, a wave of strikes swept over America. But General Mills had fewer work stoppages than most companies. A cost-of-living bonus, granted voluntarily, took the impetus out of one threatened strike and after two short interruptions, increases in wages met all objections from workers.

The peace that has come about between the milling industry and labor may be measured by the circumstances that attended the 1950 signing of agreements. An end had come, by that time, to all national contracts binding industry en masse to certain basic policies. General Mills now signed its separate understandings with union representatives. It was one of these spokesmen for labor who, when the negotiations had been completed, observed that "the constructive approach of management could not be commended highly enough" and added that "the degree of mutual understanding" between General Mills and labor was "higher than ever before." A strike in the spring of 1954 briefly interrupted this harmony. Concerned with highly technical matters of scheduling operations, this contention among experts over planning touched no basic matter of wages or conditions of work and left the morale of human relations still high.

On the assumption that any properly responsible general must have well-indoctrinated troops to move into position when the need arises, General Mills instituted in 1937 its intensive program for the training of men to be supervisors and sub-supervisors. A thorough exploration of the techniques of foremanship, of instruction in processes, in hiring, promoting, coping with grievances, and meeting union representatives has produced an extraordinarily fine army of confident young men, ready to assume the responsibilities of leadership.

So concerned with the idea of training did General Mills become that company leaders created also a training course for the development of men capable of heading any one of the many departments and familiar with them all: sales, promotion, accounting, statistics, grain, as well as such broad and inclusive services as public relations. The training program, designed to clarify the complexities of the milling process, to define types of flour, to identify by-products and suggest their great potentialities, to teach merchandising, has fulfilled its purpose by providing General Mills with some of its ablest young executives.

Belief in the humanities of business has become a firmly held tenet in the philosophy of General Mills. The companies of which the corporation was made up had shown in every instance a natural inclination toward social responsibility and their attitude was accepted as a matter of policy. The complexities of modern industry, which have made men on both sides of the conference table zealous in the protection of their rights, have not changed the fact that the tone of family discussion still pervades meetings between management and labor. Though family life in America is often shrill and sometimes tense, its most characteristic features are humorous awareness, cooperation, and mutual indulgence. Knowing that, in the climate of normal life, industrial relations, like family relations, have a sturdy power to resist corruption, Arthur Hyde once observed in a report on labor policy: "In looking to the future and to the adjustment of the problems it will bring, we have no belief in panaceas and almost none in sudden ruin."

Protection of the rights of men and women on every level of its enterprise is only one of the tasks of the great modern corporation. Another is to attract young men into its design and to train them for top executive responsibility. From the time of J. S. Bell when his "kindergarten" was the sardonic envy of companies less well supplied with apprentices, the phrase "building men" has been one of almost mystical importance and significance in the councils first of the Washburn Crosby Company and later of General Mills.

The Humanities of Business

As Bullis has said: "The success of General Mills over the past twenty-five years has been due to an ever accelerating momentum caused, in its turn, by the high morale of its operating executives, not only in the headquarters at Minneapolis but in each of its field divisions, branch offices, and plant locations. That high morale may be attributed to the belief of individuals that they could advance if they were willing to pay the price in intelligent hard work. General Mills always has allowed its executives the opportunity to use all their aptitudes and talents. To them has been delegated authority enough so that they could act without having to clear too many things with an executive in some remote 'Ivory Tower.' In this highly competitive age we need to have every executive — big and little, all over the system — giving himself to the best interests of his company, learning to take initiative and above all to carry on his daily duties in an atmosphere that develops self-respect and self-confidence."

This atmosphere of confidence prevailed in each unit before the formation of General Mills. Searle Mowat, for all his ruddy, firsthand purposefulness, felt himself to be in part the creation of James Larrowe. Thatcher, who stood tall and broad against all comers and all winds of circumstance, nonetheless liked to think of Kell as his foster father and mentor. At Buffalo, Frank Henry, who yearned to perform every labor, have every idea, make every decision, still felt the tradition strongly enough to allow G. S. Kennedy to learn leadership at his side. In San Francisco the "Sperry spirit" which called for teamwork in every operation became the most closely cherished of its assets.

As retirement has taken one dominating figure after another from the General Mills scene, an able successor has shown himself. Frank Burke of the Sperry division, when the tyranny of time required him to expend his still enormous vitality on his flower gardens, nominated E. O. Boyer to follow him. Small of stature but direct and indomitable as a bullet, Boyer surrounded himself with men of good bulk. "I'm the only little squirt I'll tolerate in this office," he once said with irresistible humor.

Boyer, too, built men by allowing them the initiative recommended by Bullis. The result was that he had a cabinet of distinguished West Coast citizens: Clarence E. Anderson, lately assigned to an important executive post at Minneapolis; George Lambert, veteran of every kind of campaign in the business; D. F. Wright, who is incidentally a distin-

302

guished leader of the Mormon church; J. S. Mitchell, dynamic Grocery Products merchandiser; and H. B. Herron.

Three principal aims, all in sympathy with Bullis' program, have dominated Boyer's West Coast regime. The first is to give every kind of proper recognition to the individual worker. From top executive to sweeper in the mill each must have his voice. Orders in the Sperry Division do not descend from on high. Rather decisions are made by the individual directly responsible for a particular phase of company business. Vast quantities of confidential information are supplied to him on which to base judgment but the final word is his.

Boyer's second concern has been to bring the support of General Mills and its resources to a great program of diversification. The West has been traditionally a credit-granting region and to this tradition the Sperry Division has made a creative contribution by financing the projects of modern pioneers, in poultry raising, for example, and turkey farming. So significant has this side line become that General Mills is now one of the four largest backers of such enterprises.

Third among Boyer's major interests is that of modernizing mill operations and of using his plants to serve General Mills as laboratories for the development of new techniques.

In 1944 H. R. McLaughlin retired from leadership in Chicago. This shrewd and witty product of the J. S. Bell training school had instituted a training program of his own in which he developed men like James E. Skidmore, who succeeded him in Chicago and later returned to the central headquarters in Minneapolis to do a basic job of allocation and stock control.

At Buffalo, Frank Henry, being old and full of years in 1949, resigned as director, ending a long career as what might be called thinker-extraordinary to two generations of Bells. No one ever served more effectively as sounding board. The resonance with which Henry gave back ideas was a feature of the creative life of General Mills for half a century.

In 1931 Henry had given up his place as chief of the Eastern Division to devote himself for the rest of his active career to guidance of policy as chairman of the Operating Board. William Morris, his successor, proved to be one of the most adaptable of men. During the lean years of the 1930s his selling team set marks for all competition to follow. As builder of men he could offer a creditable list of disciples

303

including two men who became vice presidents of General Mills, Barry and Kennedy.

There has been, however, no rigid pattern to the training school of General Mills. From his own university, Wisconsin, Bullis brought many graduates with high standing, among them E. L. Schujahn and Gordon Ballhorn. He sponsored the career of Richard J. Keeler, treasurer of the company, and employed for the company many others including Everett H. Andreson, Arthur H. Smith, Leslie B. Colfix, Glenn M. Harold, Robert W. Wiper, Stuart Wilson, Melvin Bright, LeRoy Jamison, David Fuhriman, and James McFarland.

By a very different route H. C. Lautensack reached leadership in the Eastern Division. He began as office boy to the formidable Tully Estee in New York. Having eluded all the attempts at cheerful intimidation made daily by that master of challenge, Lautensack entered on the next phase of a modest apprenticeship. He "sold the baker's trade" in the area around New York at a time when price structures were hazy and merchandising was an improvised and often reckless adventure. Having become at last manager of the New York office, he moved on to wider opportunities in the divisional headquarters at Buffalo. This on-the-job training for executives has been another familiar formula within the company.

More recently, top executives, destined to be vice presidents, have been recruited from other pursuits — men like Raymond Brang, Whitney Eastman, and Edward Thode. The latter, General Mills' chief legal adviser within the company, seems to have captured for himself a slightly paradoxical combination of traits: the ability to concentrate severely on a specialty and at the same time to invite breadth of interest. Recipient at twenty of a bachelor of arts degree, taken *magna cum laude,* Thode trained himself for law at Georgetown University, Washington, D.C. Before going into private practice he was for a time a member of the FBI serving as administrative assistant to J. Edgar Hoover and later as chief of the National Division of Identification of that bureau. Preoccupying interests have not kept him from becoming a devotee of music, for he finds playing the piano good treatment for taut nerves.

An intensely practical way in which General Mills has undertaken to build men, particularly for executive posts, has been to offer the incentive of a profit-sharing plan. Details are changed from time to time, and in 1953 basic revisions were under consideration.

The men, and quite as frequently the women, of General Mills offer evidence of the pride that they take in the tradition of the company. Such, for example, was the creation, in 1949, of a flag to be flown from the corporation's many, wide-scattered properties, declaring its prestige and its unity. It was at the suggestion of an employee that this handsome banner was created. The initials GMI occupy the hub of a stylized millwheel with sheaves of wheat gathered below. This shield rests in the center of a deep blue field symbolizing the benevolent sky, warming the grain.

Another triumphant venture in dramatizing tradition is the *Betty Crocker Picture Cook Book*. Nothing, of course, could more appropriately sum up the experiments of a quarter of a century than this official testament from the Home Service Department. Marjorie Husted, long head of the department and now consultant to General Mills, was chosen to capture in permanent form what might be called the radiant practicality of Betty Crocker's helpfulness. She selected as chief lieutenants Ruth Anderson and Mae Chestnut, both of whom have grown up in the Betty Crocker tradition.

The success of the final result, from every standpoint, has been spectacular. No volume exists that so nearly satisfied the requirements of a definitive document on American cookery. The 2000 recipes have been translated with the greatest adroitness into the language of action. The hundreds of photographs in black and white, the double spreads in color, lend visual drama to the adventure of the kitchen — defining food values, suggesting proper balances, analyzing processes. The many sketches and decorations keep the temper of the exploit spirited. Individual chapters examine every aspect of the cooking process with a maximum of gaiety and a minimum of strain. The work is admirably designed to make both a cook and a gourmet of anyone — child, hermit, ascetic, or even dyspeptic. The spontaneous witnesses to its success are the two and a half million people who have bought it and made it a runaway best-seller.

The intimate and comfortable relationship that exists between General Mills and its employees may be attributed in large part to the philosophy of its leaders. As Bullis has said, the men and women of the company are its most important asset. "They have made our past. They are the moving force that will mold our future."

21

Challenges of Tomorrow

THE COMPANY AND ITS ORGANIZATION

I̲F, A S many psychologists believe, an aptitude for self-appraisal is the definitive mark of maturity, then General Mills may be said to have reached maturity under the firm, steady discipline of J. F. Bell. Few institutions have been required to look more scrutinizingly at their own principles and procedures. From the moment when he returned to the Washburn Crosby Company after his service to the government in World War I, Bell turned the uncompromising light of theory on the activities of the milling industry in general and on the practices of his own company in particular. His criticism was often severe, but his discipline had always the stimulating value of a positive point of view.

Typical of his impulse to get an objective and impartial view of his own operations was the invitation offered in the summer of 1948 to a group of outside experts to give the company a thorough "check-up" such as any private individual should have from time to time during his maturity. As chairman of the committee on technological progress, Bell received such a team of experts sent to him by Dean Donald Kirk David of the Graduate School of Business Administration at Harvard and gave them access to all company books, manuals, and other data. In an atmosphere of free inquiry these six analysts, each a specialist in a particular field of investigation, explored every phase of the company in every part of the country. After weeks of close study they reached the conclusion in their printed report that General Mills stood stanchly among institutions of its kind as an "eminent citizen of the free enterprise system" and one in a state of abundant health.

Part of Bell's plan in asking for an outside appraisal of the company's organization was to sharpen the critical faculties of its own executives. Success, continuing over a long period, might, he believed, be more stultifying than stimulating. Many influences combined in the fall of 1950 to persuade the leading men of General Mills to believe that the time had come to shift the emphasis in planning for so large an organization from the regional to the functional basis. The affairs of the corporation had come inevitably to be directed toward harmony and consistency of effort as parts of a program designed to serve the entire country. The old geographical units had tended, consequently, to lose their significance. In October 1950, announcement was made of the creation of a Food Division, under the direction of Walter Barry as president and G. S. Kennedy as vice president, to coordinate the interests of this branch of the business on a nationwide basis.

The determination of a large company to escape from the duplication of effort involved in too great subdivision of authority on a geographical basis has animated the thinking of every corporation many times in its history. General Mills' movement toward centralization worked many useful reforms. During the presidency of Leslie Perrin all the advantages to be gained from a tight pattern of planning were triumphantly achieved in a period of great prosperity.

But it is the nature of a problem affecting the life of a healthy corporate citizen to be subject to constant change. By June 1952 when a new executive assumed the presidency of General Mills it had become apparent that adaptations of method had once more to be made. In Charles H. Bell the company found a vigorous, experienced, and resourceful young man well fitted for the task. Like his father, J. F. Bell, his grandfather, James Stroud Bell, and several generations of forebears, he had spent his entire life in the milling business.

This tall, dark young man had duplicated in many ways the pattern of his father's development. He entered the company in 1930, serving "the hard way" in successive phases as mill hand, truck driver, grain man, accountant, statistician, salesman in a poor Los Angeles district, and, finally, promotion executive. In 1942 he interrupted his career, as did three thousand of his coworkers at General Mills — men and women — to go into military service. Discharged from the air corps at the war's end with the rank of major, Bell returned to take up a new task as liaison man between research and operations, opening the door of one world upon the other so that there might be closer understanding of their mutual dependence. As he once observed: "The key to American business success has been the willingness of management to recognize change, to accept the principle of early obsolescence and to embrace all new and better techniques."

His election to the presidency of General Mills was not, as a portrait in *Fortune* has pointed out, "because of his birth, perhaps even in spite of it." General Mills, *Fortune* went on to say, "is non-dynastic and there is no family control. Charles Bell was by general agreement the outstanding candidate among younger men."

The son of J. F. Bell has followed the pattern of his father's development in acquiring a wide variety of interests. There are differences between the temperaments of father and son, as there are also differences of outlook. But their sympathy of impulse is striking. The portrait in *Fortune* emphasized Charles Bell's "easiness and affability of manner" and the significance of the family trait which makes him collect the first names of men in all ranks from office boy to vice president.

The universal, frequently recurring, problem with which he had first to deal as organizer has been effectively defined by Arthur Pound in his *Industrial America*:

"Division of authority between a central staff and decentralized units is one of the prickly problems of modern business. Too much centralization is likely to slow down energy at the rim of the industrial circle where goods are sold and contacts maintained with dealers and consumers. Too great decentralization means loss of motion and increased costs through unnecessary duplication of effort. Search for the correct balance between these forces goes on unceasingly in many large corporations which swing periodically toward one extreme or the other."

Bell was determined to avoid any dizzy reversal of motion in his campaign of reorganization announced in April 1953, less than a year after he had assumed the presidency. Four considerations prompted the new plan: the desire to conduct business on the most efficient and profitable basis; "to maintain and enhance the quality of products and services"; to release creative thinking and stimulate the company's further progress; to attract and develop superior manpower.

His fundamental reexamination of company problems persuaded him that the tendency toward centralization of effort on a functional basis had allowed the operation to become too large. Activities in the realms of flour, feed, and grocery foods each had become huge. Brought together under one managerial banner, they had a gratifyingly healthy yet formidable look. In terms of figures this growth could be expressed with impressive effect. The Food Division in 1953 was 4½ times greater in profits (before taxes) than General Mills as a whole had been in 1930; it was 2½ times larger from the point of view of sales, 3½ times greater in expense, 1⅜ times larger in manpower. Inevitably "the problems of efficient management and direction had of course multiplied manyfold."

Among many reasons demanding change was the obvious fact that it was unfair to ask any individual to assume the tremendous burden involved in the management of so huge a product-making and product-selling campaign. Bell's new plan called for a division of authority but not on the rigid and arbitrary basis of the old geographical divisions. Minneapolis continued, of course, to hold down quite firmly the center of the organization as the place where administrative policy originated. But the flexibility needed to conduct a vast business enterprise in the day-by-day functioning of the competitive principle must, Charles Bell felt, be increased.

On April 13, 1953, after painstaking study of all possibilities, he announced that the Food Division of General Mills would be dissolved immediately and that its functions would be divided among three separate operating divisions: the Grocery Products Division, the Flour Division, and the Feed Division.

These divisions, together with four more divisions representing the other activities of General Mills, constitute the broad base of its operation. Each of these divisions has its general manager who under the new plan has delegated to him authority enough to encourage initiative and responsibility enough to balance authority. The essential purpose is to give each executive a sense of "belonging" so that the company may benefit to the full from his gifts of enterprise. Within the limitations established by over-all policy directed from Minneapolis there has been a strong inclination to decentralize activities, not in the geographical but in the managerial sense. This, Bell describes picturesquely as a "Bottom-Up" type of management.

On the firm base of the divisions, Bell has raised up a second level of executive authority. General managers of divisions report to a triumvirate of administrators of "Activities." Only in one instance is the general manager and the administrator the same individual. In the realm of Grocery Products Walter Barry plays both roles. The general managers of the Flour Division (D. A. Stevens) and Feed Division (W. H. Eastman) have as their superior G. S. Kennedy, administrator of Flour and Feed Activities. The other divisions representing the diversified interests of General Mills in related fields are grouped under A. D. Hyde as administrator of Mechanical and Chemical Activities. Only the administrators report directly to the president's office.

There are in a great corporation like General Mills many departments which do not have to do directly with the business of making standardized products. They police the outlying districts of company activities as do the purchasing, traffic, and product-coordinating departments. They may keep a vigilant eye on quality of products as does Products Control. They may look toward the discovery of new activities as do Research and Management Development. They may have to do with the large interests of wooing public interest and good will as do Advertising and Public Relations. They may be concerned with the family affairs of the company as is Personnel Administration. They may be devoted to the keeping of the books as are the offices of the comptroller and of the treasurer. Or they may finally be charged with the large matters of a corporate citizen's rights and duties as is the Legal Department. General Mills has all of these each with its own organization and each presided over by an officer who is responsible in the last analysis to the president.

Each of the seven operating divisions which form the base of the present organization of General Mills has its budget. To each is delegated profit-and-loss responsibility and "control of every possible cost factor."

As Bell's report of April 1953 pointed out, four of the operating divisions already had this kind of autonomy even before the new plan was put into effect. One of these is O-Cel-O, a corporation of Buffalo, New York, purchased by General Mills in 1952. On the theory that any product designed to travel along the "avenue to the home" is a proper one for his company to handle, Charles Bell selected this one for acquisition. Three young men — J. A. Bitzer, C. R. Hardt, and G. E. Murray — all trained at Du Pont, had developed this cellulose sponge and organized a company to market it. Made of wood pulp reinforced with vegetable fiber, this sponge improves upon nature's own product in serviceability and in durability. Also it costs less to make a cellulose sponge than to gather and prepare for market the natural sponge of the sea. So the housewife is doubly served.

A recent development in another of these basic divisions was the decision of May 10, 1954, to permit the Mechanical Division to concentrate on its interest in the manufacture of electronic instruments by selling its home appliance business. The purchase was made by the Illinois McGraw Electric Company and included capital equipment, tooling, and inventories.

General Mills had begun in 1946 to make electric irons, toasters, pressure cookers, and other items chiefly as a means of maintaining a high level of employment among workers whom the company had brought together first to make supplies for the armed services. The making of home appliances accounted at no time for more than 10 per cent of the productive effort of the Mechanical Division which by the new adaptation is enabled to concentrate on the more important phase of its interest in industrial instruments and special equipment. To act as director of a newly created department of Engineering Research and Development General Mills has engaged Dr. Cledo Brunetti, late of the Stanford Research Institute in California. The director is a graduate of the University of Minnesota (1937) and before his appointment at Stanford had served the National Bureau of Standards for eight years as chief of its Engineering Electronics Section.

Guiding the general policies of all the divisions is the Board of Directors. The 1954 board reflects the diversity of interests General Mills has always sought in its counsels: Harry A. Bullis, Minneapolis, chairman; Charles H. Bell, Minneapolis, president of General Mills; Walter R. Barry, Minneapolis, vice president of General Mills; James F. Bell, Minneapolis, chairman of the committee on finance and technological progress of General Mills; John Cowles, Minneapolis, president of the *Minneapolis Star and Tribune*; Arthur D. Hyde, Minneapolis, vice president of General Mills; Gerald S. Kennedy, Minneapolis, vice president of General Mills; Henry S. Kingman, Minneapolis, president of the Farmers and Mechanics Savings Bank; Deane W. Malott, Ithaca, N.Y., president of Cornell University; Putnam D. McMillan, Minneapolis; Frank J. Morley, Minneapolis, of Morley, Cant, Taylor, Haverstock, and Beardsley; Leslie N. Perrin, Minneapolis; Frederick A. O. Schwarz,

New York, of Davis Polk Wardwell Sunderland and Kiendl; Don A. Stevens, Minneapolis, vice president of General Mills; Henry S. Sturgis, New York, vice president of the First National Bank of the City of New York; and Harold W. Sweatt, Minneapolis, chairman of the board of Minneapolis-Honeywell Regulator Company.

Shortly before he became president of General Mills Charles Bell was introduced to the large fraternity of fellow merchants as chief speaker of the occasion at the fiftieth anniversary banquet of the Millers' National Federation held on May 13, 1952, in Chicago.

The temper of the meeting was at once gay and meditative as the millers looked back over their long history of joint effort. To that session Charles Bell carried a word of youthful vigor and confidence. He surveyed briskly the problems with which these pages have been concerned and concluded: "The future is full of opportunity for men of vision, men of ingenuity, men of persuasive salesmanship. We need creative thinking; we need imagination, enthusiasm, and faith."

312

22

Anniversary Celebration

INVESTING IN TOMORROW

O_{N JUNE} 20, 1953, General Mills rounded out its first quarter of a century. It reached that anniversary in an atmosphere characterized throughout world society by a kind of tense expectation of the unexpected. Mankind, alert and wary, awaited the next development in a pattern of events that had made the spectacular seem commonplace and the most drastic revisions of political values seem to be inevitable.

Yet the daily needs of human beings continued to be what they had always been. To the people of the United States it became increasingly clear, during the 1950s, that they must assume a large responsibility for satisfying the basic needs of many allies in the free world. General Mills as the largest unit in an important division of the food industry found no reason, on its twenty-fifth anniversary, to be anything but optimistic about its opportunity for service. As Walter Barry had pointed out in an address to the Graduate School of Business Administration at Harvard, "the food industry is a growing industry in a growing nation."

The purposefulness of General Mills was dramatized in all the occasions that celebrated its twenty-fifth anniversary by the sturdy individuality of its still youthful president. Charles Bell, speaking in a conversational tone which suggested the family discussion rather than the public policy forum, rehearsed the progress of the years and found it good. Through each brisk account of reasons for confidence, a listener sensed a flow of power that had great reserves of strength behind it. The poise of Charles Bell was clearly the product of a varied experience

313

that had touched many aspects of enterprise. Having seen all these interests prosper, he did not hesitate to believe that the future would be as full of rewarding responsibilities as the past had been.

He was describing a corporation that had come into full possession of its own adult powers. Despite the fact that the climate of the business world in which General Mills began its career had been variable and by no means always salubrious, the company's own development had been uninterruptedly healthy. Like a rugged organism that seems to thrive on difficulty, this corporate citizen had passed through agricultural crisis, general economic depression, and rigid government control without losing either its strategic balance or its balance in the bank. Throughout crises that had wrecked many an institution and maimed others, General Mills had clung tenaciously and skillfully to its margin of profit and emerged from each onslaught of circumstance with its prestige higher than ever and its position in the business community more secure.

Actually the good and bad in the economic outlook had been inextricably mixed. The mid-twenties, even while agriculture suffered and endured, had been a time of significant industrial expansion. World War II, though its conditions were exacting, encouraged the ambitious to find new duties and opportunities. Indeed, the whole pattern of the quarter-century was one of alternating forces, positive and negative. After the great drive toward the construction of a new economic plant in the United States during the 1920s came the depression of the 1930s. After the surge of energy so noticeable during World War II came the adjustment period of the postwar years. But even this sometimes violent alternation of favorable with unfavorable circumstance seemed to further the development of General Mills. Good times brought opportunity; bad times brought challenge. Having met each with the flexibility of creative intelligence, General Mills grew steadily. Indicative of its belief in the ability of its leaders to maintain that pace was the fact that the preferred stockholders authorized the company in 1952 to borrow up to $50,000,000 for long-term financing of its expansion requirements. No testimony of faith in the future quite equals the spontaneous sincerity expressed by borrowing a fortune to invest in tomorrow.

The twenty-fifth annual report of General Mills — June 1, 1952, to May 31, 1953 — revealed the background of this faith. The year just past had been the most successful in all the company's history from the

314

standpoint of sales. For products and services General Mills had received nearly half a billion dollars compared with the $125,000,000 of its first year, the $300,000,000 of 1944, and the $400,000,000 of 1949. Its net earnings had been eleven and a half million; earnings had been between three and four millions during the 1920s and 1930s and between five and six millions during the early half of the 1940s before the postwar program had accelerated the drive for volume. The earnings per share of common stock had been $4.68, exactly three times what these had been in 1929.

General Mills, in the year 1953, was more securely placed than ever before as the largest miller in the world. Its daily capacity (measured now in hundredweights since the word "barrel" had become obsolescent, except in the language of low comedy) was 143,000 cwt., nearly one sixth of the effective commercial milling capacity of the United States and one and three quarters times that of its nearest rival.

President Bell provided a climax to this year of enthusiasm and progress when he announced on December 29, 1953, that General Mills would enter the market in Canada through a Canadian subsidiary. Headquarters would be in Toronto, and E. L. Schujahn, whose broad experience in grocery products and bakers' flour well qualified him for the post, was named to head the activity.

The strength of General Mills had other sources beside its large participation in an essential business, the manufacture of flour. Such sources were the various features of its diversification program. The broad base which J. F. Bell and Bullis have insisted must support the company's effort has provided ample room for adaptation to changing conditions in the present-day world. In the year 1938 the products making up the total dollar sales showed this comparative scale of value: 74 per cent for flour, 17 per cent for formula feeds, and 9 per cent for packaged foods. In 1953, flour accounted for only 52 per cent of the company's volume of sales, formula feeds for 19 per cent, packaged foods for 18 per cent, chemical and mechanical products for 11 per cent. To be sure, 52 per cent of the $483,000,000 total in flour sales was more than twice the 74 per cent of the 1938 total of $153,000,000. Flour continued to be the reliable backbone of the enterprise, carrying it steadily forward in every campaign to capture customers. At the same time the company had strengthened its position by seeking out scores of opportunities for service.

315

Anniversary Celebration

Everywhere in this empire of enterprise there was, in 1953, evidence of a buoyant enthusiasm. Things stood well in each of the seven newly created operating divisions. General Mills' thorough study of what is required to please "the little nerves that fringe the tongue" had established its whole list of grocery products firmly in the public imagination. In the face of severe competition deliveries reached an all-time-high record. Indeed, trade names tended to take on the authority of generic terms. Many a housewife asks for a box of Bisquick as she asks for a pound of sugar. Exploration of possibilities goes on constantly in the kitchens and the laboratories of General Mills, all looking toward the introduction of new products. To the family of Betty Crocker mixes, two more were added within the year along with two new breakfast cereals sweetened to the taste of the modern child and his parents.

In the realm of flour, competition grows more exacting every year. But in times of stress and change, rewards always go to those who have established a reputation for stability. During a period when strategic conditions required the gradual reduction of milling capacity in the United States and General Mills suspended production at Oklahoma City, the prestige of its products preserved its advantage in the field. Even the about-face in the eating habits of America did not disturb the progress of Gold Medal Flour. Just a generation ago, 60 per cent of all flour went straight into the family kitchen. Now only 25 per cent of it goes there, the rest into the hands of bakers. But the baker is a good buyer, too. As he has become more and more a scientist, his standards of excellence have risen and he has demanded the right to buy the best flour available. The gift of the Brown 'n Serve process has continued to make other friends for General Mills. A coast-to-coast survey lately showed that 80 per cent of the 23,000 stores questioned were in the habit of handling one or another variety of goods produced by this process.

The avenue to the home and the highway to the farm still run parallel through the thinking of General Mills' executives. Carrying formula feeds along the second of these has become an important part of the total enterprise, and it will be of increasing importance in the years to come. The highway to the farm crosses a reassuringly broad field of expansion and offers a vista of opportunity rich enough to satisfy any industrialist's imagination.

Science must go along on this trip, for the manufacture of formula feeds has become a matter of the greatest complexity. Begun in a time of comparative ignorance simply as a means of getting rid of the by-products of flour making, the creation of feeds today involves as many steps as the preparation of a ceremonial dinner for human beings. Within two years the revolution of ideas on nutrition has become sharply intensified, particularly in the world of the stock barn. Six or seven ingredients were considered, until quite recently, to be all that a reasonable animal could want; now no conscientious builder of a formula feed feels that any of a possible twenty can be omitted. Poultry and livestock raisers ask that various medicinal rations be added for the prevention of disease and that vitamins and antibiotics be added for fast and sturdy growth. Here, too, the future belongs to those who have the resources of scientific study at their disposal, as well as the readiness to pack the best of contemporary knowledge of nutrition neatly away into a formula feed.

In January 1953, General Mills inaugurated a new campaign on behalf of its formula feeds by giving them the name Larro SureFeeds. Borrowed from Sperry, this confident combination of trade mark and battle cry declares the energetic temper of the new leaders in the realm of formula feeds.

The dramatic diversity of General Mills' interests is demonstrated nowhere more effectively than in its program for livestock and poultry raisers. The Larro Research Farm where for so many years Charles Staff conducted his exhaustive researches has continued his work under highly trained experts. The tract at Detroit has proved to be inadequate to growing needs and will presently be replaced with a larger one somewhere in the heartland of American agriculture.

In the company's program, salesmen too are required to be scientists. One of the important achievements of the Larro research program was the invention by two of its men of a circular slide rule for measurement of a farm animal's productivity. Norman Dewes put his knowledge as engineer at the disposal of Charles Staff, long a user of graphs in dairy research, to evolve this method of graph analysis. The milk flow of a cow may be estimated accurately so that a farmer is left in no doubt as to the animal's economic value. It is part of the salesman's task to help the farmer understand his own animals so that the wasteful user of food may be eliminated and the high producer of food value developed. Indeed, the salesman is expected to spend many hours in "earning his business" by the interpretation of productivity figures. A "flock check" system similar to the milk graph performs a like service for the poultry raiser. The preeminent rule for today's salesman would seem to be the slide rule.

Nor is this quite all. General Mills never has been reticent about entering the entertainment field. To alert the attention of its farm customers it has encouraged the development of a kind of livestock circus designed to display the intelligence of properly reared animals. It is the creation of Keller Breland, holder of a master's degree in psychology from Louisiana State University, and of his wife, also a professional psychologist. By a training system that eliminates punishment and uses the expectation of food as stimulant, Breland has taught chickens to play poker, a fastidious sow to tidy up a room with a vacuum cleaner, and Sureshot, the Larro rabbit, to play basketball. "The reenforcing stimulus" of the promise of nourishment has produced a barnyardful of astonishing animals whose stunts never fail to enchant customers. Breland's shows have been presented in farm stores of the General Mills system, and also at fairs and rodeos. Some quarter of a million men, women, and children have watched them with incredulous delight.

The significance of the experiment is simply that of showing how, in the modern world of business, science and circuses have been brought to the support of salesmanship.

Despite the company's preoccupation with household and farm, its leaders are aware that the ferment of ideas must go on as it will and that some of the enterprises in which it has become involved are certain to lead far outside the boundaries of the food world. The Chemical Division shelters many such projects. The plant at Kankakee, for example, lately has established a new unit for the manufacture of fatty nitriles, fatty amines, and ammonium compounds. It was inevitable that this development should emerge out of the work with fatty acids. A vast new field for the modern pioneers of science has been opened up by recent discoveries, and General Mills has become indirectly involved in a curious round of tasks. It makes a contribution to the work of refining low-grade ores, especially potash, phosphate, and feldspar. It aids the textile industry by supplying material softeners. Recently the amine has been put to the task in the oil regions of helping to recover the 10 per cent of oil that is left in the sand around a gusher.

The fatty acid project has taken also, in recent months, the reflected glow of a great humanitarian drama. The fractioning of these substances has produced a rich stream of stigmasterol from which the maker of pharmaceuticals can produce in great quantity and at modest price the drug cortisone. Diseases that have proved for years to be unresponsive to other treatment may yield to this kind of cure when a sufficient supply of the drug has become available.

The two remaining divisions — Special Commodities and O-Cel-O — have broadened the base of General Mills, one stretching its interests from vitamins to vegetable gum, the other, adding in ever greater numbers a valuable kitchen aid to the list of commodities carried by General Mills along the avenue to the home.

General Mills never has been as busy, as useful, as exploratory, as fully in possession of its powers. This is the principle by which it has been guided: boldly to seek out what is new in the realm of service and to offer its own product for sale only when it has been tested for enduring value. And in the multiplicity of its interests today, as contrasted with the patient monotony of its original task, one sees dramatized the whole of a century's progress in industry. The spirit of industry at its most conscientious stands revealed in the way that this diversity of effort has been disciplined by science and warmed by a sense of social responsibility.

It is interesting that J. F. Bell, founder of a great modern corporation, should have seen his complex task always in terms of a simple duty toward the gospel of excellence. In an editorial for a company publication he once wrote of "The Passing of the Peddler" who, in an earlier generation, had been the carrier of news and wares to towns along the highway of the past.

"We knew little of whence he came or where he passed. Of the makers and qualities of his goods we knew less. He found no ready acceptance for his wares; each article required careful examination and inspection to reveal its worth or to disclose its hidden flaws. Buyer, beware! No guarantee here . . ."

But with the modern crier of wares it was quite different.

"He comes no more with tinkling bell or lyric halloo. From a known and permanent place he cries throughout the wide reaches of the air, and his story meets the eye at every turn. You know all about him. He tells you of his wares. He tells you how they are made. He hangs them up so that you may see and judge their standards and their worth.

Anniversary Celebration

"By his goods do you know him. By their worth is his reputation made. He invents new things for your benefit and enjoyment. He tells you of the developments of science and invention. He seeks your confidence, for his work is dependent upon it. His good name comes first; where you see his goods, where the goods bear his name, you know it as a guarantee of value."

It might be set down, in the end, as a capsule history of this "eminent citizen of the free enterprise system":

He cried his wares through the wide reaches of the air and his good name came first.

SOURCES AND INDEX

Sources and Acknowledgments

THE work of preparing this story of General Mills had the generous and the trusting support of hundreds of men and women in the organization who opened up to the writer three chief sources of information within the company. There were, first of all, the intelligences of the leaders themselves — executives, directors, heads of divisions, and key men in various departments. In many long interviews each surveyed the history of the company as he had seen it and rediscovered the pattern of its development. There were, second, the official documents of the several organizations that came together as General Mills — minute books, correspondence, memorandums, annual reports, reports of committees, pamphlets, brochures, cookbooks, radio scripts. And there were, finally, many valuable kinds of private papers belonging to various highly productive members of the General Mills family.

It is difficult to estimate, comparatively, the contribution made to knowledge of the company by these various sources. Thanks to the fact that General Mills has rejoiced in a tradition of expressiveness, the interviews were at all times pleasant and rewarding. The author of this story traveled during the two years of his effort to every geographical branch of the enterprise and spent a week at a time making his way conversationally through the organization from president on to a large representative group of operating executives, encountering everywhere from San Francisco to New York the same copiously communicative and perceptive spirit.

The most frequent interviews were with veterans and newcomers of the home office at Minneapolis. With James Ford Bell, founder of the corporation, and Harry A. Bullis, chairman of the board, these often were extended into sessions of many hours, interrupted only by pressing crises of the moment in the company's history. One of Harry Bullis's immeasurable services was to glean from his diaries significant items marking the progress of each succeeding year. He continued this examination into the period of the writer's effort and it was amusing to come upon such entries as "Spent the morning with Gray," or "Had a four-hour interview with Gray," and, finally, in what one can only hope was not a sigh of weariness, "Spent the entire day with Gray."

The interviews with James Ford Bell were similarly frequent and prolonged. Their value was commensurate with the high degree of critical insight possessed by that extraordinary man.

Documents in the second category were of great importance for similar reasons. Beside the routine correspondence, which the files of every company contain, there are in the day-to-day record of General Mills many souvenirs of the habit of self-examination established by Bell and represented admirably by the document that became famous among his colleagues as the "magnum opus." Bullis maintained this tradition in many highly readable studies.

Under the leadership of men so closely analytical of their own purposes, scores of department heads became crisply and dramatically adept in the preparation of significant and revealing memorandums.

Fortunately for the writer the attitude on the part of General Mills' executives toward his project was that of full and free disclosure. The principle was established on the first day of his study that from him no secrets were to be hid and he was permitted to explore these sources in perfect freedom.

The third source of material consisted of a great reservoir of the reflections of key men set down in family letters (those of the Bell group proved to be particularly rich in liveliness and insight), speeches, articles, published interviews, and diaries. Through much the greater part of his more than fifty years of association with, and direction of, this enterprise, James Ford Bell dictated to his succession of secretaries a full digest of the day's news. These pages proved to be so full of sprightliness, as well as of shrewdness, in the estimation of men and events that the writer could not rid himself of the sense of having been personally wronged whenever a barren patch, due to a momentary crisis of activity in the life of the founder of General Mills, appeared in this record.

One previous comment on the progress of one division of General

324

Mills has appeared in print. William Edgar's *Medal of Gold* rehearsed the history of the Washburn Crosby Company from its establishment by Cadwallader Washburn down to the period just following World War I. Written with the lance-breaking vigor that ever characterized its challenging and courageous author, the *Medal of Gold* offered many lively leads for further study. A manuscript account of the Sperry Company briefly outlined its general pattern of progress.

The files of the *Northwestern Miller*, admirably edited from its beginning and for many years after by William Edgar and no less admirably guided today by Carroll Michener, afford rich veins of information running in many directions from the milling industry into every corner of economic investigation.

For clarification of the Christian story the writer is indebted to Lucille Kane for her help in exploring the papers of the Christian family and of W. D. Washburn in the Minnesota Historical Society.

To acknowledge adequately obligations to the men and women of General Mills in preparing this story would be virtually to list the company's large personnel, from the successive presidents, Leslie Perrin and Charles H. Bell, down to many new recruits. Particular thanks, however, should go to Cyril W. Plattes of the Department of Public Relations for his devoted interest in the project from its beginning. It is a pleasure also to acknowledge gratitude to Ethel M. Johnson of the General Mills library whose realm the writer shared for a time during the preparation of this book and whose patience he thoroughly explored in demands that involved the no less patient cooperation of representatives of the General Mills research library, the Minneapolis Public Library, the library of the University of Minnesota, and the Minnesota Historical Society.

The writer acknowledges also with the greatest satisfaction the help of two colleagues. Clyde Bailey, dean emeritus of the Department of Agriculture at the University of Minnesota, made himself available again and again for help with problems in the field of research. Professor Herbert Heaton, of the Department of History, read the manuscript at various stages and made an enormous contribution to the task of revision. It is a pleasure also to acknowledge a very particular debt of gratitude to all the staff members of the University of Minnesota Press for their creative assistance in letting this book "escape into print."

Index

Index